THE

CHURCH HYMNARY

Third Edition

THE
CHURCH HYMNARY

Third Edition

WORDS ONLY

OXFORD UNIVERSITY PRESS

Oxford University Press, Ely House, London W. 1

GLASGOW NEW YORK TORONTO MELBOURNE WELLINGTON
CAPE TOWN IBADAN NAIROBI DAR ES SALAAM LUSAKA
ADDIS ABABA DELHI BOMBAY CALCUTTA MADRAS KARACHI
LAHORE DACCA KUALA LUMPUR SINGAPORE HONG KONG
TOKYO

First printed 1973

*Set by the Oxford University Press, Oxford
Printed by Robert MacLehose and Co. Ltd
The University Press, Glasgow*

PREFACE

IN 1963 the General Assemblies of the Church of
Scotland, the Presbyterian Church of England, the
Presbyterian Church in Ireland and the Presbyterian
Church of Wales authorized the preparation of a new
edition of *The Church Hymnary*, the previous editions
having appeared in 1898 and 1927. The Joint Committee appointed to undertake this task invited the
United Free Church of Scotland to be represented on
the Church Hymnary Revision Committee.

In the selection and preparation of the contents of
The Church Hymnary: Third Edition the Committee
has been helped by discussion in successive General
Assemblies of the participating Churches, and also by
the careful scrutiny of its work by the Presbyteries of
these Churches, leading to many useful alterations and
improvements. Moreover, much specialized knowledge,
biblical, theological, liturgical, hymnological and liter-
ary, generously shared with the Committee, is gratefully acknowledged.

The General Assembly of the Church of Scotland
gave general approval to the draft of *The Church
Hymnary : Third Edition* in 1968, and similar authoriza-
tion was received from the General Assemblies of the
Presbyterian Church in Ireland, the Presbyterian
Church of Wales, the United Free Church of Scotland,
and also the Presbyterian Church of England, which,
on 5 October 1972, was united with the Congregational
Church in England and Wales to become the United
Reformed Church.

The Committee had corporate responsibility for the
selection and preparation of the music, but acknow-
ledges its debt to those appointed as Music Consult-
ants, Dr. Kenneth Leighton, Mr. Herrick Bunney, Mr.
John Currie and Mr. David Murray; also the late
Mr. Guthrie Foote who, in addition to professional

PREFACE

competence, had wide experience in the publication of music. Mr. Ian Barrie also assisted.

Grateful acknowledgement is also made of the professional help so unsparingly given by the staff of Oxford University Press in the whole preparation of this hymnary.

The Church Hymnary : Third Edition is sent out in the prayerful hope that it may enrich the worship of congregations to the greater glory of God.

In the name of *The Church Hymnary* Revision Committee:

THOMAS H. KEIR, D.D.
Convener

R. STUART LOUDEN, D.D.
Vice-Convener

F. N. DAVIDSON KELLY, S.S.C.
Hon. Secretary

INTRODUCTION

Worship and Hymns

A Church hymn book is essentially designed for Christian worship.

Christ's earthly life and self-giving on the Cross was itself the one offering of perfect worship to the Father whose will he fulfilled. Through Word and Sacrament, as in daily obedience, his faithful disciples are united with him as his Body in the continuing offering of this worship.

Hence each action in Christian worship has a double significance. It is indeed Christ's people who pray and who praise the Father. Nevertheless they do so as the baptized community whose life is so grounded in Christ and bound up with his life that in worship he, as Head, exercises always his authoritative office as Prophet, High Priest and King.

Through the Church's worship, therefore, Christ fulfils today in the life of his people what he did on earth 'once and for all'. When Scripture is read and preached, it is not the words of the Minister the congregation awaits but the Word of Christ who is the Word of God. Through the rites of initiation, Holy Baptism and Confirmation together with Holy Communion, Christ calls his people and establishes them in the covenant of grace. In Baptism he makes the person, whether infant or adult, a member of his Body. In Confirmation he strengthens and blesses the baptized, who profess their faith, as members of his Body with both privileges and responsibilities. In the Holy Communion Christ's eternal self-giving is present still in and through his Church. So, in every action of worship, including what is sung, Christ fulfils his ministry as Prophet, Priest and King in order that through his Church he may be known as Lord by the world he came to save.

Study of the hymns offered in this book will, it is hoped, make these points clear.

The Cultural Context

It has at all times been necessary for the Committee, in the selection of material, to be aware of the special nature of its responsibility: to provide the means for high and holy worship, and at the same time to recognize the cultural limits within which this can be done.

On the one hand Christ, the Lord of the Church, is active in the midst of his worshipping people. It follows that as the spoken language used in church must be true and faithful to the Word of Christ, so the musical language also must be true to it. The Committee therefore had to take care, with what success only experience will show, to ensure that tunes are true to the words to which they are set. It is hoped, moreover, that in many instances the offer of a different tune to already well-known words will enable the words to yield up their meaning more fully.

On the other hand, this faithfulness to the Divine in worship must be balanced by a concern that the music is appropriate to the variety of emotions involved in the people's worship as well as to their musical ability. The Committee therefore had to keep in view the requirements of a number of somewhat differing communities not only in Britain but overseas. It also found it necessary to include a number of hymns of more or less local provenance or use, to meet the specific needs of some particular branch of the Church. Thus it has tried to ensure that every congregation will find in the Hymnary a sufficient number of tunes it can use.

The Contents and their Order

In selecting the *contents* of the Hymnary every effort has been made to present the essential elements in the Biblical revelation as adequately as liturgical necessity demanded and available resources permitted. Since a Church hymnal is essentially a liturgical book, the Committee in determining the *order* in which the hymns are arranged, has borne in mind that the Order of Holy Communion is normative for worship in the Reformed Church and that, where there is no regular weekly celebration of Holy Communion, the service should still follow the eucharistic pattern.

The Order of Common Worship.

The central act of Christian worship from the beginning was understood as a unity, the structure of which involved a double action: (*a*) the 'Liturgy of the Word' based on the reading and exposition of the Scriptures; and (*b*) the 'Liturgy of the faithful', sometimes called 'the Liturgy of the Upper Room'—that is, the Holy Communion or Lord's Supper.

Part I: The approach to God

In the early centuries, Christian worship seems normally to have commenced with reading and preaching. Later, however, it became customary to commence the service with brief acts of approach to God. This comprises *the first part of the service* (Part I of the Hymnary).

Part II: The Word of God

Following his people's approach, God speaks to them through his Word in Holy Scripture and sermon. This 'Liturgy of the Word' is *the second part of the service* (Part II of the Hymnary).

Part III: Response to the Word of God

The third part, to which all else leads, is the 'Liturgy of the Upper Room'—the Holy Communion.

Even where the sacramental elements are not present, there follows response to the Word of God in the Church's outpouring of faith, adoration, thanksgiving, dedication and intercession, culminating in her rejoicing in the communion of saints and the hope of glory (Parts III and IV of the Hymnary). Thus, recommissioned, the Church returns to her work in the world.

Using the Book

It will be noted that there is a certain correspondence both in style and content between the earlier portions of Parts I and III of the Hymnary, the former acknowledging the greatness of God, the latter providing acts of adoration and thanksgiving. Clearly certain hymns in Part III may with perfect propriety be used for the opening of worship, while some in Part I will provide on occasion suitable acts of response to what God has spoken in his Word. Nevertheless the distinction between the two parts of the book remains valid since the hymns in Part III do on the whole express the heightened adoration and thanksgiving which faithful worshippers are more prepared to offer after the Divine Word has been heard. This again is characteristic of the Communion Service.

The Table of Contents indicates the shape of the service both in its broad pattern and in its variable details; while cross-references at the end of the sub-sections in the body of the book point out certain cognate hymns to be found in other parts of the Hymnary.

The value of arranging a hymn-book in this way, both to ministers in selecting a praise list and to congregations at worship, will, the Committee trusts, prove itself in practice.

Psalms and Paraphrases

From the beginning the Psalter had an integral place in Christian worship. Having regard to this and also to the traditional use of metrical versions in the Reformed Church, the Committee hopes, by including a selection of psalms, both prose and metrical, to promote a fuller use of the riches of the Psalter and that the range of selection may be widened.

INTRODUCTION

The selections from the Psalter and Scottish Paraphrases are normally placed first in the appropriate section or sub-section of the Hymnary.

Hymns for Children

In selecting hymns for use by children, it should not be forgotten that in this, as in other fields, it is better that a child's reach should exceed his grasp than that he should be encouraged to sing what is banal or below his best capacity. Many of the great hymns of the Church are admirably suited for children's enjoyment and use, so that their omission from children's worship is a serious lack.

Hymns suitable only for children and for younger children are placed according to the same principle as the other hymns, hymns of approach to God in Part I and so on, except that they are invariably last in the sub-section. These hymns are designated in a distinctive way in the Index of First Lines.

The Contribution of the Centuries

Each age, including our own, has contributed something new and of value to the rich treasury of the Church's hymnody, and this is reflected in the contents of the book, which contains a number of hymns and tunes written this century, as well as a significant corpus of specially commissioned music.

Congregations will gain both in the variety and the devotional fullness of their worship by extending the range of their hymnody.

So far as possible the dates of author, composer or source are given.

Thus the Church is constantly reminded that her inheritance and her promise are alike ageless, because they are from God the Eternal;

TO WHOM, FATHER, SON AND HOLY SPIRIT, ONE GOD,

BE GLORY IN THE CHURCH TO THE AGES OF AGES.

INTRODUCTORY NOTES TO THE MUSIC

The Selection of the Music

IN the selection of music, three guiding principles have been followed:

1. that the tunes and settings should in general be easily learned and readily singable by the average congregation, and that tunes should be thoroughly suited to the words they are to serve;

2. that where a familiar tune has to be omitted, it should wherever possible be replaced by another familiar tune, or else a cross-reference given to such a tune occurring elsewhere in the book;

3. that a fine tune may well be employed more than once, thus bringing into use certain hymns previously unfamiliar because the tune was unknown or uninspiring, and also providing a known tune for special hymns only rarely required—for example at weddings, funeral services, consecration of churches and so on.

The Style and Interpretation of Congregational Music

SINGING

Every hymn has its own style, and the manner of its performance will vary, depending on a number of practical considerations—the occasion, the size of the congregation, the acoustics of the building. Consequently, few indications of *tempo* are offered, but it is hoped that the use of the crotchet instead of the minim as the standard pulse will assist towards lively musical interpretation.

The end of the verbal line in a hymn is generally indicated by the sign ∥ in the musical setting.

Unison verses should be used at times to highlight the words.

Amen has been excluded where it is not appropriate, and should be sung only where it is printed.

ACCOMPANIMENT

It is recognized that the organ will not always be the accompanying instrument. The following points are for general guidance.

(*a*) *The congregation* will best hear notes of at least an octave higher, or lower, than their own voices. Hence organ upper-work and pedals, piano lower and upper octaves, double bass, and strings and woodwind in upper octaves will prove most helpful in leading singing.

(*b*) *The accompaniment* should clearly indicate the mood for each verse, while avoiding too precious an interpretation within the verse itself.

(*c*) *Tunes* should be played over at the speed intended for singing. Normally it is only necessary for the first phrase to be played over. The practice of playing first and final phrases is to be discouraged.

MUSICAL SETTINGS

Some tunes have been revised to a limited extent. Others have been strengthened by more sweeping alterations in the harmonic structure.

A few settings more suitable for a choir than for the average congregation have been included.

Children's hymns and those recommended for unison singing have generally been given accompaniments which are both effective and readily playable.

PROSE SETTINGS

To encourage a wider and more varied use of speech rhythms four musical styles have been included.

1. In *Anglican chanting* the spoken word should always be the guide, the words being sung at the speed

of clear speech with the stresses and rhythms of normal speech. Certain details of the pointing have been left to the individual choirmaster's own initiative and preference.

2. *Psalms or Canticles in the style of Gelineau* (e.g. No. 67) are designed to be sung with the rhythm of natural speech bound only by one slow pulse in each bar. The organist must be careful to supply this pulse clearly and regularly. Further details will be found in the introductions to *The Psalms of Joseph Gelineau*, published by the Grail Press.

3. By the introduction of *chanted psalms using only a few chords* (e.g. No. 66) it is hoped that congregations who have not yet attempted to sing prose settings will be encouraged to do so. The short series of chords or 'chant' is used once to each verse. The melodic note changes on the syllables or word marked with an acute accent. These settings may be sung in unison or in harmony.

4. In classical *plainchant* the syllables should be sung with even spacing, but without stiffness. Where possible the singing should be unaccompanied. If however a keyboard accompaniment is used it should contain as few chord changes as possible, and the choice of harmony should be governed by the accepted style for the accompaniment of modal music.[1]

The following symbols, occurring in the music or in the verbal text as the case may be, will be found sufficient to direct the singing of the Tones.

[ ] Notes enclosed in a *bracket* are used only for the first verse of the psalm; succeeding verses commence on the reciting note.

[|] A *vertical* indicates the point at which the reciting note is quitted. Occasionally it will be found

---

[1] Further guidance may be found in J. H. Arnold, *The Accompaniment of Plainsong* (O.U.P., reprinted by Waltham Forest Books); and in *A Manual of Plainsong* edited by H. B. Briggs and W. H. Frere, revised and enlarged by J. H. Arnold (Novello).

that at the end of the half-verse a note is left over, for which there is no verbal syllable remaining; in such instances the note is simply omitted. This is termed the 'abrupt mediation'. In No. 166 (Psalm 2) for instance, this happens a number of times. Notes are also omitted if necessary from the traditional endings.

: A *colon* at the end of the half-verse corresponds with the bar-line in the music, at which point a short silence occurs, the duration of which is approximately equal to the two previous syllables. There should, however, be no break between verses, but the first syllable of each new verse should maintain without interruption the flow of notes from the last syllable of the previous verse.

⌒ A *tie* indicates that two syllables are to be sung at the same pitch. In other words, the note of the first syllable is simply repeated.

.. A *double dot* above the text is used where one syllable requires two notes of the chant.

— A *long dash* indicates that the reciting note is omitted altogether.

The method of chanting is as follows. The first half-verse of a psalm should, if possible, be chanted by one or two solo voices, the second half of the verse being sung by the choir or congregation or both. Thereafter complete verses should be sung alternately by, for example, the choir (verse 2) and congregation (verse 3) and so on; or else by a chanter (verse 2) and choir (verse 3). Or some other similar pattern may be followed, such as the ladies' voices of the choir (verse 2) being answered by the men's voices (verse 3), always provided that the alternation is that of complete verses. Only the first verse should be divided between voices or sections of singers at the half-way point.

ACKNOWLEDGEMENTS

The Church Hymnary Trust wishes to thank the following who have given permission for copyright material to be printed. *A blank in the second column indicates that the author is also the owner of the copyright.*

WORDS

AUTHOR	COPYRIGHT OWNER	NO. OF HYMN
Adams, J.	National Adult School Union	444
Agnew, E.	© W. L. Jenkins 1953	230 lines 1–12 from *Songs & Hymns for Primary Children,*
	© The Geneva Press 1972	230 lines 13–16 from *Teachers' Guide Book Revised*
Alexander, J. N. S.		162, 203
Alington, C. A.	The Proprietors of *Hymns Ancient and Modern*	270, 120, 599, 555
Alston, A. E.	Mr. C. Alston	31 (tr.)
Andrew, Father	A. R. Mowbray & Co. Ltd.	252
Arlott, J.		619
Armitage, E. S.	United Reformed Church	553
Baring-Gould, S.	Mr. G. Hitchcock	423, 480, 653
Barkley, J. M.		595
Barnard, W. E.		625
Bax, C.	A. D. Peters & Co.	84
Bayly, A. F.		554 (alt.), 141, 503 (alt.), 426, 458
Bell, G. K. A.	Oxford University Press	474
Blatchford, A. N.	Archberg, Hopwood & Crew Ltd.	148
Bourne, G. H.	Oxford University Press	583
Bowie, W. Russell	Abingdon Press	255, 509
Bridges, R.	Oxford University Press	55, 57, 119, 156, 251, 403, 405, 408, 471 (i), 642
Briggs, G. W.	Oxford University Press	215, 219, 452, 505, 572
Brownlie, J.	Mr. A. Rutherford Brownlie	95
Buchanan, V.	Oxford University Press	327

ACKNOWLEDGEMENTS

AUTHOR	COPYRIGHT OWNER	NO. OF HYMN
Chesterton, G. K.	Oxford University Press	520, from *The English Hymnal*
Clarkson, E. M.	Inter Varsity Press	337, 592
Cropper, M.		467, 228
Crum, J. M. C.	Oxford University Press	278, from *The Oxford Book of Carols*
Darbyshire, J. R.	Oxford University Press	260
Dearmer, P.	Oxford University Press	341, from *The Oxford Book of Carols* 43, 111, 515, 588, from *The English Hymnal* 128, 416, from *Songs of Praise*
Draper, W. H.	Roberton Publications	30
Dudley-Smith, T.		164
Dugmore, E. E.	Mr. E. M. Mills	451
East, J. T.	Methodist Youth Department	222
Editors of *The B.B.C. Hymn Book*	Oxford University Press	305
Ferguson, J. M. Macdougall	Religious Education Press	631, 654
Fletcher, F.	Oxford University Press	309
Fosdick, H. E.	Mrs. E. Fosdick Downs	88
Frere, M. Temple	The National Society	622
Gelineau, J.	A. P. Watt & Son Ltd.	66, 350, 389
Gill, D. M.		384
Gillet, G. G. S.	Oxford University Press	328
Green, F. Pratt	Oxford University Press	152
Greenaway, A. R.	The Proprietors of *Hymns Ancient and Modern*	244, 248
Head, B. P.	The Revd. A. Hanbury Head	339
Housman, L.	Oxford University Press	196, 507
Hoyle, R. Birch	World Student Christian Federation	279
Huey, M. E.	©W. L. Jenkins 1963	17, from *Songs and Hymns for Primary Children*
Hull, E.	Chatto & Windus Ltd.	87 (coll.)
Hunter, A. M.		399
Hunter-Clare, T. C.		513
Ikeler, C. R.	©W. L. Jenkins 1963	427, from *Songs and Hymns for Primary Children*
Jackson, F. A.	National Christian Education Council	633, 630
Jefferies, C.	Joint Action for Christian Literature Overseas (Feed the Minds)	469

ACKNOWLEDGEMENTS

AUTHOR	COPYRIGHT OWNER	NO. OF HYMN
Jones, A. M.	United Society for Christian Literature	340
Kipling, R.	A. P. Watt & Son Ltd.	446
Kirkland, P. M.	The Misses Kirkland	283
Kitchin, G. W. and M. R. Newbolt	The Proprietors of *Hymns Ancient and Modern*	550
Littlewood, R. Wesley	Methodist Youth Department	528
Lowry, S. C.	Oxford University Press	454
Macalister, E. F. Boyle	National Christian Education Council	16, 557
Macalister, R. A. S.	Oxford University Press	129, 401
Macnicol, N.	Trustees of the late Helen Macnicol	82
Masterman, J. H. B.		508
Mathams, B. J.	Oxford University Press	501
Mathews, W. J.	Oxford University Press	100
Mealy, N. and M.	Seabury Press Inc.	155, from *Sing for Joy*
Merrill, W. P.	*The Presbyterian Outlook*	477
Milner, Barry A. M.	The National Society	280
Moore, J. Boyd		601
Moore, J. E.	United Church Press	466, from *Pilgrim Bible Stories for Children*
Niles, D. T.	East Asia Christian Conference	415
Oxenham, John	Westminster Bank Ltd. and Miss T. Dunkerley	425
Parker, W. H.	National Christian Education Council	124
Perkins, J. E.	United Church Press	157, from *As Children Worship*
Phillips, A. N.		506
Phillips, E. M.		690
Piggot, W. Charter	Oxford University Press	134, 538
Pitt-Watson, I.		126, 64, 68 (paraphrased from *The New English Bible*)
Quinn, J.	Geoffrey Chapman Ltd.	276, 308, 568 (adpt.), 581, 589, 175
Reed, E. M.	Evans Bros. Ltd.	186
Rees, T.	A. R. Mowbray & Co. Ltd.	334, 473
Roberts, K. E.	Oxford University Press	185, from *The Oxford Book of Carols*
Roberts, R. E.	Oxford University Press	330
Scott, R. B. T.		511
Shields, E. McE.	©Presbyterian Board of Christian Education 1935 and 1963	229

ACKNOWLEDGEMENTS

AUTHOR	COPYRIGHT OWNER	NO. OF HYMN
Shillito, E.	Oxford University Press	292
Skemp, A.	National Christian Education Council	156
Smith, F. M.	The National Society	447
Snow, G.		91
Stephenson, L.	Oxford University Press	375
Struther, J.	Oxford University Press	92, 206
Terry, R. R.	Oxford University Press	652, from *The Oxford Book of Carols*
Tucker, F. Bland	The Church Pension Fund	586 (alt.), 297, 522, 24.
Tweedy, H. Hallam	Hymn Society of America	133, 499
Tynan-Hinkson, K.	Search Press Ltd.	524
Waddell, H.	The Girls Auxiliary	486
Watt, L. MacLean	Mr. A. L. MacLean Watt	667
Wilkinson, K. Barclay	Mr. D. H. Gould	432
Winslow, J. C.		428, 51
Woodward, G. R.	A. R. Mowbray & Co. Ltd.	271
Woodward, G. R.	Schott & Co. Ltd.	604, 640, from *The B.B.C. Hymn Book*
Wright, W.	Young Men's Christian Association	614

The Church Hymnary Trust also wishes to thank Dr. Bernard Rose for carrying out the pointing of the psalms set to PLAINSONG CHANTS in this book: Nos. 63, 158, 166, 231, 239, 262, 284, 310, 326.

The pointing is copyright and may not be reproduced in any form without application in the first instance to Oxford University Press.

CONTENTS

PREFACE   *page* v

INTRODUCTION   vii

INTRODUCTORY NOTES TO THE MUSIC   xiii

ACKNOWLEDGEMENTS   xvii

                                               HYMNS
I. APPROACH TO GOD   1–134
   The House of God   1–18
   The Majesty of God   19–40
   Morning   41–49
   Evening   50–59
   Confession and Supplication   60–100
   Invocation   101–12
   Illumination   113–24
   Holy Scripture   125–34

II. THE WORD OF GOD: HIS MIGHTY ACTS   135–344
    Creation and Providence   135–57
    The Promise of the Messiah   158–65
    Christ's Incarnation   166–203
    Christ's Life and Ministry   204–30
    Christ's Passion and Cross   231–61
    Christ's Resurrection and Exaltation   262–92
    Christ's Reign and Priesthood   293–309
    Christ's Coming with Power   310–25
    Pentecost   326–32
    The Holy Spirit in the Church   333–44

III. RESPONSE TO THE WORD OF GOD   345–545
     Adoration and Thanksgiving   345–86
     Affirmation   387–427
     Dedication and Discipleship   428–50
     Stewardship and Service   451–67

CONTENTS

		HYMNS
Witness and Encouragement		468–88
Intercession:		
	For the Church	489–92
	For the Church's Mission	493–502
	For the World	503–15
	For the Nation	516–21
	For the Family	522–24
	For the Ministry of Healing	525–6
	For Travellers and the Absent	527–9
The Church Triumphant		530–45

IV. THE SACRAMENTS	546–90
Holy Baptism	546–57
Holy Communion	558–90

V. OTHER ORDINANCES	591–610
Confirmation	591–5
Ordination	596–7
Marriage	598–602
Funeral Services	603–8
Dedication of Church Buildings	609–10

VI. TIMES AND SEASONS	611–33
New Year	611–16
Spring	617–22
Summer	623–5
Seedtime and Harvest	626–31
Winter	632–3

VII. CLOSE OF SERVICE	634–62
Close of Service	634–40
Evening	641–56
Doxologies	657–62

VIII. PERSONAL FAITH AND DEVOTION	663–95

INDEXES	
	page
Index of Psalms	249
Table of Liturgical Items	251
Index of First Lines	252

I

APPROACH TO GOD

THE HOUSE OF GOD

I

PSALM 100

ALL people that on earth do
dwell,
Sing to the Lord with cheerful
voice,
Him serve with mirth, his praise
forth tell,
Come ye before him and rejoice.

2 Know that the Lord is God in-
deed;
Without our aid he did us make;
We are his folk, he doth us feed,
And for his sheep he doth us
take.

3 O enter then his gates with
praise,
Approach with joy his courts
unto:
Praise, laud, and bless his Name
always,
For it is seemly so to do.

4 For why? the Lord our God is
good,
His mercy is for ever sure;
His truth at all times firmly
stood,
And shall from age to age endure.

5 *To Father, Son, and Holy Ghost,
The God whom earth and heaven
adore,
Be glory, as it was of old,
Is now, and shall be evermore.*
Amen.

2

BEFORE Jehovah's awesome
throne,
Ye nations, bow with sacred
joy;

Know that the Lord is God
alone;
He can create, and he de-
stroy.

2 His sovereign power, without
our aid,
Made us of clay, and formed
us men;
And, when like wandering sheep
we strayed,
He brought us to his fold
again.

3 We are his people, we his care,—
Our souls and all our mortal
frame:
What lasting honours shall we
rear,
Almighty Maker, to thy
Name?

4 We'll crowd thy gates with
thankful songs,
High as the heavens our
voices raise;
And earth, with her ten thousand tongues,
Shall fill thy courts with
sounding praise.

5 Wide as the world is thy com-
mand,
Vast as eternity thy love;
Firm as a rock thy truth must
stand,
When rolling years shall
cease to move.
ISAAC WATTS, 1674–1748, and
JOHN WESLEY, 1703–91
From Psalm 100

3

PSALM 100
Jubilate Deo

O BE joyful in the Lord ' all
ye ' lands : serve the
Lord with gladness ⸱and
come before his ' presence '
with a ' song.

1

2 Be ye sure that the Lord ' he
 is ' God : it is he that hath
 made us and we are his
 own we are his ' people ·
 and the ' sheep of his '
 pasture.

3 O go your way into his gates
 with thanksgiving and
 into his ' courts with '
 praise : be thankful unto him
 and speak ' good ' of his '
 Name.

4 For the Lord is gracious his
 mercy is ' ever- ' lasting :
 and his truth endureth from
 gener- ' ation to ' gener- '
 ation.

*Glory ' be to the ' Father : and to
 the Son ' and to the ' Holy '
 Ghost :*

*As it ' was in the be- ' ginning :
 is now and ever shall be '
 world without ' end.*
                    A- ' men.

4   PSALM 84, verses 1–5

HOW lovely is thy dwelling-
 place,
 O Lord of hosts, to me!
The tabernacles of thy grace
 How pleasant, Lord, they be!

2 My thirsty soul longs
 vehemently,
 Yea faints, thy courts to see:
My very heart and flesh cry
 out,
 O living God, for thee.

3 Behold, the sparrow findeth out
 An house wherein to rest;
The swallow also for herself
 Hath purchasèd a nest;

4 Even thine own altars, where
 she safe
 Her young ones forth may
 bring,
O thou almighty Lord of hosts,
 Who art my God and King.

5 Blest are they in thy house that
 dwell,
 They ever give thee praise.

Blest is the man whose strength
 thou art,
 In whose heart are thy ways.

6 *To Father, Son, and Holy Ghost,
 The God whom we adore,
Be glory, as it was, and is,
 And shall be evermore. Amen.*

5   PSALM 15

WITHIN thy tabernacle,
 Lord,
 Who shall abide with thee?
And in thy high and holy hill
 Who shall a dweller be?

2 The man that walketh up-
 rightly,
 And worketh righteousness,
And as he thinketh in his heart,
 So doth he truth express.

3 Who doth not slander with his
 tongue,
 Nor to his friend doth hurt;
Nor yet against his neighbour
 doth
 Take up an ill report.

4 In whose eyes vile men are des-
 pised;
 But those that God do fear
He honoureth; and changeth
 not,
 Though to his hurt he swear.

5 His coin puts not to usury,
 Nor take reward will he
Against the guiltless. Who doth
 thus
 Shall never movèd be.

6 *To Father, Son, and Holy Ghost,
 The God whom we adore,
Be glory, as it was, and is,
 And shall be evermore. Amen.*

6   PSALM 36, verses 5–9

THY mercy, Lord, is in the
 heavens;
 Thy truth doth reach the
 clouds:

Thy justice is like mountains
    great;
    Thy judgments deep as
        floods:

2 Lord, thou preservest man and
        beast.
    How precious is thy grace!
    Therefore in shadow of thy
        wings
    Men's sons their trust shall
        place.

3 They with the fatness of thy
        house
    Shall be well satisfied;
    From rivers of thy pleasures
        thou
    Wilt drink to them provide.

4 Because of life the fountain pure
    Remains alone with thee;
    And in that purest light of
        thine
    We clearly light shall see.

5 *To Father, Son, and Holy Ghost,*
    The God whom we adore,
    Be glory, as it was, and is,
    And shall be evermore. Amen.

7   PSALM 43, verses 3–5

O SEND thy light forth and
    thy truth;
    Let them be guides to me,
And bring me to thine holy hill,
    Even where thy dwellings be.

2 Then will I to God's altar go,
    To God my chiefest joy:
    Yea, God, my God, thy Name to
        praise
    My harp I will employ.

3 Why art thou then cast down,
        my soul?
    What should discourage thee?
    And why with vexing thoughts
        art thou
    Disquieted in me?

4 Still trust in God; for him to
        praise
    Good cause I yet shall have:
    He of my countenance is the
        health,
    My God that doth me save.

5 *To Father, Son, and Holy Ghost,*
    The God whom we adore,
    Be glory, as it was, and is,
    And shall be evermore. Amen.

8   PSALM 116, verses 1–7

I LOVE the Lord, because my
    voice
    And prayers he did hear.
I, while I live, will call on him,
    Who bowed to me his ear.

2 The cords of death on every side
    Encompassed me around;
    The sorrows of the grave me
        seized,
    I grief and trouble found.

3 Upon the Name of God the Lord
    Then did I call, and say,
Deliver thou my soul, O Lord,
    I do thee humbly pray.

4 God merciful and righteous is,
    Yea, gracious is our Lord.
    God saves the meek: I was
        brought low,
    He did me help afford.

5 O thou my soul, do thou return
    Unto thy quiet rest;
    For largely, lo, the Lord to thee
    His bounty hath expressed.

6 *To Father, Son, and Holy Ghost,*
    The God whom we adore,
    Be glory, as it was, and is,
    And shall be evermore. Amen.

9   *Lobe den Herren*

P RAISE to the Lord, the
    Almighty, the King of crea-
        tion;
O my soul, praise him, for he is
    thy health and salvation;
    All ye who hear,
    Now to his temple draw near,
Joining in glad adoration.

2 Praise to the Lord, who o'er
    all things so wondrously
        reigneth,

Shieldeth thee gently from
   harm, or when fainting
   sustaineth;
Hast thou not seen
How thy heart's wishes have
   been
Granted in what he ordaineth?

3 Praise to the Lord, who doth
      prosper thy work and de-
      fend thee;
   Surely his goodness and mercy
      shall daily attend thee;
   Ponder anew
   What the Almighty can do,
   Who with his love doth befriend
      thee.

4 Praise to the Lord! O let all that
      is in me adore him!
   All that hath life and breath,
      come now with praises be-
      fore him!
   Let the Amen
   Sound from his people again:
   Gladly for aye we adore him.

JOACHIM NEANDER, 1650–80
Tr. CATHERINE WINKWORTH
1827–78, and others
From Psalms 103, 150

10 *Angularis fundamentum lapis*
    Christus missus est

CHRIST is made the sure
   foundation,
   Christ the head and corner-
      stone,
   Chosen of the Lord, and
      precious,
   Binding all the Church in one,
   Holy Zion's help for ever,
   And her confidence alone.

2 To this temple, where we call
      thee,
   Come, O Lord of Hosts, to-
      day:
   With thy wonted loving-kind-
      ness,
   Hear thy servants as they
      pray,
   And thy fullest benediction
   Shed within its walls alway.

3 Here vouchsafe to all thy ser-
      vants
   What they ask of thee to
      gain,

What they gain from thee for
   ever
With the blessèd to retain,
And hereafter in thy glory
   Evermore with thee to reign.

4 *Laud and honour to the Father,*
   Laud and honour to the Son,
Laud and honour to the Spirit,
   Ever Three and ever One,
One in might, and One in glory,
   While unending ages run.
                           Amen.

Latin, 7th or 8th century
Tr. JOHN MASON NEALE, 1818–66
altered

11

JESUS, stand among us
   In thy risen power;
Let this time of worship
   Be a hallowed hour.

2 Breathe the Holy Spirit
   Into every heart;
Bid the fears and sorrows
   From each soul depart.

3 Thus with quickened footsteps
   We pursue our way,
Watching for the dawning
   Of eternal day.

WILLIAM PENNEFATHER, 1816–73

12 *Macht hoch die Thür, das Thor*
    macht weit

LIFT up your heads, ye
   mighty gates,
         Alleluia!
Behold, the King of glory waits;
         Alleluia!
The King of kings is drawing
   near,
The Saviour of the world is here.
         Alleluia!

2 O blest the land, the city blest,
         Alleluia!
Where Christ the ruler is confessed.
         Alleluia!
O happy hearts and happy
   homes
To whom this King in triumph
   comes.
         Alleluia!

4

3 Redeemer, come! with us abide,
  Alleluia!
Our hearts to thee we open wide,
  Alleluia!
Thy presence with us let us feel,
Thy grace and love in us reveal.
  Alleluia!

GEORG WEISSEL, 1590–1635
Tr. CATHERINE WINKWORTH, 1827–78
altered

13

Lux alma Jesu mentium

LIGHT of the anxious
    heart,
Jesus, thou dost appear,
To bid the gloom of guilt de-
    part,
  And shed thy sweetness here.

2 Joyous is he with whom,
  God's Word, thou dost abide,
Sweet Light of our eternal
    home,
  To fleshly sense denied.

3 Brightness of God above,
  Unfathomable grace,
Thy presence be a fount of love
  Within thy chosen place.

c. 1200
Tr. JOHN HENRY NEWMAN, 1801–90

14

WE come unto our fathers'
    God;
  Their Rock is our Salvation;
The eternal arms, their dear
    abode,
  We make our habitation;
We bring thee, Lord, the praise
    they brought;
  We seek thee as thy saints have
    sought
In every generation.

2 The fire divine their steps that
    led
  Still goeth bright before us;
The heavenly shield around
    them spread
  Is still high holden o'er us;

The grace those sinners that
    subdued,
The strength those weaklings
    that renewed,
  Doth vanquish, doth restore
    us.

3 Their joy unto their Lord we
    bring;
  Their song to us descendeth;
The Spirit who in them did sing
  To us his music lendeth;
His song in them, in us, is one;
  We raise it high, we send it
    on,—
The song that never endeth.

4 Ye saints to come, take up the
    strain,
  The same sweet theme en-
    deavour;
Unbroken be the golden chain;
  Keep on the song for ever;
Safe in the same dear dwelling-
    place,
Rich with the same eternal
    grace,
  Bless the same boundless
    Giver.

THOMAS HORNBLOWER GILL
1819–1906

15

WE love the place, O God,
    Wherein thine honour
    dwells;
The joy of thine abode
  All earthly joy excels.

2 It is the house of prayer,
  Wherein thy servants meet;
And thou, O Lord, art there,
  Thy chosen flock to greet.

3 We love the word of life,
  The word that tells of peace,
Of comfort in the strife,
  And joys that never cease.

4 We love to sing below
  For mercies freely given;
But O we long to know
  The triumph song of heaven!

APPROACH TO GOD

5 Lord Jesus, give us grace,
   On earth to love thee more,
In heaven to see thy face,
   And with thy saints adore.

WILLIAM BULLOCK, 1798–1874
and HENRY WILLIAMS BAKER
1821–77

16 *For younger children*

LORD Jesus, be thou with us
   now,
As in thy house in prayer we
   bow;
And when we sing, and when
   we pray,
Help us to mean the words we
   say,
Help us to listen to thy word,
And keep our thoughts from
   wandering, Lord.

EDITH FLORENCE BOYLE MACALISTER
1873–1950

17 *For younger children*

SERVE the Lord with joy and
   gladness,
Come into his gates with song;
Serve the Lord with loving-
   kindness,
Love and praise him all day
   long.

MARY ELIZABETH HUEY
Based on Psalm 100, verse 2

18 *For younger children*

THIS is God's holy house
   And he is here today;
He hears each song of praise;
And listens while we pray.

LOUISE M. OGELVEE

THE MAJESTY OF GOD

19 PSALM 95, verses 1–6

O COME, and let us to the
   Lord
In songs our voices raise,
With joyful noise let us the
   Rock
Of our salvation praise.

2 Let us before his presence come
   With praise and thankful
      voice;
Let us sing psalms to him with
   grace,
And make a joyful noise.

3 The Lord's a great God and
      great King,
   Above all gods he is.
Depths of the earth are in his
      hand,
   The strength of hills is his.

4 To him the spacious sea belongs,
   For he the same did make;
The dry land also from his
      hands
   Its form at first did take.

5 O come and let us worship him,
   Let us bow down withal,
And on our knees before the
      Lord
   Our Maker let us fall.

6 *To Father, Son, and Holy Ghost,*
   The God whom we adore,
Be glory, as it was, and is,
   And shall be evermore. Amen.

20 PSALM 95, verses 1–7
Venite, exultemus

O COME let us ' sing unto
   the ' Lord : let us heartily
rejoice in the ' strength of '
our sal- ' vation.

2 Let us come before his ' presence with ' thanksgiving :
and show ourselves ' glad in '
him with ' psalms.

3 For the Lord is a ' great '
   God : and a great ' King
a- ' bove all ' gods.

4 In his hand are all the '
  corners . of the ' earth : and
  the strength of the ' hills is '
  his ' also.

5 The sea is ' his and he ' made
  it : and his hands pre- '
  pared the ' dry ' land.

6 O come let us ' worship and
  fall ' down : and ' kneel
  be · fore the ' Lord our '
  Maker.

7 For he is our God and ' we
  are his ' people : he is our '
  shepherd and ' we are his '
  flock.

  Glory ' be to the ' Father : and
    to the Son ' and to the '
    Holy ' Ghost :

  As it ' was in the be- ' ginning '
    is now and ever shall be '
    world without ' end.
                            A- ' men.

2I Psalm 95, verses 1–7

*O COME let us sing unto the
    Lórd:
  lét us make a joyful noise to the
    rock of our salvátion.
Let us come before his présence
    with thánksgiving,,
  ánd make a joyful noise unto
    him with psálms.
For the Lórd is a greát God,
  ánd a great Kíng above all góds.
In his hands are the deép places of
    the éarth:
  the strength of the hills is his
    álso.
The sea is hís and he máde it:
  ánd his hands fórmed the drý
    land.
O come let us wórship and bow
    dówn:
  lét us kneel before the Lórd our
    máker.

For he is our Gód;
  ánd we are the people of his
    pasture and the sheép of his
    hánd.

Glory bé to the Fáther,
  ánd to the Són, and to the Hóly
    Ghost ;
As it was in the beginning, is nów
    and ever shall be :,
  wórld without énd. Amen.

  * For pointing system, see p. xv.

22 Psalm 96, verses 1, 2, 6–8

O SING a new song to the
    Lord:
  Sing all the earth to God.
  To God sing, bless his Name,
    show still
  His saving health abroad.

2 Great honour is before his face,
    And majesty divine;
  Strength is within his holy
    place,
  And there doth beauty shine.

3 Do ye ascribe unto the Lord,
    Of people every tribe,
  Glory do ye unto the Lord,
    And mighty power ascribe.

4 Give ye the glory to the Lord
    That to his Name is due;
  Come ye into his courts, and
    bring
  An offering with you.

5 *To Father, Son, and Holy Ghost,*
    The God whom we adore,
  Be glory, as it was, and is,
    And shall be evermore. Amen.

23 Psalm 9, verses 7–11

G OD shall endure for aye ; he
    doth
  For judgment set his throne;
  In righteousness to judge the
    world,
  Justice to give each one.

2 God also will a refuge be
    For those that are oppressed;
  A refuge will he be in times
    Of trouble to distressed.

3 And they that know thy Name,
    in thee
  Their confidence will place:
  For thou hast not forsaken them
    That truly seek thy face.

4 O sing ye praises to the Lord
    That dwells in Zion hill;
  Among all nations of the earth
    His deeds record ye still.

5 *To Father, Son, and Holy Ghost,*
    The God whom we adore,
  Be glory, as it was, and is,
    And shall be evermore. Amen.

24   PSALM 46, verses 1–5

GOD is our refuge and our
    strength,
  In straits a present aid;
  Therefore, although the earth
    remove,
  We will not be afraid:

2 Though hills amidst the seas be
    cast;
  Though waters roaring make,
  And troubled be; yea, though
    the hills
  By swelling seas do shake.

3 A river is, whose streams make
    glad
  The city of our God,
  The holy place, wherein the
    Lord
  Most high hath his abode.

4 God in the midst of her doth
    dwell;
  Nothing shall her remove:
  God unto her an helper will,
    And that right early, prove.

5 *To Father, Son, and Holy Ghost,*
    The God whom we adore,
  Be glory, as it was, and is,
    And shall be evermore. Amen.

25   PSALM 62, verses 5–8

ONLY on God do thou, my
    soul,
  Still patiently attend;
  My expectation and my hope
    On him alone depend.

2 He only my salvation is,
    And my strong rock is he;
  He only is my sure defence:
    I shall not movèd be.

3 In God my glory placèd is,
    And my salvation sure;
  In God the rock is of my
    strength,
  My refuge most secure.

4 Ye people, place your con-
    fidence
  In him continually;
  Before him pour ye out your
    heart;
  God is our refuge high.

5 *To Father, Son, and Holy Ghost,*
    The God whom we adore,
  Be glory, as it was, and is,
    And shall be evermore. Amen.

26   PSALM 27, verses 1, 3–5, 14

THE Lord's my light and
    saving health,
  Who shall make me dis-
    mayed?
  My life's strength is the Lord,
    of whom
  Then shall I be afraid?

2 Against me though an host en-
    camp,
  My heart yet fearless is:
  Though war against me rise, I
    will
  Be confident in this.

3 One thing I of the Lord desired,
    And will seek to obtain,
  That all days of my life I may
    Within God's house remain;

4· That I the beauty of the Lord
    Behold may and admire,
  And that I in his holy place
    May reverently enquire.

5 For he in his pavilion shall
  Me hide in evil days;
In secret of his tent me hide,
  And on a rock me raise.

6 Wait on the Lord, and be thou
    strong,
  And he shall strength afford
Unto thine heart; yea, do thou
    wait,
  I say, upon the Lord.

7 *To Father, Son, and Holy Ghost,*
  The God whom we adore,
Be glory, as it was, and is,
  And shall be evermore. Amen.

27   PSALM 33, verses 1–5

YE righteous, in the Lord re-
    joice;
  It comely is and right,
That upright men, with thank-
    ful voice,
  Should praise the Lord of
    might.

2 Praise God with harp, and unto
    him
  Sing with the psaltery;
Upon a ten-stringed instru-
    ment
  Make ye sweet melody.

3 A new song to him sing, and
    play
  With loud noise skilfully;
For right is God's word, all his
    works
  Are done in verity.

4 To judgment and to righteous-
    ness
  A love he beareth still;
The loving-kindness of the
    Lord
  The earth throughout doth
    fill.

5 *To Father, Son, and Holy Ghost,*
  The God whom we adore,
Be glory, as it was, and is,
  And shall be evermore. Amen.

28   PSALM 65, verses 1–4

PRAISE waits for thee in
    Zion, Lord:
  To thee vows paid shall be.
O thou that hearer art of prayer,
  All flesh shall come to thee.

2 Iniquities, I must confess,
  Prevail against me do:
But as for our transgressions
    all,
  Them purge away shalt thou.

3 Blest is the man whom thou
    dost choose
  And makest approach to
    thee,
That he within thy courts, O
    Lord,
  May still a dweller be:

4 We surely shall be satisfied
  With thy abundant grace,
And with the goodness of thy
    house,
  Even of thy holy place.

5 *To Father, Son, and Holy Ghost,*
  The God whom we adore,
Be glory, as it was, and is,
  And shall be evermore. Amen.

29   PSALM 92, verses 1–4

TO render thanks unto the
    Lord
  It is a comely thing,
And to thy Name, O thou most
    high,
  Due praise aloud to sing.

2 Thy loving-kindness to show
    forth
  When shines the morning
    light;
And to declare thy faithful-
    ness
  With pleasure every night,

3 Upon a ten-stringed instru-
    ment,
  And on the psaltery,
Upon the harp with solemn
    sound
  And grave sweet melody.

4 For thou, Lord, by thy mighty
        works
    Hast made my heart right
        glad ;
    And I will triumph in the works
    Which by thine hands were
        made.

5 *To Father, Son, and Holy Ghost,*
    The God whom we adore,
    Be glory, as it was, and is,
    And shall be evermore. Amen.

30   *Laudato sia Dio mio Signore*

ALL creatures of our God and
    King,
Lift up your voice and with us
    sing
    Alleluia, Alleluia!
Thou burning sun with golden
    beam,
Thou silver moon with softer
    gleam,
    O praise him, O praise him,
    Alleluia, Alleluia, Alleluia!

*2 Thou rushing wind that art so
        strong,
    Ye clouds that sail in heaven
        along,
        O praise him, Alleluia!
    Thou rising morn, in praise
        rejoice,
    Ye lights of evening, find a
        voice:

*3 Thou flowing water, pure and
        clear,
    Make music for thy Lord to
        hear,
        Alleluia, Alleluia!
    Thou fire so masterful and
        bright,
    That givest man both warmth
        and light:

4 Dear mother earth, who day by
        day
    Unfoldest blessings on our
        way,
        O praise him, Alleluia!
    The flowers and fruits that in
        thee grow,
    Let them his glory also show:

5 And all ye men of tender heart,
    Forgiving others, take your
        part,
        O sing ye, Alleluia!
    Ye who long pain and sorrow
        bear,
    Praise God and on him cast
        your care:

6 And thou, most kind and
        gentle death,
    Waiting to hush our latest
        breath,
        O praise him, Alleluia!
    Thou leadest home the child
        of God,
    And Christ our Lord the way
        hath trod:

7 *Let all things their Creator bless,*
    And worship him in humble-
        ness,
        O praise him, Alleluia
    Praise, praise the Father,
        praise the Son,
    And praise the Spirit, Three in
        One: *Amen.*
            ST. FRANCIS OF ASSISI, 1182–1226
        Tr. WILLIAM HENRY DRAPER, 1855–1933
        * These verses may be omitted if desired.

31   *O Pater sancte*

FATHER most holy, merciful
    and loving,
    Jesus, Redeemer, ever to be
        worshipped,
Life-giving Spirit, Comforter
        most gracious,
    God everlasting;

2 Three in a wondrous unity un-
        broken,
    One perfect Godhead, love
        that never faileth,
    Light of the angels, succour of
        the needy,
    Hope of all living;

3 All thy creation serveth its
        Creator;
    Thee every creature praiseth
        without ceasing;
    We too would sing thee psalms
        of true devotion;
    Hear, we beseech thee.

4 *Lord God Almighty, unto thee*
    be glory,
  One in Three Persons, over all
    exalted;
Thine, as is meet, be honour,
    praise, and blessing,
  Now and for ever. Amen.

c. 10th century
Tr. ALFRED EDWARD ALSTON
1862–1927

32

IMMORTAL, invisible, God
    only wise,
In light inaccessible hid from
    our eyes,
Most blessèd, most glorious, the
    Ancient of Days,
Almighty, victorious, thy great
    Name we praise.

2 Unresting, unhasting, and silent
    as light,
  Nor wanting, nor wasting,
    thou rulest in might;
  Thy justice like mountains high
    soaring above
  Thy clouds, which are fountains
    of goodness and love.

3 To all, life thou givest—to both
    great and small;
  In all life thou livest, the true
    life of all;
  We blossom and flourish as
    leaves on the tree,
  And wither and perish—but
    naught changeth thee.

4 Great Father of Glory, pure
    Father of Light,
  Thine angels adore thee, all
    veiling their sight;
  All laud we would render: O
    help us to see
  'Tis only the splendour of light
    hideth thee.

WALTER CHALMERS SMITH, 1824–1908
Based on 1 Timothy, 1:17

33

LET us with a gladsome mind
  Praise the Lord, for he is
    kind:
  For his mercies aye endure,
  Ever faithful, ever sure.

2 Let us blaze his Name abroad,
  For of gods he is the God:

3 He, with all-commanding
    might,
  Filled the new-made world with
    light:

4 He his chosen race did bless
  In the wasteful wilderness:

5 All things living he doth feed;
  His full hand supplies their
    need:

6 Let us then with gladsome mind
  Praise the Lord, for he is kind:

JOHN MILTON, 1608–74
From Psalm 136

34

LORD of all being, throned
    afar,
Thy glory flames from sun and
    star;
Centre and soul of every sphere,
Yet to each loving heart how
    near!

2 Sun of our life, thy quickening
    ray
  Sheds on our path the glow of
    day;
  Star of our hope, thy softened
    light
  Cheers the long watches of the
    night.

3 Our midnight is thy smile with-
    drawn,
  Our noontide is thy gracious
    dawn,
  Our rainbow arch thy mercy's
    sign;
  All, save the clouds of sin, are
    thine.

4 Lord of all life, below, above,
  Whose light is truth, whose
    warmth is love,
  Before thy ever-blazing throne
  We ask no lustre of our own.

5 Grant us thy truth to make us
    free,
  And kindling hearts that burn
    for thee,

11   B

Till all thy living altars claim
One holy light, one heavenly
flame.

OLIVER WENDELL HOLMES, 1809–9

35

O WORSHIP the King all-
glorious above,
O gratefully sing his power and
his love,
Our Shield and Defender, the
Ancient of Days,
Pavilioned in splendour, and
girded with praise.

2 O tell of his might, O sing of his
grace,
Whose robe is the light, whose
canopy space.
His chariots of wrath the deep
thunder-clouds form,
And dark is his path on the
wings of the storm.

3 The earth with its store of
wonders untold,
Almighty, thy power hath
founded of old,
Hath stablished it fast by a
changeless decree,
And round it hath cast, like
a mantle, the sea.

4 Thy bountiful care what tongue
can recite?
It breathes in the air; it shines
in the light;
It streams from the hills; it
descends to the plain,
And sweetly distils in the dew
and the rain.

5 Frail children of dust, and
feeble as frail,
In thee do we trust, nor find
thee to fail;
Thy mercies how tender, how
firm to the end,
Our Maker, Defender, Re-
deemer, and Friend!

6 O measureless Might! ineffable
Love!
While angels delight to hymn
thee above,

The humbler creation, though
feeble their lays,
With true adoration shall sing
to thy praise.

ROBERT GRANT, 1779–1838
From Psalm 104

36

THE Lord is King! lift up
thy voice,
O earth, and all ye heavens,
rejoice;
From world to world the joy
shall ring,
'The Lord Omnipotent is King!'

2 The Lord is King! who then
shall dare
Resist his will, distrust his care,
Or murmur at his wise decrees,
Or doubt his royal promises?

3 The Lord is King! child of the
dust,
The Judge of all the earth is
just;
Holy and true are all his ways:
Let every creature speak his
praise.

4 Come, make your wants, your
burdens known;
Christ will present them at the
throne;
For he is at the Father's side,
The Man of Love, the Crucified.

5 One Lord, one empire, all
secures;
He reigns, and life and death
are yours:
Through earth and heaven one
song shall ring,
'The Lord Omnipotent is King!'

JOSIAH CONDER, 1789–1855
altered

37

PRAISE the Lord! ye
heavens, adore him;
Praise him, angels, in the
height;

Sun and moon, rejoice before
him,
   Praise him, all ye stars and
   light.
Praise the Lord! for he hath
spoken;
   Worlds his mighty voice
   obeyed;
Laws which never shall be
broken
   For their guidance hath he
   made.

2 Praise the Lord! for he is
glorious;
   Never shall his promise fail;
God hath made his saints
victorious;
   Sin and death shall not pre-
   vail.
Praise the God of our salva-
tion!
   Hosts on high, his power
   proclaim;
Heaven, and earth, and all
creation,
   Laud and magnify his Name.
   Amen.

Foundling Hospital Hymns, c. 1796
From Psalm 148

38

SONGS of praise the angels
sang,
Heaven with alleluias rang,
When creation was begun,
When God spake, and it was
done.

2 Songs of praise awoke the morn
When the Prince of Peace was
born;
Songs of praise arose when he
Captive led captivity.

3 Heaven and earth must pass
away:
Songs of praise shall crown that
day;
God will make new heavens,
new earth:
Songs of praise shall hail their
birth.

4 And can man alone be dumb,
Till that glorious · Kingdom
come?
No! the Church delights to raise
Psalms, and hymns, and songs
of praise.

5 Saints below, with heart and
voice,
Still in songs of praise rejoice,
Learning here, by faith and
love,
Songs of praise to sing above.

6 Borne upon their latest breath,
Songs of praise shall conquer
death;
Then, amidst eternal joy,
Songs of praise their powers
employ.

JAMES MONTGOMERY, 1771–1854

39

STAND up, and bless the
Lord,
   Ye people of his choice;
Stand up, and bless the Lord
your God
   With heart and soul and
   voice.

2 Though high above all praise,
Above all blessing high,
Who would not fear his holy
Name,
And laud and magnify?

3 O for the living flame
From his own altar brought,
To touch our lips, our minds
inspire,
And wing to heaven our
thought!

4 God is our strength and song,
And his salvation ours;
Then be his love in Christ pro-
claimed
With all our ransomed
powers.

5 Stand up, and bless the Lord;
The Lord your God adore;
Stand up, and bless his glorious
Name
Henceforth for evermore.

JAMES MONTGOMERY, 1771–1854

40

WORSHIP the Lord in the
beauty of holiness;
Bow down before him, his
glory proclaim;
Gold of obedience and incense
of lowliness
Bring, and adore him; the
Lord is his Name!

2 Low at his feet lay thy burden
of carefulness;
High on his heart he will bear
it for thee,
Comfort thy sorrows, and
answer thy prayerfulness,
Guiding thy steps as may
best for thee be.

3 Fear not to enter his courts, in
the slenderness
Of the poor wealth thou
canst reckon as thine;

Truth in its beauty and love in
its tenderness,
These are the offerings to lay
on his shrine.

4 These, though we bring them in
trembling and fearfulness,
He will accept for the Name
that is dear,
Mornings of joy give for even-
ings of tearfulness,
Trust for our trembling, and
hope for our fear.

5 Worship the Lord in the beauty
of holiness;
Bow down before him, his
glory proclaim;
Gold of obedience and incense
of lowliness
Bring, and adore him; the
Lord is his Name!

JOHN SAMUEL BEWLEY MONSELL
1811–75

MORNING

41

PSALM 63, verses 1–4

LORD, thee my God, I'll
early seek:
My soul doth thirst for thee;
My flesh longs in a dry parched
land,
Wherein no waters be.

2 That I thy power may behold,
And brightness of thy face,
As I have seen thee heretofore
Within thy holy place.

3 Since better is thy love than
life,
My lips thee praise shall give.
I in thy Name will lift my hands,
And bless thee while I live.

4 To Father, Son, and Holy Ghost,
The God whom we adore,
Be glory, as it was, and is,
And shall be evermore. Amen.

42

AWAKE, my soul, and with the
sun
Thy daily stage of duty run;
Shake off dull sloth, and joyful
rise,
To pay thy morning sacrifice.

2 Wake, and lift up thyself, my
heart,
And with the angels bear thy
part,
Who all night long unwearied
sing
High praise to the eternal King.

3 Lord, I my vows to thee renew;
Disperse my sins as morning
dew;
Guard my first springs of
thought and will,
And with thyself my spirit fill.

Direct, control, suggest, this day,
All I design, or do, or say,
That all my powers, with all their might,
In thy sole glory may unite.

Praise God, from whom all blessings flow;
Praise him, all creatures here below;
Praise him above, ye heavenly host;
Praise Father, Son, and Holy Ghost. Amen.

THOMAS KEN, 1637–1711

43
Nocte surgentes

FATHER, we praise thee, now the night is over;
Active and watchful, stand we all before thee;
Singing, we offer prayer and meditation:
        Thus we adore thee.

2 Monarch of all things, fit us for thy mansions;
Banish our weakness, health and wholeness sending;
Bring us to heaven, where thy saints united
        Joy without ending.

3 *All-holy Father, Son, and equal Spirit,*
Trinity blessèd, send us thy salvation;
Thine is the glory, gleaming and resounding
        Through all creation. Amen.

10th century or earlier
Tr. PERCY DEARMER, 1867–1936

44

MOST glorious Lord of life, that on this day
Didst make thy triumph over death and sin,
And having harrowed hell, didst bring away
    Captivity thence captive, us to win:

2 This joyous day, dear Lord, with joy begin,
And grant that we, for whom thou diddest die,
Being with thy dear blood clean washed from sin,
    May live for ever in felicity:

3 And that thy love we, weighing worthily,
May likewise love thee for the same again;
And for thy sake, that all like dear didst buy,
    With love may one another entertain.

4 So let us love, dear Love, like as we ought,
Love is the lesson which the Lord us taught.

EDMUND SPENSER, c. 1552–99

45
Iam lucis orto sidere

NOW that the daylight fills the sky,
We lift our hearts to God on high,
That he, in all we do or say,
Would keep us free from harm today:

2 Would guard our hearts and tongues from strife,
From anger's din would hide our life,
From all ill sights would turn our eyes,
Would close our ears from vanities:

3 Would keep our inmost conscience pure,
Our souls from folly would secure,
Would bid us check the pride of sense
With due and holy abstinence.

4 So we, when this new day is gone
And night in turn is drawing on,
With conscience by the world unstained,
Shall praise his Name for victory gained.

Before 8th century
Tr. JOHN MASON NEALE, 1818–66

46

THIS is the day of light:
　Let there be light today;
O Dayspring, rise upon our night,
And chase its gloom away.

2　This is the day of prayer:
　Let earth to heaven draw near;
Lift up our hearts to seek thee there,
Come down to meet us here.

3　This is the first of days:
　Send forth thy quickening breath,
And wake dead souls to love and praise,
O Vanquisher of death!

　　　　JOHN ELLERTON, 1826–93

47

NEW every morning is the love
　Our wakening and uprising prove,
Through sleep and darkness safely brought,
Restored to life, and power, and thought.

2　New mercies, each returning day,
Hover around us while we pray,—
New perils past, new sins forgiven,
New thoughts of God, new hopes of heaven.

3　If, on our daily course, our mind
Be set to hallow all we find,
New treasures still, of countless price,
God will provide for sacrifice.

4　The trivial round, the common task,
Will furnish all we ought to ask,—
Room to deny ourselves, a road
To bring us daily nearer God.

5　Only, O Lord, in thy dear love
Fit us for perfect rest above;
And help us, this and every day
To live more nearly as we pray.

　　　　JOHN KEBLE, 1792–186

48

O LORD of life, thy quicken
　ing voice
Awakes my morning song!
In gladsome words I woul rejoice
That I to thee belong.

2　I see thy light, I feel thy wind
The world, it is thy word;
Whatever wakes my heart an mind
Thy presence is, my Lord.

3　Therefore I choose my highes part,
And turn my face to thee;
Therefore I stir my inmos heart
To worship fervently.

4　Lord, let me live and will thi day—
Keep rising from the dead;
Lord, make my spirit good an gay—
Give me my daily bread.

5　Within my heart speak, Lord speak on,
My heart alive to keep,
Till comes the night, and labour done,
In thee I fall asleep.

　　　　GEORGE MACDONALD, 1824–190.

49　　*For younger children*

THE morning bright, wit rosy light,
　Has waked me up from sleep;
Father, I own, thy love alon
Thy little one doth keep.

2 All through the day, I humbly
    pray,
  Be thou my Guard and Guide;
    My sins forgive, and let me
    live,
  Blest Jesus, near thy side.

3 O make thy rest within my
    breast,
  Great Spirit of all grace;
    Make me like thee, then shall
    I be
  Prepared to see thy face.

THOMAS OSMOND SUMMERS
1812–82

EVENING

50

Sol praeceps rapitur

THE sun is sinking fast,
    The daylight dies;
Let love awake, and pay
    Her evening sacrifice.

2 As Christ upon the Cross
    His head inclined,
  And to his Father's hands
    His parting soul resigned,

3 So now herself my soul
    Would wholly give
  Into his sacred charge
    In whom all spirits live;

4 Thus would I live; yet now
    Not I, but he
  In all his power and love
    Henceforth alive in me:

5 One sacred Trinity,
    One Lord Divine;
  Myself for ever his,
    And he for ever mine.

Anonymous 18th century Latin Hymn
Tr. EDWARD CASWALL, 1814–78

51

AS now the day draws near its
    ending,
  While evening steals o'er
    earth and sky,
Once more to thee our hymns
    ascending
  Sound forth thy praises,
    Lord Most High.

Thine is the splendour of the
    morning,
  Thine is the evening's tran-
    quil light;
Thine too the veil which till the
    dawning
  Shrouds all the earth in
    peaceful night.

2 Maker of worlds beyond our
    knowing,
  Realms which no human eye
    can scan,
Yet in thy wondrous love be-
    stowing
  Through Christ thy saving
    aid to man;
Lord, while the hymns of all
    creation
  Rise ever to thy throne above,
We too would join in adoration,
  Owning thee God of change-
    less love.

JACK COPLEY WINSLOW
Partly based on a hymn by
JOHN ELLERTON, 1826–93

52

AT even, when the sun was
    set,
  The sick, O Lord, around thee
    lay;
O in what divers pains they met!
  O with what joy they went
    away!

2 O Saviour Christ, our woes
    dispel:
  For some are sick, and some
    are sad,

And some have never loved thee
    well,
    And some have lost the love
      they had.

3 O Saviour Christ, thou too art
    Man;
Thou hast been troubled,
    tempted, tried;
Thy kind but searching glance
    can scan
    The very wounds that shame
      would hide.

4 Thy touch has still its ancient
    power;
No word from thee can fruit-
    less fall:
Hear in this solemn evening
    hour,
    And in thy mercy heal us all.
        HENRY TWELLS, 1823–1900

53

BEFORE the day draws near
    its ending,
And evening steals o'er earth
    and sky,
Once more to thee our hymns
    ascending
    Shall speak thy praises, Lord
      Most High.

2 Thy Name is blessed by count-
    less numbers
In vaster worlds unseen, un-
    known,
Whose duteous service never
    slumbers,
    In perfect love and faultless
      tone.

3 Yet thou wilt not despise the
    weakest
Who here in spirit bend the
    knee;
Thy Christ hath said, 'Thou,
    Father, seekest
    For such as these to worship
      thee.'

4 And through the swell of chant-
    ing voices,
    The blended notes of age and
      youth,

Thine ear discerns, thy love
    rejoices,
    When hearts rise up to thee
      in truth.

5 O Light all clear, O Truth most
    holy,
O boundless Mercy pardoning
    all,
Before thy feet, abashed and
    lowly,
    With fervent prayer thy
    children fall:——

6 When we no more on earth
    adore thee,
And others worship here in
    turn,
O may we sing that song before
    thee,
    Which none but thy redeemed
      can learn.

        JOHN ELLERTON, 1826–93

54   Φῶς ἱλαρὸν ἁγίας δόξης

HAIL, gladdening Light, of
    his pure glory poured
Who is the immortal Father,
    heavenly, blest,
Holiest of Holies, Jesus Christ,
    our Lord!

2 Now we are come to the sun's
    hour of rest,
The lights of evening round us
    shine.
We hymn the Father, Son, and
    Holy Spirit Divine.

3 Worthiest art thou at all times
    to be sung with undefiled
    tongue,
Son of our God, Giver of life,
    alone:
Therefore in all the world, thy
    glories, Lord, they own.
    Amen.

        Before 4th century
        Tr. JOHN KEBLE, 1792–1866

55   Φῶς ἱλαρὸν ἁγίας δόξης

O GLADSOME Light, O
    grace
Of God the Father's face,

The eternal splendour wearing;
Celestial, holy, blest,
Our Saviour Jesus Christ,
Joyful in thine appearing.

2 Now, ere day fadeth quite,
We see the evening light,
Our wonted hymn outpouring;
Father of might unknown,
Thee, his incarnate Son,
And Holy Spirit adoring.

3 To thee of right belongs
All praise of holy songs,
O Son of God, Lifegiver;
Thee therefore, O Most High,
The world doth glorify,
And shall exalt for ever.

Before 4th century
Tr. ROBERT BRIDGES, 1844–1930

56   *O Lux beata Trinitas*

O TRINITY, O blessèd
Light,
O Unity, most principal,
The fiery sun now leaves our
sight:
Cause in our hearts thy
beams to fall.

2 Let us with songs of praise
divine
At morn and evening thee
implore;
And let our glory, bowed to
thine,
Thee glorify for evermore.

3 To God the Father, glory great,
And glory to his only Son,
And to the Holy Paraclete,
Both now and still while ages
run. Amen.

Attributed to ST. AMBROSE
340–97
Tr. WM. DRUMMOND OF
HAWTHORNDEN, 1585–1649

57   *Nun ruhen alle Wälder*

THE duteous day now closeth,
Each flower and tree re-
poseth,
Shade creeps o'er wild and
wood:

Let us, as night is falling,
On God our Maker calling,
Give thanks to him, the
Giver good.

2 Now all the heavenly splendour
Breaks forth in starlight tender
From myriad worlds un-
known;
And man, the marvel seeing,
Forgets his selfish being,
For joy of beauty not his own.

3 Awhile his mortal blindness
May miss God's loving-kindness,
And grope in faithless strife:
But when life's day is over,
Shall death's fair night discover
The fields of everlasting life.

PAUL GERHARDT, 1607–76
Par. ROBERT BRIDGES, 1844–1930

58   *For younger children*

IF I come to Jesus,
He will make me glad;
He will give me pleasure
When my heart is sad.
*If I come to Jesus,
Happy shall I be;
He is gently calling
Little ones like me.*

2 If I come to Jesus,
He will hear my prayer;
He will love me dearly;
He my sins did bear.

3 If I come to Jesus,
He will take my hand,
He will kindly lead me
To a better land.

FRANCES (CROSBY) VAN ALSTYNE
1820–1915

59   *For younger children*

JESUS Christ, our Lord and
King,
Listen to the prayer we sing
Now the lovely light, that shone
Through our happy day, has
gone.

2 Thou, by whom the birds were
    fed,
  Gavest us our daily bread ;
  Thou the gentle dark hast sent—
  May we sleep in hushed content.

3 Bless thy grateful children now,
  As our sleepy heads we bow ;
  May thy Holy Spirit's might
  Guard us through the hours of
    night.

4 Teach us, Lord, thy way to
    know,
  We must in thy pattern grow ;
  And, when thou at last shalt
    come,
  Take us to thy heavenly home.

Based on a hymn by
EMILY MARY SHAPCOTE, 1828–1909

The following are also suitable :

No.
489 I joyed when to the house of God
347 Praise ye the Lord, God's praise
    within
348 Sing a new song to Jehovah
143 The spacious firmament on high
236 Children of Jerusalem
359 Praise the Lord, his glories show
455 Angel voices ever singing

*Certain hymns in Part III, section 1
(Adoration, Thanksgiving), and section 2
(Affirmation) are also suitable.*

CONFESSION AND SUPPLICATION

60   KYRIE ELEISON

First Form
Minister   Lord have mercy
People   Christ have mercy
Minister   Lord have mercy

Second Form
*Lord, have mercy upon us
 Christ have mercy upon us
 Lord have mercy upon us

* *When sung, each line is repeated
three times.*

61   TRISAGION

Holy God, holy and mighty, holy
  and immortal, have mercy upon
  us.

For Trisagion with The Reproaches, *see
No.* 240.

62   GLORIA IN EXCELSIS

GLORY be to God on high,
    and in earth peace, good
will towards men.
We praise thee, we bless thee,
  we worship thee, we glorify
  thee,
We give thanks to thee for
  thy great glory,

O Lord God, heavenly King,
  God the Father Almighty.
O Lord, the only begotten Son,
  Jesus Christ ;
O Lord God, Lamb of God,
  Son of the Father,
That takest away the sins of
  the world, have mercy upon
  us.
Thou that takest away the sins
  of the world, have mercy
  upon us.
Thou that takest away the
  sins of the world, receive
  our prayer.
Thou that sittest at the right
  hand of God the Father, have
  mercy upon us.
For thou only art holy, thou
  only art the Lord ;
Thou only, O Christ, with the
  Holy Ghost, art most high
  in the glory of God the
  Father. Amen.

63   Psalm 51, verses 1–4, 6–12

HAVE mercy upon me O
    God according to thy
loving-kindness : according
to the multitude of thy
tender mercies blot ' out my
transgressions.

Wash me throughly from ' mine iniquity : and ' cleanse me from my sins.

For I acknowledge ' my transgressions : and my sin is ' ever before me.

Against thee thee only have I sinned and done this evil ' in thy sight : that thou mightest be justified when thou speakest and be ' clear when thou judgest.

Behold thou desirest truth in the ' inward parts : and in the hidden part thou shalt make ' me to know wisdom.

Purge me with hyssop and I ' shall be clean : wash me and I ' shall be whiter than snow.

Make me to hear ' joy and gladness : that the bones which thou hast ' broken may re-joice.

Hide thy face ' from my sins : and blot out ' all mine iniqui-ties.

Create in me a clean ' heart O God : and renew a right ' spirit within me.

Cast me not away ' from thy presence : and take not thy' Holy Spirit from me.

Restore unto me the joy of ' thy salvation : and uphold me ' with thy free spirit.

Glory be to the Father and ' to the Son: and ' to the Holy Ghost :

As it was in the beginning is now and ' ever shall be : world ' without end Amen.

64

O GOD be gracious to me in thy love,
And in thy mercy pardon my misdeeds ;

Wash me from guilt and cleanse me from my sin,
For well I know the evil I have done.

2 Against thee, Lord, thee only have I sinned,
And what to thee is hateful have I done;
I own thy righteousness in charging me,
I know thee justified should'st thou condemn.

3 Take hyssop, sprinkle me and make me clean,
Wash me and make me whiter than the snow ;
Fill me with gladness and re-joicing, Lord,
And let my broken frame know joy once more.

4 Turn thou thy face, O God, from my misdeeds,
And blot out all the sins that sully me ;
Create a clean and contrite heart in me,
Renew my soul in faithfulness and love.

5 Drive me not from thy presence, gracious Lord,
Nor keep thy Holy Spirit far from me ;
Restore my soul with thy salvation's joy,
And with a willing spirit strengthen me.

IAN PITT-WATSON
From *The New English Bible* version
of Psalm 51

65 PSALM 130, verses 1–6a, 7b, 8

LORD, from the depths to thee I cried.
My voice, Lord, do thou hear:
Unto my supplications' voice
Give an attentive ear.

2 Lord, who shall stand, if thou, O Lord,
Shouldest mark iniquity ?
But yet with thee forgiveness is,
That feared thou mayest be.

3 I wait for God, my soul doth
    wait,
    My hope is in his word.
  More than they that for morn-
    ing watch,
    My soul waits for the Lord;

4 Redemption also plenteous
    Is ever found with him.
  And from all his iniquities
    He Israel shall redeem.

5 *To Father, Son, and Holy
      Ghost,*
    The God whom we adore,
  Be glory, as it was, and is,
    And shall be evermore. Amen.

66
PSALM 130

*O̱UT of the depths have I
    cried unto thee O Lórd.
  Lord hear my voice let
    thine ears be attentive to
    the voice of my supplica-
    tions.

If thou Lord shouldest mark
    iniquities   O Lórd who
    shall stánd?

But there is forgiveness with
    thee   that thou mayest be
    feared.

I wait for the Lord my soul
    doth wait   and in his
    word do I hope.

My soul waiteth for the Lord
    more than they that watch
    for the mórning   I say
    more than they that watch
    for the mórning.

Let Israel hope in the Lórd
    for with the Lord there is
    mercy   and with him is
    plenteous redémption.

And he shall redeem Israel
    from all his iniquities.

*Glory be to the Father and to
    the Son   and to the Hóly
    Ghost:*

*As it was in the beginning is
    now   and ever shall be
    world without end. Amen.*
    * See No. 21 footnote.

67
PSALM 130, Gelineau version

*O̱UT of the depths I cry to
      you, O Lórd,
  Lord, hear my voice!
  O let your ears be attentive
  To the voice of my pleading.

2 If you, O Lórd, should mark our
      guilt,
  Lord, who would survive?
  But with you is found forgive-
      ness:
  For this we revere you.

3 My soul is waiting for the Lórd,
  I count on his word.
  My soul is longing for the Lórd
  More than watchman for day-
      break.

4 Because with the Lórd there is
      mercy
  And fullness of redemption,
  Israel indeed he will redeem
  From all its iniquity.

5 To the Father Almighty give
      glory,
  Give glory to his Son,
  To the Spirit most Holy give
      praise,
  Whose reign is for ever.

*It is suggested that either of the following
Antiphons be sung by the congregation
after each verse of the psalm.*

Antiphon 1
I place all my trust in you, my God: all my hope is in your saving word.

Antiphon 2
With the Lord there is mercy without end.

The accented words and syllables should be stressed rhythmically.

68 From PSALM 139

THOU art before me, Lord,
    thou art behind,
And thou above me hast spread
    out thy hand;
Such knowledge is too wonderful
    for me,
Too high to grasp, too great to
    understand.

2 Then whither from thy Spirit
    shall I go,
And whither from thy presence
    shall I flee?
If I ascend to heaven thou art
    there,
And in the lowest depths I meet
    with thee.

3 If I should take my flight into
    the dawn,
If I should dwell on ocean's
    farthest shore,
Thy mighty hand would rest
    upon me still,
And thy right hand would
    guard me evermore.

4 If I should say 'Darkness will
    cover me,
And I shall hide within the
    veil of night',
Surely the darkness is not dark
    to thee,
The night is as the day, the
    darkness light.

5 Search me, O God, search me
    and know my heart,
Try me, O God, my mind and
    spirit try;
Keep me from any path that
    gives thee pain,

And lead me in the everlasting
    way.

IAN PITT-WATSON
From *The New English Bible*
version of Psalm 139

69 PARAPHRASE 30

COME, let us to the Lord our
    God
With contrite hearts return;
Our God is gracious, nor will
    leave
The desolate to mourn.

2 His voice commands the tem-
    pest forth,
And stills the stormy wave;
And though his arm be strong to
    smite,
'Tis also strong to save.

3 Long hath the night of sorrow
    reigned,
The dawn shall bring us light:
God shall appear, and we shall
    rise
With gladness in his sight.

4 Our hearts, if God we seek to
    know,
Shall know him, and rejoice;
His coming like the morn
    shall be,
Like morning songs his voice.

5 As dew upon the tender herb,
    Diffusing fragrance round;
As showers that usher in the
    spring,
And cheer the thirsty ground:

6 So shall his presence bless our
    souls,
And shed a joyful light;
That hallowed morn shall chase
    away
The sorrows of the night.

Scottish Paraphrases, 1781
From *Hosea* 6: 1–4

70 PSALM 143 (ii), from verses 1, 6, 8

O, HEAR my prayer, Lord,
    Unto me answer make,
And, in thy righteousness,
Upon me pity take.

Lo, I do stretch my hands
To thee, my help alone;
For thou well understands
All my complaint and moan:

2 My thirsting soul desires,
And longeth after thee,
As thirsty ground requires
With rain refreshed to be.
Because I trust in thee,
O Lord, cause me to hear
Thy loving-kindness free,
When morning doth appear:

3 Cause me to know the way
Wherein my path should be;
For why, my soul on high
I do lift up to thee.
Now glory be to God
The Father, and the Son,
And to the Holy Ghost,
All-glorious Three in One.
                          Amen.

71 PSALM 61, verses 1–4

O GOD, give ear unto my cry;
    Unto my prayer attend.
From the utmost corner of the
    land
    My cry to thee I'll send.

2 What time my heart is over-
    whelmed
    And in perplexity,
Do thou me lead unto the Rock
    That higher is than I.

3 For thou hast for my refuge
    been
    A shelter by thy power;
And for defence against my
    foes
    Thou hast been a strong tower.

4 Within thy tabernacle I
    For ever will abide;
And under covert of thy wings
    With confidence me hide.

5 *To Father, Son, and Holy Ghost,*
    The God whom we adore,
Be glory, as it was, and is,
    And shall be evermore. Amen.

72 PARAPHRASE 2

O GOD of Bethel! by whose
    hand
    Thy people still are fed;
Who through this weary pil-
    grimage
    Hast all our fathers led:

2 Our vows, our prayers, we now
    present
    Before thy throne of grace:
God of our fathers! be the God
    Of their succeeding race.

3 Through each perplexing path
    of life
    Our wandering footsteps
    guide;
Give us each day our daily
    bread,
    And raiment fit provide.

4 O spread thy covering wings
    around,
    Till all our wanderings cease,
And at our Father's loved
    abode
    Our souls arrive in peace.

5 Such blessings from thy gra-
    cious hand
    Our humble prayers implore;
And thou shalt be our chosen
    God,
And portion evermore.

                Scottish Paraphrases, 1781
                From Genesis 28: 20–22

73 PSALM 40, verses 1–4

I WAITED for the Lord my
    God,
    And patiently did bear;
At length to me he did incline
    My voice and cry to hear.

2 He took me from a fearful pit,
    And from the miry clay,
And on a rock he set my feet,
    Establishing my way.

3 He put a new song in my
    mouth,
    Our God to magnify:
Many shall see it, and shall fear,
    And on the Lord rely.

4 O blessèd is the man whose trust
    Upon the Lord relies;
Respecting not the proud, nor such
    As turn aside to lies.

5 *To Father, Son, and Holy Ghost,*
    The God whom we adore,
Be glory, as it was, and is,
    And shall be evermore. Amen.

74 PSALM 25, verses 4, 5a, 6–10

SHOW me thy ways, O Lord;
    Thy paths, O teach thou me:
And do thou lead me in thy truth,
    Therein my teacher be:

2 Thy tender mercies, Lord,
    I pray thee to recall,
And loving-kindnesses; for they
    Have been through ages all.

3 My sins and faults of youth
    Do thou, O Lord, forget:
After thy mercy think on me,
    And for thy goodness great.

4 God good and upright is:
    The way he'll sinners show.
The meek in judgment he will guide,
    And make his path to know.

5 The whole paths of the Lord
    Are truth and mercy sure,
To those that do his covenant keep,
    And testimonies pure.

6 *To thee be glory, Lord,*
    Whom heaven and earth adore,
To Father, Son, and Holy Ghost,
    One God for evermore. Amen.

75 PSALM 85 (ii), verses 1, 2, 5–7

LORD, thine heart in love
    hath yearned
    On thy lost and fallen land;
Israel's race is homeward turned,
    Thou hast freed thy captive band:

2 Thou hast borne thy people's sin,
    Covered all their deeds of ill;
All thy wrath is gathered in,
    And thy burning anger still.

3 Wilt thou not in mercy turn?
    Turn, and be our life again,
That thy people's heart may burn
    With the gladness of thy reign.

4 Show us now thy tender love;
    Thy salvation, Lord, impart;
I the voice divine would prove,
    Listening in my silent heart:

5 Listening what the Lord will say—
    'Peace' to all that own his will:
To his saints that love his way,
    'Peace', and 'turn no more to ill'.

6 *Glory to the Father be,*
    Glory, Christ our Lord, to thee,
Glory to the Holy Ghost,
    Praised by men and Heavenly Host. Amen.

76

DEAR Lord and Father of
    mankind,
    Forgive our foolish ways;
Reclothe us in our rightful mind;
In purer lives thy service find,
*In deeper reverence, praise.

2 In simple trust like theirs who heard,
    Beside the Syrian sea,
The gracious calling of the Lord,
Let us, like them, without a word
    Rise up and follow thee.

3 O Sabbath rest by Galilee!
    O calm of hills above,
Where Jesus knelt to share with thee
The silence of eternity,
    Interpreted by love!

4 With that deep hush subduing
   all
  Our words and works that
    drown
The tender whisper of thy call,
As noiseless let thy blessing fall
As fell thy manna down.

5 Drop thy still dews of quietness,
  Till all our strivings cease;
Take from our souls the strain
   and stress,
And let our ordered lives con-
   fess
  The beauty of thy peace.

6 Breathe through the heats of
   our desire
  Thy coolness and thy balm;
Let sense be dumb, let flesh
   retire;
Speak through the earthquake,
   wind, and fire,
  O still small voice of calm!

JOHN GREENLEAF WHITTIER, 1807–92

  *The last line of each verse is to be
repeated, when Tune* (ii) REPTON *is sung.*

77

FATHER of heaven, whose
   love profound
A ransom for our souls hath
   found,
Before thy throne we sinners
   bend;
To us thy pardoning love extend.

2 Almighty Son, Incarnate Word,
Our Prophet, Priest, Redeemer,
   Lord,
Before thy throne we sinners
   bend;
To us thy saving grace extend.

3 Eternal Spirit, by whose breath
The soul is raised from sin and
   death,
Before thy throne we sinners
   bend;
To us thy quickening power
   extend.

4 Jehovah—Father, Spirit, Son—
Mysterious Godhead, Three in
   One,
Before thy throne we sinners
   bend;
Grace, pardon, life to us extend.

EDWARD COOPER, 1770–1833

78

JESUS, Lover of my soul,
  Let me to thy bosom fly,
While the nearer waters roll,
  While the tempest still is
   high;
Hide me, O my Saviour, hide,
  Till the storm of life is past;
Safe into the haven guide,
  O receive my soul at last!

2 Other refuge have I none;
  Hangs my helpless soul on
   thee;
Leave, ah! leave me not alone;
  Still support and comfort me.
All my trust on thee is stayed;
  All my help from thee I
   bring;
Cover my defenceless head
  With the shadow of thy
   wing.

3 Thou, O Christ, art all I want;
  More than all in thee I find;
Raise the fallen, cheer the faint,
  Heal the sick, and lead the
   blind.
Just and holy is thy Name,
  I am all unrighteousness;
False and full of sin I am,
  Thou art full of truth and
   grace.

4 Plenteous grace with thee is
   found,
  Grace to cover all my sin;
Let the healing streams
   abound;
  Make and keep me pure
   within.
Thou of life the fountain art,
  Freely let me take of thee;
Spring thou up within my heart,
  Rise to all eternity.

CHARLES WESLEY, 1707–88

79

JUST as I am, without one plea
But that thy blood was shed for me,
And that thou bidd'st me come to thee,
O Lamb of God, I come.

2 Just as I am, though tossed about
With many a conflict, many a doubt,
Fightings and fears within, without,
O Lamb of God, I come.

3 Just as I am, thou wilt receive,
Wilt welcome, pardon, cleanse, relieve;
Because thy promise I believe,
O Lamb of God, I come.

4 Just as I am—thy love unknown
Has broken every barrier down—
Now to be thine, yea, thine alone,
O Lamb of God, I come.

5 Just as I am, of that free love
The breadth, length, depth, and height to prove,
Here for a season, then above,—
O Lamb of God, I come.

CHARLOTTE ELLIOTT, 1789–1871

80

Μνώεο Χριστέ

LORD Jesus, think on me,
And purge away my sin;
From earthborn passions set me free,
And make me pure within.

2 Lord Jesus, think on me,
With care and woe oppressed;
Let me thy loving servant be,
And taste thy promised rest.

3 Lord Jesus, think on me,
Amid the battle's strife;
In all my pain and misery
Be thou my health and life.

4 Lord Jesus, think on me,
Nor let me go astray;
Through darkness and perplexity
Point thou the heavenly way.

5 Lord Jesus, think on me,
When flows the tempest high:
When on doth rush the enemy,
O Saviour, be thou nigh.

6 Lord Jesus, think on me,
That, when the flood is past,
I may the eternal brightness see,
And share thy joy at last.

SYNESIUS OF CYRENE, c. 375–430
Tr. ALLEN WILLIAM CHATFIELD
1808–96

81

MY faith looks up to thee,
Thou Lamb of Calvary,
Saviour Divine:
Now hear me while I pray;
Take all my guilt away;
O let me from this day
Be wholly thine.

2 May thy rich grace impart
Strength to my fainting heart,
My zeal inspire;
As thou hast died for me,
O may my love to thee
Pure, warm, and changeless be,
A living fire.

3 While life's dark maze I tread,
And griefs around me spread,
Be thou my Guide;
Bid darkness turn to day,
Wipe sorrow's tears away,
Nor let me ever stray
From thee aside.

4 When ends life's transient dream,
When death's cold, sullen stream
Shall o'er me roll,
Blest Saviour, then, in love,
Fear and distrust remove;
O bear me safe above,
A ransomed soul.

RAY PALMER, 1808–87

82 *Śiṣyaht̪ ganāyā naht̪ yogya jo tayālā*

ONE who is all unfit to count
As scholar in thy school,
Thou of thy love hast named a friend—
O kindness wonderful!

2 So weak am I, O gracious Lord,
So all unworthy thee,
That even the dust upon thy feet
Outweighs me utterly.

3 Thou dwellest in unshadowed light,
All sin and shame above—
That thou shouldst bear our sin and shame,
How can I tell such love?

4 Ah, did not he the heavenly throne
A little thing esteem,
And not unworthy for my sake
A mortal body deem?

5 When in his flesh they drove the nails,
Did he not all endure?
What name is there to fit a life
So patient and so pure?

6 So, Love itself in human form,
For love of me he came;
I cannot look upon his face
For shame, for bitter shame.

7 If there is aught of worth in me,
It comes from thee alone;
Then keep me safe, for so, O Lord,
Thou keepest but thine own.

From the Marathi of
NARAYAN VAMAN TILAK
1862–1919
Tr. NICOL MACNICOL
1870–1952

83

ROCK of Ages, cleft for me,
Let me hide myself in thee;
Let the water and the blood,
From thy riven side which flowed,
Be of sin the double cure,
Cleanse me from its guilt and power.

2 Not the labours of my hands
Can fulfil thy law's demands;
Could my zeal no respite know,
Could my tears for ever flow,
All for sin could not atone:
Thou must save, and thou alone.

3 Nothing in my hand I bring,
Simply to thy cross I cling;
Naked, come to thee for dress;
Helpless, look to thee for grace;
Foul, I to the fountain fly;
Wash me, Saviour, or I die.

4 While I draw this fleeting breath,
When mine eyelids close in death,
When I soar through tracts unknown,
See thee on thy judgment throne,
Rock of Ages, cleft for me,
Let me hide myself in thee.

AUGUSTUS MONTAGUE TOPLADY
1740–78

84

TURN back, O man, forswear thy foolish ways;
Old now is earth, and none may count her days,
Yet thou, her child, whose head is crowned with flame,
Still wilt not hear thine inner God proclaim—
'Turn back, O man, forswear thy foolish ways.'

2 Earth might be fair and all men glad and wise:
Age after age their tragic empires rise,
Built while they dream, and in that dreaming weep:
Would man but wake from out his haunted sleep,
Earth might be fair and all men glad and wise.

3 Earth shall be fair, and all her people one:
Nor till that hour shall God's whole will be done.

Now, even now, once more from
   earth to sky,
Peals forth in joy man's old un-
   daunted cry—
'Earth shall be fair, and all her
   folk be one.'

CLIFFORD BAX, 1886–1962

85

O FOR a heart to praise my
   God!
   A heart from sin set free;
A heart that always feels thy
   blood,
   So freely shed for me;

2 A heart resigned, submissive,
   meek,
   My great Redeemer's throne,
Where only Christ is heard to
   speak,
   Where Jesus reigns alone;

3 A humble, lowly, contrite heart,
   Believing, true, and clean,
Which neither life nor death
   can part
   From him that dwells within;

4 A heart in every thought re-
   newed,
   And full of love divine,
Perfect and right and pure and
   good,
   A copy, Lord, of thine!

5 Thy nature, gracious Lord,
   impart;
   Come quickly from above;
Write thy new Name upon my
   heart,
   Thy new, best Name of Love.

CHARLES WESLEY, 1707–88

86 *Je te salue, mon certain Redempteur*

I GREET thee, who my sure
   Redeemer art,
My only Trust and Saviour of
   my heart,
Who pain didst undergo for my
   poor sake;
I pray thee from our hearts all
   cares to take.

2 Thou art the King of mercy and
   of grace,
Reigning omnipotent in every
   place:
So come, O King, and our whole
   being sway;
Shine on us with the light of thy
   pure day.

3 Thou art the Life, by which
   alone we live,
And all our substance and our
   strength receive;
Sustain us by thy faith and by
   thy power,
And give us strength in every
   trying hour.

4 Thou hast the true and perfect
   gentleness,
No harshness hast thou and no
   bitterness:
O grant to us the grace we
   find in thee,
That we may dwell in perfect
   unity.

5 Our hope is in no other save in
   thee;
Our faith is built upon thy
   promise free;
Lord, give us peace, and make
   us calm and sure,
That in thy strength we evermore endure.

Attributed to JOHN CALVIN
1509–64
Tr. ELIZABETH LEE SMITH
1817–98, altered

87 Ṡuṗaḃ ċú mo ḃóıle

BE thou my Vision, O Lord of
   my heart;
Naught be all else to me, save
   that thou art,—
Thou my best thought, by day
   or by night,
Waking or sleeping, thy presence my light.

2 Be thou my Wisdom, thou my
   true Word;
I ever with thee, thou with me,
   Lord;

29

Thou my great Father, I thy
    true son;
Thou in me dwelling, and I
    with thee one.

3 Be thou my battle-shield,
    sword for the fight;
Be thou my dignity, thou my
    delight,
Thou my soul's shelter, thou
    my high tower:
Raise thou me heaven-ward,
    O Power of my power.

4 Riches I heed not, nor man's
    empty praise,
Thou mine inheritance, now
    and always:
Thou and thou only, first in my
    heart,
High King of Heaven, my
    treasure thou art.

5 High King of Heaven, after
    victory won,
May I reach heaven's joys, O
    bright heaven's Sun!
Heart of my own heart, what-
    ever befall,
Still be my Vision, O Ruler of
    all.

Ancient Irish, tr. MARY BYRNE
                1880–1931
versified ELEANOR HULL
                1860–1935

88

GOD of grace and God of
    glory,
    On thy people pour thy
    power;
Now fulfil thy Church's story;
    Bring her bud to glorious
    flower.
Grant us wisdom, grant us
    courage,
    For the facing of this hour.

2 Lo, the hosts of evil round us
    Scorn thy Christ, assail his
    ways;
From the fears that long have
    bound us
    Free our hearts to faith and
    praise.

Grant us wisdom, grant us
    courage,
    For the living of these days.

3 Cure thy children's warring
    madness,
    Bend our pride to thy control;
Shame our wanton selfish glad-
    ness,
    Rich in goods and poor in
    soul.
Grant us wisdom, grant us
    courage,
    Lest we miss thy kingdom's
    goal.

4 Set our feet on lofty places,
    Gird our lives that they may
    be
Armoured with all Christ-like
    graces
    In the fight to set men free.
Grant us wisdom, grant us
    courage,
    That we fail not man nor
    thee.

HARRY EMERSON FOSDICK
        1878–1969, and Compilers
        of The BBC Hymn Book

89

Arglwydd, arwain trwy'r anialwch

GUIDE me, O thou great
    Jehovah,
    Pilgrim through this barren
    land;
I am weak, but thou art mighty;
    Hold me with thy powerful
    hand:
    Bread of heaven, Bread of
    heaven,
*Feed me till my want is o'er.

2 Open now the crystal fountain,
    Whence the healing stream
    doth flow;
Let the fire and cloudy pillar
    Lead me all my journey
    through:
    Strong Deliverer, strong
    Deliverer,
    Be thou still my strength and
    shield.

3 When I tread the verge of Jor-
    dan,
    Bid my anxious fears subside!

Death of death, and hell's De-
  struction,
  Land me safe on Canaan's
    side!
    Songs of praises, songs of
      praises,
  I will ever give to thee.

WILLIAM WILLIAMS, 1717–91
Tr. PETER WILLIAMS, 1727–96

* *When tune (ii) CWM RHONDDA is used,*
the last line of each verse must be repeated.

90

LEAD us, heavenly Father,
  lead us
  O'er the world's tempestuous
    sea;
  Guard us, guide us, keep us, feed
    us,
  For we have no help but thee;
  Yet possessing every blessing
  If our God our Father be.

2 Saviour, breathe forgiveness
    o'er us,
  All our weakness thou dost
    know;
  Thou didst tread this earth
    before us,
  Thou didst feel its keenest
    woe;
  Lone and dreary, faint and
    weary,
  Through the desert thou didst
    go.

3 Spirit of our God, descending,
  Fill our hearts with heavenly
    joy,
  Love with every passion blend-
    ing,
  Pleasure that can never cloy;
  Thus provided, pardoned,
    guided,
  Nothing can our peace de-
    stroy.

JAMES EDMESTON, 1791–1867

91

DEFEND me, Lord, from
  hour to hour,
  And bless thy servant's way;

Increase thy Holy Spirit's
    power
  Within me day by day.

2 Help me to be what I should be,
  And do what I should do,
  And ever with thy Spirit free
  My daily life renew.

3 Grant me the courage from
    above
  Which thou dost give to all
  Who hear thy word and know
    thy love
  And answer to thy call.

4 So may I daily grow in grace,
  Continuing thine alone,
  Until I come to sing thy
    praise
  With saints around thy
    throne.

GEORGE SNOW

92

LORD of all hopefulness
  Lord of all joy,
  Whose trust, ever childlike, no
  cares could destroy,
  Be there at our waking, and
  give us, we pray,
  Your bliss in our hearts, Lord,
  at the break of the day.

2 Lord of all eagerness, Lord of
    all faith,
  Whose strong hands were
  skilled at the plane and the
    lathe,
  Be there at our labours, and
  give us, we pray,
  Your strength in our hearts,
  Lord, at the noon of the day.

3 Lord of all kindliness, Lord of
    all grace,
  Your hands swift to welcome,
  your arms to embrace,
  Be there at our homing, and
  give us, we pray,
  Your love in our hearts, Lord,
  at the eve of the day.

4 Lord of all gentleness, Lord of
    all calm,
    Whose voice is contentment,
        whose presence is balm,
    Be there at our sleeping, and
        give us, we pray,
    Your peace in our hearts, Lord,
        at the end of the day.
                JAN STRUTHER, 1901–53

93

LOVING Shepherd of thy
    sheep,
Keep me, Lord, in safety keep;
Nothing can thy power with-
    stand;
None can pluck me from thy
    hand.

2 Loving Shepherd, thou didst
    give
    Thine own life that I might live;
    May I love thee day by day,
    Gladly thy sweet will obey.

3 Loving Shepherd, ever near,
    Teach me still thy voice to hear;
    Suffer not my feet to stray
    From the straight and narrow
        way.

4 Where thou leadest may I go,
    Walking in thy steps below;
    Then, before thy Father's
        throne,
    Jesus, claim me for thine own.
        JANE ELIZA LEESON, 1807–82, altered
                From St. John 10: 11, 27, 28

94

O JESUS, strong and pure
    and true,
    Before thy feet we bow;
The grace of earlier years re-
    new,
    And lead us onward now.

2 The joyous life that year by
    year
    Within these walls is stored,
The golden hope, the gladsome
    cheer,
    We bring to thee, O Lord.

3 Our faith endow with keener
    powers,
    With warmer glow our love;
And draw these halting hearts
    of ours
    From earth to things above.

4 In paths our bravest ones have
    trod,
    O make us strong to go,
That we may give our lives to
    God,
    In serving man below.

5 So hence shall flow fresh
    strength and grace,
    As from a full-fed spring,
To make the world a better
    place,
    And life a worthier thing.
        WILLIAM WALSHAM HOW, 1823–97

95
Ἄτερ ἀρχῆς ἀπέραντον

O LIGHT that knew no
    dawn,
    That shines to endless day,
All things in earth and heaven
    Are lustred by thy ray;
No eye can to thy throne as-
    cend,
Nor mind thy brightness com-
    prehend.

2   Thy grace, O Father, give,
        That I may serve in fear;
    Above all boons, I pray,
        Grant me thy voice to
            hear;
    From sin thy child in mercy
        free,
    And let me dwell in light with
        thee;

3   That, cleansed from stain of
        sin,
        I may meet homage give,
    And, pure in heart, behold
        Thy beauty while I live;
    Clean hands in holy worship
        raise,
    And thee, O Christ my Saviour,
        praise.

4   In supplication meek
        To thee I bend the knee;
    O Christ, when thou shalt
        come,
        In love remember me,

32

And in thy Kingdom, by thy grace,
Grant me a humble servant's place.

5   Thy grace, O Father, give,
    I humbly thee implore;
And let thy mercy bless
    Thy servant more and more.
All grace and glory be to thee,
From age to age eternally.

ST. GREGORY NAZIANZEN, 329–89
Tr. JOHN BROWNLIE, 1859–1925

96   *Verborgne Gottesliebe du*

THOU hidden Love of God, whose height,
  Whose depth unfathomed, no man knows,
I see from far thy beauteous light,
  Inly I sigh for thy repose;
My heart is pained, nor can it be
At rest till it finds rest in thee.

2 Thy secret voice invites me still
  The sweetness of thy yoke to prove;
And fain I would; but, though my will
  Seem fixed, yet wide my passions rove;
Yet hindrances strew all the way;
I aim at thee, yet from thee stray.

3 'Tis mercy all, that thou hast brought
  My mind to seek her peace in thee;
Yet, while I seek but find thee not,
  No peace my wandering soul shall see.
O when shall all my wanderings end,
And all my steps to thee-ward tend?

4 Is there a thing beneath the sun
  That strives with thee my heart to share?

Ah! tear it thence, and reign alone,
  The Lord of every motion there;
Then shall my heart from earth be free,
When it has found repose in thee.

GERHARD TERSTEEGEN, 1697–1769
Tr. JOHN WESLEY, 1703–91

97   *For children*

FATHER, lead me, day by day,
Ever in thy perfect way;
Teach me to be pure and true;
Show me what I ought to do.

2 When in danger, make me brave;
Make me know that thou canst save;
Keep me safe by thy dear side;
Let me in thy love abide.

3 When I'm tempted to do wrong,
Make me steadfast, wise, and strong;
And, when all alone I stand,
Shield me with thy mighty hand.

4 When my heart is full of glee,
Help me to remember thee,
Happy most of all to know
That my Father loves me so.

5 May I do the good I know,
Be thy loving child below,
Then at last go home to thee,
Evermore thy child to be.

JOHN PAGE HOPPS, 1834–1912
altered

98   *For children*

JESUS, Saviour ever mild,
  Born for us a little Child
Of the Virgin undefiled:
    Hear us, Holy Jesus.

2 Jesus, Son of God most high,
Who didst in the manger lie,
Who upon the cross didst die,
　　　Hear us, Holy Jesus.

3 From all pride and vain conceit,
From all spite and angry heat,
From all lying and deceit,
　　　Save us, Holy Jesus.

4 From refusing to obey,
From the love of our own way,
From forgetfulness to pray,
　　　Save us, Holy Jesus.

5 By the Name we bow before,
Human Name, which evermore
All the hosts of heaven adore,
　　　Save us, Holy Jesus.
　　　RICHARD FREDERICK LITTLEDALE
　　　1833–90, and others

99　　　*For younger children*

FATHER, we thank thee for
　　the night,
And for the pleasant morning
　　light;
For rest and food and loving
　　care,
And all that makes the day so
　　fair.

2 Help us to do the things we
　　should,
To be to others kind and good;
In all we do at work or play
To grow more loving every day.
　　　Ascribed to REBECCA J. WESTON
　　　19th century

100　　　*For younger children*

JESUS, Friend of little children,
　　　Be a friend to me;
Take my hand and ever keep
　　me
　　　Close to thee.

2 Teach me how to grow in goodness
　　　Daily as I grow;
Thou hast been a child, and surely
　　　Thou dost know.

3 Never leave me nor forsake me,
　　　Ever be my Friend;
For I need thee from life's
　　dawning
　　　To its end.
　　　WALTER JOHN MATHAMS
　　　1853–1931

INVOCATION

101　　PSALM 106, verses 1–5, 48

GIVE praise and thanks unto
　　the Lord,
　　　For bountiful is he;
His tender mercy doth endure
　　　Unto eternity.

2 God's mighty works who can
　　express?
　　　Or show forth all his praise?
Blessèd are they that judgment keep,
　　　And justly do always.

3 Remember me, Lord, with that
　　love
　　　Which thou to thine dost bear;
With thy salvation, O my God,
　　　To visit me draw near.

4 That I thy chosen's good may
　　see,
　　　And in their joy rejoice;
And may with thine inheritance
　　　Triumph with cheerful voice.

5 Blest be Jehovah, Israel's God,
　　　To all eternity:
Let all the people say, Amen.
　　　Praise to the Lord give ye.

34

102

PSALM 90, verses
1, 2, 14, 16, 17

LORD, thou hast been our
dwelling-place
In generations all.
Before thou ever hadst brought
forth
The mountains great or
small;

2 Ere ever thou hadst formed the
earth,
And all the world abroad;
Even thou from everlasting art
To everlasting God.

3 O with thy tender mercies,
Lord,
Us early satisfy;
So we rejoice shall all our days,
And still be glad in thee.

4 O let thy work and power ap-
pear
Thy servants' face before;
And show unto their children
dear
Thy glory evermore:

5 And let the beauty of the Lord
Our God be us upon:
Our handy-works establish
thou,
Establish them each one.

6 *To Father, Son, and Holy Ghost,
The God whom we adore,
Be glory, as it was, and is,
And shall be evermore. Amen.*

103

BREATHE on me, Breath
of God;
Fill me with life anew,
That I may love what thou dost
love,
And do what thou wouldst
do.

2 Breathe on me, Breath of
God,
Until my heart is pure,
Until with thee I will one will,
To do and to endure.

3 Breathe on me, Breath of
God,
Till I am wholly thine,
Until this earthly part of me
Glows with thy fire divine.

4 Breathe on me, Breath of
God,
So shall I never die,
But live with thee the perfect
life
Of thine eternity.

EDWIN HATCH, 1835–89

104

COME, Holy Spirit, come;
Let thy bright beams
arise;
Dispel the darkness from our
minds,
And open all our eyes.

2 Cheer our desponding hearts,
Thou heavenly Paraclete;
Give us to lie with humble hope
At our Redeemer's feet.

3 Revive our drooping faith;
Our doubts and fears remove;
And kindle in our breasts the
flame
Of never-dying love.

4 Convince us of our sin;
Then lead to Jesus' blood,
And to our wondering view re-
veal
The secret love of God.

5 'Tis thine to cleanse the
heart,
To sanctify the soul,
To pour fresh life on every part,
And new create the whole.

6 Dwell, therefore, in our
hearts;
Our minds from bondage
free;
Then shall we know and praise
and love
The Father, Son, and thee.

JOSEPH HART, 1712–68

105

Veni, sancte Spiritus

COME, thou Holy Paraclete,
 And from thy celestial
 seat
 Send thy light and brilliancy.
Father of the poor, draw near;
Giver of all gifts, be met;
*Come, the soul's true radiancy.

2 Come, of comforters the best,
 Of the soul the sweetest guest,
 Come in toil refreshingly.
Thou in labour rest most sweet,
Thou art shadow from the heat,
 Comfort in adversity.

3 O thou Light, most pure and
 blest,
 Shine within the inmost breast
 Of thy faithful company.
Where thou art not, man hath
 naught;
Every holy deed and thought
 Comes from thy Divinity.

4 What is soilèd make thou pure;
What is wounded, work its
 cure;
 What is parchèd fructify.
Fill thy faithful, who confide
In thy power to guard and
 guide,
 With thy sevenfold mystery.

13th century
Tr. JOHN MASON NEALE, 1818–66

* *The last line of each verse is repeated.*

106

HOLY Spirit, Truth Divine,
 Dawn upon this soul of
 mine;
 Word of God, and inward
 Light,
 Wake my spirit, clear my sight.

2 Holy Spirit, Love Divine,
 Glow within this heart of mine;
 Kindle every high desire;
 Perish self in thy pure fire.

3 Holy Spirit, Power Divine,
 Fill and nerve this will of mine;
 By thee may I strongly live,
 Bravely bear, and nobly strive.

4 Holy Spirit, Right Divine,
 King within my conscience
 reign;
 Be my law, and I shall be
 Firmly bound, for ever free.

5 Holy Spirit, Peace Divine,
 Still this restless heart of mine;
 Speak to calm this tossing sea,
 Stayed in thy tranquillity.

6 Holy Spirit, Joy Divine,
 Gladden thou this heart of
 mine;
 In the desert ways I sing,
 'Spring, O Well, for ever
 spring!'

SAMUEL LONGFELLOW, 1819–92

107

SPIRIT Divine, attend our
 prayers,
 And make this house thy
 home;
 Descend with all thy gracious
 powers;
 O come, great Spirit, come!

2 Come as the light: to us reveal
 Our emptiness and woe;
 And lead us in those paths of
 life
 Where all the righteous go.

3 Come as the fire: and purge our
 hearts
 Like sacrificial flame;
 Let our whole soul an offering
 be
 To our Redeemer's Name.

4 Come as the dove: and spread
 thy wings,
 The wings of peaceful love;
 And let thy Church on earth
 become
 Blest as the Church above.

5 Come as the wind, with rushing
 sound
 And Pentecostal grace,
 That all of woman born may
 see
 The glory of thy face.

6 Spirit Divine, attend our
    prayers;
Make a lost world thy home;
Descend with all thy gracious
    powers;
    O come, great Spirit, come!
        ANDREW REED, 1787–1862

108

SPIRIT of God, descend upon
    my heart;
    Wean it from earth; through
      all its pulses move;
Stoop to my weakness, mighty
    as thou art,
    And make me love thee as
      I ought to love.

2 I ask no dream, no prophet-
    ecstasies,
    No sudden rending of the
      veil of clay,
No angel-visitant, no opening
    skies;
    But take the dimness of my
      soul away.

3 Hast thou not bid me love thee,
    God and King—
    All, all thine own, soul, heart,
      and strength, and mind?
I see thy cross—there teach my
    heart to cling:
    O let me seek thee, and O let
      me find!

4 Teach me to feel that thou art
    always nigh;
    Teach me the struggles of the
      soul to bear,
To check the rising doubt, the
    rebel sigh;
    Teach me the patience of un-
      answered prayer.

5 Teach me to love thee as thine
    angels love,
    One holy passion filling all my
      frame—
The baptism of the heaven-
    descended Dove,
    My heart an altar, and thy
      love the flame.
        GEORGE CROLY, 1780–1860

109

SPIRIT of God, that moved of
    old
    Upon the waters' darkened
      face,
Come, when our faithless hearts
    are cold,
    And stir them with an in-
      ward grace.

2 Thou that art power and peace
    combined,
    All highest strength, all
      purest love,
The rushing of the mighty
    wind,
    The brooding of the gentle
      dove,

3 Come, give us still thy powerful
    aid,
    And urge us on, and keep us
      thine;
Nor leave the hearts that once
    were made
    Fit temples for thy grace
      divine;

4 Nor let us quench thy sevenfold
    light;
    But still with softest breath-
      ings stir
Our wayward souls, and lead us
    right,
    O Holy Ghost, the Com-
      forter.
        CECIL FRANCES ALEXANDER
               1818–95

110

O THOU who camest from
    above,
    The pure celestial fire to im-
      part,
Kindle a flame of sacred love
    On the mean altar of my
      heart.

2 Jesus, confirm my heart's de-
    sire
    To work, and speak, and
      think for thee;
Still let me guard the holy fire,
    And still stir up thy gift in
      me:

3 Ready for all thy perfect will,
  My acts of faith and love re-
    peat,
Till death thy endless mercies
    seal,
  And make the sacrifice com-
    plete.
                CHARLES WESLEY, 1707–88

III

JESUS, good above all other,
  Gentle child of gentle mother,
In a stable born our brother,
  Give us grace to persevere.

2 Jesus, cradled in a manger,
  For us facing every danger,
Living as a homeless stranger,
  Make we thee our King most
    dear.

3 Jesus, for thy people dying,
  Risen Master, death defying,
Lord in heaven, thy grace sup-
    plying,
  Keep us to thy presence near.

Jesus, who our sorrows bearest,
All our thoughts and hopes thou
    sharest;

Thou to man the truth de-
    clarest;
  Help us all thy truth to hear.

5 Lord, in all our doings guide us;
  Pride and hate shall ne'er
    divide us;
We'll go on with thee beside us,
  And with joy we'll persevere!
                PERCY DEARMER, 1867–1936

112 *For younger children*

JESUS Christ, I look to thee;
  Thou shalt my example be;
Thou art holy, just, and mild;
Thou wast once a little child.

2 Make me, Jesus, what thou art;
  Give me thy obedient heart;
Thou art merciful and kind;
Let me have thy loving mind.

3 I shall then show forth thy
    praise,
Serve thee all my happy days;
Then the world shall always see
Christ, the Holy Child, in me.
                CHARLES WESLEY, 1707–88, altered

ILLUMINATION

113

BLEST are the pure in heart,
  For they shall see their
    God:
The secret of the Lord is theirs;
  Their soul is Christ's abode.

2 The Lord, who left the sky
  Our life and peace to bring,
And dwelt in lowliness with
    men,
  Their Pattern and their
    King,—

3 Still to the lowly soul
  He doth himself impart,
And for his dwelling and his
    throne
  Chooseth the pure in heart.

4 Lord, we thy presence seek;
  Ours may this blessing be;
O give the pure and lowly heart,
  A temple meet for thee.
                vv. 1 and 3 JOHN KEBLE
                            1792–1866
                vv. 2 and 4 from Hall's
                    Psalms and Hymns, 1836

114

CHRIST, whose glory fills the
    skies,
  Christ, the true, the only
    Light,
Sun of Righteousness, arise,
  Triumph o'er the shades of
    night.

38

Dayspring from on high, be near;
Daystar, in my heart appear.

2 Dark and cheerless is the morn
　　Unaccompanied by thee;
Joyless is the day's return,
　　Till thy mercy's beams I see,
Till they inward light impart,
Glad my eyes, and warm my
　　heart.

3 Visit, then, this soul of mine,
　　Pierce the gloom of sin and
　　　grief;
Fill me, Radiancy Divine;
　　Scatter all my unbelief;
More and more thyself display,
Shining to the perfect day.

CHARLES WESLEY, 1707–88

115　　*Discendi, Amor santo*

COME down, O Love
　　Divine,
Seek thou this soul of mine,
And visit it with thine own
　　ardour glowing;
O Comforter, draw near,
Within my heart appear,
And kindle it, thy holy flame
　　bestowing.

2　O let it freely burn,
　　Till earthly passions turn
To dust and ashes, in its heat
　　consuming;
And let thy glorious light
Shine ever on my sight,
And clothe me round, the while
　　my path illuming.

3　Let holy charity
　　Mine outward vesture be,
And lowliness become mine
　　inner clothing;
True lowliness of heart,
Which takes the humbler
　　part,
And o'er its own shortcomings
　　weeps with loathing.

4　And so the yearning strong,
　　With which the soul will long,
Shall far outpass the power of
　　human telling;

For none can guess its grace,
Till he become the place
Wherein the Holy Spirit makes
　　his dwelling.

BIANCO DA SIENA, ?–1434
Tr. RICHARD FREDERICK
LITTLEDALE, 1833–90

116

COME, gracious Spirit,
　　heavenly Dove,
With light and comfort from
　　above;
Be thou our Guardian, thou our
　　Guide;
O'er every thought and step
　　preside.

2 The light of truth to us display,
And make us know and choose
　　thy way;
Plant holy fear in every
　　heart,
That we from God may ne'er
　　depart.

3 Lead us to Christ, the living
　　Way;
Nor let us from his pastures
　　stray:
Lead us to holiness, the road
That we must take to dwell
　　with God.

4 Lead us to heaven, that we
　　may share
Fullness of joy for ever there;
Lead us to God, our final rest,
To be with him for ever blest.

SIMON BROWNE, 1680–1732

117

COMMAND thy blessing from
　　above,
　　O God, on all assembled here

Behold us with a Father's love,
    While we look up with filial
      fear.

2 Command thy blessing, Jesus,
    Lord;
    May we thy true disciples be;
Speak to each heart the mighty
    word;
    Say to the weakest, 'Follow
      Me.'

3 Command thy blessing in this
    hour,
    Spirit of truth, and fill this
      place
With humbling and exalting
    power,
    With quickening and con-
      firming grace.

4 O thou, our Maker, Saviour,
    Guide,
    One true eternal God con-
      fessed,
May naught in life or death
    divide
    The saints in thy communion
      blest.

5 With thee and these for ever
    bound,
    May all who here in prayer
      unite,
With harps and songs thy
    throne surround,
    Rest in thy love, and reign in
      light.

JAMES MONTGOMERY, 1771–1854

118

Veni, Creator Spiritus

CREATOR Spirit! by whose
   aid
The world's foundations first
    were laid,
Come, visit every pious mind,
Come, pour thy joys on human
    kind;
From sin and sorrow set us free,
*And make thy temples worthy
    thee.

2 O Source of uncreated light,
    The Father's promised Para-
      clete,

Thrice holy Fount, thrice holy
    Fire,
Our hearts with heavenly love
    inspire;
Come, and thy sacred unction
    bring
To sanctify us while we sing.

3 Plenteous of grace, descend
    from high,
    Rich in thy sevenfold energy;
Thou Strength of his almighty
    hand
Whose power does heaven and
    earth command,
Give us thyself, that we may
    see
The Father and the Son by thee.

4 *Immortal honour, endless fame*
    Attend the Almighty Father's
      Name;
The Saviour Son be glorified,
Who for lost man's redemption
    died;
And equal adoration be,
Eternal Paraclete, to thee. Amen.

9th century
Tr. JOHN DRYDEN, 1631–1700
Adapted JOHN WESLEY, 1703–91

* *The last line of each verse is repeated.*

119

ENTER thy courts, thou
   Word of life,
My joy and peace;
Let the glad sound therein be
    heard,
Bid plaintive sadness cease.
Comfort my heart, thou Truth
    most fair;
O enter in,
Chasing despair and earthborn
    care,
My woe and slothful sin.

2 Glad was the time when I would
    sing
The heavenly praise;
Happy my heart when thou
    wert nigh,
Directing all my ways.
O let thy light, thy joy again
Return to me;
Nor in disdain from me refrain,
Who lift my soul to thee.

In heaven and earth thy law
    endures,
Thy word abides:
My troubled flesh trembleth in
    awe,
My heart in terror hides.
Yet still on thee my hope is set;
On thee, O Lord,
I will await and not forget
The promise of thy word.

           ROBERT BRIDGES, 1844–1930

120

LORD of beauty, thine the
   splendour
    Shown in earth and sky and
      sea,
Burning sun and moonlight
    tender,
    Hill and river, flower and
      tree;
Lest we fail our praise to ren-
    der,
    Touch our eyes that we may
      see!

2 Lord of wisdom, whom obeying
    Mighty waters ebb and flow,
While unhasting, undelaying,
    Planets on their courses go;
In thy laws thyself displaying,
    Teach our minds thy truth to
      know!

3 Lord of life, alone sustaining
    All below and all above,
Lord of love, by whose ordain-
    ing
    Sun and stars sublimely
      move;
In our earthly spirits reigning,
    Lift our hearts, that we may
      love!

4 Lord of beauty, bid us own
    thee,
Lord of truth, our footsteps
    guide,
Till as love our hearts enthrone
    thee,
    And, with vision purified,
Lord of all, when all have
    known thee,
    Thou in all art glorified!

         CYRIL ARGENTINE ALINGTON
                  1872–1955

121

THOU art the Way: to thee
   alone
    From sin and death we flee;
And he who would the Father
    seek
    Must seek him, Lord, by thee.

2 Thou art the Truth: thy word
    alone
    True wisdom can impart;
Thou only canst inform the
    mind,
    And purify the heart.

3 Thou art the Life: the rending
    tomb
    Proclaims thy conquering
      arm;
And those who put their trust in
    thee
    Nor death nor hell shall harm.

4 Thou art the Way, the Truth,
    the Life:
    Grant us that way to know,
That truth to keep, that life to
    win,
    Whose joys eternal flow.

        GEORGE WASHINGTON DOANE
                  1799–1859

122

COME, Holy Ghost, our
   hearts inspire;
    Let us thine influence prove,
Source of the old prophetic fire,
    Fountain of life and love.

2 Come, Holy Ghost, for moved
    by thee
    The prophets wrote and
      spoke;
Unlock the truth, thyself the
    key;
    Unseal the sacred book.

3 Expand thy wings, celestial
    Dove;
    Brood o'er our nature's night;
On our disordered spirits move,
    And let there now be light.

4 God through himself we then
    shall know,
    If thou within us shine,

And sound, with all thy saints
   below,
  The depths of love divine.
          CHARLES WESLEY, 1707–88

123 *For children*

HUSHED was the evening
   hymn,
  The temple courts were
   dark,
  The lamp was burning dim
   Before the sacred ark,
When suddenly a voice Divine
Rang through the silence of the
   shrine.

2 The old man, meek and mild,
    The priest of Israel, slept;
  His watch the temple child,
    The little Levite, kept;
And what from Eli's sense was
   sealed
The Lord to Hannah's son re-
   vealed.

3 O give me Samuel's ear,
    The open ear, O Lord,
  Alive and quick to hear
    Each   whisper   of   thy
     word,—
Like him to answer at thy call,
And to obey thee first of all.

4 O give me Samuel's heart,
    A lowly heart, that waits
  Where in thy house thou art,
    Or watches at thy gates
By day and night,—a heart that
   still
Moves at the breathing of thy
   will.

5 O give me Samuel's mind,
    A   sweet   unmurmuring
     faith,
  Obedient and resigned
    To thee in life and death,
That I may read, with childlike eyes,
Truths that are hidden from the
   wise.
        JAMES DRUMMOND BURNS
              1823–6

124 *For younger children*

HOLY Spirit, hear us;
   Help us while we sing;
Breathe into the music
Of the praise we bring.

2 Holy Spirit, prompt us
   When we kneel to pray;
Nearer come, and teach us
What we ought to say.

3 Holy Spirit, shine thou
   On the book we read;
Gild its holy pages
With the light we need.

4 Holy Spirit, give us
   Each a lowly mind;
Make us more like Jesus,
Gentle, pure, and kind.

5 Holy Spirit, help us
   Daily, by thy might,
What is wrong to conquer,
And to choose the right.
        WILLIAM HENRY PARKER
              1845–192

HOLY SCRIPTURE

125 PSALM 19, verses 7–10, 14

GOD'S law is perfect, and
   converts
  The soul in sin that lies;
God's testimony is most sure,
  And makes the simple wise.

2 The statutes of the Lord are
   right,
  And do rejoice the heart:
The Lord's command is pure
   and doth
  Light to the eyes impart.

Unspotted is the fear of God,
  And doth endure for ever:
The judgments of the Lord are
    true
  And righteous altogether.

They more than gold, yea, much
    fine gold,
  To be desirèd are:
Than honey, honey from the
    comb
  That droppeth, sweeter far.

The words which from my
    mouth proceed,
  The thoughts sent from my
    heart,
Accept, O Lord, for thou my
    strength
  And my Redeemer art.

To Father, Son, and Holy Ghost,
  The God whom we adore,
Be glory, as it was, and is,
  And shall be evermore. Amen.

126   From PSALM 19, verses
          7–14

GOD'S perfect law revives the
    soul,
His word makes wise the simple;
God's clear commands rejoice
    the heart,
His light the eye enlightens;
God's fear is pure, his judg-
    ments just,
More to be sought than pure
    fine gold,
Sweeter by far than honey.

Lord, who can tell the secret
    faults
That have dominion o'er me?
Hold back thy servant from
    self-will
And break its power to bind me.
May all I think and all I say
Be now acceptable to thee,
My Rock and my Redeemer.
                   IAN PITT-WATSON
          From *The New English Bible* version
                       of Psalm 19

127   PSALM 119, verses 33–40

TEACH me, O Lord, the per-
    fect way
  Of thy precepts divine,

And to observe it to the end
  I shall my heart incline.

2 Give understanding unto me,
    So keep thy law shall I;
  Yea, even with my whole heart
      I shall
    Observe it carefully.

3 In thy law's path make me to
      go;
    For I delight therein;
  My heart unto thy testimonies,
    And not to greed, incline.

4 Turn thou away my sight and
      eyes
    From viewing vanity;
  And in thy good and holy way
    Be pleased to quicken me.

5 Confirm to me thy gracious
      word,
    Which I did gladly hear,
  Even to thy servant, Lord, who
      is
    Devoted to thy fear.

6 Turn thou away my feared re-
      proach;
    For good thy judgments be.
  Lo, for thy precepts I have
      longed;
    In thy truth quicken me.

7 *To Father, Son, and Holy Ghost,*
    The God whom we adore,
  Be glory, as it was, and is,
    And shall be evermore. Amen.

128

BOOK of books, our people's
    strength,
  Statesman's, teacher's, hero's
      treasure,
Bringing freedom, spreading
      truth,
  Shedding light that none can
      measure—
Wisdom comes to those
    who know thee,
  All the best we have we
      owe thee.

43   c

Thank we those who toiled in
  thought,
    Many diverse scrolls complet-
      ing,
Poets, prophets, scholars, saints,
    Each his word from God re-
      peating;
        Till they came, who told
          the story
        Of the Word, and showed
          his glory.

3 Praise we God, who hath in-
      spired
    Those whose wisdom still
      directs us;
Praise him for the Word made
    flesh,
  For the Spirit who protects
      us.
      Light of Knowledge, ever
        burning,
      Shed on us thy deathless
        learning.

PERCY DEARMER, 1867–1936

I29 *Liebster Jesu, wir sind hier*

LOOK upon us, blessèd Lord,
  Take our wandering thoughts
    and guide us:
  We have come to hear thy
    word:
With thy teaching now provide
    us,
  That, from earth's distrac-
    tions turning,
  We thy message may be
    learning.

2   For thy Spirit's radiance
      bright
  We, assembled here, are hop-
    ing:
    If thou shouldst withold the
      light,
  In the dark our souls were
    groping:
    In word, deed, and thought
      direct us;
    Thou, none other, canst cor-
      rect us.

3   Brightness of the Father's
      face,
  Light of Light, from God pro-
    ceeding,
    Make us ready in this place:

Ear and heart await thy leading
  In our study, prayers, and
    praising,
  May our souls find their
    upraising.

TOBIAS CLAUSNITZER, 1619–84
Tr. ROBERT MACALISTER
1870–1950

I30

LORD, thy word abideth,
  And our footsteps guideth;
Who its truth believeth
Light and joy receiveth.

2 When our foes are near us,
  Then thy word doth cheer us,
  Word of consolation,
  Message of salvation.

3 When the storms are o'er us,
  And dark clouds before us,
  Then its light directeth,
  And our way protecteth.

4 Who can tell the pleasure,
  Who recount the treasure,
  By thy word imparted
  To the simple-hearted?

5 Word of mercy, giving
  Succour to the living;
  Word of life, supplying
  Comfort to the dying!

6 O that we, discerning
  Its most holy learning,
  Lord, may love and fear thee,
  Evermore be near thee!

HENRY WILLIAMS BAKER
1821–77

I3I

LIGHT of the world! for ever
  ever shining,
    There is no change in thee;
True Light of Life, all joy and
    health enshrining,
    Thou canst not fade nor flee.

2 Thou hast arisen, but thou
    descendest never;
    Today shines as the past;
  All that thou wast thou art, and
    shalt be ever,
    Brightness from first to last.

44

Night visits not thy sky, nor
   storm, nor sadness;
Day fills up all its blue,—
Unfailing beauty, and unfalter-
   ing gladness,
   And love for ever new.

Light of the world, undimming
   and unsetting!
  O shine each mist away;
Banish the fear, the falsehood,
   and the fretting;
  Be our unchanging Day.
        HORATIUS BONAR, 1808–89

32

TELL me the old, old story
   Of unseen things above,
Of Jesus and his glory,
  Of Jesus and his love.
Tell me the story simply,
  As to a little child;
For I am weak and weary,
  And helpless, and defiled.
   Tell me the old, old story,
   Tell me the old, old story,
   Tell me the old, old story,
   Of Jesus and his love.

Tell me the story slowly,
  That I may take it in,—
That wonderful redemption,
  God's remedy for sin.
Tell me the story often,
  For I forget so soon;
The early dew of morning
  Has passed away at noon.

Tell me the story softly,
  With earnest tones and grave;
Remember, I'm the sinner
  Whom Jesus came to save.
Tell me the story always,
  If you would really be,
In any time of trouble,
  A comforter to me.

Tell me the same old story
  When you have cause to fear
That this world's empty glory
  Is costing me too dear.
Yes, and when that world's
   glory
Shall dawn upon my soul,

Tell me the old, old story,
  'Christ Jesus makes thee
   whole.'
     ARABELLA CATHERINE HANKEY
          1834–1911

133

BREAK forth, O living light
   of God,
Upon the world's dark hour!
Show us the way the Master
   trod;
Reveal his saving power.

2 Remove the veil of ancient
   words,
  Their message long obscure;
Restore to us thy truth, O God,
  And make its meaning sure.

3 O let thy Word be light anew
  To every nation's life;
Unite us in thy will, O Lord,
  And end all sinful strife.

4 O may one Lord, one Faith, one
   Word,
  One Spirit lead us still;
And one great Church go forth
   in might
To work God's perfect will.
      FRANK VON CHRISTIERSON

134

HEAVENLY Father, may
   thy blessing
  Rest upon thy children now,
When in praise thy Name they
   hallow,
  When in prayer to thee they
   bow:
In the wondrous story reading
  Of the Lord of truth and
   grace,
May they see thy love reflected
  In the light of his dear face.

2 May they learn from this great
   story
  All the arts of friendliness;
Truthful speech and honest
   action,
  Courage, patience, steadfastness;

How to master self and temper,
　How to make their conduct
　　fair;
When to speak and when be
　silent,
　When to do and when forbear.

3 May his Spirit wise and holy
　With his gifts their spirits
　　bless,
　Make them loving, joyous,
　　peaceful,
　Rich in goodness, gentleness,
Strong in self-control, and
　faithful,
　Kind in thought and deed;
　　for he
Sayeth, 'What ye do for others
　Ye are doing unto me'.

WILLIAM CHARTER PIGGOTT,
1872–1943

See also certain hymns in Part ☐
Section 3 (The Holy Spirit in the Chur☐

The following hymns are appropriate
opening processional hymns on spec☐
occasions:

Advent: O come, O come Immanuel, 1
Christmas: Of the Father's love begotte☐
　198
Palm Sunday: All glory, laud and hono☐
　233
Passiontide: Sing, my tongue, 256
Easter: 'Welcome, happy morning', 2☐
Ascension: The head that once, 286
Pentecost: Come, Holy Ghost, our sou☐
　inspire, 342
Trinity: Holy, holy, holy, 352
　　　　I bind unto myself today, 40☐
All Saints: For all the saints, 534
Rogation and Harvest: We plough t☐
　fields, 620
Holy Communion: Deck thyself, my so☐
　567

II

THE WORD OF GOD:
HIS MIGHTY ACTS

CREATION AND PROVIDENCE

35 PSALM 148 (ii)

THE Lord of heaven confess,
  On high his glory raise.
Him let all angels bless,
  Him all his armies praise.
    Him glorify
      Sun, moon, and stars;
      Ye higher spheres,
    And cloudy sky.

From God your beings are,
  Him therefore famous make;
You all created were,
  When he the word but spake.
    And from that place,
      Where fixed you be
      By his decree,
    You cannot pass.

Praise God from earth below,
  Ye dragons, and ye deeps:
Fire, hail, clouds, wind, and
    snow,
  Whom in command he keeps.
    Praise ye his Name,
      Hills great and small,
      Trees low and tall;
    Beasts wild and tame.

All things that creep or fly,
  Ye kings, ye vulgar throng,
All princes mean or high;
  Both men and virgins young,
    Even young and old,
      Exalt his Name;
      For much his fame
    Should be extolled.

O let God's Name be praised
  Above both earth and sky;

For he his saints hath raised,
  And set their horn on high;
    Even those that be
      Of Israel's race,
      Near to his grace.
    The Lord praise ye.

6 *To God the Father, Son,*
  And Spirit ever blest,
Eternal Three in One,
  All worship be addressed,
    As heretofore
      It was, is now,
      And still shall be
    For evermore. Amen.

136 PSALM 147, verses 1–5

PRAISE ye the Lord; for it is
    good
  Praise to our God to sing:
For it is pleasant, and to praise
  It is a comely thing.

2 God doth build up Jerusalem;
    And he it is alone
  That the dispersed of Israel
    Doth gather into one.

3 Those that are broken in their
    heart,
    And grievèd in their minds,
  He healeth, and their painful
    wounds
    He tenderly up-binds.

4 He counts the number of the
    stars;
    He names them every one.
  Great is our Lord, and of great
    power;
    His wisdom search can none.

47

5 To Father, Son, and Holy Ghost,
   The God whom we adore,
Be glory, as it was, and is,
   And shall be evermore. Amen.

137 PSALM 136 (ii), verses 1–5,
        23–26

PRAISE God, for he is kind:
   His mercy lasts for aye.
Give thanks with heart and
   mind
To God of gods alway:
   For certainly
      His mercies dure
      Most firm and sure
   Eternally.

2 The Lord of lords praise ye,
   Whose mercies still endure.
Great wonders only he
   Doth work by his great power:

3 Give praise to his great name,
   Who, by his wisdom high,
The heaven above did frame,
   And built the lofty sky:

4 Who hath remembered us
   When in our low estate;
And hath delivered us
   From foes who did us hate:

5 Who to all flesh gives food;
   For his grace faileth never.
Give thanks to God most good,
   The God of heaven, for ever:

6 To God the Father, Son,
   And Spirit ever blest,
Eternal Three in One,
   All worship be addressed,
      As heretofore
         It was, is now,
         And still shall be
      For evermore. Amen.

138 PSALM 8, verses 1, 3–5

HOW excellent in all the
   earth,
Lord, our Lord, is thy Name!
Who hast thy glory far advanced
   Above the starry frame.

2 When I look up unto t[
   heavens,
   Which thine own finge[
      framed,
Unto the moon, and to t[
   stars,
   Which were by thee ordaine[

3 Then say I, What is man, th[
   he
   Remembered is by thee?
Or what the son of man, th[
   thou
   So kind to him should'st be[

4 For thou a little lower hast
   Him than the angels made
With glory and with dignity
   Thou crowned hast his hea[

5 To Father, Son, and Holy Gho[
   The God whom we adore,
Be glory, as it was, and is,
   And shall be evermore. Ame[

139 PSALM 121

I TO the hills will lift mine eye[
   From whence doth con[
      mine aid?
My safety cometh from t[
   Lord,
   Who heaven and earth ha[
      made.

2 Thy foot he'll not let slide, n[
   will
   He slumber that thee keeps[
Behold, he that keeps Israel,
   He slumbers not, nor sleeps[

3 The Lord thee keeps, the Lo[
   thy shade
   On thy right hand doth sta[
The moon by night thee sha[
   not smite,
   Nor yet the sun by day.

4 The Lord shall keep thy sou[
   he shall
   Preserve thee from all ill.
Henceforth thy going out ar[
   in
   God keep for ever will.

5 To Father, Son, and Holy Gho[
   The God whom we adore,
Be glory, as it was, and is,
   And shall be evermore. Ame[

140

PSALM 93

THE Lord doth reign, and
    clothed is he
  With majesty most bright;
His works do show him clothed
    to be,
  And girt about with might.
The world is also stablishèd,
  That it cannot depart.
Thy throne is fixed of old, and
    thou
  From everlasting art.

2 The floods, O Lord, have lifted
    up,
  They lifted up their voice;
The floods have lifted up their
    waves,
  And made a mighty noise.
But yet the Lord, that is on
    high,
  Is more of might by far
Than noise of many waters is,
  Or great sea-billows are.

3 Thy testimonies every one
  In faithfulness excel;
And holiness for ever, Lord,
  Thine house becometh well.
*To Father, Son, and Holy Ghost,
  The God whom we adore,
Be glory, as it was, and is,
  And shall be evermore. Amen.*

141

O LORD of every shining
    constellation
  That wheels in splendour
    through the midnight sky;
Grant us thy Spirit's true
    illumination
  To read the secrets of thy
    work on high.

2 And thou who mad'st the
    atom's hidden forces,
  Whose laws its mighty ener-
    gies fulfil;
Teach us, to whom thou giv'st
    such rich resources,
  In all we use, to serve thy
    holy will.

3 O Life, awaking life in cell and
    tissue,
  From flower to bird, from
    beast to brain of man;
O help us trace, from birth to
    final issue,
  The sure unfolding of thine
    ageless plan.

4 Thou who hast stamped thine
    image on thy creatures,
  And though they marred that
    image, lov'st them still;
Uplift our eyes to Christ, that
    in his features
  We may discern the beauty
    of thy will.

5 Great Lord of nature, shaping
    and renewing,
  Who mad'st us more than
    nature's sons to be;
Help us to tread, with grace our
    souls enduing,
  The road to life and immor-
    tality.

ALBERT FREDERICK BAYLY

142   *Sei Lob und Ehr' dem
              höchsten Gut*

SING praise to God who reigns
    above,
  The God of all creation,
The God of power, the God of
    love,
  The God of our salvation;
With healing balm my soul he
    fills,
  And every faithless murmur
    stills:
    To God all praise and glory!

2 The angel host, O King of kings,
  Thy praise for ever telling,
In earth and sky all living
    things
  Beneath thy shadow dwelling,
Adore the wisdom which could
    span,
  And power which formed crea-
    tion's plan.

3 O ye who name Christ's holy
    Name,
  Give God all praise and glory:

49

All ye who own his power, pro-
claim
Aloud the wondrous story.
Cast each false idol from his
throne,
The Lord is God, and he alone:

JOHANN JAKOB SCÜHTZ, 1640–90
Tr. FRANCES ELIZABETH COX
1812–97

143

THE spacious firmament on
high,
With all the blue ethereal sky,
And spangled heavens, a shin-
ing frame,
Their great Original proclaim.
The unwearied sun, from day to
day,
Does his Creator's power dis-
play,
And publishes to every land
The work of an almighty hand.

2 Soon as the evening shades
prevail,
The moon takes up the won-
drous tale,
And nightly to the listening
earth
Repeats the story of her birth;
While all the stars that round
her burn,
And all the planets, in their
turn,
Confirm the tidings, as they roll,
And spread the truth from pole
to pole.

3 What though in solemn silence
all
Move round the dark terres-
trial ball?
What though no real voice nor
sound
Amidst their radiant orbs be
found?
In reason's ear they all rejoice,
And utter forth a glorious voice,
For ever singing, as they shine,
'The hand that made us is
divine.' Amen.   (Tune ii)

JOSEPH ADDISON, 1672–1719

144

GOD is Love: his mercy
brightens
All the path in which we rove
Bliss he wakes, and woe he
lightens:
God is Wisdom, God is Love.

2 Chance and change are busy
ever;
Man decays, and ages move
But his mercy waneth never:

3 Even the hour that darkest
seemeth
Will his changeless goodness
prove;
From the mist his brightness
streameth:

4 He with earthly cares entwineth
Hope and comfort from
above;
Everywhere his glory shineth:

JOHN BOWRING, 1792–1872

145

O LORD of heaven and earth
and sea,
To thee all praise and glory be
How shall we show our love to
thee,
Who givest all?

2 The golden sunshine, vernal air,
Sweet flowers and fruits thy
love declare;
Where harvests ripen, thou art
there,
Who givest all.

3 For peaceful homes and health-
ful days,
For all the blessings earth displays,
We owe thee thankfulness and
praise,
Who givest all.

4 Thou didst not spare thine only
Son,
But gav'st him for a world
undone,
And freely with that blessèd
One
Thou givest all.

For souls redeemed, for sins
   forgiven,
For means of grace and hopes
   of heaven,
Father, all praise to thee be
   given,
      Who givest all.
         CHRISTOPHER WORDSWORTH
                  1807–85

146

MY God, I thank thee, who
   hast made
   The earth so bright,
So full of splendour and of joy,
   Beauty and light;
So many glorious things are
   here,
   Noble and right.

2 I thank thee, too, that thou
   hast made
   Joy to abound,
So many gentle thoughts and
   deeds
   Circling us round
That in the darkest spot of
   earth
   Some love is found.

3 I thank thee more that all our
   joy
   Is touched with pain,
That shadows fall on brightest
   hours,
   That thorns remain,
So that earth's bliss may be our
   guide,
   And not our chain.

4 I thank thee, Lord, that here
   our souls,
   Though amply blest,
Can never find, although they
   seek,
   A perfect rest,
Nor ever shall, until they lean
   On Jesus' breast.
         ADELAIDE ANNE PROCTER
            1825–64, altered slightly

147

GOD moves in a mysterious
   way,
   His wonders to perform;

He plants his footsteps in the
   sea,
   And rides upon the storm.

2 Deep in unfathomable mines
   Of never-failing skill
He treasures up his bright
   designs,
   And works his sovereign will.

3 Ye fearful saints, fresh courage
   take;
   The clouds ye so much dread
Are big with mercy, and shall
   break
   In blessings on your head.

4 Judge not the Lord by feeble
   sense,
   But trust him for his grace;
Behind a frowning providence
   He hides a smiling face.

5 Blind unbelief is sure to err,
   And scan his work in vain,
God is his own interpreter,
   And he will make it plain.
         WILLIAM COWPER, 1731-1800

148

A GLADSOME hymn of
      praise we sing,
   And thankfully we gather
To bless the love of God above,
   Our everlasting Father.
In him rejoice with heart and
   voice,
   Whose glory fadeth never,
Whose providence is our de-
   fence,
   Who lives and loves for ever.

2 Full in his sight his children
   stand,
   By his strong arm defended,
And he whose wisdom guides
   the world
   Our footsteps hath attended.
For nothing falls unknown to
   him,
   Or care or joy or sorrow,
And he whose mercy ruled the
   past
   Will be our stay tomorrow.
         AMBROSE NICHOLS BLATCHFORD
                  1842–1924

149 *Rebus creatis nil egens*

O GOD, the joy of heaven
  above,
Thou didst not need thy creatures' love,
When from thy secret place
  was said
The word that earth's foundation laid.

2 Thou spakest:—worlds began
  to be;
They stand before thy majesty;
And all to their Creator raise
A wondrous harmony of praise.

3 But ere, O Lord, this lovely
  earth
From thy creative will had
  birth,
Thou in thy counsels didst unfold
Another world of fairer mould.

4 That world doth our Redeemer
  frame,
And build upon his mighty
  Name;
His Holy Church shall last for
  aye
Till time itself hath passed
  away.

CHARLES COFFIN, 1676–1749
Tr. Compilers of *A Plainsong
Hymnbook,* 1932, altered

150

WHEN all thy mercies, O my
  God!
My rising soul surveys,
Transported with the view, I'm
  lost
In wonder, love, and praise.

2 Unnumbered comforts to my
  soul
Thy tender care bestowed,
Before my infant heart conceived
From whom these comforts
  flowed.

3 When in the slippery paths of
  youth
With heedless steps I ran,

Thine arm, unseen, conveyed
  me safe,
And led me up to man.

4 Ten thousand thousand pre-
  cious gifts
My daily thanks employ;
Nor is the least a cheerful heart
  That tastes those gifts with
  joy.

5 Through every period of my
  life
Thy goodness I'll pursue;
And after death, in distant
  worlds,
The glorious theme renew.

JOSEPH ADDISON, 1672–1719

151 *For children*

GOD, who made the earth,
  The air, the sky, the sea,
Who gave the light its birth,
  Careth for me.

2 God, who made the grass,
  The flower, the fruit, the tree,
The day and night to pass,
  Careth for me.

3 God, who made the sun,
  The moon, the stars, is he
Who, when life's clouds come
  on,
  Careth for me.

4 God, who made all things,
  On earth, in air, in sea,
Who changing seasons brings,
  Careth for me.

5 God, who sent his Son
  To die on Calvary,
He, if I lean on him,
  Will care for me.

SARAH BETTS RHODES, 1829–1904

152 *For children*

HOW wonderful this world of
  thine,
A fragment of a fiery sun,
How lovely and how small!
Where all things serve thy
  great design,
Where life's adventure is begun
In thee, the life of all.

2 The smallest seed in secret
    grows,
  And thrusting upward answers
    soon
  The bidding of the light;
  The bud unfurls into a rose;
  The wings within the white
    cocoon
  Are perfected for flight.

3 The migrant bird, in winter
    fled,
  Shall come again with spring
    and build
  In this same shady tree;
  By secret wisdom surely led,
  Homeward across the clover-
    field
  Hurries the honey-bee.

4 O thou, whose greater gifts are
    ours:
  A conscious will, a thinking
    mind,
  A heart to worship thee—
  O take these strange unfolding
    powers
  And teach us through thy Son
    to find
  The life more full and free.

FREDERICK PRATT GREEN

153 *For younger children*

A LITTLE child may know
  Our Father's name of 'Love';
'Tis written on the earth below,
And on the sky above.

2 Around me when I look,
  His handiwork I see;
This world is like a picture-book
To teach his Name to me.

3 The thousand little flowers
  Within our garden found,
The rainbow and the soft spring
    showers,
And every pleasant sound;

4 The birds that sweetly sing,
  The moon that shines by night,
With every tiny living thing
Rejoicing in the light;

5 And every star above,
  Set in the deep blue sky,
All tell me that our God is Love,
And tell me he is nigh.

JANE ELIZA LEESON, 1807–82

154 *For younger children*

* A LL things bright and beautiful,
    All creatures great and
      small,
  All things wise and wonderful—
    The Lord God made them all.

2 Each little flower that opens,
    Each little bird that sings,—
  He made their glowing colours,
    He made their tiny wings.

3 The purple-headed mountain,
    The river running by,
  The sunset, and the morning
    That brightens up the sky,

4 The cold wind in the winter,
    The pleasant summer sun,
  The ripe fruits in the garden,—
    He made them every one:

5 He gave us eyes to see them,
    And lips that we might tell
  How great is God Almighty,
    Who has made all things well.

CECIL FRANCES ALEXANDER
1818–95

* Verse 1 is also sung as a refrain after
each other verse.

155 *For younger children*

G OD who put the stars in
    space,
Who made the world we share,
In his making made a place
For me, and put me here.

2 Thank you, God, for stars in
    space
And for the world we share.
Thank you for my special place
To love and serve you here.

NORMAN and MARGARET MEALY
based on a poem by
LUCILE S. REID

156 *For younger children*

I LOVE to think that Jesus saw
The same bright sun that shines today;
It gave him light to do his work,
And smiled upon his play.

2 The same white moon, with silver face,
That sails across the sky at night,
He used to see in Galilee,
And watch it with delight.

3 The same great God that hears my prayers
Heard his, when Jesus knelt to pray;

He is my Father, who will keep
His child through every day.

ADA SKEMP, 1857–1927

157 *For younger children*

WE thank thee, God, for eyes to see
The beauty of the earth;
For ears to hear the words of love
And happy sounds of mirth;
For minds that find new thoughts to think,
New wonders to explore;
For health and freedom to enjoy
The good thou hast in store.

JEANNETTE PERKINS BROWN
1887–1960

THE PROMISE OF THE MESSIAH

158 PSALM 72, verses 1, 2, 5, 11, 17–19

GIVE the king thy judgments O ' God : and thy righteous-ness un ' to the king's son.

He shall judge thy people with ' righteousness : and thy ' poor with judgment.

They shall fear thee as long as the sun and moon en ' dure : throughout all ' generations.

Yea all kings shall fall down be ' fore him : all na ' tions shall serve him.

His Name shall endure for ever his Name shall be continued as long as the ' sun : and men shall be blessèd in him all nations shall ' call him blessèd.

Blessèd be the Lord God the God of ' Israel : who only ' doeth wondrous things.

And blessèd be his glorious Name for ' ever : and let the whole earth be filled with his glory·A ' men and Amen.

Glory be to the Father and to the ' Son : and ' to the Holy Ghost :

As it was in the beginning is now and ever ' shall be : world with ' out end Amen.

159 PARAPHRASE 26, verses 5–10

BEHOLD he comes! your leader comes,
With might and honour crowned;
A witness who shall spread my Name
To earth's remotest bound.

2 See! nations hasten to his call
From every distant shore;
Isles, yet unknown, shall bow to him,
And Israel's God adore.

3 Seek ye the Lord while yet his
    ear
    Is open to your call;
  While offered mercy still is near,
    Before his footstool fall.

4 Let sinners quit their evil ways,
    Their evil thoughts forgo:
  And God, when they to him
    return,
    Returning grace will show.

5 He pardons with o'erflowing
    love:
  For, hear the voice divine!
  My nature is not like to yours,
    Nor like your ways are mine:

6 But far as heaven's resplendent
    orbs
    Beyond earth's spot extend,
  As far my thoughts, as far my
    ways,
    Your ways and thoughts
      transcend.

          Scottish Paraphrases, 1781
          From Isaiah 55:4–9

160 PARAPHRASE 39

HARK, the glad sound! the
    Saviour comes,
  The Saviour promised long;
  Let every heart exult with joy,
    And every voice be song!

2 He comes, the prisoners to re-
    lieve,
    In Satan's bondage held;
  The gates of brass before him
    burst,
    The iron fetters yield.

3 He comes, the broken hearts to
    bind,
    The bleeding souls to cure;
  And with the treasures of his
    grace
    To enrich the humble poor.

4 The sacred year has now re-
    volved,
    Accepted of the Lord,
  When heaven's high promise is
    fulfilled,
    And Israel is restored.

5 Our glad hosannas, Prince of
    Peace,
    Thy welcome shall proclaim;
  And heaven's exalted arches
    ring
    With thy most honoured
      Name.

          Scottish Paraphrases, 1781
          From St. Luke 4:18, 19

161 BENEDICTUS

BLESSED be the Lord '
    God of ' Isra-el : for he
  hath visited ' and re-'
  deemed his ' people :
  And hath raised up a mighty
    sal-' vation ' for us : in the '
    house of his ' servant '
    David.

2 As he spake by the mouth of
    his ' holy ' prophets : which
    have ' been since the ' world
    be-' gan :
  That we should be ' saved
    from our ' enemies : and
    from the ' hands of ' all
    that ' hate us.

3 To perform the mercy ' pro-
    mised to our ' forefathers :
    and to re-' member his '
    holy ' covenant :
  To perform the oath which he
    sware to our ' forefather '
    Abraham : that ' he would '
    give ' us.

4 That we being delivered out
    of the ' hands of our '
    enemies : might ' serve him
    with-' out ' fear :
  In holiness and ' righteousness
    be-' fore him : all the ' days '
    of our ' life.

5 And thou child shalt be called
    the ' prophet of the ' Highest :
    for thou shalt go before
    the face of the ' Lord to
    pre-' pare his ' ways :
  To give knowledge of salva-
    tion ' unto his ' people : for
    the re-' mission ' of their '
    sins.

6 Through the tender ' mercy of
  our ' God : whereby the '
  dayspring from on ' high
  hath ' visited us :
To give light to them that
  sit in darkness and in the '
  shadow of ' death : and to
  guide our feet ' into the '
  way of ' peace.

*Glory ' be to the ' Father : and to
  the Son ' and to the ' Holy '
  Ghost :
As it ' was in the be- ' ginning :
  is now and ever shall be '
  world without ' end.
  A- ' men.*
From St. Luke 1: 68–79

*162

BEFORE all time the Word
  existed ;
Before all time he was with God ;
With God in fellowship eternal,
In essence one with all God was.
Through him all things received
  their birth ;
No thing without him came to
  be.

2 The Word was life in all creation—
That life the Light of all mankind.
Through countless ages in the
  darkness
The Light shone out, and still
  it shines.
No matter how the dark
  might strive,
Its force could not the Light
  subdue.

3 To witness to the Light there
  came,
Sent forth from God, a man
  named John ;
That through him all men
  might believe
The Light to whom he testi-
  fied.
This True Light, lighting every
  man,
Ev'n then was entering the
  world.

4 The world he entered failed to
  know him,
Although through him the
  world was made:
To his own realm it was he
  came,
Yet his own folk no welcome
  gave.
But some there were who did
  receive
The Light of men, the Word of
  God.

5 To these, to all in him be-
  lieving,
Who put their faith in his great
  Name,
He gave authority and war-
  rant—
The power God's children to
  become.
No human blood or seed or will
Gave them this birth, but God
  alone!

6 The Word became a human
  being,
And made his dwelling in our
  midst.
We saw his majesty and splen-
  dour—
His glory, full of grace and
  truth:
Such as to One alone belongs
Who is the Father's only Son.

JAMES N. S. ALEXANDER
From St. John 1:1–7, 9–14

* *When the whole paraphrase is not
sung, a selection of verses may be made as
follows: verses 1, 2, (3), and 6, or verses
3, 4, 5, and 6.*

163   MAGNIFICAT

MY soul doth magnify the
  Lord   and my spirit
  hath rejoiced in ' God my '
  Saviour : for he hath re-
  garded the ' lowliness ' of
  his ' hand-maiden :
For be- ' hold from ' henceforth : all gener- ' ations
  shall ' call me ' blessèd.

2 For he that is mighty hath '
  magnified ' me : and holy '
  is his ' Name :

And his mercy is on ' them
    that ' fear him : through- '
    out all ' gener- ' ations.

3 He hath showed ' strength
    with his ' arm : he hath
    scattered the proud in the
    imagi- ' nation ' of their '
    hearts :
He hath put down the '
    mighty from their ' seat :
    and hath ex- ' alted the '
    humble and ' meek.

4 He hath filled the ' hungry
    with ' good things : and the '
    rich he hath sent ' empty
    a- ' way :
He remembering his mercy
    hath holpen his ' servant '
    Isra-el : as he promised to
    our forefathers ' Abraham
    and his ' seed for ' ever.

Glory ' *be to the* ' *Father : and to*
    the ' *Son* ' *and to the* ' *Holy* '
    Ghost :
As it ' *was in the be-* ' *ginning :*
    is now and ever shall be '
    world without ' *end.*
                A- ' men.
    From St. Luke 1: 46–55

164

TELL out, my soul, the
    greatness of the Lord!
Unnumbered blessings, give my
    spirit voice;
Tender to me the promise of his
    word;
In God my Saviour shall my
    heart rejoice.

2 Tell out, my soul, the greatness
    of his Name!
Make known his might, the
    deeds his arm has done;
His mercy sure, from age to age
    the same;
His holy Name—the Lord, the
    Mighty One.

3 Tell out, my soul, the greatness
    of his might!
Powers and dominions lay their
    glory by.

Proud hearts and stubborn wills
    are put to flight,
The hungry fed, the humble
    lifted high.

4 Tell out, my soul, the glories of
    his word!
Firm is his promise, and his
    mercy sure.
Tell out, my soul, the greatness
    of the Lord
To children's children and for
    evermore!
          TIMOTHY DUDLEY-SMITH
    Based on the Magnificat as in *The*
          New English Bible

165   *Veni, Emmanuel*

O COME, O come, Emmänuel,
    And ransom captive Ïsrael,
That mourns in lonely ëxile here
Until the Son of Göd appear.
    Rejoice! rejoice! Emmänuel
    Shall come to thee, O Ïsrael.

2 O come, O come, thou Lörd of
    might,
Who to thy tribes, on Šinai's
    height,
In ancient times didst give the
    law
In cloud and majesty and awe.

3 O come, thou Rod of Jësse, free
Thine own from Satan's
    tÿranny;
From depths of hell thy pëople
    save,
And give them victory o'er the
    grave.

4 O come, thou Dayspring, cöme
    and cheer
Our spirits by thine ädvent
    here;
Disperse the gloomy cloüds of
    night,
And death's dark shadows püt
    to flight.

5 O come, thou Key of David,
come,
And open wide our heavenly
home;

Make safe the way that leads on
high,
And close the path to misery:

18th century, based on the ancient
Advent Antiphons
Tr. JOHN MASON NEALE, 1818–66

CHRIST'S INCARNATION

166 PSALM 2, verses 1–3, 6–8,
10, 11, 12b

WHY do the heathen ' rage :
and the people i ' ma-gine
a vain thing?

The kings of the earth set
themselves and the rulers
take counsel to ' gether :
against the Lord and against
his a ' nointed saying,

Let us break their bonds a ' sunder :
and cast a ' way their cords
from us.

Yet have I set my ' king : upon
my holy ' hill of Zion.

I will declare the decree the
Lord hath said unto ' me :
thou art my son this day
have ' I begotten thee.

Ask of me and I shall give thee
the heathen for thine in- '
heritance : and the uttermost
parts of the earth for ' thy
possession.

Be wise now therefore O ye '
kings : be instructed ye '
judges of the earth.

Serve the Lord with ' fear : and
re ' joice with trembling.

Blessèd are ' all they : that ' put
their trust in him.

*Glory be to the Father and to the '
Son : and ' to the Holy Ghost.*

*As it was in the beginning is
now and ever ' shall be : world
with ' out end Amen.*

167 PSALM 72, verses 8, 10, 11,
17–19

HIS large and great dominion
shall
From sea to sea extend:
It from the river shall reach
forth
Unto earth's utmost end.

2 The kings of Tarshish, and the
isles,
To him shall presents bring;
And unto him shall offer gifts
Sheba's and Seba's king.

3 Yea, all the mighty kings on
earth
Before him down shall fall;
And all the nations of the world
Do service to him shall.

4 His Name for ever shall endure;
Last like the sun it shall:
Men shall be blest in him, and
blest
All nations shall him call.

5 Now blessèd be the Lord our
God,
The God of Israel,
For he alone doth wondrous
works,
In glory that excel.

6 And blessèd be his glorious
Name
To all eternity:
The whole earth let his glory
fill.
Amen, so let it be.

168 PARAPHRASE 19

THE race that long in darkness pined
Have seen a glorious light;

The people dwell in day, who
    dwelt
  In death's surrounding night.

2 To us a Child of hope is born;
    To us a Son is given;
  Him shall the tribes of earth
    obey,
  Him all the hosts of heaven.

3 His name shall be the Prince of
    Peace,
    For evermore adored,
  The Wonderful, the Counsellor,
    The great and mighty Lord.

4 His power increasing still shall
    spread,
    His reign no end shall know;
  Justice shall guard his throne
    above,
    And peace abound below.

Scottish Paraphrases, 1781
From Isaiah 9: 2, 6, 7

169

HARK! the herald angels
    sing,
'Glory to the new-born King,
Peace on earth, and mercy
    mild,
God and sinners reconciled!'
Joyful, all ye nations, rise,
Join the triumph of the skies,
With the angelic host proclaim,
'Christ is born in Bethlehem'.
  Hark! the herald angels sing,
    'Glory to the new-born King'.

2 Christ, by highest heaven
    adored,
Christ, the everlasting Lord,
Late in time behold him come,
Offspring of a virgin's womb.
Veiled in flesh the Godhead see;
Hail, the Incarnate Deity,
Pleased as Man with man to
    dwell,
Jesus, our Immanuel!

3 Hail, the heaven-born Prince of
    Peace!
Hail, the Sun of Righteousness!
Light and life to all he brings,
Risen with healing in his wings.

Mild he lays his glory by,
Born that man no more may die,
Born to raise the sons of earth,
Born to give them second birth:
    CHARLES WESLEY, 1707–88
    and others

170

IT came upon the midnight
    clear,
That glorious song of old,
From angels bending near the
    earth
  To touch their harps of
    gold:—
'Peace on the earth, good will to
    men,
  From heaven's all-gracious
    King!'
The world in solemn stillness lay
  To hear the angels sing.

2 Still through the cloven skies
    they come
  With peaceful wings un-
    furled;
And still their heavenly music
    floats
  O'er all the weary world;
Above its sad and lowly plains
  They bend on hovering wing,
And ever o'er its Babel sounds
  The blessèd angels sing.

3 But with the woes of sin and
    strife
  The world has suffered long;
Beneath the angel strain have
    rolled
  Two thousand years of
    wrong;
And man, at war with man,
    hears not
  The love song which they
    bring;
O hush the noise, ye men of
    strife,
  And hear the angels sing.

4 For, lo! the days are hastening
    on,
  By prophet bards foretold,
When with the ever-circling
    years
  Comes round the Age of Gold,

When peace shall over all the
    earth
  Its ancient splendours fling,
And the whole world give back
    the song
  Which now the angels sing.
                    EDMUND HAMILTON SEARS
                              1810–76

171 *Fröhlich soll mein Herze springen*

ALL my heart this night re-
    joices,
  As I hear, far and near,
    Sweetest angel voices,
'Christ is born!' their choirs are
    singing,
  Till the air, everywhere,
    Now with joy is ringing.

2 Hark! a voice from yonder
    manger,
  Soft and sweet, doth entreat:
    'Flee from woe and danger;
Brethren, come: from all doth
    grieve you
  You are freed; all you need
    I will surely give you'.

3 Come, then, let us hasten
    yonder;
  Here let all, great and small,
    Kneel in awe and wonder.
Love him who with love is
    yearning;
  Hail the Star that, from far,
    Bright with hope is burn-
    ing.
                    PAUL GERHARDT, 1607–76
                    Tr. CATHERINE WINKWORTH
                              1827–78

172

O LITTLE town of Bethle-
    hem,
  How still we see thee lie!
Above thy deep and dreamless
    sleep
  The silent stars go by:
Yet in thy dark streets shineth
  The everlasting Light;

The hopes and fears of all the
    years
  Are met in thee tonight.

2 O morning stars, together
    Proclaim the holy birth,
And praises sing to God the
    King,
    And peace to men on earth.
For Christ is born of Mary;
  And, gathered all above,
While mortals sleep, the angels
    keep
    Their watch of wondering
    love.

3 How silently, how silently,
    The wondrous gift is given!
So God imparts to human
    hearts
    The blessings of his heaven.
No ear may hear his coming;
  But in this world of sin,
Where meek souls will receive
    him, still
    The dear Christ enters in.

4 O Holy Child of Bethlehem,
    Descend to us, we pray;
Cast out our sin, and enter in;
    Be born in us today.
We hear the Christmas angels
    The great glad tidings tell;
O come to us, abide with us,
    Our Lord Immanuel.
                    PHILLIPS BROOKS, 1835–93

173

THE first Nowell the angel
    did say
Was to certain poor shepherds
    in fields as they lay:
In fields where they lay a-keep-
    ing their sheep
On a cold winter's night that
    was so deep.
  Nowell, Nowell, Nowell,
    Nowell,
  Born is the King of Israel.

60

They lookèd up and saw a star,
Shining in the east, beyond
  them far;
And to the earth it gave great
  light,
And so it continued both day
  and night.

And by the light of that same
  star,
Three wise men came from
  country far;
To seek for a King was their
  intent,
And to follow the star wherever
  it went.

This star drew nigh to the
  north-west,
O'er Bethlehem it took its rest,
And there it did both stop and
  stay
Right over the place where
  Jesus lay.

Then entered in those wise men
  three,
Full reverently upon their knee,
And offered there in his pre-
  sènce
Their gold and myrrh and
  frankincense.

Then let us all with one accord
Sing praises to our Heavenly
  Lord,
That hath made heaven and
  earth of naught,
And with his blood mankind
  hath bought.

Traditional Carol

74   PARAPHRASE 37

WHILE humble shepherds
  watched their flocks
  In Bethlehem's plains by
    night,
An angel sent from heaven ap-
  peared,
  And filled the plains with
    light.

'Fear not', he said, for sudden
  dread
  Had seized their troubled
    mind;
'Glad tidings of great joy I bring
  To you and all mankind.

3 'To you in David's town, this
    day,
  Is born, of David's line,
The Saviour, who is Christ the
  Lord;
  And this shall be the sign:

4 'The heavenly Babe you there
    shall find
  To human view displayed,
All meanly wrapped in swath-
  ing-bands,
  And in a manger laid.'

5 Thus spake the seraph; and
    forthwith
  Appeared a shining throng
Of angels praising God, and
    thus
  Addressed their joyful song:

6 'All glory be to God on high,
  And to the earth be peace;
Good will is shown by heaven
    to men
  And never more shall cease.'
Scottish Paraphrases, 1781
Based on St. Luke 2:8–14

175   *Quem pastores laudavere*

ANGEL voices, richly blending,
Shepherds to the manger sending,
Sing of peace from heav'n
  descending!
Shepherds, greet your Shep-
  herd-King!

2 Lo! a star is brightly glowing!
Eastern kings their gifts are
  showing
To the King whose gifts pass
  knowing!
Gentiles, greet the Gentiles'
  King!

3 To the manger come adoring,
Hearts in thankfulness out-
  pouring
To the child, true peace re-
  storing,
Mary's Son, our God and King!
German, 14th century
Tr. JAMES QUINN

61

176 *Stille Nacht, heilige Nacht*

STILL the night, holy the
night!
Sleeps the world; hid from sight,
Mary and Joseph in stable bare
Watch o'er the Child beloved
and fair,
Sleeping in heavenly rest,
Sleeping in heavenly rest.

2 Still the night, holy the night!
Shepherds first saw the light,
Heard resounding clear and
long,
Far and near, the angel-song,
'Christ the Redeemer is
here!
Christ the Redeemer is
here!'

3 Still the night, holy the night!
Son of God, O how bright
Love is smiling from thy face!
Strikes for us now the hour of
grace,
Saviour, since thou art
born!
Saviour, since thou art
born!

JOSEPH MOHR, 1792–1848
Tr. STOPFORD BROOKE, 1832–1916
and the Compilers of *The Church
Hymnary*, 1927 Edition

177

GLOOMY night embraced the
place
Where the noble Infant lay;
The Babe looked up and showed
his face,
In spite of darkness it was
day!
It was thy day, Sweet, and did
rise,
Not from the East, but from
thine eyes.

2 We saw thee in thy balmy nest,
Bright dawn of our eternal
day!
We saw thine eyes break from
their east
And chase the trembling
shades away;

We saw thee, and we blesse[d]
the sight,
We saw thee by thine own swe[et]
light.

3 Welcome, all wonder in on[e]
sight,
Eternity shut in a span,
Summer in winter, day [in]
night,
Heaven in earth, and God [in]
man!
Great Little One! whose al[l-]
embracing birth
Lifts earth to heaven, stoo[ps]
heaven to earth.

RICHARD CRASHAW, c. 1613–[]
From *Hymn in the Holy Nativi[ty]*
16[]

178

IN the bleak mid-winter
Frosty wind made moan,
Earth stood hard as iron,
Water like a stone;
Snow had fallen, snow on sno[w]
Snow on snow,
In the bleak mid-winter,
Long ago.

2 Our God, heaven cannot hol[d]
him,
Nor earth sustain:
Heaven and earth shall fl[ee]
away
When he comes to reign:
In the bleak mid-winter
A stable-place sufficed
The Lord God Almighty,
Jesus Christ.

3 Angels and archangels
May have gathered there,
Cherubim and seraphim
Thronged the air;
But only his mother,
In her maiden bliss,
Worshipped the Belovèd
With a kiss.

4 What can I give him,
Poor as I am?
If I were a shepherd,
I would bring a lamb;

If I were a wise man,
  I would do my part;
Yet what I can I give him—
  Give my heart.
CHRISTINA ROSSETTI, 1830–94

79

SEE! in yonder manger low,
  Born for us on earth below,
See! the tender Lamb appears
Promised from eternal years.
  Hail, thou ever-blessèd morn!
  Hail,   redemption's   happy
    dawn!
  Sing through all Jerusalem,
  'Christ is born in Bethlehem!'

Lo! within a manger lies
He who built the starry skies,
He who, throned in height sub-
    lime,
Sits amid the cherubim.

Sacred Infant, all Divine,
What a tender love was thine,
Thus to come from highest bliss
Down to such a world as this!
EDWARD CASWALL, 1814–78

80   *Leanabh an aigh*

CHILD in the manger,
  Infant of Mary;
Outcast and stranger,
  Lord of all!
Child who inherits
  All our transgressions,
All our demerits
  On him fall.

Once the most holy
  Child of salvation
Gently and lowly
  Lived below;
Now, as our glorious
  Mighty Redeemer,
See him victorious
  O'er each foe.

Prophets foretold him,
  Infant of wonder;
Angels behold him
  On his throne;

Worthy our Saviour
  Of all their praises;
Happy for ever
  Are his own.
MARY MACDONALD, 1817–c. 1890
TR. LACHLAN MACBEAN, 1853–1931

181

*ON Christmas night all Chris-
  tians sing,
To hear the news the angels
  bring—
News of great joy, news of great
  mirth,
News of our merciful King's
  birth.

2 Then why should men on earth
    be so sad,
  Since our Redeemer made us
    glad,
  When from our sin he set us
    free,
  All for to gain our liberty?

3 When sin departs before his
    grace,
  Then life and health come in its
    place;
  Angels and men with joy may
    sing,
  All for to see the new-born
    King.

4 All out of darkness we have
    light,
  Which made the angels sing
    this night;
  'Glory to God and peace to
    men,
  Now and for evermore. Amen.'
Traditional carol

* *The first two lines of each verse are*
repeated.

182

ANGELS from the realms of
  glory,
Wing your flight o'er all the
  earth;
Ye who sang creation's story,
  Now   proclaim   Messiah's
    birth;

Come and worship
  Christ, the new-born King.
Come and worship,
  Worship Christ, the new-born
    King.

2 Shepherds, in the fields abiding,
    Watching o'er your flock by
      night,
  God with man is now residing,
    Yonder shines the infant
      Light;

3 Wise men, leave your contem-
      plations;
    Brighter visions beam afar;
  Seek the great Desire of
      nations;
    Ye have seen his natal star;

4 *All creation, join in praising*
    God the Father, Spirit, Son,
  Evermore your voices raising
    To the eternal Three in One:
        JAMES MONTGOMERY, 1771–1854

183

GOOD Christian men, rejoice
  With heart and soul and
    voice;
Give ye heed to what we say,
Jesus Christ is born today:
Ox and ass before him bow,
And he is in the manger now.
  Christ is born today!
  Christ is born today!

2 Good Christian men, rejoice
  With heart and soul and voice;
    Now ye hear of endless bliss,
  Jesus Christ was born for this:
  He hath oped the heavenly
      door,
  And man is blessèd evermore.
    Christ was born for this!
    Christ was born for this!

3 Good Christian men, rejoice
  With heart and soul and voice;
    Now ye need not fear the
        grave,
  Jesus Christ was born to save,
  Calls you one, and calls you all,
  To gain his everlasting hall.
    Christ was born to save!
    Christ was born to save!
        JOHN MASON NEALE, 1818–66

184

GOD rest you merry, gentle
    men,
Let nothing you dismay,
For Jesus Christ our Saviour
Was born upon this day,
To save us all from Satan[']s
    power
When we were gone astray:
  O tidings of comfort and jo[y]
    comfort and joy!
  O tidings of comfort and joy!

2 From God our Heav'nly Fath[er]
  A blessèd angel came,
  And unto certain shepherds
  Brought tidings of the same,
  How that in Bethlehem wa[s]
      born
  The Son of God by name:

3 The shepherds at those tiding[s]
  Rejoicèd much in mind,
  And left their flocks a-feeding
  In tempest, storm and wind,
  And went to Bethlehe[m]
      straightway
  This blessèd Babe to find:

4 But when to Bethlehem the[y]
      came,
  Whereat this Infant lay,
  They found him in a manger,
  Where oxen feed on hay;
  His mother Mary kneeling
  Unto the Lord did pray:

5 Now to the Lord sing praises[,]
  All you within this place,
  And with true love and brothe[r]
      hood
  Each other now embrace;
  This holy tide of Christmas
  All others doth deface:
        Traditional ca[rol]

85   *O Deued Pob Cristion*

ALL poor men and humble,
  All lame men who stumble[,]
Come haste ye nor feel ye afrai[d]
For Jesus, our treasure,
With love pást all measure,
In lowly poor manger was lai[d]

*2 Though wise men who found him
Laid rich gifts around him,
Yet oxen they gave him their hay:
And Jesus in beauty
Accepted their duty;
Contented in manger he lay.

3 Then haste we to show him
The praises we owe him;
Our service he ne'er can despise:
Whose love still is able
To show us that stable
Where softly in manger he lies.

KATHARINE EMILY ROBERTS, 1877–
1962 based on a Welsh carol

* Verses 2 and 3 are sung to the second half of the tune.

186   W Żłobie Leży

INFANT holy,
Infant lowly,
For his bed a cattle stall;
Oxen lowing,
Little knowing
Christ the babe is Lord of all.
Swift are winging
Angels singing,
Nowells ringing,
Tidings bringing,
Christ the babe is Lord of all,
Christ the babe is Lord of all.

2 Flocks were sleeping,
Shepherds keeping
Vigil till the morning new
Saw the glory,
Heard the story,
Tidings of a gospel true.
Thus rejoicing,
Free from sorrow,
Praises voicing,
Greet the morrow,
Christ the babe was born for you!
Christ the babe was born for you!

Polish carol
Tr. EDITH M. G. REED, 1885–1933

187   Puer nobis nascitur

UNTO us is born a Son.
King of Quires supernal:
See on earth his life begun,
Of lords the Lord eternal,
Of lords the Lord eternal.

2 Christ, from heav'n descending low,
Comes on earth a stranger:
Ox and ass their Owner know
Becradled in the manger,
Becradled in the manger.

3 This did Herod sore affray,
And grievously bewilder;
So he gave the word to slay,
And slew the little childer,
And slew the little childer.

4 Of his love and mercy mild
This the Christmas story:
And O that Mary's gentle Child
Might lead us up to glory,
Might lead us up to glory!

5 O and A and A and O,
Cum cantibus in choro,
Let our merry organ go,
Benedicamus Domino,
Benedicamus Domino.

Piae Cantiones, 1582
Tr. GEORGE RATCLIFFE WOODWARD
1848–1934

188   Vom Himmel hoch da komm ich her

GIVE heed, my heart, lift up thine eyes:
Who is it in yon manger lies?
Who is this child so young and fair?
The blessèd Christ-child lieth there.

2 Welcome to earth, thou noble Guest,
Through whom even wicked men are blest!
Thou com'st to share our misery;
What can we render, Lord, to thee?

3 Were earth a thousand times as
    fair,
Beset with gold and jewels rare,
She yet were far too poor to be
A narrow cradle, Lord, for
    thee.

4 Ah! dearest Jesus, Holy Child,
Make thee a bed, soft, un-
    defiled,
Within my heart, that it may
    be
A quiet chamber kept for thee.

5 My heart for very joy doth leap;
My lips no more can silence
    keep;
I too must raise with joyful
    tongue
That sweetest ancient cradle
    song.

6 'Glory to God in highest
    heaven,
Who unto man his Son hath
    given!'
While angels sing with pious
    mirth
A glad New Year to all the
    earth.

MARTIN LUTHER, 1483–1546
Tr. CATHERINE WINKWORTH
1827–78

189

A solis ortus cardine

FROM east to west, from
    shore to shore,
Let every heart awake and
    sing
The holy Child whom Mary bore,
The Christ, the everlasting
    King.

2 Behold, the world's Creator
    wears
The form and fashion of a
    slave;
Our very flesh our Maker shares,
His fallen creature, man, to
    save.

3 For this how wondrously he
    wrought!
A maiden, in her lowly place,
Became, in ways beyond all
    thought,
The chosen vessel of his
    grace.

4 He shrank not from the oxen's
    stall,
He lay within the manger
    bed,
And he, whose bounty feedeth
    all,
At Mary's breast himself was
    fed.

5 And while the angels in the sky
Sang praise above the silent
    field,
To shepherds poor the Lord
    most high,
The one great Shepherd, was
    revealed.

6 *All glory for this blessèd morn*
    To God the Father ever be;
All praise to thee, O Virgin-born,
    All praise, O Holy Ghost, to
    thee. Amen.

CAELIUS SEDULIUS, d. c. 450
Tr. JOHN ELLERTON, 1826–93

190

CHRISTIANS, awake, salute
    the happy morn,
Whereon the Saviour of the
    world was born;
Rise to adore the mystery of
    love,
Which hosts of angels chanted
    from above;
With them the joyful tidings
    first begun
Of God Incarnate and the Vir-
    gin's Son:

2 Then to the watchful shepherds
    it was told,
Who heard the angelic herald's
    voice, 'Behold,
I bring good tidings of a
    Saviour's birth
To you and all the nations upon
    earth;
This day hath God fulfilled his
    promised word,
This day is born a Saviour,
    Christ the Lord.'

To Bethl'em straight the en-
lightened shepherds ran
To see the wonder God had
wrought for man,
And found, with Joseph and the
blessèd Maid,
Her Son, the Saviour, in a
manger laid;
Joyful, the wondrous story they
proclaim,
The first apostles of his infant
fame.

O may we keep and ponder in
our mind
God's wondrous love in saving
lost mankind;
Trace we the Babe, who hath
retrieved our loss,
From his poor manger to his
bitter cross;
Saved by his love, incessant we
shall sing
Eternal praise to heaven's
almighty King.

JOHN BYROM, 1691–1763
and the Compilers of *The BBC
Hymn Book*, 1951

191

Adeste fideles

O COME, all ye faithful,
Joyful and triumphant,
O come ye, O come ye to
Bethlehem;
Come and behold him
Born the King of angels;
*O come, let us adore him,
O come, let us adore him,
O come, let us adore him, Christ
the Lord.*

God of God,
Light of Light,
Lo! he abhors not the Virgin's
womb;
Very God,
Begotten, not created;

Sing, choirs of angels,
Sing in exultation,
Sing, all ye citizens of heaven
above,
'Glory to God
In the highest':

For Christmas Day

4 Yea, Lord, we greet thee,
Born this happy morning;
Jesus, to thee be glory given;
Word of the Father,
Now in flesh appearing;

Possibly by JOHN WADE, c. 1711–86
Tr. FREDERICK OAKELEY, 1802–80
and others

192 *Μέγα καὶ παράδοξον θαῦμα*

A GREAT and mighty wonder
A full and holy cure!
The Virgin bears the Infant
With virgin-honour pure.
*Repeat the hymn again!
'To God on high be glory,
And peace on earth to men!'*

2 The Word becomes incarnate
And yet remains on high!
And Cherubim sing anthems
To shepherds, from the sky:

3 While thus they sing your
Monarch,
Those bright angelic bands,
Rejoice, ye vales and moun-
tains,
Ye oceans, clap your hands:

4 Since all he comes to ransom,
By all be he adored,
The Infant born in Bethl'em,
The Saviour and the Lord:

5 And idol forms shall perish,
And error shall decay,
And Christ shall wield his
sceptre,
Our Lord and God for aye:

ST. GERMANUS, c. 634–c. 734
Tr. JOHN MASON NEALE
1818–66, and others

193

O NCE in royal David's city
Stood a lowly cattle-shed,
Where a mother laid her Baby
In a manger for his bed.
Mary was that mother mild,
Jesus Christ her little Child.

2 He came down to earth from
    heaven
  Who is God and Lord of all,
And his shelter was a stable,
  And his cradle was a stall.
With the poor and mean and
    lowly
Lived on earth our Saviour
  holy.

3 And through all his wondrous
    childhood
  He would honour and obey,
Love, and watch the lowly
    maiden
  In whose gentle arms he lay.
Christian children all must be
Mild, obedient, good as he.

4 For he is our childhood's pat-
    tern:
  Day by day like us he grew;
He was little, weak, and help-
    less;
  Tears and smiles like us he
    knew;
And he feeleth for our sadness,
And he shareth in our gladness.

5 And our eyes at last shall see
    him,
  Through his own redeeming
    love;
For that Child so dear and
    gentle
  Is our Lord in heaven above;
And he leads his children on
To the place where he is gone.

6 Not in that poor lowly stable,
  With the oxen standing by,
We shall see him, but in heaven,
  Set at God's right hand on
    high,
When, like stars, his children
    crowned
All in white shall wait around.
      CECIL FRANCES ALEXANDER
      1818–95

194

LOVE came down at Christ-
    mas,
  Love all lovely, Love Divine;
Love was born at Christmas,
  Star and angels gave the
    sign.

2 Worship we the Godhead,
    Love Incarnate, Love Divine;
Worship we our Jesus:
  But wherewith for sacre
    sign?

3 Love shall be our token,
    Love be yours and love b
    mine,
Love to God and all men,
  Love for plea and gift an
    sign.
      CHRISTINA ROSSETTI, 1830–9

195   *For younger children*

AWAY in a manger, no crib fo
    a bed,
The little Lord Jesus laid dow
  his sweet head.
The stars in the bright sk
  looked down where he lay,
The little Lord Jesus asleep o
  the hay.

2 The cattle are lowing, the Bab
    awakes,
But little Lord Jesus no cryin
  he makes.
I love thee, Lord Jesus! loo
  down from the sky,
And stay by my side unti
  morning is nigh.

3 Be near me, Lord Jesus; I as
    thee to stay
Close by me for ever, and lov
  me, I pray.
Bless all the dear children i
  thy tender care,
And fit us for heaven, to liv
  with thee there.
      Anonymou

196   *Holy Innocents' Day*

WHEN Christ was born i
    Bethlehem,
Fair peace on earth to bring
In lowly state of love he came
  To be the children's King.

2 And round him, then, a holy
    band
Of children blest was born,
Fair guardians of his throne to
    stand
    Attendant night and morn.

3 And unto them this grace was
    given
    A Saviour's Name to own,
And die for him who out of
    heaven
    Had found on earth a throne.

4 O blessèd babes of Bethlehem,
    Who died to save our King,
Ye share the martyrs' diadem,
    And in their anthem sing!
        LAURENCE HOUSMAN, 1865–1959

197

BEHOLD the great Creator
    makes
Himself a house of clay,
A robe of human flesh he takes
Which he will wear for aye.

2 Hark, hark, the wise eternal
    Word,
Like a weak infant cries!
In form of servant is the Lord,
And God in cradle lies.

3 Glad shepherds came to view
    this sight;
    A choir of angels sings,
And eastern sages with delight
Adore this King of kings.

4 Join then, all hearts that are
    not stone,
And all our voices prove,
To celebrate this holy One
    The God of peace and love.
        THOMAS PESTEL, 1584–1659
                altered

198
Corde natus ex Parentis

OF the Father's love begötten
    Ere the worlds begän to
    be,
He is Alpha and Omëga,
    He the source, the ënding he,

Of the things that are, that havë
    been,
    And that future years shall
    see,
        Evermore and evermöre.

2 O that birth for ever blëssèd,
    When the Virgin, füll of grace,
By the Holy Ghost concëiving,
    Bare the Saviour öf our race,
And the Babe, the world's
    Redeëmer,
    First revealed his sacred face,

3 This is he whom seers in öld
    time
    Chanted of with öne accord,
Whom the voices of the prö-
    phets
    Promised in their faïthful
    word;
Now he shines, the Long-
    expected;
    Let creation praise its Lord,

4 O ye heights of heaven, adöre
    him;
    Angel hosts, his praïses sing;
All dominions, bow befóre him,
    And extol our Göd and King;
Let no tongue on earth be
    silent,
    Every voice in concert ring,

5 *Christ, to thee, with God the*
    Fäther,
    And, O Holy Ghöst, to thee,
Hymn, and chant, and high
    thanksgïving,
    And unwearied praïses be,
Honour, glory, and domïnion,
    And eternal victory,
Evermore and evermöre. Amen.

        PRUDENTIUS, 348–c. 413
        Tr. JOHN MASON NEALE
              1818–66
    and HENRY WILLIAMS BAKER
              1821–77

199 *O sola magnarum urbium*

BETHLEHEM, of noblest
cities
None can once with thee compare;
Thou alone the Lord from
heaven
Didst for us incarnate bear.

2 Fairer than the sun at morning
Was the star that told his
birth;
To the world its God announc-
ing,
Seen in fleshly form on earth.

3 Eastern sages at his cradle
Make oblations rich and rare;
See them give, in deep devo-
tion,
Gold and frankincense and
myrrh.

4 Sacred gifts of mystic meaning:
Incense doth their God dis-
close,
Gold the King of kings pro-
claimeth,
Myrrh his sepulchre fore-
shows.

5 *Holy Jesu, in thy brightness*
To the Gentile world displayed,
With the Father and the Spirit
Endless praise to thee be paid.
Amen.

PRUDENTIUS, 348–c. 413
Tr. EDWARD CASWALL, 1814–78

200

AS with gladness men of old
Did the guiding star be-
hold,
As with joy they hailed its light,
Leading onward, beaming
bright,—
So, most gracious Lord, may we
Evermore be led to thee.

2 As with joyful steps they sped,
Saviour, to thy lowly bed,
There to bend the knee before
Thee, whom heaven and earth
adore,—
So may we with willing feet
Ever seek thy mercy-seat.

3 As they offered gifts most rare
At thy cradle rude and bare,—
So may we with holy joy,
Pure, and free from sin's alloy,
All our costliest treasures bring,
Christ, to thee, our heavenly
King.

4 Holy Jesus, every day
Keep us in the narrow way;
And, when earthly things are
past,
Bring our ransomed souls at
last
Where they need no star to
guide,
Where no clouds thy glory
hide.

5 In the heavenly country bright
Need they no created light;
Thou its light, its joy, its crown,
Thou its sun which goes not
down;
There for ever may we sing
Alleluias to our King.

WILLIAM CHATTERTON DIX
1837–98

201

BRIGHTEST and best of the
sons of the morning,
Dawn on our darkness, and
lend us thine aid;
Star of the east, the horizon
adorning,
Guide where our infant Redeemer is laid.

2 Cold on his cradle the dew-drops
are shining;
Low lies his head with the
beasts of the stall;
Angels adore him in slumber
reclining,
Maker and Monarch and
Saviour of all.

3 Say, shall we yield him, in
costly devotion,
Odours of Edom, and offerings divine,
Gems of the mountains and
pearls of the ocean,
Myrrh from the forest or gold
from the mine?

4 Vainly we offer each ample
    oblation,
Vainly with gifts would his
    favour secure;
Richer by far is the heart's
    adoration;
Dearer to God are the prayers
    of the poor.

5 Brightest and best of the sons of
    the morning,
Dawn on our darkness, and
    lend us thine aid;
Star of the east, the horizon
    adorning,
Guide where our infant Re-
    deemer is laid.

REGINALD HEBER, 1783–1826

202   *Wie schön leuchtet der
            Morgenstern*

HOW brightly beams the
    morning star!
What sudden radiance from afar
Doth glad us with its shin-
    ing?
Brightness of God, that breaks
    our night
And fills the darkened souls
    with light
Who long for truth were
    pining!
Thy word, Jesus, inly feeds us,
    Rightly leads us,
    Life bestowing:
Praise, oh praise such love
    o'erflowing!

2 O praise to him who came to
    save,
Who conquer'd death and burst
    the grave;
    Each day new praise re-
        soundeth
To him the Lamb who once
    was slain,
The friend whom none shall
    trust in vain,
    Whose grace for aye aboun-
        deth;
Sing, ye heavens, tell the story,
    Of his glory,
    Till his praises
Flood with light earth's darkest
    places!

PHILIPP NICOLAI, 1556–1608
and JOHANN SCHLEGEL, 1721–93
Tr. CATHERINE WINKWORTH, 1827–78

203

KING of kings and Lord of
    lords, and Maker of all is
    he;
Leaving the glory of heav'n he
    comes, incarnate now to
    be,
    Incarnate now to be.

2 Lord of the world, he comes
    among us, bearing love
    and grace;
Born of the womb of Virgin
    Mary, there in David's
    place,
    There in David's place.

3 Angels clothed in robes of
    whiteness, far above the
    earth,
Filling the heav'ns with praise
    and wonder, sing of
    Jesus' birth,
    Sing of Jesus' birth.

4 Joyful, joyful, all you people,
    give the Saviour praise!
Welcome the new-born King
    with gladness, shouts of
    triumph raise!
    Shouts of triumph raise!

5 All for *your* sake, all for *my*
    sake; yes, for *all*, I say;
Now for the *world* comes news of
    salvation: 'Christ is born
    today!'
    'Christ is born today!'

6 Worship now, but do not leave
    him out in stable bare;
Give him your heart for home!
    Enthrone him, King of
    glory there!
    King of glory there!

KAHANGI MADHAVY, 1869–1916
adapted JAMES N. S. ALEXANDER

The following are also suitable

No.
40 Worship the Lord in the beauty of
    holiness
369 God and Father, we adore thee
399 Though in God's form he was
12 Lift up your heads, ye mighty gates
158 Give the king thy judgments O
    God

CHRIST'S LIFE AND MINISTRY

204 NUNC DIMITTIS

LORD now lettest thou thy
servant de- ' part in '
peace : ac- ' cording ' to thy '
word.

2 For mine eyes have ' seen thy
sal- ' vation : which thou
hast prepared before the '
face of ' all ' people.

3 To be a light to ' lighten
the ' Gentiles : and to be
the ' glory of thy ' people '
Isra-el.

*Glory ' be to the ' Father : and
to the Son ' and to the '
Holy ' Ghost :*

*As it ' was in the be- ' ginning :
is now and ever shall be '
world without ' end.*
A- ' men.
From St. Luke 2: 29–32

205

'JESUS!' Name of wondrous
love ;
Name all other names above,
Unto which must every knee
Bow in deep humility.

2 'Jesus!' Name of priceless worth
To the fallen sons of earth,
For the promise that it gave,—
'Jesus shall his people save'.

3 'Jesus!' Name of mercy mild,
Given to the Holy Child
When the cup of human woe
First he tasted here below.

4 'Jesus!' only Name that's given
Under all the mighty heaven
Whereby man, to sin enslaved,
Bursts his fetters, and is saved.

5 'Jesus!' Name of wondrous
love ;
Human Name of God above ;
Pleading only this, we flee,
Helpless, O our God, to thee.
WILLIAM WALSHAM HOW, 1823–97

206 *Candlemas*

WHEN Mary brought her
treasure
Unto the holy place,
No eye of man could measure
The joy upon her face.
He was but six weeks old,
Her plaything and her pleasure,
Her silver and her gold.

2 Then Simeon, on him gazing
With wonder and with love,
His agèd voice up-raising
Gave thanks to God above :
'Now welcome sweet re-
lease!
For I, my Saviour praising,
May die at last in peace'.

3 And she, all sorrow scorning,
Rejoiced in Jesus' fame.
The child her arms adorning
Shone softly like a flame
That burns the long night
through,
And keeps from dusk till morn-
ing
Its vigil clear and true.

4 As by the sun in splendour
The flags of night are furled,
So darkness shall surrender
To Christ who lights the
world :
To Christ the Star of day,
Who once was small and tender,
A candle's gentle ray.
JAN STRUTHER, 1901–53

207

BEHOLD a little Child,
Laid in a manger bed ;
The wintry blasts blow wild
around his infant head.
But who is this, so lowly laid ?
'Tis he by whom the worlds
were made.

Where Joseph plies his trade,
  Lo, Jesus labours too;
The hands that all things
    made an earthly craft
    pursue,
That weary men in him may
    rest,
And faithful toil through him
    be blest.

Among the doctors see
  The Boy so full of grace;
Say, wherefore taketh he the
    scholar's lowly place?
That Christian boys, with
    reverence meet,
May sit and learn at Jesus' feet.

Christ, once thyself a boy!
  Our boyhood guard and
    guide;
Be thou its light and joy, and
    still with us abide,
That thy dear love, so great and
    free,
May draw us evermore to thee.
                WILLIAM WALSHAM HOW
                          1823–97

o8   *Iordanis oras praevia*

ON Jordan's bank the Bap-
    tist's cry
Announces that the Lord is
    nigh;
Come then and hearken, for he
    brings
Glad tidings from the King of
    kings.

Then cleansed be every breast
    from sin;
Make straight the way for God
    within;
Prepare we in our hearts a
    home,
Where such a mighty Guest
    may come.

For thou art our salvation,
    Lord,
Our refuge, and our great
    reward;
Without thy grace we waste
    away,
Like flowers that wither and
    decay.

4 Stretch forth thine hand, to
    heal our sore,
And make us rise to fall no
    more;
Once more upon thy people
    shine,
And fill the world with love
    divine.

5 *All praise, eternal Son, to thee*
Whose advent sets thy people free,
Whom with the Father we adore,
And Holy Ghost, for evermore.
                              Amen.
                CHARLES COFFIN, 1676–1749
                Tr. JOHN CHANDLER, 1806–76
                          and others

209   *Hostis Herodes impie*

HOW vain the cruel Herod's
    fear,
When told that Christ the King
    is near!
He takes not earthly realms
    away,
Who gives the realms that ne'er
    decay.

2 The eastern sages saw from far
And followed on his guiding
    star;
By light their way to Light they
    trod,
And by their gifts confessed
    their God.

3 Within the Jordan's sacred
    flood
The heavenly Lamb in meek-
    ness stood,
That he, to whom no sin was
    known,
Might cleanse his people from
    their own.

4 And oh, what miracle divine,
When water reddened into wine!
He spake the word, and forth
    there flowed
A stream that nature ne'er be-
    stowed.

5 *All glory, Jesus, be to thee*
For this thy glad Epiphany:
Whom with the Father we adore,
And Holy Ghost, for evermore.
Amen.

CAELIUS SEDULIUS, d. c. 450
Tr. JOHN MASON NEALE, 1818–66
and Compilers of *Hymns Ancient and
Modern*, 1875 edn.

210

FORTY days and forty nights
Thou wast fasting in the
wild;
Forty days and forty nights
Tempted still, yet undefiled.

*2 Sunbeams scorching day by
day;
Chilly dewdrops nightly shed;
Prowling beasts about thy way;
Stones thy pillow; earth thy
bed.

3 Shall not we thy sorrows share,
Learn thy discipline of will,
And like thee, by fast and
prayer
Wrestle with the powers of
ill?

4 What if Satan, vexing sore,
Flesh and spirit shall assail,
Thou, his vanquisher before,
Will not suffer us to fail.

5 Watching, praying, struggling
thus,
Victory ours at last shall be;
Angels minister to us
As they ministered to thee.

GEORGE SMYTTAN, 1822–70
and FRANCIS POTT, 1832–1909
altered

* *This verse may be omitted if desired.*

211

JESUS calls us! O'er the
tumult
Of our life's wild restless sea,
Day by day his voice is sounding,
Saying, 'Christian, follow
me':

2 As, of old, Saint Andrew hear
it
By the Galilean lake,
Turned from home and toil an
kindred,
Leaving all for his dear sak

3 Jesus calls us from the worshi
Of the vain world's golde
store,
From each idol that would kee
us,
Saying, 'Christian, love m
more'.

4 In our joys and in our sorrow
Days of toil and hours o
ease,
Still he calls, in cares an
pleasures,
'Christian, love me more tha
these'.

5 Jesus calls us! By thy mercies
Saviour, make us hear th
call,
Give our hearts to th
obedience,
Serve and love thee best o
all.

CECIL FRANCES ALEXANDER
1818–95, altere

212

I HEARD the voice of Jesu
say,
'Come unto me and rest;
Lay down, thou weary one, la
down
Thy head upon my breast':
I came to Jesus as I was,
Weary, and worn, and sad;
I found in him a resting-place,
And he has made me glad.

2 I heard the voice of Jesus say,
'Behold, I freely give
The living water; thirsty on
Stoop down and drink, an
live':
I came to Jesus, and I drank
Of that life-giving stream;
My thirst was quenched, m
soul revived,
And now I live in him.

I heard the voice of Jesus say,
'I am this dark world's Light;
Look unto me, thy morn shall
rise,
And all thy day be bright':
I looked to Jesus, and I found
In him my Star, my Sun;
And in that light of life I'll
walk,
Till travelling days are done.

HORATIUS BONAR, 1808–89

13

IT fell upon a summer day,
When Jesus walked in
Galilee,
The mothers from a village
brought
Their children to his knee.

He took them in his arms, and
laid
His hands on each remembered
head;
'Suffer these little ones to come
To me', he gently said.

'Forbid them not; unless ye
bear
The childlike heart your hearts
within,
Unto my Kingdom ye may
come,
But may not enter in.'

Master, I fain would enter
there;
O let me follow thee, and share
Thy meek and lowly heart, and
be
Freed from all worldly care.

O happy thus to live and move!
And sweet this world, where I
shall find
God's beauty everywhere, his
love,
His good in all mankind.

Then, Father, grant this childlike heart,
That I may come to Christ, and
feel
His hands on me in blessing
laid,
Love-giving, strong to heal.

STOPFORD AUGUSTUS BROOKE
1832–1916

214

THINE arm, O Lord, in days
of old,
Was strong to heal and save;
It triumphed o'er disease and
death,
O'er darkness and the grave.
To thee they went—the blind,
the dumb,
The palsied, and the lame,
The leper with his tainted life,
The sick with fevered frame;

2 And, lo! thy touch brought life
and health,
Gave speech, and strength,
and sight;
And youth renewed and frenzy
calmed
Owned thee, the Lord of
light.
And now, O Lord, be near to
bless,
Almighty as of yore,
In crowded street, by restless
couch,
As by Gennesaret's shore.

3 Be thou our great Deliverer
still,
Thou Lord of life and death;
Restore and quicken, soothe
and bless,
With thine almighty breath;
To hands that work and eyes
that see
Give wisdom's heavenly lore,
That whole and sick, and weak
and strong,
May praise thee evermore.

EDWARD HAYES PLUMPTRE
1821–91

215

JESUS, whose all-redeeming
love
No penitent did scorn,
Who didst the stain of guilt
remove,
Till hope anew was born:

2 To thee, Physician of the soul,
The lost, the outcast, came:
Thou didst restore and make
them whole,
Disburdened of their shame.

3 'Twas love, thy love, their
  bondage brake,
  Whose fetters sin had bound:
For faith to love did answer
  make,
  And free forgiveness found.

4 Jesus, that pardoning grace to
  find,
  I too would come to thee:
O merciful to all mankind,
  Be merciful to me.

GEORGE WALLACE BRIGGS
1875–1959

216

WHAT grace, O Lord, and
  beauty shone
Around thy steps below!
What patient love was seen in
  all
Thy life and death of woe!

2 Thy foes might hate, despise,
  revile,
  Thy friends unfaithful prove:
Unwearied in forgiveness still,
  Thy heart could only love.

3 O give us hearts to love like
  thee,
  Like thee, O Lord, to grieve
Far more for others' sins than
  all
  The wrongs that we receive.

4 One with thyself, may every
  eye
  In us, thy brethren, see
That gentleness and grace that
  spring
  From union, Lord, with
  thee.

EDWARD DENNY, 1796–1889

217 *For the Transfiguration*
Caelestis formam gloriae

O WONDROUS type, O
  vision fair
Of glory that the Church shall
  share,
Which Christ upon the mountain shows,
Where brighter than the sun he
  lows!

2 With shining face and brigh
  array,
Christ deigns to manifest toda
What glory shall be their
  above,
Who joy in God with perfec
  love.

3 The law and prophets ther
  have place,
The chosen witnesses of Grace
The Father's voice from out th
  cloud
Proclaims his only Son aloud.

4 And Christian hearts are raise
  on high
By that great vision's mystery
For which, in thankful strain
  we raise
On this glad day the voice c
  praise.

5 O Father, with the eternal So
And Holy Spirit ever One,
Vouchsafe to bring us, by th
  grace,
To see thy glory face to face.

15th centur
Tr. JOHN MASON NEALE, 1818–6
and othe

218

THERE'S a wideness in God'
  mercy,
Like the wideness of the sea
There's a kindness in his justice
  Which is more than liberty.

2 There is no place where earth
  sorrows
  Are more felt than up i
  heaven:
There is no place where earth
  failings
  Have such kindly judgmen
  given.

3 For the love of God is broader
  Than the measures of man'
  mind;
And the heart of the Eterna
  Is most wonderfully kind.

4 There is plentiful redemption
  In the blood that has bee
  shed;
There is joy for all the member
  In the sorrows of the Head.

If our love were but more
    simple,
We would take him at his
    word;
And our lives be filled with
    glory
From the glory of the Lord.

FREDERICK WILLIAM FABER
1814–63, altered

219

SON of the Lord Most High,
    Who gave the worlds their
    birth,
He came to live and die
    The Son of Man on earth:
      In Bethlem's stable born
        was he,
      And humbly bred in
        Galilee.

2 Born in so low estate,
    Schooled in a workman's
    trade,
Not with the high and great
    His home the Highest made:
      But labouring by his
        brethren's side,
      Life's common lot he
        glorified.

3 Then, when his hour was come,
    He heard his Father's call:
And leaving friends and home,
    He gave himself for all:
      Glad news to bring, the
        lost to find;
      To heal the sick, the lame,
        the blind.

4 Toiling by night and day,
    Himself oft burdened sore,
Where hearts in bondage lay,
    Himself their burden bore:
      Till, scorned by them he
        died to save,
      Himself in death; as life, he
        gave.

5 O lowly Majesty,
    Lofty in lowliness!
Blest Saviour, who am I
    To share thy blessedness?
      Yet thou hast called me,
        even me,
      Servant Divine, to follow
        thee.

GEORGE WALLACE BRIGGS
1875–1959

220

O SING a song of Bethlehem,
    Of shepherds watching
    there,
And of the news that came to
    them
    From angels in the air:
The light that shone on Bethle-
    hem
    Fills all the world today;
Of Jesus' birth and peace on
    earth
    The angels sing alway.

2 O sing a song of Nazareth,
    Of sunny days of joy;
O sing of fragrant flowers'
    breath,
    And of the sinless Boy:
For now the flowers of Nazareth
    In every heart may grow;
Now spreads the fame of his
    dear Name
    On all the winds that blow.

3 O sing a song of Galilee,
    Of lake and woods and hill,
Of him who walked upon the
    sea,
    And bade its waves be still:
For though, like waves on
    Galilee,
    Dark seas of trouble roll,
When faith has heard the
    Master's word,
    Falls peace upon the soul.

4 O sing a song of Calvary,
    Its glory and dismay;
Of him who hung upon the
    tree,
    And took our sins away:
For he who died on Calvary
    Is risen from the grave,
And Christ, our Lord, by heaven
    adored,
    Is mighty now to save.

LOUIS FITZGERALD BENSON
1855–1930

221

WHO is he in yonder stall,
    At whose feet the shepherds
    fall?
'Tis the Lord, O wondrous story!
'Tis the Lord, the King of glory!

2 Who is he in deep distress,
Fasting in the wilderness?

3 Who is he the gathering throng
Greet with loud triumphant
song?

4 Lo, at midnight, who is he
Prays in dark Gethsemane?

5 Who is he on yonder tree
Dies in shame and agony?

6 Who is he that from the grave
Comes to heal and help and
save?

7 Who is he that from his throne
Rules through all the world
alone?

BENJAMIN RUSSELL HANBY
1833–67, altered

222

WISE men seeking Jesus
Travelled from afar,
Guided on their journey
By a beauteous star.

2 But if we desire him,
He is close at hand;
For our native country
Is our Holy Land.

3 Prayerful souls may find him
By our quiet lakes,
Meet him on our hillsides
When the morning breaks.

4 In our fertile cornfields
While the sheaves are bound,
In our busy markets,
Jesus may be found.

5 Fishermen talk with him
By the great north sea,
As the first disciples
Did in Galilee.

6 Every peaceful village
In our land might be
Made by Jesus' presence
Like sweet Bethany.

7 He is more than near us,
If we love him well;
For he seeketh ever
In our hearts to dwell.

JAMES THOMAS EAST
1860–1937

223 *O amor quam ecstaticus*

O LOVE, how deep, how
broad, how high!
How passing thought and fan
tasy
That God, the Son of God
should take
Our mortal form for mortals
sake.

2 He sent no angel to our race
Of higher or of lower place
But wore the robe of human
frame,
And he himself to this world
came.

3 For us baptized, for us he bore
His holy fast, and hungered
sore;
For us temptations sharp he
knew;
For us the tempter overthrew.

4 For us to wicked men betrayed,
Scourged, mocked, in crown of
thorns arrayed,
He bore the shameful cross and
death;
For us at length gave up his
breath.

5 For us he rose from death again,
For us he went on high to reign,
For us he sent his Spirit here,
To guide, to strengthen, and to
cheer.

6 *To him whose boundless love has
won*
Salvation for us through his Son,
To God the Father, glory be
Both now and through eternity.
Amen.

15th century
Tr. BENJAMIN WEBB, 1820–85
altered

224

MY song is love unknown,
My Saviour's love to me,
Love to the loveless shown, that
they might lovely be.
O who am I, that for my sake
My Lord should take frail flesh
and die?

He came from his blest throne,
    Salvation to bestow:
But men made strange, and
    none the longed-for Christ
    would know.
      But O, my Friend, my
        Friend indeed,
Who at my need his life did
    spend!

Sometimes they strew his way,
    And his sweet praises sing;
Resounding all the day hosannas
    to their King.
      Then 'Crucify!' is all their
        breath,
And for his death they thirst and
    cry.

Why, what hath my Lord
    done?
    What makes this rage and
      spite?
He made the lame to run, he
    gave the blind their sight.
      Sweet injuries! yet they at
      these
Themselves displease and 'gainst
    him rise.

They rise, and needs will have
    My dear Lord done away;
A murderer they save, the Prince
    of Life they slay.
      Yet cheerful he to suffering
      goes,
That he his foes from thence
    might free.

In life, no house, no home
    My Lord on earth might
    have;
In death, no friendly tomb but
    what a stranger gave.
What may I say? heav'n was
    his home:
      But mine the tomb wherein he
      lay.

Here might I stay and sing,
    No story so divine;
Never was love, dear King, never
    was grief like thine!
      This is my Friend, in whose
      sweet praise
I all my days could gladly
    spend.

SAMUEL CROSSMAN, c. 1624–83

225   PARAPHRASE 52, verses 1,
            3–6

YE who the Name of Jesus
    bear,
    His sacred steps pursue;
And let that mind which was in
    him
    Be also found in you.

2 His greatness he for us abased,
    For us his glory veiled;
In human likeness dwelt on
    earth,
    His majesty concealed:

3 Nor only as a man appears,
    But stoops a servant low;
Submits to death, nay, bears
    the cross,
    In all its shame and woe.

4 Hence God this generous love to
    men
    With honours just hath
    crowned,
And raised the Name of Jesus
    far
    Above all names renowned:

5 That at this Name, with sacred
    awe,
    Each humble knee should
    bow,
Of hosts immortal in the skies,
    And nations spread below.

Scottish Paraphrases, 1781
Phil. 2: 5, 7–10

226   *For children*

I CAN picture Jesus toiling,
    Carpenter of Nazareth
    town:
In his face a great love shining,
    Working till the sun goes
    down.
By his children still he stands,
Blessing labour of their hands.

2 I can picture Jesus stooping,
    Lifting up a heavy weight;
Stiff with toil, his arms out-
    stretching,
    Weary, when the hour is late.
Still he stoops from heaven
    above,
Drawing all men by his love.

3 Christ the Workman, make me
    holy,
  Christ the Saviour, make me
    true ;
Make of me a thing of beauty,
  Show me how to labour too ;
Fellow-worker would I be
Ever, blessèd Lord, with thee.
           D. HELEN STONE

227   *For children*

I LOVE to hear the story
  Which angel voices tell,
How once the King of Glory
    *Came down on earth to
    dwell.

2 I am both weak and sinful,
  But this I surely know,
The Lord came down to save me
  Because he loved me so.

3 I'm glad my blessèd Saviour
  Was once a child like me,
To show how pure and holy
  His little ones might be ;

4 And, if I try to follow
  His footsteps here below,
He never will forsake me,
  Because he loves me so.

5 To sing his love and mercy
  My sweetest songs I'll raise,
And, though I cannot see him,
  I know he hears my praise ;

6 For he has kindly promised
  That even I may go
To sing among his angels,
  Because he loves me so.
      EMILY HUNTINGTON MILLER
          1833–1913

  * *The last line of each verse is repeated.*

228   *For younger children*

JESUS' hands were kind
  hands, doing good to all,
Healing pain and sickness,
  blessing children small ;
Washing tired feet, and saving
  those who fall ;
Jesus' hands were kind hands,
  doing good to all.

2 Take my hands, Lord Jesus
  let them work for you,
Make them strong and gentle
  kind in all I do ;
Let me watch you, Jesus, till
  I'm gentle too,
Till my hands are kind hands
  quick to work for you.
        MARGARET CROPPER

229   *For younger children*

I LIKE to think of Jesus
  So loving, kind, and true
That when he walked among
  his friends
His friends were loving too.

2 I like to think of Jesus
  With children at his knee ;
And hear his gentle words
  again,
'Let children come to me'.

3 I like to think of Jesus
  So loving, kind, and true
That somehow when I think of
  him,
It makes me loving too.
    ELIZABETH MCEWEN SHIELDS

230   *For younger children*

WHEN Jesus saw the fisher
  men
In boats upon the sea,
He called to them 'Come, leave
  your nets
And follow, follow me'.
They followed where he healed
  the sick
And gave the hungry bread,
And others joined them as they
  went
Wherever Jesus led.

2 And now his friends are every
  where ;
The circle once so small
Extends around the whole
  wide world,
For Jesus calls us all.

In this great circle we belong,
Wherever we may be,
If we will answer when he calls,
'Come, follow, follow me'.

EDITH AGNEW

The following are also suitable
No.
52 At even, when the sun was set
76 Dear Lord and Father of mankind

CHRIST'S PASSION AND CROSS

231 PSALM 42, verses 1–5, 8–11

AS the hart panteth after the water
    brooks : so panteth my soul
after ' thee O God.

My soul thirsteth for God ' for
the living God : when shall
I come and appear ' before
God ?

My tears have been my ' meat
day and night : while they
continually say unto me
where ' is thy God ?

When I remember these things
I pour out ' my soul in me :
for I had gone with the
multitude I went with them
to the house of God with
the voice of joy and praise
with a multitude that kept '
holy day.

Why art thou cast down O
my soul ? and why art thou
dis ' quieted in me : hope
thou in God for I shall yet
praise him for the help of
his ' countenance.

Yet the Lord will command his
loving-kindness ' in the daytime : and in the night his
song shall be with me and
my prayer unto the God ' of
my life.

I will say unto God my rock
Why hast ' thou forgotten me :
why go I mourning because
of the oppression of the '
enemy ?

As with a sword in my bones
mine ene ' mies reproach me :
while they say daily unto me
where ' is thy God ?

Why art thou cast down O my
soul ? and why art thou
disquiet ' ed within me : hope
thou in God for I shall yet
praise him who is the
health of my countenance '
and my God.

232 PSALM 118, verses 19–29

OPEN to me the gates of righ-'
teousness : I will go into them
and I ' will praise the Lord.

This gate of ' the Lord : into which
the righ ' teous shall enter.

I will ' praise thee : for thou hast
heard me and art become ' my
salvation.

The stone which the builders '
refused : is become the head
stone ' of the corner.

This is the Lord's ' doing : it is
marvel ' lous in our eyes.

This is the day which the
Lord ' hath made : we will
rejoice and ' be glad in it.

Save now I beseech thee ' O
Lord : O Lord I beseech thee
send now ' prosperity.

Blessèd be he that cometh in
the Name of ' the Lord : we
have blessed you out of the '
house of the Lord.

God is the Lord which hath
showed ' us light : bind the
sacrifice with cords even unto
the horns ' of the altar.

Thou art my God and I will '
praise thee : thou art my God
I ' will exalt thee.

O give thanks unto the Lord
for he ' is good : for his mercy
endur ' eth for ever.

*Glory be to the Father and to '
the Son : and to ' the Holy
Ghost.
As it was in the beginning is
now and ever ' shall be : world
with ' out end Amen.*

233 *Gloria, laus et honor*

*ALL glory, laud, and honour
To thee, Redeemer King,
To whom the lips of children
Made sweet hosannas ring!*
Thou art the King of Israel,
Thou David's royal Son,
Who in the Lord's Name comest,
The King and Blessèd One.

2 The company of angels
Are praising thee on high,
And mortal men and all things
Created make reply.

3 The people of the Hebrews
With palms before thee went ;
Our praise and prayer and an-
thems
Before thee we present.

4 To thee before thy Passion
They sang their hymns of
praise ;
To thee now high exalted
Our melody we raise.

5 Thou didst accept their praises ;
Accept the prayers we bring,
Who in all good delightest,
Thou good and gracious King.
ST. THEODULPH OF ORLEANS, d. 821
Tr. JOHN MASON NEALE, 1818–66
altered

** This refrain is sung before each
verse and also after the final verse.*

234

RIDE on! ride on in majesty
Hark! all the tribes
'Hosanna!' cry ;
O Saviour meek, pursue thy
road
With palms and scattered gar-
ments strowed.

2 Ride on! ride on in majesty!
In lowly pomp ride on to die ;
O Christ, thy triumphs now
begin
O'er captive death and con-
quered sin.

3 Ride on! ride on in majesty!
The wingèd squadrons of the
sky
Look down with sad and wondering eyes
To see the approaching sacrifice.

4 Ride on! ride on in majesty!
Thy last and fiercest strife is
nigh ;
The Father on his sapphire
throne
Awaits his own anointed Son.

5 Ride on! ride on in majesty!
In lowly pomp ride on to die ;
Bow thy meek head to mortal
pain,
Then take, O God, thy power,
and reign.
HENRY HART MILMAN, 1791–1868

235 *For children*

HOSANNA, loud hosanna,
The little children sang ;
Through pillared court and
temple
The joyful anthem rang ;
To Jesus, who had blessed them
Close folded to his breast,
The children sang their praises
The simplest and the best.

2 From Olivet they followed,
'Mid an exultant crowd,
The victor palm-branch waving
And chanting clear and loud

Bright angels joined the chorus,
  Beyond the cloudless sky,—
'Hosanna in the highest!
  Glory to God on high!'

Fair leaves of silvery olive
  They strowed upon the
    ground,
While Salem's circling moun-
    tains
  Echoed the joyful sound;
The Lord of men and angels
  Rode on in lowly state,
Nor scorned that little children
  Should on his bidding wait.

'Hosanna in the highest!'
  That ancient song we sing,
For Christ is our Redeemer,
  The Lord of heaven our
    King.
O may we ever praise him
  With heart and life and
    voice,
And in his blissful presence
  Eternally rejoice.

JEANNETTE THRELFALL, 1821–80

236   *For children*

CHILDREN of Jerusalem
  Sang the praise of Jesus'
    name;
Children, too, of modern days
  Join to sing the Saviour's
    praise.
    *Hark! while infant voices sing
    Loud hosannas to our King.*

We are taught to love the Lord,
We are taught to read his Word,
We are taught the way to
    heaven:
Praise for all to God be given.

Parents, teachers, old and
    young,
All unite to swell the song,
Higher and yet higher rise,
Till hosannas reach the skies.

JOHN HENLEY, 1800–42

237   *Thursday in Holy Week*
            PARAPHRASE 35

'TWAS on that night when
    doomed to know
The eager rage of every foe,
That night in which he was
    betrayed,
The Saviour of the world took
    bread;

2 And, after thanks and glory
    given
To him that rules in earth and
    heaven,
That symbol of his flesh he
    broke,
And thus to all his followers
    spoke:

3 'My broken body thus I give
For you, for all; take, eat, and
    live:
And oft the sacred rite renew
That brings my wondrous love
    to view.'

4 Then in his hands the cup he
    raised,
And God anew he thanked and
    praised,
While kindness in his bosom
    glowed,
And from his lips salvation
    flowed.

5 'My blood I thus pour forth,' he
    cries,
'To cleanse the soul in sin that
    lies;
In this the covenant is sealed,
And heaven's eternal grace
    revealed.

6 'With love to man this cup is
    fraught,
Let all partake the sacred
    draught;
Through latest ages let it pour
In memory of my dying hour.'

Scottish Paraphrases, 1781
St. Matthew 26:26–29

238

PRAISE to the Holiest in the
    height,
  And in the depth be praise,—
In all his words most wonderful,
  Most sure in all his ways.

2 O loving wisdom of our God!
    When all was sin and shame,
A second Adam to the fight
    And to the rescue came.

3 O wisest love! that flesh and
    blood,
    Which did in Adam fail,
Should strive afresh against the
    foe,
    Should strive and should
    prevail;

4 O generous love! that he who
    smote
    In Man, for man, the foe,
The double agony in Man,
    For man, should undergo,

5 And in the garden secretly,
    And on the cross on high,
Should teach his brethren, and
    inspire
    To suffer and to die.

6 Praise to the Holiest in the
    height,
    And in the depth be praise,—
In all his words most wonderful,
    Most sure in all his ways.

        JOHN HENRY NEWMAN, 1801–90

239 PSALM 22, verses 1–9, 15–
    19, 22–24, 27, 30, 31

MY GOD my God why hast
    thou for ' saken me : why
art thou so far from helping
me and from the words of '
my roaring?

O my God I cry in the daytime
    but thou ' hearest not : and in
    the night season and am ' not
    silent.

But thou art holy O thou that
    inhabitest the praises of Is-
    rael   Our fathers trusted in '
    thee : they trusted and thou
    didst de ' liver them.

They cried unto thee and were
    de ' liver'd : they trusted in
    thee   and   were   not ' con-
    founded.

But I am a worm and ' no man
    a reproach of men and de
    spised of ' the people.

All they that see me laugh me to
    scorn : they shoot out the lip
    they shake the ' head saying,

He trusted on the ' Lord that he
    would de ' liver him: let him
    deliver him seeing he de
    ligh ' ted in him.

But thou art he that took me
    out of the ' womb : thou didst
    make me hope when I was
    upon my ' mother's breasts.

Be not far from me for trouble
    is ' near : for there is ' none to
    help.

My strength is dried up like a
    potsherd   and my tongue
    cleaveth to my ' jaws : and thou
    hast brought me into the ' dust
    of death.

For dogs have ' compassed me
    the assembly of the wicked
    have inclosed me   they
    pierced my ' hands and my feet

I may tell ' all my bones : they
    look and stare ' upon me.

They part my garments a ' mong
    them : and cast lots upon ' my
    vesture.

But be not thou far from me
    O ' Lord : O my strength haste
    thee ' to help me.

I will declare thy Name unto
    my ' brethren : in the midst of
    the congregation will ' I praise
    thee.

Ye that fear the Lord ' praise
    him : all ye the seed of Jacob
    glorify him and fear him all
    ye the seed ' of Israel.

For he hath not despised nor
    abhorred the affliction of the
    af ' flicted : neither hath he hid
    his face from him   but when
    he cried unto ' him he heard

All the ends of the world shall remember and turn unto the ' Lord : and all the kindreds of the nations shall worship ' before thee.

A seed shall ' serve him : it shall be accounted to the Lord for a ge ' neration.

They shall come and shall declare his righteousness unto a people that shall be ' born: that he ' hath done this.

240
TRISAGION
AND THE
REPROACHES

Choir or Cantor
Holy God, holy and mighty, holy and immortal, have mercy upon us.

Congregation
Holy God, holy and mighty, holy and immortal, have mercy upon us.

Choir or Cantor
O my people, what ' have I done to thee ?
or wherein have I wear'ied thee ? Answer me.
Because I brought thee forth out of the land of Egypt, and led thee to a land ex'ceeding good: thou hast prepared a cross ' for thy Saviour.

Congregation
Holy God, holy and mighty, holy and immortal, have mercy upon us.

Choir or Cantor
Before thee I o'pened the sea:
and with a spear thou hast o'pened my side.
I went before thee in a pil ' lar of cloud:
and thou hast brought me to the judgment 'hall of Pilate.

Congregation
Holy God, holy and mighty, holy and immortal, have mercy upon us.

Choir or Cantor
I fed thee with manna ' in the desert:
and thou hast beaten me with ' blows and stripes.
I made thee to drink the water of salvation ' from the rock:
and thou hast made me to drink ' gall and vinegar.

Congregation
Holy God, holy and mighty, holy and immortal, have mercy upon us.

Choir or Cantor
I gave thee a ' royal sceptre:
and thou hast given my head a ' crown of thorns.
I lifted thee up' with great power:
and thou hast hung me upon the gibbet ' of the cross.

Congregation
Holy God, holy and mighty, holy and immortal, have mercy upon us.

EARLY GALLICAN CHURCH

241

THERE is a green hill far away,
Outside a city wall,
Where the dear Lord was crucified,
Who died to save us all.

2 We may not know, we cannot tell
What pains he had to bear;
But we believe it was for us
He hung and suffered there.

3 He died that we might be forgiven,
He died to make us good,
That we might go at last to heaven,
Saved by his precious blood.

4 There was no other good enough
To pay the price of sin;
He only could unlock the gate
Of heaven, and let us in.

5 O dearly, dearly has he loved,
    And we must love him too,
And trust in his redeeming
        blood,
    And try his works to do.
                    CECIL FRANCES ALEXANDER
                            1818–95

242 *Solus ad victimam procedis,
        Domine*

ALONE thou goest forth, O
    Lord,
    In sacrifice to die;
Is this thy sorrow naught to us
Who pass unheeding by?

2 Our sins, not thine, thou bearest,
        Lord;
    Make us thy sorrow feel,
Till through our pity and our
        shame
    Love answers love's appeal.

3 This is earth's darkest hour, but
        thou
    Dost light and life restore;
Then let all praise be given thee
Who livest evermore.

4 Grant us to suffer with thee,
        Lord,
    That, as we share this hour,
Thy cross may bring us to thy
        joy
    And resurrection power.
                    PETER ABELARD, 1079–1142
                    Tr. FRANCIS BLAND TUCKER
                            altered

243

O COME and mourn with me
    awhile;
    O come ye to the Saviour's
        side;
O come, together let us mourn:
    Jesus, our Lord, is crucified!

2 Have we no tears to shed for
        him,
    While soldiers scoff and foes
        deride?
Ah! look how patiently he
        hangs:

3 Seven times he spake, seven
        words of love;
    And all three hours his silence
        cried
For mercy on the souls of men

4 O break, O break, hard heart of
        mine!
    Thy weak self-love and guilty
        pride
His Pilate and his Judas were:

5 O love of God! O sin of man!
    In this dread act your
        strength is tried,
And victory remains with love
                    FREDERICK WILLIAM FABER
                            1814–63, altered

244 *'Father, forgive them; for they
        know not what they do.'*

O WORD of pity, for our par-
    don pleading,
    Breathed in the hour of
        loneliness and pain;
O voice, which, through the ages
        interceding,
    Calls us to fellowship with
        God again.

2 O word of comfort, through the
        silence stealing,
    As the dread act of sacrifice
        began;
O infinite compassion, still re-
        vealing
    The infinite forgiveness won
        for man.

3 O word of hope, to raise us near-
        er heaven,
    When courage fails us, and
        when faith is dim;
The souls for whom Christ prays
        to Christ are given,
    To find their pardon and
        their joy in him.

4 O Intercessor, who art ever liv-
        ing
    To plead for dying souls that
        they may live,
Teach us to know our sin which
        needs forgiving,
    Teach us to know the love
        which can forgive.
                    ADA RUNDALL GREENAWAY
                            1861–1937

245

*Verily I say unto thee, Today
shalt thou be with me in Paradise.'*

'LORD, when thy Kingdom
comes, remember me!'
Thus spake the dying lips to
dying ears.
O faith, which in that darkest
hour could see
The promised glory of the
far-off years!

2 Hark! through the gloom. the
dying Saviour saith,
'Thou too shalt rest in Paradise today';
O words of love to answer
words of faith!
O words of hope for those
who live to pray!

3 Lord, when with dying lips my
prayer is said,
Grant that in faith thy Kingdom I may see,
And, thinking on thy cross, and
bleeding head,
May breathe my parting
words, 'Remember me'.

4 Remember me; and, ere I pass
away,
Speak thou the assuring
word that sets us free,
And make thy promise to my
heart, 'Today
Thou too shalt rest in Paradise with me'.

WILLIAM DALRYMPLE MACLAGAN
1826–1910

246

*'Woman, behold thy son!...
Behold thy mother!'*

Stabat mater dolorosa

AT the cross, her station keep-
ing,
Stood the mournful mother
weeping,
Where he hung, the dying
Lord;
For her soul, of joy bereavèd,
Bowed with anguish, deeply
grievèd,
Felt the sharp and piercing
sword.

2 O, how sad and sore distressèd
Now was she, that mother
blessèd
Of the sole-begotten One;
Deep the woe of her affliction,
When she saw the crucifixion
Of her ever-glorious Son.

3 Who, on Christ's dear mother
gazing,
Pierced by anguish so amazing,
Born of woman, would not
weep?
Who, on Christ's dear mother
thinking,
Such a cup of sorrow drinking,
Would not share her sorrows
deep?

4 For his people's sins chastisèd,
She beheld her Son despisèd,
Scourged, and crowned with
thorns entwined;
Saw him then from judgment
taken,
And in death by all forsaken,
Till his spirit he resigned.

5 Jesus, may her deep devotion
Stir in me the same emotion,
Fount of love, Redeemer
kind,
That my heart, fresh ardour
gaining,
And a purer love attaining,
May with thee acceptance
find.

13th century
Tr. EDWARD CASWALL, 1814–78
and others

247

*'My God, my God, why hast
thou forsaken me?'*

THRONED upon the awe-
some Tree,
King of grief, I watch with thee.
Darkness veils thine anguished
face:
None its lines of woe can trace:
None can tell what pangs un-
known
Hold thee silent and alone,—

2 Silent through those three dread
hours,
Wrestling with the evil powers,
Left alone with human sin,

87

Gloom around thee and within,
Till the appointed time is nigh,
Till the Lamb of God may die.

3 Hark, that cry that peals aloud
Upward through the whelming
  cloud!
Thou, the Father's only Son,
Thou, his own anointed One,
Thou dost ask him—can it
  be?—
'Why hast thou forsaken me?'

4 Lord, should fear and anguish
  roll
Darkly o'er my sinful soul,
Thou, who once wast thus bereft
That thine own might ne'er be
  left,
Teach me by that bitter cry
In the gloom to know thee nigh.

JOHN ELLERTON, 1826–93

248   *'I thirst.'*

O PERFECT God, thy love
  As perfect Man did share
Here upon earth each form of ill
Thy fellow-men must bear.

2 Now from the tree of scorn
We hear thy voice again;
Thou who didst take our mortal
  flesh,
Hast felt our mortal pain.

3 Thy body suffers thirst,
Parched are thy lips and dry:
How poor the offering man can
  bring
Thy thirst to satisfy!

4 O Saviour, by thy thirst
Borne on the cross of shame,
Grant us in all our sufferings
  here
To glorify thy Name:

5 That through each pain and
  grief
Our souls may onward move
To gain more likeness to thy
  life,
More knowledge of thy love.

ADA RUNDALL GREENAWAY
1861–1937

249   *'It is finished.'*

O PERFECT life of love!
  All, all is finished now,
All that he left his throne above
To do for us below.

2 No work is left undone
Of all the Father willed;
His toils and sorrows, one by
  one,
The Scriptures have fulfilled.

3 No pain that we can share
But he has felt its smart;
All forms of human grief and
  care
Have pierced that tender
  heart.

4 And on his thorn-crowned
  head,
And on his sinless soul,
Our sins in all their guilt were
  laid,
That he might make us
  whole.

5 In perfect love he dies;
For me he dies, for me!
O all-atoning Sacrifice,
I cling by faith to thee.

6 In every time of need,
Before the judgment throne,
Thy work, O Lamb of God, I'll
  plead,
Thy merits, not my own.

7 Yet work, O Lord, in me,
As thou for me hast wrought;
And let my love the answer be
To grace thy love has brought.

HENRY WILLIAMS BAKER, 1821–77

250   *'Father, into thy hands
I commend my spirit.'*

A ND now, belovèd Lord, thy
  soul resigning
Into thy Father's arms with
  conscious will,
Calmly, with reverend grace,
  thy head inclining,
The throbbing brow and
  labouring breast grow still.

Freely thy life thou yieldest,
    meekly bending
Even to the last beneath our
    sorrows' load,
Yet strong in death, in perfect
    peace commending
Thy spirit to thy Father and
    thy God.

3 My Saviour, in mine hour of
    mortal anguish,
    When earth grows dim, and
    round me falls the night,
O breathe thy peace, as flesh
    and spirit languish;
    At that dread eventide let
    there be light.

4 To thy dear cross turn thou
    mine eyes in dying;
    Lay but my fainting head
    upon thy breast;
Thine outstretched arms receive
    my latest sighing;
And then, O then, thine ever-
    lasting rest!

ELIZA SIBBALD ALDERSON
1818–89

251 *Herzliebster Jesu*

AH, holy Jesus, how hast thou
    offended,
That man to judge thee hath in
    hate pretended?
By foes derided, by thine own
    rejected,
    O most afflicted.

2 Lo, the good Shepherd for the
    sheep is offered;
The slave hath sinnèd, and the
    Son hath suffered;
For man's atonement, while he
    nothing heedeth,
    God intercedeth.

3 For me, kind Jesus, was thy
    incarnation,
Thy mortal sorrow, and thy
    life's oblation;
Thy death of anguish and thy
    bitter passion,
    For my salvation.

4 Therefore, kind Jesus, since I
    cannot pay thee,
I do adore thee, and will ever
    pray thee,
Think on thy mercy and thy
    love unswerving,
    Not my deserving.

JOHANN HEERMANN, 1585–1647
Par. ROBERT BRIDGES, 1844–1930

252

O DEAREST Lord, thy
    sacred head
    With thorns was pierced for
    me;
O pour thy blessing on my head,
    That I may think for thee.

2 O dearest Lord, thy sacred
    hands
    With nails were pierced for
    me;
O shed thy blessing on my
    hands,
    That they may work for thee.

3 O dearest Lord, thy sacred feet
    With nails were pierced for
    me;
O pour thy blessing on my feet,
    That they may follow thee.

4 O dearest Lord, thy sacred
    heart
    With spear was pierced for
    me;
O pour thy spirit in my heart,
    That I may live for thee.

FATHER ANDREW, 1869–1946

253 *O Haupt voll Blut und Wunden*

O SACRED Head, sore woun-
    ded,
    With grief and shame weigh-
    ed down!
O Kingly Head, surrounded
    With thorns, thine only
    crown!
How pale art thou with anguish,
    With sore abuse and scorn!
How does that visage languish,
    Which once was bright as
    morn!

2 O Lord of life and glory,
  What bliss till now was thine!
I read the wondrous story;
  I joy to call thee mine.
Thy grief and bitter passion
  Were all for sinners' gain;
Mine, mine was the trans-
    gression,
  But thine the deadly pain.

3 What language shall I borrow
    To praise thee, heavenly
      Friend,
For this thy dying sorrow,
  Thy pity without end?
O make me thine for ever,
  And, should I fainting be,
Lord, let me never, never
  Outlive my love to thee.

4 Be near me, Lord, when dying;
  O show thy cross to me;
And, for my succour flying,
  Come, Lord, to set me free;
These eyes, new faith receiving,
  From thee shall never move;
For he who dies believing
  Dies safely through thy love.
                PAUL GERHARDT, 1607–76
        Tr. JAMES WADDELL ALEXANDER
                                1804–59

254

WHEN I survey the wondrous
    cross
  On which the Prince of Glory
    died,
My richest gain I count but loss,
  And pour contempt on all my
    pride.

2 Forbid it, Lord, that I should
    boast,
  Save in the death of Christ,
    my God;
All the vain things that charm
    me most,
  I sacrifice them to his blood.

3 See! from his head, his hands,
    his feet,
  Sorrow and love flow mingled
    down;

Did e'er such love and sorrow
    meet,
  Or thorns compose so rich a
    crown?

4 Were the whole realm of nature
    mine,
  That were an offering far too
    small;
Love so amazing, so divine,
  Demands my soul, my life,
    my all.
                ISAAC WATTS, 1674–1748

255

LORD Christ, when first thou
    cam'st to men,
  Upon a cross they bound
    thee,
And mocked thy saving king-
    ship then
  By thorns with which they
    crowned thee:
And still our wrongs may weave
    thee now
New thorns to pierce that
    steady brow,
  And robe of sorrow round
    thee.

2 New advent of the love of
    Christ,
  Shall we again refuse thee,
Till in the night of hate and war
  We perish as we lose thee?
From old unfaith our souls
    release
To seek the Kingdom of thy
    peace,
  By which alone we choose
    thee.

3 O wounded hands of Jesus,
    build
  In us thy new creation;
Our pride is dust, our vaunt is
    stilled,
  We wait thy revelation:
O Love that triumphs over loss,
We bring our hearts before thy
    cross,
  To finish thy salvation.
                WALTER RUSSELL BOWIE
                                1882–1969

256   *Pange, lingua, gloriosi*
    proelium certaminis

* SING, my tongue, how glor-
   ious battle
  Glorious victory became;
And above the cross, his trophy,
  Tell the triumph and the
   fame:
Tell how he, the earth's Re-
  deemer,
  By his death for man o'er-
   came.

2 Thirty years fulfilled among
  us—
  Perfect life in low estate—
Born for this, and self-surren-
  dered,
  To his Passion dedicate,
On the cross the Lamb is
  lifted,
  For his people immolate.

3 His the nails, the spear, the
  spitting,
  Reed and vinegar and gall;
From his patient body pierced
  Blood and water streaming
  fall:
Earth and sea and stars and
  mankind
  By that stream are cleansèd
  all.

4 Faithful cross, above all other,
  One and only noble tree,
None in foliage, none in blos-
  som,
  None in fruit compares with
  thee:
Sweet the wood and sweet the
  iron,
  And thy load how sweet is
  he.

5 *Unto God be praise and honour:*
  To the Father, to the Son,
To the mighty Spirit, glory—

Ever Three and ever One:
Power and glory in the highest
  While eternal ages run. Amen.
    VENANTIUS FORTUNATUS, c. 535–600
      Tr. WILLIAM MAIR, 1830–1920
             and
  ARTHUR WELLESLEY WOTHERSPOON
            1853–1936
  and verse 4 JOHN MASON NEALE
            1818–66

* *The pointing is for use with Tune (i)*
PANGE LINGUA *only.*

257   *Vexilla Regis prodeunt*

THE royal banners forward
  go;
The cross shines forth in mystic
  glow,
Where he, the Life, did death
  endure,
And yet by death did life pro-
  cure.

2 His feet and hands outstretch-
  ing there,
He willed the piercing nails to
  bear,
For us and our redemption's
  sake
A victim of himself to make.

3 There whilst he hung, his sacred
  side
By soldier's spear was opened
  wide,
To cleanse us in the precious
  flood
Of water mingled with his
  blood.

4 Fulfilled is now what David
  told
In true prophetic song of old,
To all the nations 'Lo', saith
  he,
'Our God is reigning from the
  tree'.

5 *Blest Three in One, our praise we*
  sing
To thee from whom all graces
  spring:

As by the cross thou dost restore,
So rule and guide us evermore.
Amen.

VENANTIUS FORTUNATUS
c. 535–600
Tr. JOHN MASON NEALE, 1818–66
and others

258

WE sing the praise of him
who died,
Of him who died upon the
cross;
The sinner's hope let men
deride,
For this we count the world
but loss.

2 Inscribed upon the cross we
see,
In shining letters, 'God is
love';
He bears our sins upon the
tree;
He brings us mercy from
above.

3 The cross! it takes our guilt
away;
It holds the fainting spirit
up;
It cheers with hope the gloomy
day,
And sweetens every bitter
cup;

4 It makes the coward spirit
brave,
And nerves the feeble arm for
fight;
It takes its terror from the
grave,
And gilds the bed of death
with light;

5 The balm of life, the cure of
woe,
The measure and the pledge
of love,
The sinner's refuge here below,
The angels' theme in heaven
above.

THOMAS KELLY, 1769–1854

259

IN the cross of Christ I glory,
Towering o'er the wrecks of
time;
All the light of sacred story
Gathers round its head sub-
lime.

2 When the woes of life o'ertake
me,
Hopes deceive and fears
annoy,
Never shall the cross forsake
me;
Lo! it glows with peace and
joy.

3 When the sun of bliss is beam-
ing
Light and love upon my way,
From the cross the radiance
streaming
Adds more lustre to the day.

4 Bane and blessing, pain and
pleasure,
By the cross are sanctified;
Peace is there that knows no
measure,
Joys that through all time
abide.

5 In the cross of Christ I glory,
Towering o'er the wrecks of
time;
All the light of sacred story
Gathers round its head sub-
lime.

JOHN BOWRING, 1792–1872

260   *Good Friday evening*

AT eve, when now he breathed
no more,
The faithful few in anguish sore
The Lord they loved to burial
bore.

2 To those who mourned him,
who can say
How long the hours of sullen
day,
How long the nights while hid
he lay?

3 O ye who shrink beneath the blow
That death can deal, henceforth ye know
Not hopeless is your human woe.

4 For then, before their tears had ceased,
Love woke to joy the crimson east,
And Jesus rose, from death released.

JOHN RUSSELL DARBYSHIRE
1880–1948

261 *Saturday in Holy Week*

BY Jesus' grave on either hand,
While night is brooding o'er the land,
The sad and silent mourners stand.

2 At last the weary life is o'er,
The agony and conflict sore
Of him who all our suffering bore.

3 Deep in the rock's sepulchral shade
The Lord, by whom the worlds were made,
The Saviour of mankind, is laid.

4 O hearts bereaved and sore distressed,
Here is for you a place of rest;
Here leave your griefs on Jesus' breast.

5 So, when the dayspring from on high
Shall chase the night and fill the sky,
Then shall the Lord again draw nigh.

ISAAC GREGORY SMITH, 1826–1920

The following is also suitable
No. 224 My song is love unknown

CHRIST'S RESURRECTION AND EXALTATION

262 PSALM 118, verses 15–24

THE voice of rejoicing and salvation is in the taber-nacles of the ' righteous : the right hand of the Lord ' doëth valiantly.

The right hand of the Lord is ex ' alted : the right hand of the Lord ' doëth valiantly.

I shall not die ' but live : and declare ' the wórks of the Lord.

The Lord hath chastened ' me sore : but he hath not given me ' over unto death.

Open to me the gates of righ- ' teousness : I will go into them and ' I will praise the Lord.

This gate of ' the Lord : into which the righ ' teous shall enter.

I will ' praise thee : for thou hast heard me and art become ' my salvation.

The stone which the builders ' refused : is become the head stone ' of the corner.

This is the Lord's ' doing : it is marvel ' lous in our eyes.

This is the day which the Lord ' hath made : we will rejoice ' and be glad in it.

Glory be to the Father and to ' the Son : and ' to the Holy Ghost.

As it was in the beginning is now and ever ' shall be : world with- ' out end Amen.

263 PSALM 118, verses 19–25, 28, 29

O SET ye open unto me
    The gates of righteousness;
Then will I enter into them,
    And I the Lord will bless.

2 This is the gate of God, by it
    The just shall enter in.
Thee will I praise, for thou me
      heard'st,
    And hast my safety been.

That stone is made head cornerstone,
    Which builders did despise:
This is the doing of the Lord,
    And wondrous in our eyes.

4 This is the day God made, in it
    We'll joy triumphantly.
Save now, I pray thee, Lord; I
      pray,
    Send now prosperity.

5 Thou art my God, I'll thee
      exalt;
    My God, I will thee praise.
Give thanks to God, for he is
      good:
    His mercy lasts always.

6 *To Father, Son, and Holy Ghost,*
    The God whom we adore,
Be glory, as it was, and is,
    And shall be evermore. Amen.

264

JESUS CHRIST is risen today, *Alleluia!*
Our triumphant holy day,
    Alleluia!
Who did once, upon the cross,
    Alleluia!
Suffer to redeem our loss.
    Alleluia!

2 Hymns of praise, then, let us sing
Unto Christ, our heavenly King,
Who endured the cross and
      grave,
Sinners to redeem and save.

3 But the anguish he endured
Our salvation hath procured;
Now above the sky he's King,
Where the angels ever sing.

4 *Sing we to our God above*
Praise eternal as his love;
Praise him, all ye heavenly host,
Father, Son, and Holy Ghost:
    Amen.
    Lyra Davidica, 1708

265

'THE Lord is risen indeed';
    Now is his work performed;
Now is the mighty Captive
      freed,
    And Death's strong castle
      stormed.

2 'The Lord is risen indeed':
    The grave has lost his prey;
With him is risen the ransomed
      seed,
    To reign in endless day.

3 'The Lord is risen indeed';
    He lives, to die no more;
He lives, the sinner's cause to
      plead,
    Whose curse and shame he
      bore.

4 Then, angels, tune your lyres,
    And strike each cheerful
      chord;
Join, all ye bright celestial
      choirs,
    To sing our risen Lord!
    THOMAS KELLY, 1769–1854

266 *Finita iam sunt proelia*

THE strife is o'er, the battle
    done;
Now is the Victor's triumph
    won;
Now be the song of praise
    begun,—
    Alleluia! Alleluia! Alleluia!

2 The powers of death have done
    their worst,

But Christ their legions hath
   dispersed;
Let shouts of holy joy out-
   burst,—

3 The three sad days have quickly
   sped;
He rises glorious from the dead;
All glory to our risen Head!

4 He brake the age-bound chains
   of hell;
The bars from heaven's high
   portals fell;
Let hymns of praise his triumph
   tell.

5 Lord, by the stripes which
   wounded thee,
From death's dread sting thy
   servants free,
That we may live, and sing to
   thee:

               17th century
Tr. FRANCIS POTT, 1832–1909, altered

267   *Ἀναστάσεως ἡμέρα*

THE day of resurrection!
   Earth, tell it out abroad;
The passover of gladness,
   The passover of God!
From death to life eternal,
   From earth unto the sky,
Our Christ hath brought us over
   With hymns of victory.

2 Our hearts be pure from evil,
   That we may see aright
The Lord in rays eternal
   Of resurrection light;
And, listening to his accents,
   May hear, so calm and plain,
His own 'All hail!' and, hearing,
   May raise the victor strain.

3 Now let the heavens be joyful;
   Let earth her song begin;
Let the round world keep
   triumph,
   And all that is therein;
Let all things seen and unseen
   Their notes of gladness blend,
For Christ the Lord hath risen,
   Our Joy that hath no end.

   ST. JOHN OF DAMASCUS, d. c. 750
   Tr. JOHN MASON NEALE, 1818–66
                  altered

268   *Christ lag in Todesbanden*

CHRIST Jesus lay in death's
   strong bands,
   For our offences given,
But now at God's right hand he
   stands,
   And brings us life from
     heaven:
Wherefore let us joyful be,
And sing to God right thank-
   fully
Loud songs of Alleluia!
   Alleluia!

2 It was a strange and dreadful
   strife
   When life and death conten-
     ded;
The victory remained with life,
   The reign of death was ended:
Stripped of power, no more he
   reigns,
An empty form alone remains;
   His sting is lost for ever.

3 So let us keep the festival
   Whereto the Lord invites us;
Christ is himself the joy of all,
   The sun that warms and
     lights us;
By his grace he doth impart
Eternal sunshine to the heart;
   The night of sin is ended.

4 Then let us feast this Easter day
   On the true Bread of heaven.
The word of grace hath purged
   away
   The old and wicked leaven;
Christ alone our soul will feed,
He is our meat and drink indeed,
   Faith lives upon no other.

   MARTIN LUTHER, 1483–1546
   Tr. RICHARD MASSIE, 1800–87

269   *Ἄισωμεν πάντες λαοί*

COME, ye faithful, raise the
   strain
   Of triumphant gladness;
God hath brought his Israel
   Into joy from sadness;
Loosed from Pharaoh's bitter
   yoke
Jacob's sons and daughters;

Led them with unmoistened
    foot
Through the Red Sea waters.

2 'Tis the spring of souls today;
    Christ hath burst his prison,
And from three days' sleep in
    death
As a sun hath risen:
All the winter of our sins,
    Long and dark, is flying
From his light, to whom we give
    Laud and praise undying.

3 Now the queen of seasons, bright
    With the day of splendour,
With the royal feast of feasts,
    Comes its joy to render;
Comes to gladden Christian
    men,
    Who with true affection
Welcome in unwearied strains
    Jesus' resurrection.

4 Neither might the gates of
    death,
    Nor the tomb's dark portal,
Nor the watchers, nor the seal,
    Hold thee as a mortal;
But arising, thou dost stand
    'Midst thine own, bestowing
Thine own peace, which ever-
    more
    Passeth human knowing.

ST. JOHN OF DAMASCUS, d. c. 750
Tr. JOHN MASON NEALE, 1818–66
and others

270

GOOD Christian men, rejoice
    and sing!
Now is the triumph of our King!
To all the world glad news we
    bring:
    Alleluia! Alleluia! Alleluia!

2 The Lord of life is risen for aye;
Bring flowers of song to strew
    his way;
Let all mankind rejoice and say:

3 Praise we in songs of victory
That love, that life which can-
    not die,
And sing with hearts uplifted
    high:

4 Thy Name we bless, O risen
    Lord,
And sing today with one
    accord
The life laid down, the life re-
    stored:

CYRIL ARGENTINE ALINGTON
1872–1955

271

THIS joyful Eastertide,
    Away with sin and sorrow
My Love, the Crucified,
    Hath sprung to life this
      morrow:
    *Had Christ, that once was
      slain,*
      *Ne'er burst his three-day
      prison,*
    *Our faith had been in vain:
      But now hath Christ
      arisen,*
    Arisen, arisen, arisen!

2 My flesh in hope shall rest,
    And for a season slumber:
Till trump from east to west
    Shall wake the dead in
      number:

3 Death's flood hath lost his chill,
    Since Jesus crossed the river:
Lover of souls, from ill
    My passing soul deliver:

GEORGE RATCLIFFE WOODWARD
1848–1934

272
                Salve, festa dies

'WELCOME, happy morn-
    ing!'—age to age shall
    say:
'Hell today is vanquished,
    heaven is won today.'
Lo! the Dead is living, God for
    evermore:
Him, their true Creator, all his
    works adore.

2 Earth with joy confesses, cloth-
    ing her for spring,
All good gifts return with her
    returning King:
Bloom in every meadow, leaves
    on every bough,
Speak his sorrows ended, hail
    his triumph now.

3 Thou, of life the Author, death
    didst undergo,
Tread the path of darkness,
    saving strength to show.
Come then, True and Faithful,
    now fulfil thy word;
'Tis thine own third morning:
    rise, O buried Lord!

4 Loose the souls long prisoned,
    bound with Satan's chain:
All that now is fallen raise to
    life again:
Show thy face in brightness, bid
    the nations see:
Bring again our daylight: day
    returns with thee.

VENANTIUS FORTUNATUS
c. 535–600
Par. JOHN ELLERTON, 1826–93

273

B LEST morning, whose first
    dawning rays
Beheld the Son of God
Arise triumphant from the
    grave,
And leave his dark abode!

2 Wrapt in the silence of the
    tomb
The great Redeemer lay,
Till the revolving skies had
    brought
The third, the appointed day.

3 Hell and the grave combined
    their force
To hold our Lord, in vain;
Sudden the Conqueror arose,
And burst their feeble chain.

4 To thy great Name, Almighty
    Lord,
We sacred honours pay,
And loud hosannas shall pro-
    claim
The triumphs of the day.

5 Salvation and immortal praise
To our victorious King!
Let heaven and earth, and rocks
    and seas,
With glad hosannas ring.

6 *To Father, Son, and Holy Ghost,*
    The God whom we adore,
Be glory, as it was, and is,
    And shall be evermore. Amen.

ISAAC WATTS, 1674–1748

274

T HE world itself keeps Easter
    Day,
And Easter larks are singing;
And Easter flowers are bloom-
    ing gay,
And Easter buds are spring-
    ing:
    Alléluia, Alléluia:
The Lord of all things lives
    anew,
And all his works are rising too:
    Hosanna in excelsis!

2 There stood the women by the
    tomb,
    On Easter morning early;
When day had scarcely chased
    the gloom,
    And dew was white and
    pearly:
    Alléluia, Alléluia:
With loving but with erring
    mind,
They came the Prince of Life to
    find:

3 But earlier still the angel sped,
    His news of comfort giving;
And 'Why', he said, 'among the
    dead
    Thus seek ye for the Living?'
    Alléluia, Alléluia:
The Lord hath risen, as all
    things tell:
Good Christians, see ye rise
    as well!

JOHN MASON NEALE, 1818–66
altered

275

'C HRIST the Lord is risen to-
    day',
Sons of men and angels say;
Raise your joys and triumphs
    high;
Sing, ye heavens, and earth
    reply.

2 Love's redeeming work is done,
Fought the fight, the battle
won;
Lo! our Sun's eclipse is o'er;
Lo! he sets in blood no more.

3 Vain the stone, the watch, the
seal;
Christ has burst the gates of
hell:
Death in vain forbids his rise;
Christ has opened Paradise.

4 Lives again our glorious King;
Where, O Death, is now thy
sting?
Once he died, our souls to save;
Where thy victory, O grave?

5 Soar we now where Christ has
led,
Following our exalted Head;
Made like him, like him we rise;
Ours the cross, the grave, the
skies.

6 Hail, the Lord of earth and
heaven!
Praise to thee by both be given;
Thee we greet triumphant now;
Hail, the Resurrection thou!
CHARLES WESLEY, 1707–88

276

EASTER glory fills the sky!
Christ now lives, no more to
die!
Darkness has been put to flight
By the living Lord of light!
Alleluia!

2 See, the stone is rolled away
From the tomb where once he
lay!
He has risen as he said,
Glorious Firstborn from the
dead!

3 Seek not life within the tomb;
Christ stands in the upper room!
Risen glory he conceals,
Risen Body he reveals!

4 Though we see his face no more,
He is with us as before!
Glory veiled, he is our Priest,
His own flesh and blood our
feast!

5 Christ, the Victor over death,
Breathes on us the Spirit's
breath!
Paradise is our reward,
Endless Easter with our Lord!
JAMES QUINN

277   *O filii et filiae*

ALLELUIA! ALLELUIA! ALLELUIA

O SONS and daughters, let
us sing!
The King of heaven, the
glorious King,
O'er death today rose trium-
phing.
Alleluia!

2 That Easter morn, at break of
day,
The faithful women went their
way
To seek the tomb where Jesus
lay:

3 An angel clad in white they see,
Who sat, and spake unto the
three,
'Your Lord doth go to Galilee.'

4 That night the apostles met in
fear;
Amidst them came their Lord
most dear,
And said, 'My peace be on all
here.'

5 When Thomas first the tidings
heard,
He doubted if it were their
Lord,
Until he came and spake the
word:

6 'My piercèd side, O Thomas,
see;
Behold my hands, my feet,'
said he,
'Not faithless, but believing be.'

7 No longer Thomas then denied;
He saw the feet, the hands, the
side;
'Thou art my Lord and God', he
cried:

98

How blest are they who have
    not seen,
And yet whose faith hath con-
    stant been,
For they eternal life shall win:

On this most holy day of days,
To God your hearts and voices
    raise
In laud and jubilee and praise:

           JEAN TISSERAND, ? –1494
    Tr. JOHN MASON NEALE, 1818–66
                     altered

* These Alleluias are sung before the
rst verse only.

278

NOW the green blade riseth
    from the buried grain,
Wheat that in dark earth many
    days has lain;
Love lives again, that with
    the dead has been:
Love is come again,
Like wheat that springeth
green.

2 In the grave they laid him,
    Love whom men had
    slain,
Thinking that never he would
    wake again,
Laid in the earth like grain
    that sleeps unseen:

3 Forth he came at Easter, like
    the risen grain,
He that for three days in the
    grave had lain,
Quick from the dead my
    risen Lord is seen:

4 When our hearts are wintry,
    grieving, or in pain,
Thy touch can call us back to
    life again,
Fields of our hearts that
    dead and bare have
    been:

    JOHN MACLEOD CAMPBELL CRUM
                 1872–1958

279
A toi la gloire, O Ressuscité

THINE be the glory, risen,
    conquering Son,
Endless is the victory thou o'er
    death hast won;
Angels in bright raiment rolled
    the stone away,
Kept the folded grave-clothes,
    where thy body lay.
    Thine be the glory, risen, con-
    quering Son,
    Endless is the victory thou o'er
    death hast won.

2 Lo! Jesus meets us, risen from
    the tomb;
Lovingly he greets us, scatters
    fear and gloom;
Let the Church with gladness
    hymns of triumph sing,
For her Lord now liveth; death
    hath lost its sting.

3 No more we doubt thee, glorious
    Prince of Life;
Life is naught without thee:
    aid us in our strife;
Make us more than conquerors,
    through thy deathless love:
Bring us safe through Jordan to
    thy home above.

        EDMOND BUDRY, 1854–1932
    Tr. R. BIRCH HOYLE, 1875–1939

280
For children

GOOD Joseph had a garden,
    Close by that sad green hill
Where Jesus died a bitter
    death
To save mankind from ill.

2 One evening in that garden,
Their faces dark with gloom,
They laid the Saviour's body
Within good Joseph's tomb.

3 There came the holy women
With spices and with tears;
The angels tried to comfort
    them,
But could not calm their fears.

4 Came Mary to that garden
　And sobbed with heart forlorn;
　She thought that she heard the gar-
　　dener ask,
　'Whom　seekest　thou　this
　　morn?'

5 She　heard　her　own　name
　　spoken,
　And then she lost her care:
　All in his strength and beauty
　The risen Lord stood fair!

6 Good Joseph had a garden;
　Amid its trees so tall
　The Lord Christ rose on Easter
　　Day;
　He lives to save us all.

7 And as he rose at Easter
　He is alive for aye.
　The　very　same　Lord　Jesus
　　Christ
　Who hears us sing today.

8 Go tell the Lord Christ's mes-
　　sage,
　The Easter triumph sing,
　Till all his waiting children
　　know
　That Jesus is their King.

ALDA M. MILNER-BARRY
1877–1941

281　*For younger children*

AT Eastertime the lilies fair
And lovely flowers bloomed
everywhere.
At Eastertime, at Eastertime,
How glad the world at Eastertime!

2 At Eastertime the angels said
　That Christ had risen from the
　　dead:

FREDERICK JACKSON, 1867–1942

282　*For younger children*

COME, ye children, sing to
　Jesus
On this happy Easter Day;

All the bells are gladly ringing
Come, ye children, praise and
　pray.
All the flowers are gaily spring-
　ing,
All the birds with joy are sing-
　ing;
Come, ye children, sing to Jesus,
Come, ye children, praise and
　pray.

2 'Christ　our　Saviour　now　is
　　risen',
　Let his little children say.
　All the bells are gladly ringing
　On this happy Easter Day;
　All the flowers are gaily spring-
　　ing,
　All the birds with joy are sing-
　　ing;

FREDERICK SMITH, 1800–7
altered by compiler

283　*For Easter evening*

JESUS, Lord, Redeemer,
　Once for sinners slain,
Crucified in weakness,
　Raised in power, to reign,
Dwelling with the Father,
　Endless in thy days,
Unto thee be glory,
　Honour, blessing, praise.

2 Faithful ones, communing,
　　Towards the close of day,
Desolate and weary,
　　Met thee in the way.
So, when sun is setting,
　Come to us, and show
All the truth; and in us
　Make our hearts to glow.

3 In the upper chamber,
　　Where the ten, in fear,
Gathered sad and troubled,
　　There thou didst appear.
So, O Lord, this evening,
　Bid our sorrows cease;
Breathing on us, Saviour,
　Say, 'I give you peace'.

PATRICK MILLER KIRKLAND
1857–1943

284 PSALM 47

O CLAP your hands all ye ' people : shout unto God with the ' voice of triumph.

For the Lord most high is ' terri-ble : he is a great King ' over all the earth.

He shall subdue the people ' under us : and the nations ' under our feet.

He shall choose our inheri-tance ' for us : the excellency of Jacob ' whom he lov'd.

God is gone up with a ' shout : the Lord with the sound ' of a trumpet.

Sing praises to God sing ' praises : sing praises unto our ' King sing praises.

For God is the King of all the ' earth : sing ye praises with ' understanding.

God reigneth over the ' heathen : God sitteth upon the throne ' of his holi-ness.

The princes of the people are gathered together even the people of the God of ' Abraham : for the shields of the earth belong unto God he is great ' ly exalted.

Glory be to the Father and to the ' Son : and ' to the Holy Ghost.

As it was in the beginning is now and ever ' shall' be : world with ' out end Amen.

285 PSALM 68, verses 18a, 19, 20

THOU hast, O Lord, most glorious,
Ascended up on high ;
And in triumph victorious led
Captive captivity.

2 Blest be the Lord, who is to us
Of our salvation God ;
Who daily with his benefits
Us plenteously doth load.

3 He of salvation is the God,
Who is our God most strong ;
And unto God the Lord from death
The issues do belong.

4 *To Father, Son, and Holy Ghost,
The God whom we adore,
Be glory, as it was, and is,
and shall be evermore. Amen.*

286

THE Head that once was
crowned with thorns
Is crowned with glory now ;
A royal diadem adorns
The mighty Victor's brow.

2 The highest place that heaven affords
Is his, is his by right,
The King of kings, and Lord of lords,
And heaven's eternal Light ;

3 The joy of all who dwell above,
The joy of all below
To whom he manifests his love,
And grants his Name to know.

4 To them the cross, with all its shame,
With all its grace, is given,
Their name an everlasting name,
Their joy the joy of heaven.

5 They suffer with their Lord below,
They reign with him above,
Their profit and their joy to know
The mystery of his love.

6 The cross he bore is life and health,
Though shame and death to him,
His people's hope, his people's wealth,
Their everlasting theme.
THOMAS KELLY, 1769–1854

287

THE Lord ascendeth up on
  high,
  The Lord hath triumphed
    gloriously,
In power and might excell-
  ing;
The grave and hell are captive
  led,
Lo! he returns, our glorious
  Head,
  To his eternal dwelling.

2 The heavens with joy receive
    their Lord,
  By saints, by angel hosts
    adored;
  O day of exultation!
O earth, adore thy glorious
  King!
His rising, his ascension sing
  With grateful adoration!

3 Our great High Priest hath
    gone before,
  Now on his Church his grace to
    pour,
  And still his love he giveth:
O may our hearts to him ascend;
May all within us upward tend
  To him who ever liveth.

  ARTHUR TOZER RUSSELL, 1806–74

288

THE eternal gates are lifted
  up,
  The doors are opened wide;
The King of Glory is gone in
  Unto his Father's side.

2 Thou art gone up before us,
    Lord,
  To make for us a place,
That we may be where now thou
  art,
  And look upon God's face.

3 And ever on our earthly path
  A gleam of glory lies;
A light still breaks behind the
  cloud
  That veiled thee from our
    eyes.

4 Lift up our hearts, lift up our
    minds,
  And let thy grace be given,
That, while we live on earth
  below,
  Our treasure be in heaven;

5 That where thou art, at God's
    right hand,
  Our hope, our love may be:
Dwell thou in us, that we may
  dwell
  For evermore in thee.

  CECIL FRANCES ALEXANDER
    1818–95, altered

289

LOOK, ye saints! the sight is
  glorious;
  See the Man of Sorrows now
From the fight returned vic-
  torious,
  Every knee to him shall bow:
Crown him! crown him! crown
  him! crown him!
  Crowns become the Victor's
    brow.

2 Crown the Saviour! angels
    crown him!
  Rich the trophies Jesus
    brings;
In the seat of power enthrone
  him,
  While the vault of heaven
    rings:
Crown him! crown him! crown
  him! crown him!
Crown the Saviour King of
  kings!

3 Sinners in derision crowned him,
  Mocking thus the Saviour's
    claim;
Saints and angels crowd around
  him,
  Own his title, praise his
    Name:
Crown him! crown him! crown
  him! crown him!
Spread abroad the Victor's
  fame.

Hark, those bursts of ac-
    clamation!
    Hark, those loud triumphant
        chords!
Jesus takes the highest station:
    O what joy the sight affords!
Crown him! crown him! crown
        him! crown him
King of kings, and Lord of
        lords!

THOMAS KELLY, 1769–1854

90 *Gen Himmel aufgefahren ist*

GOD is ascended up on high,
    With merry noise of trum-
        pet's sound,
And princely seated in the sky,
Rules over all the world around:
    Alléluia!

In human shape and flesh he
        went,
Adornèd with his Passion's
        scars,
Which in heaven's sight he did
        present
More glorious than the glitter-
        ing stars:

Lord, raise our sinking minds
        therefore
Up to our proper country dear,
And purify us evermore,
To fit us for those regions clear:

HENRY MORE, 1614–87
from the German carol

291

AGAIN the morn of gladness,
    The morn of light, is here,
And earth itself looks fairer,
    And heaven itself more near:
The bells, like angel voices,
    Speak peace to every breast;
And all the land lies quiet,
    To keep the day of rest.
    'Glory be to Jesus!'
        Let all his children say;
    'He rose again, he rose again,
        On this glad day!'

2 Again, O loving Saviour,
    The children of thy grace
Prepare themselves to seek thee
    Within thy chosen place.

Our song shall rise to greet thee,
    If thou our hearts wilt raise;
If thou our lips wilt open,
    Our mouth shall show thy
        praise.

3 Tell out, sweet bells, his
        praises!
    Sing, children, sing his Name!
Still louder and still farther
    His mighty deeds proclaim,
Till all whom he redeemèd
    Shall own him Lord and King,
Till every knee shall worship,
    And every tongue shall sing.
    'Glory be to Jesus!'
        Let all creation say;
    'He rose again, he rose again,
        On this glad day!'

JOHN ELLERTON, 1826–93

292

AWAY with gloom, away with
    doubt!
With all the morning stars we
        sing;
With all the sons of God we
        shout
    The praises of a King,
        Alleluia! Alleluia!
    Of our returning King.

2 Away with death, and welcome
        life;
    In him we died and live
        again;
And welcome peace, away with
        strife;
    For he returns to reign.
        Alleluia! Alleluia!
    The Crucified shall reign.

3 Then welcome beauty, he is
        fair;
    And welcome youth, for he is
        young;
And welcome spring; and every-
        where
    Let merry songs be sung!
        Alleluia! Alleluia!
    For such a King be sung!

EDWARD SHILLITO, 1872–1948

The following are also suitable
No.
  11 Jesus, stand among us
  44 Most glorious Lord of life
605 Jesus lives! thy terrors now

CHRIST'S REIGN AND PRIESTHOOD

293 PARAPHRASE 48, verses
5–9

THE Saviour died, but rose
again
Triumphant from the grave;
And pleads our cause at God's
right hand,
Omnipotent to save.

2 Who then can e'er divide us
more
From Jesus and his love,
Or break the sacred chain that
binds
The earth to heaven above?

3 Let troubles rise, and terrors
frown,
And days of darkness fall;
Through him all dangers we'll
defy,
And more than conquer all.

4 Nor death nor life, nor earth
nor hell,
Nor time's destroying sway,
Can e'er efface us from his
heart,
Or make his love decay.

5 Each future period that will
bless,
As it has blessed the past;
He loved us from the first of
time,
He loves us to the last.

Scottish Paraphrases, 1781
From Romans 8:34–end

294 PARAPHRASE 20, verses
1–5

HOW glorious Zion's courts
appear,
The city of our God!
His throne he hath established
here,
Here fixed his loved abode.

2 Its walls, defended by his grace,
No power shall e'er o'erthrow,
Salvation is its bulwark sure
Against the assailing foe.

3 Lift up the everlasting gates,
The doors wide open fling;
Enter, ye nations, who obey
The statutes of our King.

4 Here shall ye taste unmingled
joys,
And dwell in perfect peace,
Ye, who have known Jehovah's
Name,
And trusted in his grace.

5 Trust in the Lord, for ever trust
And banish all your fears;
Strength in the Lord Jehovah
dwells
Eternal as his years.

Scottish Paraphrases, 1781
From Isaiah 26:1–4

295 PARAPHRASE 58

WHERE high the heavenly
temple stands,
The house of God not made with
hands,
A great High Priest our nature
wears,
The Guardian of mankind appears.

2 He who for men their surety
stood,
And poured on earth his precious blood,
Pursues in heaven his mighty
plan,
The Saviour and the Friend of
man.

3 Though now ascended up on
high,
He bends on earth a brother's
eye;
Partaker of the human name,
He knows the frailty of our
frame.

4 Our fellow-sufferer yet retains
A fellow-feeling of our pains;
And still remembers in the skies
His tears, his agonies, and cries.

In every pang that rends the heart
The Man of Sorrows had a part;
He sympathizes with our grief,
And to the sufferer sends relief.

With boldness, therefore, at the throne,
Let us make all our sorrows known;
And ask the aids of heavenly power
To help us in the evil hour.

Scottish Paraphrases, 1781
From Hebrews 4:14–end

296

REJOICE, the Lord is King;
Your Lord and King adore;
Mortals, give thanks and sing
And triumph evermore:
Lift up your heart, lift up your voice;
Rejoice; again I say, 'Rejoice'.

Jesus, the Saviour, reigns,
The God of truth and love;
When he had purged our stains,
He took his seat above:
Lift up your heart, lift up your voice;
Rejoice; again I say, 'Rejoice'.

His Kingdom cannot fail;
He rules o'er earth and heaven;
The keys of death and hell
Are to our Jesus given:
Lift up your heart, lift up your voice;
Rejoice; again I say, 'Rejoice'.

He sits at God's right hand
Till all his foes submit,
And bow to his command,
And fall beneath his feet:
Lift up your heart, lift up your voice;
Rejoice; again I say, 'Rejoice'.

Rejoice in glorious hope;
Jesus, the Judge, shall come,
And take his servants up
To their eternal home;

We then shall hear the arch-angel's voice;
The trump of God shall sound, 'Rejoice'.

CHARLES WESLEY, 1707–88, altered

297

ALL praise to thee, for thou, O King divine,
Didst yield the glory that of right was thine,
That in our darkened hearts thy grace might shine:
Alleluia!

2 Thou cam'st to us in lowliness of thought;
By thee the outcast and the poor were sought,
And by thy death was God's salvation wrought:

3 Let this mind be in us which was in thee,
Who wast a servant that we might be free,
Humbling thyself to death on Calvary:

4 Wherefore, by God's eternal purpose, thou
Art high exalted o'er all creatures now,
And given the Name to which all knees shall bow:

5 Let every tongue confess with one accord
In heaven and earth that Jesus Christ is Lord;
And God the Father be by all adored:

FRANCIS BLAND TUCKER
Based on Philippians 2:5–11

298

CROWN him with many crowns,
The Lamb upon his throne:
Hark how the heavenly anthem drowns
All music but its own.
Awake, my soul, and sing
Of him who died for thee,

And hail him as thy matchless
　　King
　　Through all eternity.

2　Crown him the Lord of life,
　　Who triumphed o'er the
　　　grave,
And rose victorious in the strife
　For those he came to save.
　　His glories now we sing
　　Who died and rose on high,
　Who died eternal life to bring,
　And lives that death may die.

3　Crown him the Lord of love;
　　Behold his hands and side,
Rich wounds yet visible above,
　In beauty glorified.
　　All hail, Redeemer, hail!
　　For thou hast died for me:
　Thy praise shall never, never
　　fail
　　　Throughout eternity.
　　　　MATTHEW BRIDGES, 1800–94
　　　and GODFREY THRING, 1823–1903

299

BLESSING and honour and
　glory and power,
Wisdom and riches and strength
　evermore
Give ye to him who our battle
　hath won,
Whose are the Kingdom, the
　crown, and the throne.

2 Into the heaven of the heavens
　　hath he gone;
Sitteth he now in the joy of the
　　throne;
Weareth he now of the Kingdom
　　the crown;
Singeth he now the new song
　　with his own.

3 Soundeth the heaven of the
　　heavens with his Name;
Ringeth the earth with his
　　glory and fame;
Ocean and mountain, stream,
　　forest, and flower
Echo his praises and tell of his
　　power.

4 Ever ascendeth the song and
　　the joy;
Ever descendeth the love from
　　on high;
Blessing and honour and glory
　　and praise,—
This is the theme of the hymn
　　that we raise.

5 Give we the glory and praise to
　　the Lamb;
Take we the robe and the harp
　　and the palm;
Sing we the song of the Lamb
　　that was slain,
Dying in weakness, but rising
　　to reign.
　　　　　HORATIUS BONAR, 1808–8

300

AT the Name of Jesus
　　Every knee shall bow,
Every tongue confess him
　　King of Glory now;
'Tis the Father's pleasure
　　We should call him Lord,
Who from the beginning
　　Was the mighty Word.

2 Humbled for a season,
　　To receive a name
From the lips of sinners,
　　Unto whom he came,
Faithfully he bore it
　　Spotless to the last;
Brought it back victorious,
　　When from death he passed.

3 Name him, brothers, name him,
　　With love strong as death,
But with awe and wonder
　　And with bated breath!
He is God the Saviour,
　　He is Christ the Lord,
Ever to be worshipped,
　　Trusted, and adored.

4 In your hearts enthrone him;
　　There let him subdue
All that is not holy,
　　All that is not true:
Crown him as your Captain
　　In temptation's hour;
Let his will enfold you
　　In its light and power.

Brothers, this Lord Jesus
Shall return again,
With his Father's glory,
With his angel train;
For all wreaths of empire
Meet upon his brow,
And our hearts confess him
King of Glory now.

CAROLINE MARIA NOEL, 1817–77

01   *Christus Redemptor gentium*

CHRIST is the world's Re-
deemer,
The lover of the pure,
The fount of heav'nly wisdom,
Our trust and hope secure;
The armour of his soldiers,
The Lord of earth and sky;
Our health while we are living,
Our life when we shall die.

Christ hath our host surrounded
With clouds of martyrs
bright,
Who wave their palms in
triumph,
And fire us for the fight.
For Christ the cross ascended
To save a world undone,
And, suffering for the sinful,
Our full redemption won.

Down in the realm of darkness
He lay a captive bound,
But at the hour appointed
He rose, a Victor crowned;
And now, to heav'n ascended,
He sits upon the throne,
In glorious dominion,
His Father's and His own.

Glory to God the Father,
The unbegotten One;
All honour be to Jesus,
His sole-begotten Son;
And to the Holy Spirit—
The perfect Trinity,
Let all the worlds give answer,
'Amen—so let it be'.

ST. COLUMBA, 521–97
Tr. DUNCAN MACGREGOR
1854–1923, altered

302   *Jesu, nostra redemptio*

JESUS, our hope, our heart's
desire,
Thy work of grace we sing;
Redeemer of the world art thou,
Its Maker and its King.

2 How vast the mercy and the love
Which laid our sins on thee,
And led thee to a cruel death
To set thy people free!

3 But now the bonds of death are
burst;
The ransom has been paid;
And thou art on thy Father's
throne,
In majesty arrayed.

4 Jesus, our only joy be thou,
As thou our prize wilt be;
In thee be all our glory now,
And through eternity.

7th–8th century
Tr. JOHN CHANDLER, 1806–76
and Compilers of *Hymns Ancient and
Modern*

303

GOD is working his purpose
out, as year succeeds to
year:
God is working his purpose out,
and the time is drawing
near—
Nearer and nearer draws the
time—the time that shall
surely be,
When the earth shall be filled
with the glory of God, as
the waters cover the sea.

2 What can we do to work God's
work, to prosper and in-
crease
The brotherhood of all mankind
—the reign of the Prince of
Peace?
What can we do to hasten the
time—the time that shall
surely be,
When the earth shall be filled
with the glory of God, as
the waters cover the sea?

107   E

3 March we forth in the strength
    of God, with the banner of
    Christ unfurled,
That the light of the glorious
    Gospel of truth may shine
    throughout the world:
Fight we the fight with sorrow
    and sin, to set their cap-
    tives free,
That the earth may be filled
    with the glory of God, as
    the waters cover the sea.

4 All we can do is nothing worth,
    unless God blesses the deed;
Vainly we hope for the harvest-
    tide, till God gives life to
    the seed;
Yet nearer and nearer draws
    the time—the time that
    shall surely be,
When the earth shall be filled
    with the glory of God, as
    the waters cover the sea.

ARTHUR CAMPBELL AINGER
1841–1919

304

JOIN all the glorious names
    Of wisdom, love, and
    power,
That ever mortals knew,
    That angels ever bore:
All are too mean to speak his
    worth,
Too mean to set my Saviour
    forth.

2 Great Prophet of my God,
    My tongue would bless thy
    Name;
By thee the joyful news
    Of our salvation came,—
The joyful news of sins for-
    given,
Of hell subdued, and peace
    with heaven.

3 Jesus, my great High Priest,
    Offered his blood and died;
My guilty conscience seeks
    No sacrifice beside:
His powerful blood did once
    atone,
And now it pleads before the
    throne.

4 My dear Almighty Lord,
    My Conqueror and m
    King,
Thy sceptre and thy sword,
    Thy reigning grace, I sing
Thine is the power: behold, I si
In willing bonds before thy fee

5 Now let my soul arise,
    And tread the tempte
    down:
My Captain leads me forth
    To conquest and a crown:
A feeble saint shall win the day
Though death and hell obstruc
    the way.

ISAAC WATTS, 1674–174

305   *Hymnum canamus gloriae*

SING we triumphant hymn
    of praise,
New hymns to heaven exultin
    raise:
Christ, by a road before untrod
Ascendeth to the throne c
    God.

2 O grant that we may thithe
    tend,
And with unwearied heart
    ascend
Toward thy kingdom's throne
    where thou,
Our great high priest, ar
    seated now.

3 Be thou our joy and stron
    defence,
Who art our future recompense
So shall the light that spring
    from thee
Be ours through all eternity.

4 O risen Christ, ascended Lord,
    All praise to thee let earth
    accord,
Who art, while endless age
    run,
With Father and with Spiri
    One. Amen.

THE VENERABLE BEDE 673–73
Tr. BENJAMIN WEBB, 1820–8
and Compilers of *The BB*
Hymn Boo

306

IMMORTAL Love, for ever
  full,
    For ever flowing free,
For ever shared, for ever whole,
    A never-ebbing sea!

2 Blow, winds of God, awake and
    blow
  The mists of earth away:
Shine out, O Light Divine, and
    show
  How wide and far we stray.

3 We may not climb the heavenly
    steeps
  To bring the Lord Christ
    down;
In vain we search the lowest
    deeps,
  For him no depths can drown.

4 And not for signs in heaven
    above,
  Or earth below, they look
Who know with John his smile
    of love,
  With Peter his rebuke.

5 In joy of inward peace, or sense
  Of sorrow over sin,
He is his own best evidence;
  His witness is within.

6 And, warm, sweet, tender, even
    yet
  A present help is he;
And faith has still its Olivet,
  And love its Galilee.

7 The healing of his seamless
    dress
  Is by our beds of pain;
We touch him in life's throng
    and press,
  And we are whole again.
          JOHN GREENLEAF WHITTIER
                  1807–92

307

'LIFT up your hearts': I hear
  the summons calling
Forth from the heavenly
    altar where he stands—
Our great High Priest, the
    Father's love revealing,
In priestly act, with pleading
    outspread hands.

2 'Lift up your hearts': with
    hearts to heaven soaring
  The Church exulting makes
    her glad reply—
'We lift them up unto the Lord',
    adoring;
  Our God and thine, through
    thee, we glorify.

3 'Lift up your hearts': alas, O
    Lord, I cannot
  Lift up aright my burdened
    heart to thee;
Thou knowest, Lord, the cares
    that weigh upon it,
  The chains that bind it
    struggling to be free.

4 O Love divine! thy promise
    comes to cheer me,
  O Voice of pity! blessing and
    thrice blest—
'Come unto me, ye laden hearts
    and weary,
  Take up my yoke, and learn:
    I pledge you rest'.

5 I dare not waver by such grace
    invited,
  I yield my heart, dear Lord:
    I close the strife.
Lift thou my heart until, with
    thine united,
  I taste anew the joy of endless
    life.
          JOHN MACLEOD, 1840–98, altered

308

NOW at last he takes his
  throne; Alleluia!
From all ages his alone!
    Alleluia!
With his praise creation rings,
Lord of lords and King of kings.

2 Hands and feet and side reveal
Wounds of love, High Priest-
    hood's seal!
Advocate, for us he pleads;
Heavenly Priest, he intercedes!

3 Christians, raise your eyes
    above!
He will come again in love,
On that great and wondrous
    Day
When this world will pass away!

THE WORD OF GOD: HIS MIGHTY ACTS

4 At his word new heavens and earth
Will in glory spring to birth!
Joy of angels, joy of men,
Come, Lord Jesus, come again!

JAMES QUINN

309 *For children*

O SON of Man, our Hero strong
and tender,
Whose servants are the brave
in all the earth,
Our living sacrifice to thee we
render,
Who sharest all our sorrows,
all our mirth.

O feet so strong to climb the
path of duty,
O lips divine that taught the
words of truth,
Kind eyes that marked the
lilies in their beauty,

And heart that kindled at the
zeal of youth;

2 Lover of children, boyhood's
inspiration,
Of all mankind the Servant
and the King;
O Lord of joy and hope and con
solation,
To thee our fears and joy
and hopes we bring.
Not in our failures only and our
sadness
We seek thy presence, Com
forter and Friend;
O rich man's Guest, be with us
in our gladness,
O poor man's Mate, our low
liest tasks attend.

FRANK FLETCHER, 1870–1954

The following are also suitable

No.
158 Give the king thy judgments, O
God
36 The Lord is King! Lift up thy voice

CHRIST'S COMING WITH POWER

310 PSALM 50, verses 1–6, 14 and 23

THE mighty God even the '
Lord hath spoken : and
called the earth from the
rising of the sun unto the
going ' down thereof.

Out of Zion the per ' fection of
beauty : — ' God hath shined.

Our God shall come and shall '
not keep silence : a fire shall
devour before him and it
shall be very tempestuous
round ' about him.

He shall call to the ' heavens from
above : and to the earth that
he may ' judge his people.

Gather my saints to ' gether unto
me : those that have made a
covenant with me by ' sacrifice.

And the heavens shall de ' clare
his righteousness : for God is
judge himself.

Offer unto ' God thanksgiving :
and pay thy vows unto ' the
most High.

Whoso offereth praise ' glori-fieth
me : and to him that ordereth
his conversation aright will
I show the salva ' tion of
God.

Glory be to the ' Father ' and
to the Son : and to the ' Holy
Ghost.

As it was in the beginning is
now and ' ever shall be : world
without ' end Amen.

311
PSALM 96, verses 9, 11–13

IN beauty of his holiness,
　O do the Lord adore;
Likewise let all the earth
　throughout
　　Tremble his face before.
Let heavens be glad before the
　Lord,
　And let the earth rejoice;
Let seas and all their fullness
　roar,
　　And make a mighty noise.

2 Let fields rejoice, and every-
　thing
　That springeth of the earth;
Then of the forest all the trees
　Shall shout aloud with mirth
Before the Lord; because he
　comes,
　To judge the earth comes he;
He'll judge the world with
　righteousness,
　　The people faithfully.

3 All glory be to God on high,
　And to the earth be peace;
Goodwill is shown by heaven to
　men,
　And never more shall cease.
To Father, Son, and Holy Ghost,
　The God whom we adore,
Be glory, as it was, and is,
　And shall be evermore. Amen

The King who reigns in Salem's
　towers
　Shall all the world command.

4 Among the nations he shall
　judge;
　His judgments truth shall
　　guide;
His sceptre shall protect the
　just,
　And quell the sinner's pride.

5 No strife shall rage, nor hostile
　feuds
　Disturb those peaceful years;
To ploughshares men shall beat
　their swords,
　To pruning-hooks their
　　spears.

6 No longer hosts encountering
　hosts
　Shall crowds of slain deplore:
They hang the trumpet in the
　hall,
　And study war no more.

7 Come then, O house of Jacob!
　come
　To worship at his shrine;
And, walking in the light of
　God,
　With holy beauties shine.

Scottish Paraphrases, 1781
From Isaiah 2:2–5

312
PARAPHRASE 18

BEHOLD! the mountain of
　the Lord
In latter days shall rise
On mountain tops above the
　hills,
　And draw the wondering
　　eyes.

2 To this the joyful nations round,
　All tribes and tongues, shall
　　flow;
Up to the hill of God, they'll
　say,
　And to his house we'll go.

3 The beam that shines from
　Zion hill
　Shall lighten every land;

313

CHRIST is coming! let crea-
　tion
　From her groans and travail
　　cease;
Let the glorious proclamation
　Hope restore and faith in-
　　crease:
Christ is coming! Christ is
　coming!
　Come, thou blessèd Prince of
　　Peace.

2 Earth can now but tell the story
　Of thy bitter cross and pain;
She shall yet behold thy glory,
　When thou comest back to
　　reign:

111

Christ is coming! Christ is
coming!
Let each heart repeat the
strain.

3 Long thine exiles have been
pining,
Far from rest, and home, and
thee:
But, in heavenly vestures shining,
They their loving Lord shall
see:
Christ is coming! Christ is
coming!
Haste the joyous jubilee.

4 With that blessèd hope before
us,
Let no harp remain unstrung;
Let the mighty advent chorus
Onward roll from tongue to
tongue:
'Christ is coming! Christ is
coming!
Come, Lord Jesus, quickly
come!'

JOHN ROSS MACDUFF, 1818–95

314

HARK what a sound, and too
divine for hearing,
Stirs on the earth and
trembles in the air!
Is it the thunder of the Lord's
appearing?
Is it the music of his people's
prayer?

2 Surely he cometh, and a thousand voices
Shout to the saints, and to
the deaf are dumb;
Surely he cometh, and the
earth rejoices,
Glad in his coming who hath
sworn, 'I come'.

3 This hath he done, and shall
we not adore him?
This shall he do, and can we
still despair?
Come, let us quickly fling ourselves before him,
Cast at his feet the burden of
our care.

4 Yea, through life, death,
through sorrow and
through sinning
He shall suffice me, for he
hath sufficed:
Christ is the end, for Christ
was the beginning,
Christ the beginning, for
the end is Christ.

FREDERIC WILLIAM HENRY MYERS
1843–1901

315

Wachet auf! ruft uns die
Stimme

'WAKE, awake! for night
is flying,'
The watchmen on the heights
are crying,
'Awake, Jerusalem, at
last!'
Midnight hears the welcome
voices,
And at the thrilling cry rejoices:
'Come forth, ye virgins,
night is past!
The Bridegroom comes;
awake,
Your lamps with glad-
ness take;
Alleluia!
And for his marriage feast
prepare,
For ye must go to meet
him there.'

2 Zion hears the watchmen
singing,
And all her heart with joy is
springing;
She wakes, she rises from
her gloom;
For her Lord comes down all-
glorious,
The strong in grace, in truth
victorious,
Her Star is risen, her Light
is come!
Ah come, thou blessèd
One,
God's own belovèd Son;
Alleluia!
We follow till the halls we
see
Where thou hast bid us sup
with thee.

3   Now let all the heavens adore thee,
And men and angels sing before thee,
    With harp and cymbal's clearest tone;
Of one pearl each shining portal,
Where we are with the choir immortal
    Of angels round thy dazzling throne;
    Nor eye hath seen, nor ear
    Hath yet attained to hear
    What there is ours;
But we rejoice, and sing to thee
Our hymn of joy eternally.
        PHILIPP NICOLAI, 1556–1608
        Tr. CATHERINE WINKWORTH
        1827–78

316

LO! he comes, with clouds descending,
    Once for favoured sinners slain;
Thousand thousand saints attending
    Swell the triumph of his train;
    Alleluia! Alleluia! Alleluia!
    God appears on earth to reign.

2 Every eye shall now behold him,
    Robed in dreadful majesty;
Those who set at naught and sold him,
    Pierced, and nailed him to the tree,
    Deeply wailing, deeply wailing,
Shall the true Messiah see.

3 Those dear tokens of his Passion
    Still his dazzling body bears;
Cause of endless exaltation
    To his ransomed worshippers;
    Alleluia! Alleluia! Alleluia!
    See! the day of God appears!

4 Yea, Amen! let all adore thee,
    High on thine eternal throne;
Saviour, take the power and glory,
    Claim the kingdom for thine own:
    O come quickly; O come quickly; O come quickly;
    Alleluia! come, Lord, come!
        CHARLES WESLEY, 1707–88
        altered
    Based on a hymn by JOHN CENNICK
        1718–55

317

HAIL to the Lord's Anointed,
    Great David's greater Son!
Hail, in the time appointed,
    His reign on earth begun!
He comes to break oppression,
    To set the captive free,
To take away transgression,
    And rule in equity.

2 He comes with succour speedy
    To those who suffer wrong,
To help the poor and needy,
    And bid the weak be strong;
To give them songs for sighing,
    Their darkness turn to light
Whose souls, condemned and dying,
    Were precious in his sight.

3 He shall come down like showers
    Upon the fruitful earth,
And love, joy, hope, like flowers,
    Spring in his path to birth.
Before him, on the mountains,
    Shall peace, the herald, go;
And righteousness in fountains
    From hill to valley flow.

4 For him shall prayer unceasing
    And daily vows ascend,
His Kingdom still increasing,
    A Kingdom without end.
The mountain dews shall nourish
    A seed, in weakness sown,
Whose fruit shall spread and flourish
    And shake like Lebanon.

5 O'er every foe victorious,
   He on his throne shall rest,
From age to age more glorious,
   All blessing and all-blest.
The tide of time shall never
   His covenant remove;
His Name shall stand for ever;
   That Name to us is Love.

JAMES MONTGOMERY, 1771–1854
From Psalm 72

318(i)

MINE eyes have seen the
   glory of the coming of the
   Lord:
He is trampling out the vintage
   where the grapes of wrath
   are stored;
He hath loosed the fatal lighting of his terrible swift
   sword:
      His truth is marching on.

2 He hath sounded forth the
   trumpet that shall never
   call retreat;
He is sifting out the hearts of
   men before his judgment-
   seat:
O, be swift, my soul, to answer
   him; be jubilant, my feet!
      Our God is marching on.

3 In the beauty of the lilies Christ
   was born across the sea,
With a glory in his bosom that
   transfigures you and me:
As he died to make men holy,
   let us live to make men free,
      While God is marching
        on.

4 He is coming like the glory of
   the morning on the wave;
He is wisdom to the mighty; he
   is succour to the brave;
So the world shall be his foot-
   stool, and the soul of time
   his slave:
      Our God is marching on!

JULIA WARD HOWE, 1819–1910
and others

318(ii)

MINE eyes have seen the
   glory of the coming of the
   Lord:
He is trampling out the vintage
   where the grapes of wrath are
   stored;
He hath loosed the fatal lighting of his terrible swift
   sword:
      His truth is marching on.
      Glory, glory, Alleluia!
      Glory, glory, Alleluia!
      Glory, glory, Alleluia!
      His truth is marching on.

2 He hath sounded forth the
   trumpet that shall never
   call retreat;
He is sifting out the hearts of
   men before his judgment-
   seat:
O, be swift, my soul, to answer
   him; be jubilant, my feet!
      Our God is marching on.
      Glory, glory, Alleluia!
      Glory, glory, Alleluia!
      Glory, glory, Alleluia!
      Our God is marching on.

3 In the beauty of the lilies Christ
   was born across the sea,
With a glory in his bosom that
   transfigures you and me:
As he died to make men holy,
   let us live to make men free,
      While God is marching on.
      Glory, glory, Alleluia!
      Glory, glory, Alleluia!
      Glory, glory, Alleluia!
      While God is marching
        on.

4 He is coming like the glory of
   the morning on the wave;
He is wisdom to the mighty; he
   is succour to the brave;
So the world shall be his foot-
   stool, and the soul of time
   his slave:
      Our God is marching on.
      Glory, glory, Alleluia!
      Glory, glory, Alleluia!
      Glory, glory, Alleluia!
      Our God is marching on.

JULIA WARD HOWE, 1819–1910
and others

319

YE servants of the Lord,
　　Each in his office wait,
Observant of his heavenly word,
　And watchful at his gate.

Let all your lamps be bright,
　And trim the golden flame;
Gird up your loins, as in his
　　sight,
　For awesome is his name.

Watch: 'tis your Lord's com-
　　mand,
　And while we speak he's near;
Mark the first signal of his hand,
　And ready all appear.

O happy servant he,
　In such a posture found!
He shall his Lord with rapture
　　see,
　And be with honour crowned.

Christ shall the banquet
　　spread
　With his own royal hand,
And raise that faithful servant's
　　head
　Amid the angelic band.

　　　　PHILIP DODDRIDGE, 1702–51

320

COME, thou long-expected
　　Jesus,
　Born to set thy people free;
From our fears and sins release
　　us;
　Let us find our rest in thee.

Israel's Strength and Consola-
　　tion,
　Hope of all the earth thou art,
Dear Desire of every nation,
　Joy of every longing heart.

Born thy people to deliver,
　Born a Child and yet a King,
Born to reign in us for ever,
　Now thy gracious Kingdom
　　bring.

4 By thine own eternal Spirit
　　Rule in all our hearts alone;
By thine all-sufficient merit
　　Raise us to thy glorious
　　　throne.

　　　　CHARLES WESLEY, 1707–88

321

THE Lord will come and not
　　be slow,
　His footsteps cannot err;
Before him righteousness shall
　　go,
　His royal harbinger.
Truth from the earth, like to a
　　flower,
　Shall bud and blossom then;
And justice, from her heavenly
　　bower,
　Look down on mortal men.

2 Surely to such as do him fear
　　Salvation is at hand!
And glory shall ere long appear
　　To dwell within our land.
Rise, God, judge thou the earth
　　in might,
　This wicked earth redress;
For thou art he who shall by
　　right
　The nations all possess.

3 The nations all whom thou hast
　　made
　　Shall come, and all shall
　　　frame
To bow them low before thee,
　　Lord,
　And glorify thy Name.
For great thou art, and wonders
　　great
　By thy strong hand are done:
Thou in thy everlasting seat
　　Remainest God alone.

　　　　JOHN MILTON, 1608–74
　　　　From Psalms 85, 82, 86

322

THY Kingdom come, O God;
　　Thy rule, O Christ, begin;
Break with thine iron rod
　　The tyrannies of sin.

2 Where is thy reign of peace
   And purity and love?
When shall all hatred cease,
   As in the realms above?

3 When comes the promised time
   That war shall be no more,
And lust, oppression, crime,
   Shall flee thy face before?

4 We pray thee, Lord, arise,
   And come in thy great might;
Revive our longing eyes,
   Which languish for thy sight.

5 Men scorn thy sacred Name,
   And wolves devour thy fold;
By many deeds of shame
   We learn that love grows
      cold.

6 O'er lands both near and far
   Thick darkness broodeth yet;
Arise, O Morning Star,
   Arise, and never set.

LEWIS HENSLEY, 1824–1905
altered

323

'THY Kingdom come!'—on
   bended knee
The passing ages pray;
And faithful souls have yearned
      to see
   On earth that Kingdom's
      day.

2 But the slow watches of the
      night
Not less to God belong;
And for the everlasting right
   The silent stars are strong.

3 And lo! already on the hills
   The flags of dawn appear;
Gird up your loins, ye prophet
      souls,
   Proclaim the day is near:

4 The day in whose clear-shining
      light
All wrong shall stand re-
      vealed,
When justice shall be throned
      with might,
   And every hurt be healed:

5 When knowledge, hand in hand
      with peace,
   Shall walk the earth
      abroad,—
The day of perfect righteous-
      ness,
   The promised day of God.

FREDERICK LUCIAN HOSMER
1840–192

324

BLEST is the man, O God
   That stays himself on thee
Who wait for thy salvation
      Lord,
   Shall thy salvation see.

2 When we in darkness walk,
   Nor feel the heavenly flame
Then is the time to trust ou
      God,
   And rest upon his Name.

3 Soon shall our doubts and
      fears
   Subside at his control;
His loving-kindness shall break
      through
   The midnight of the soul.

4 Wait till the shadows flee;
   Wait thy appointed hour;
Wait till the Bridegroom of thy
      soul
   Reveals his love with power

AUGUSTUS MONTAGUE TOPLADY
1740–78

325

*Ἀπὸ δόξης εἰς δόξαν
πορευόμενοι*

FROM glory to glory advanc-
      ing, we praise thee, O
      Lord;
Thy Name with the Father and
   Spirit be ever adored.

2 From strength unto strength
   we go forward on Zion's
      highway,
To appear before God in the
   city of infinite day.

3 Thanksgiving, and glory and
   worship, and blessing and
   love,
One heart and one song have
   the saints upon earth and
   above.

4 O Lord, evermore to thy servants thy presence be nigh;
Ever fit us by service on earth
   for thy service on high.

From the Liturgy of St. James
Tr. CHARLES WILLIAM HUMPHREYS
1840–1921

The following are also suitable

No.
  12 Lift up your heads, ye mighty gates
 505 Christ is the world's true light

PENTECOST

326   PSALM 104, verses 1–5,
             30–4

BLESS the Lord ' O my soul :
  O Lord my God thou art
very great thou art clothed
with honour and ' majesty.

Who coverest thyself with light
as ' with a garment : who
stretchest out the heavens '
like a curtain.

Who layeth the beams of his
chambers ' in the waters : who
maketh the clouds his chariot
who walketh upon the wings '
of the wind.

Who maketh his ' angels spirits : his ministers a ' flaming
fire.

Who laid the foun ' dations of
the earth : that it should not
be re ' moved for ever.

Thou sendest forth thy spirit
they ' are created : and thou
renewest the face ' of the
earth.

The glory of the Lord shall
en ' dure for ever : the Lord
shall rejoice in ' all his works.

He looketh on the earth ' and it
trembleth : he toucheth the
hills ' and they smoke.

I will sing unto the Lord as '
long as I live : I will sing
praise to my God while I '
have my being.

My meditation of ' him shall be
sweet : I will be glad ' in the
Lord.

*Glory be to the ' Father and to the
Son : and to the ' Holy Ghost.*

*As it was in the beginning is
now and ' ever shall be : world
without ' end Amen.*

327

O DAY of joy and wonder!
  Christ's promise now ful-
  filled!
The coming of his Spirit
The Father's love has willed;
Our Lord in human body,
To mortal eye is lost,
Yet he returns for ever
At blessèd Pentecost!

2 The world in sheer amazement,
The truth must now declare,
That men who once were
   cowards,
Are brave beyond compare,
And tongues which could not
   utter
Their faith in Jesus' name,
Defy all persecution,
His glory to proclaim!

3 We too may know thy power,
Thy courage makes us strong,
Thy love, thy joy, thy patience,
Can all to us belong,

If thou wilt dwell within us,
A Comforter divine;
Come to our hearts, we pray
thee,
And keep them ever thine.

VIOLET BUCHANAN

328 *Salve, festa dies, toto venerabilis aevo*

* HAIL thee, Festival Day! blest
day that art hallowed for ever;
*Day wherein God from heaven
shone on the world with his
grace.*

2 Lo! in the likeness of fire, on
them that await his appearing,
He whom the Lord foretold,
suddenly, swiftly, descends.

3 Forth from the Father he comes
with his sevenfold mystical
dowry,
Pouring on human souls infinite
riches of God.

4 Hark! in a hundred tongues
Christ's own, his chosen
Apostles,
Preach to a hundred tribes
Christ and his wonderful
works.

5 Praise to the Spirit of life, all
praise to the Fount of our
being,
Light that dost lighten all,
Life that in all dost abide.

c. 14th century (York Processional)
Tr. GABRIEL GILLETT, 1873–1948

* *Verse 1 is also sung as a refrain
after each verse.*

329 *Beata nobis gaudia*

O JOY! because the circling
year
Hath brought our day of blessing here,
The day when first the light
divine
Upon the Church began to
shine.

2 Like unto quivering tongues of
flame
Upon each one the Spirit
came,—
Tongues, that the earth might
hear their call,
And fire, that love might burn
in all.

3 Thus wondrously were spread
abroad
To all the wondrous works of
God;
To each in his familiar tone
The glorious marvel was made
known.

4 While hardened scoffers vainly
jeered,
The listening strangers heard
and feared;
They knew the prophet's word
fulfilled,
And owned the work which God
had willed.

5 *Praise we the Father and the Son,
And Holy Spirit with them One:
And may the Son on us bestow
The gifts that from the Spirit
flow.*
Amen.

c. 4th century
Tr. JOHN ELLERTON, 1826–93
and Compilers of *Hymns Ancient
and Modern*
Based on Acts 2: 1–4.

330 *Beata nobis gaudia*

REJOICE! the year upon its
way
Has brought again that blessèd
day,
When on the chosen of the Lord
The Holy Spirit was outpoured.

2 On each the fire, descending,
stood
In quivering tongues' simi-
litude—
Tongues, that their words might
ready prove,
And fire, to make them flame
with love.

118

3 And now, O holy God, this day
Regard us as we humbly pray,
And send us, from thy heavenly seat,
The blessings of the Paraclete.

4 *To God the Father, God the Son,*
And God the Spirit, praise be done;
May Christ the Lord upon us pour
The Spirit's gift for evermore.
Amen.

c. 4th century
Tr. RICHARD ELLIS ROBERTS
1879–1953
Based on Acts 2:1–4

5 So, when the Spirit of our God
Came down his flock to find,
A voice from heaven was heard abroad,
A rushing mighty wind.

6 It fills the Church of God; it fills
The sinful world around;
Only in stubborn hearts and wills
No place for it is found.

7 Come, Lord; come, Wisdom, Love, and Power;
Open our ears to hear;
Let us not miss the accepted hour;
Save, Lord, by love or fear.

JOHN KEBLE, 1792–1866
* *This verse may be omitted.*

331

WHEN God of old came down from heaven,
In power and wrath he came;
Before his feet the clouds were riven,
Half darkness and half flame.

2 But, when he came the second time,
He came in power and love;
Softer than gale at morning prime
Hovered his holy Dove.

*3 The fires that rushed on Sinai down
In sudden torrents dread,
Now gently light, a glorious crown,
On every sainted head.

4 And, as on Israel's awe-struck ear
The voice exceeding loud,
The trump that angels quake to hear,
Thrilled from the deep, dark cloud,

332

LORD God, the Holy Ghost,
In this accepted hour,
As on the day of Pentecost,
Descend in all thy power.

2 We meet with one accord
In our appointed place,
And wait the promise of our Lord,
The Spirit of all grace.

3 Like mighty rushing wind
Upon the waves beneath,
Move with one impulse every mind;
One soul, one feeling breathe.

4 The young, the old inspire
With wisdom from above;
And give us hearts and tongues of fire,
To pray and praise and love.

5 Spirit of light, explore
And chase our gloom away,
With lustre shining more and more
Unto the perfect day.

JAMES MONTGOMERY, 1771–1854

THE HOLY SPIRIT IN THE CHURCH

333 PSALM 102 (ii), verses
13–18

THOU shalt arise, and mercy
yet
Thou to mount Zion shalt extend:
The time is come for favour
set,
The time when thou shalt blessing send.

2 Thy saints take pleasure in her
stones,
Her very dust to them is dear.
All heathen lands and kingly
thrones
On earth thy glorious Name shall
fear.

3 God in his glory shall appear,
When Zion he builds and re-
pairs.
He shall regard and lend his ear
Unto the needy's humble
prayers:

4 The afflicted's prayer he will not
scorn.
All times this shall be on record:
And generations yet unborn
Shall praise and magnify the
Lord.

5 *To Father, Son, and Holy Ghost,*
The God whom earth and heaven
adore,
Be glory, as it was of old,
Is now, and shall be evermore.
Amen.

334

HOLY Spirit, ever living
As the Church's very life;
Holy Spirit, ever striving
Through her in a ceaseless
strife;
Holy Spirit, ever forming
In the Church the mind of
Christ;
Thee we praise with endless
worship
For thy fruit and gifts unpriced.

2 Holy Spirit, ever working
Through the Church's ministry;
Quick'ning, strength'ning, and
absolving,
Setting captive sinners free;
Holy Spirit, ever binding
Age to age, and soul to soul,
In a fellowship unending
Thee we worship and extol.
TIMOTHY REES, 1874–1939

335

LOVE of the Father, Love of
God the Son,
From whom all came, in whom
was all begun;
Who formest heavenly beauty
out of strife,
Creation's whole desire and
breath of life:

2 Thou the All-holy, thou
supreme in might,
Thou dost give peace, thy presence maketh right;
Thou with thy favour all things
dost enfold,
With thine all-kindness free
from harm wilt hold.

3 Purest and highest, wisest and
most just,
There is no truth save only in
thy trust;
Thou dost the mind from
earthly dreams recall,
And bring, through Christ, to
him for whom are all.

4 Eternal Glory, all men thee
adore,
Who art and shalt be wor-
shipped evermore:
Us whom thou madest, comfort
with thy might,
And lead us to enjoy thy
heavenly light.
ROBERT BRIDGES, 1844–1930
Based on *Amor Patris et Filii*
12th century

336

OUR blest Redeemer, ere he breathed
His tender last farewell,
A Guide, a Comforter bequeathed,
With us to dwell.

2 He came in tongues of living flame,
To teach, convince, subdue;
All-powerful as the wind he came,
As viewless too.

3 He came sweet influence to impart,
A gracious, willing Guest,
While he can find one humble heart
Wherein to rest.

4 And his that gentle voice we hear,
Soft as the breath of even,
That checks each fault, that calms each fear,
And speaks of heaven.

5 And every virtue we possess,
And every victory won,
And every thought of holiness,
Are his alone.

6 Spirit of purity and grace,
Our weakness, pitying, see;
O make our hearts thy dwelling-place,
And worthier thee.
HENRIETTE AUBER, 1773–1862

337

FOR thy gift of God the Spirit,
With us, in us, e'er to be,
Pledge of life and hope of glory,
Saviour, we would worship thee.

2 He who in creation's dawning
Brooded o'er the pathless deep,
Still across our nature's darkness
Moves to wake our souls from sleep.

3 He it is, the living Author,
Wakes to life the sacred Word;
Reads with us its holy pages,
And reveals our risen Lord.

4 He it is who works within us,
Teaching rebel hearts to pray;
He whose holy intercessions
Rise for us both night and day.

5 Fill us with thy holy fullness,
God the Father, Spirit, Son;
In us, through us, then, forever,
Shall thy perfect will be done.
EDITH MARGARET CLARKSON

338

SPIRIT of mercy, truth and love,
O shed thine influence from above,
And still from age to age convey
The wonders of this sacred day.

2 In every clime, by every tongue,
Be God's surpassing glory sung:
Let all the listening earth be taught
The acts our great Redeemer wrought.

3 Unfailing Comfort, heavenly Guide,
Still o'er thy Holy Church preside;
Still let mankind thy blessings prove;
Spirit of mercy, truth and love.
Anonymous. Foundling Hospital Collection, 1774

339

O BREATH of life, come sweeping through us,
Revive thy Church with life and power;
O Breath of life, come, cleanse, renew us,
And fit thy Church to meet this hour.

2 O Wind of God, come bend us,
    break us,
  Till humbly we confess our
    need;
  Then in thy tenderness remake
    us,
  Revive, restore; for this we
    plead.

3 O Breath of love, come breathe
    within us,
  Renewing thought and will and
    heart:
  Come, Love of Christ, afresh to
    win us,
  Revive thy Church in every
    part.

4 Revive us, Lord! is zeal abating
  While harvest fields are vast
    and white?
  Revive us, Lord, the world is
    waiting,
  Equip thy Church to spread the
    light.
          BESSIE PORTER HEAD, 1850–1936

340

SPIRIT of Light—Holy,
  Shine in this world of thine;
Lighten thou our darkness,
    clear
Blindness from out our minds.
Guide thou our ways, so may
    we
Walk in the light of thy truth,
Come, Spirit, come.

2 Spirit of Love—Holy,
  Fire thou this world of thine;
  Chasten thou the pride of race
  Marring our common life.
  Kindle our love, that loving,
  All may true brotherhood find,
  Come, Spirit, come.

3 Spirit of Life—Holy,
  Breathe o'er this world of
    thine;
  Teach us all to know and do
  All that will make men free.
  Thy kingdom come, on earth as
  In thy blest heaven above,
  Come, Spirit, come.

4 Spirit of Power—Holy,
  Mighty and infinite;
  Work within this world of thine
  Breaking the powers of sin.
  Take thou thy throne, and
    reigning,
  Claim the whole world for thine
    own.
  Great Spirit, come.
          ARTHUR MORRIS JONES

341

HOW great the harvest is
    Of him who came to save
    us!
The hearts of men are his,
    Our law the love he gave us.
The world lay cruel, blind,
    Naught holding, naught
    divining;
He came to human kind,
    And now the light is shining,
    Is shining, is shining.

2 And though the news did seem
    Too good for man's believing,
  'Tis not an empty dream
    Too high for our achieving.
  He triumphed in the strife,
    O'er all his foes he towered;
  They killed the Prince of Life,
    But he hath death o'er-
    powered, o'erpowered,
    O'erpowered, o'erpowered.

3 Then came the Father's call;
    His work on earth was
    ended;
  That he might light on all,
    To heaven the Lord ascended.
  To heaven so near to earth
    Our hearts we do surrender:
  There all things find their worth
    And human life its splendour,
    Its splendour, its splendour.

4 The power by which there came
    The Word of God among us
  Was love's eternal flame,
    Whose light and heat are
    flung us;
  That Spirit sent from God,
    Within our hearts abiding,

Hath brought us on our road
   And still the world is guiding,
     is guiding,
   Is guiding, is guiding.

In Three made manifest,
   Thou source of all our being,
Thou loveliest, truest, best,
   Beyond our power of seeing;
Thou power of light and love,
   Thou life that never diest—
To thee in whom all move
   Be glory in the highest, the
     highest,
   The highest, the highest,
     PERCY DEARMER, 1867–1936

42   *Veni, Creator Spiritus*

COME, Hŏly Ghŏst, our souls
   inspire
And lighten wĭth celĕstial fire;
Thou thĕ anŏinting Spĭrit art,
Who dost thy sĕvenfold gĭfts
   impart.

Thy blĕssèd ŭnction frŏm above
Is comfort, lĭfe, and fĭre of love;
Enăble wĭth perpĕtual light
The dulness ŏf our blĭnded
   sight:

Anŏint and chĕer our sŏilèd
   face
With the abŭndance ŏf thy
   grace:
Keep făr our fŏes; give pĕace at
   home:
Where thou art Guĭde no ĭll can
   come.

Teach ŭs to knŏw the Făther,
   Son,
And thee of Bŏth, to bĕ but
   One,

That thrŏugh the ăges ăll along
Thĭs may bĕ our ĕndless song,
   'Praĭse   to thĭne etĕrnal
     merit,
   Făther, Sŏn, and Hŏly Spĭrit.'
            Ămen.
             9th century
    Tr. JOHN COSIN, 1594–1672
   The following are also suitable
No.
103 Breathe on me, Breath of God
104 Come, Holy Spirit, come
105 Come, thou Holy Paraclete
115 Come down, O Love Divine
*See also hymns on the Holy Spirit in
Part I, Section 2 and Part I, Section 3*

343(i)

          Alleluia!

343(ii)

     Alleluia, Alleluia, Alleluia!

343(iii)

Alleluia, Alleluia,
Praise God the Lord most high.
Alleluia, Alleluia,
His word doth last for aye.

344

GLORY be to the Father,
   and to the Son, and to the
   Holy Ghost:
As it was in the beginning, is
   now, and ever shall be,
   world without end. Amen.

III

RESPONSE TO THE WORD OF GOD

ADORATION AND THANKSGIVING

345 TE DEUM LAUDAMUS

Chant A

WE praise ' thee O ' God :
we ac- ' knowledge thee
to ' be the ' Lord :
All the ' earth doth ' worship
thee : the ' Father ' everlasting.

2 To thee all angels ' cry a- '
loud : the ' heavens and ' all
the ' powers therein :
To thee ' cherubim and '
seraphim : con- ' tinual- ' ly
do ' cry.

3 Holy holy holy Lord ' God of
Sa- ' baoth : heaven and
earth are full of the '
majesty ' of thy ' glory :
The glorious company of the
a- ' postles ' praise thee : the
goodly ' fellowship of the '
prophets ' praise thee.

4 The noble army of ' martyrs '
praise thee : the ' holy
Church throughout ' all the '
world doth ac- ' knowledge
thee :
The Father of an ' infinite '
majesty : thine honourable
true and only Son also
the ' Holy ' Ghost the ' Comforter.

Chant B

5 Thou art the King of ' Glory
O ' Christ : thou art the ever- '
lasting ' Son of the ' Father :
When thou tookest upon thee
to de- ' liver ' man : thou
didst not ab- ' hor the '
Virgin's ' womb.

6 When thou hadst overcom[e]
the ' sharpness of ' death
thou didst open the King[-]
dom of ' heaven to ' a
be- ' lievers :
Thou sittest at the ' righ[t]
hand of ' God : in the
glory ' of the ' Father.

7 We believe that thou sha[lt]
come to ' be our ' Judge
we therefore pray thee hel[p]
thy servants whom tho[u]
hast re- ' deemed with thy '
precious ' blood :
Make them to be ' numbere[d]
with thy ' saints : in ' glory
ever- ' lasting.

Chant C

8 O Lord save thy people and
bless thine ' heritage :
govern them and ' lift them
up for ' ever :
Day by day we ' magnify
thee : and we worshi[p]
thy ' Name ever ' worl[d]
without ' end.

9 Vouchsafe O Lord to keep u[s]
this ' day without ' sin
O Lord have mercy up- ' o[n]
us have ' mercy up- ' on us
O Lord let thy mercy lighte[n]
upon us as our ' trust is in
thee : O Lord in thee hav[e]
I trusted let me ' never
be con- ' founded.

346 PSALM 145 (ii), verses 1–6

O LORD, thou art my Go[d]
and King ;
Thee will I magnify and prais[e]
I will thee bless, and gladly sin[g]
Unto thy holy Name always.

Each day I rise I will thee bless,
And praise thy Name time with-
out end.
Much to be praised, and great
God is;
His greatness none can compre-
hend.

Race shall thy works praise
unto race,
The mighty acts show done by
thee.
I will speak of the glorious
grace,
And honour of thy majesty;

Thy wondrous works I will
record.
By men the might shall be ex-
tolled
Of all thy dreadful acts, O
Lord:
And I thy greatness will unfold.

To Father, Son, and Holy Ghost,
The God whom earth and
heaven adore,
Be glory, as it was of old,
Is now, and shall be evermore.
Amen.

47   PSALM 150

PRAISE ye the Lord. God's
praise within
His sanctuary raise;
And to him in the firmament
Of his power give ye praise.

Because of all his mighty acts,
With praise him magnify:
O praise him, as he doth excel
In glorious majesty.

Praise him with trumpet's
sound; his praise
With psaltery advance:
With timbrel, harp, stringed
instruments,
And organs, in the dance.

Praise him on cymbals loud;
him praise
On cymbals sounding high.
Let each thing breathing praise
the Lord.
Praise to the Lord give ye.

5 *To Father, Son, and Holy Ghost,*
    The God whom we adore,
   Be glory, as it was, and is,
     And shall be evermore. Amen.

348   PSALM 98, verses 1–3, 5–9

SING a new song to Jehovah,
    For he wondrous things
    hath wrought;
His right hand and arm most
    holy
    Victory to him have brought.

2 Lo! the Lord his great salvation
    Openly hath now made
    known;
In the sight of every nation
    He his righteousness hath
    shown.

3 Mindful of his truth and
    mercy
    He to Israel's house hath
    been;
And the Lord our God's salva-
    tion
    All the ends of earth have
    seen.

4 Sound the trumpet and the
    cornet,
    Shout before the Lord the
    King;
Sea, and all its fullness,
    thunder;
    Earth, and all its people,
    sing.

5 Let the rivers in their gladness
    Clap their hands with one
    accord;
Let the mountains sing together
    Joyfully before the Lord.

6 For to judge the earth he
    cometh;
    And with righteousness shall
    he
Judge the world, and all the
    nations
    With most perfect equity.

7 *Glory be to God, the Father;*
    Glory be to God, the Son;
    Glory be to God, the Spirit;
    While eternal ages run. Amen.

349

PSALM 98

O SING unto the Lord a
new song for he hath
done ' marvellous ' things :
his right hand and his holy '
arm hath ' gotten him · the '
victory :
The Lord hath made ' known
his sal- ' vation : his righteousness hath he openly '
showed in the ' sight of the '
heathen.

2 He hath remembered his
mercy and his truth to-
ward the ' house of ' Israel :
all the ends of the earth
have seen the sal- ' vation '
of our ' God :
Make a joyful noise unto the
Lord ' all the ' earth : make
a loud ' noise and re- ' joice
and sing ' praise.

3 Sing unto the ' Lord with the '
harp : with the ' harp and
the ' voice of a ' psalm :
With trumpets and ' sound of '
cornet : make a joyful ' noise
before the ' Lord the ' King.

4 Let the sea roar, and the ' fullness there- ' of : the ' world
and ' they that ' dwell
therein :
Let the ' floods clap their '
hands : let the hills be joyful to- ' gether be- ' fore
the ' Lord.

5 For he cometh to ' judge the '
earth : with righteousness
shall he judge the ' world
and the ' people with '
equity.

Glory ' *be to the* ' *Father : and to*
the Son ' *and to the* ' *Holy* '
Ghost :
As it ' *was in the be-* ' *ginning :*
is now and ever shall be '
world without ' *end.*
A- ' men.

350

PSALM 136, Gelineau
version

O give thanks to the Lor
for he is good,
*Great is his love, love withou
end.*

Give thanks to the God of gods
*Great is his love, love withou
end.*

Give thanks to the Lord c
lords,
*Great is his love, love withou
end.*

2 Who alone has wrought mar
vellous works,
*Great is his love, love withou
end.*
Whose wisdom it was made th
skies,
*Great is his love, love withou
end.*
Who, spread the earth on th
seas,
*Great is his love, love withou
end.*

3 It was he who made the grea
lights,
*Great is his love, love withou
end.*
The sun to rule in the day,
*Great is his love, love withou
end.*
The moon and stars in the night
*Great is his love, love withou
end.*

4 The first-born of the Egyptian
he smote,
*Great is his love, love withou
end.*
Brought Israel out from thei
midst,
*Great is his love, love withou
end.*
Arm outstretched with powe
in his hand,
*Great is his love, love withou
end.*

He let Israel inherit their land,
*Great is his love, love without
end.*

On his servant their land he
bestowed,
*Great is his love, love without
end.*

He remembered us in our distress
*Great is his love, love without
end.*

And he snatched us away from
our foes,
*Great is his love, love without
end.*

He gives food to all living
things,
*Great is his love, love without
end.*

To the God of heaven give
thanks,
*Great is his love, love without
end.*

* A more literal translation of the
Refrain is: 'For his great love is without
end.' But this does not fit the musical
setting so well.

351

PSALM 103, verses 1–5

O THOU my soul, bless God
the Lord;
And all that in me is
Be stirred up his holy Name
To magnify and bless.

2 Bless, O my soul, the Lord thy
God,
And not forgetful be
Of all his gracious benefits
He hath bestowed on thee.

3 All thine iniquities who doth
Most graciously forgive;
Who thy diseases all and pains
Doth heal, and thee relieve.

4 Who doth redeem thy life, that
thou
To death mayest not go
down;

Who thee with loving-kindness
doth
And tender mercies crown:

5 Who with abundance of good
things
Doth satisfy thy mouth;
So that, even as the eagle's age,
Renewed is thy youth.

6 *To Father, Son, and Holy Ghost,
The God whom we adore,
Be glory, as it was, and is,
And shall be evermore. Amen.*

352

HOLY, holy, holy, Lord
God Almighty!
Early in the morning our song
shall rise to thee;
Holy, holy, holy, merciful and
mighty,
God in Three Persons, blessèd
Trinity!

2 Holy, holy, holy! all the saints
adore thee,
Casting down their golden
crowns around the glassy
sea,
Cherubim and seraphim falling
down before thee,
Which wert, and art, and
evermore shalt be.

3 Holy, holy, holy! though the
darkness hide thee,
Though the eye of sinful man
thy glory may not see,
Only thou art holy; there is
none beside thee,
Perfect in power, in love, and
purity.

*Holy, holy, holy, Lord God
Almighty!
All thy works shall praise thy
Name in earth and sky and
sea;
Holy, holy, holy, merciful and
mighty,
God in Three Persons, blessèd
Trinity! Amen.*
REGINALD HEBER, 1783–1826

RESPONSE TO THE WORD OF GOD

353

ROUND the Lord in glory
   seated,
Cherubim and seraphim
Filled his temple, and repeated
Each to each the alternate
   hymn:
   'Lord thy glory fills the
      heaven;
   Earth is with its fullness
      stored;
   Unto thee be glory given,
   Holy, holy, holy Lord.'

2 Heaven is still with glory ring-
   ing,
Earth takes up the angels'
   cry,
'Holy, holy, holy,' singing,
   'Lord of hosts, the Lord
     most high.'

3 With his seraph train before
   him,
With his holy Church below,
Thus conspire we to adore him,
Bid we thus our anthem flow:
    RICHARD MANT, 1776–1848

354

GLORY be to God the Father,
   Glory be to God the Son,
Glory be to God the Spirit,—
   Great Jehovah, Three in
     One!
   Glory, glory, glory, glory
   While eternal ages run!

2 Glory be to him who loved us,
   Washed us from each spot
     and stain!
Glory be to him who bought us,
   Made us kings with him to
     reign!
   Glory, glory, glory, glory
   To the Lamb that once was
     slain!

3 Glory to the King of angels,
   Glory to the Church's King,
Glory to the King of nations!
   Heaven and earth, your
     praises bring;
   Glory, glory, glory, glory
   To the King of Glory bring!

4 'Glory, blessing, praise eternal!'
   Thus the choir of angels sings
'Honour, riches, power, do-
    minion!'
Thus its praise creation
    brings;
   Glory, glory, glory, glory
   Glory to the King of kings!
             Amen
    HORATIUS BONAR, 1808–8

355
       Gott ist gegenwärtig

GOD reveals his presence:
   Let us now adore him,
And with awe appear before
   him.
God is in his temple:
   All within keep silence,
Prostrate lie with deepest re-
   verence.
     Him alone
     God we own,
Him our God and Saviour:
Praise his Name for ever.

2 God reveals his presence:
   Hear the harps resounding,
See the crowds the throne sur-
   rounding;
   Holy, holy, holy!
Hear the hymn ascending,
Angels, saints, their voice
   blending.
     Bow thine ear
     To us here;
Hearken, O Lord Jesus,
To our meaner praises.

3 O thou Fount of blessing
   Purify my spirit,
Trusting only in thy merit:
   Like the holy angels
   Who behold thy glory,
May I ceaselessly adore thee.
     Let thy will
     Ever still
Rule thy Church terrestrial,
As the hosts celestial.

    GERHARD TERSTEEGEN, 1697–176
    Tr. FREDERICK WILLIAM FOSTE
               1760–183
      and JOHN MILLER, 1756–9
    revised WILLIAM MERCER 1811–7

356

MY God, how wonderful thou
art,
Thy majesty how bright!
How beautiful thy mercy-seat,
In depths of burning light!

2 How dread are thine eternal
years,
O everlasting Lord,
By prostrate spirits day and
night
Incessantly adored!

3 O how I fear thee, living God,
With deepest, tenderest fears,
And worship thee with trembl-
ing hope
And penitential tears!

4 Yet I may love thee too, O Lord,
Almighty as thou art,
For thou hast stooped to ask of
me
The love of my poor heart.

5 No earthly father loves like
thee;
No mother, e'er so mild,
Bears and forbears as thou hast
done
With me, thy sinful child.

6 How beautiful, how beautiful
The sight of thee must be,
Thine endless wisdom, bound-
less power,
And awesome purity!
FREDERICK WILLIAM FABER
1814–63

357

ETERNAL Light! eternal
Light!
How pure the soul must be,
When, placed within thy search-
ing sight,
It shrinks not, but, with calm
delight,
Can live, and look on thee!

2 The spirits that surround thy
throne
May bear the burning bliss;
But that is surely theirs alone,
Since they have never, never
known
A fallen world like this.

3 O how shall I, whose native
sphere
Is dark, whose mind is dim,
Before the Ineffable appear,
And on my naked spirit bear
The uncreated beam?

4 There is a way for man to rise
To that sublime abode:
An offering and a sacrifice,
A Holy Spirit's energies,
An Advocate with God.

5 These, these prepare us for the
sight
Of holiness above:
The sons of ignorance and night
May dwell in God's eternal
Light,
Through his eternal Love!
THOMAS BINNEY, 1798–1874
altered

358

THE God of Abraham
praise,
Who reigns enthroned above,
Ancient of everlasting days,
And God of love.
Jehovah, Great I AM!
By earth and heaven con-
fessed,
I bow, and bless the sacred
Name
For ever blest.

2 The God of Abraham praise,
At whose supreme command
From earth I rise, and seek the
joys
At his right hand.
I all on earth forsake—
Its wisdom, fame, and
power—
And him my only portion make,
My shield and tower.

3 He by himself hath sworn,
I on his oath depend:
I shall, on eagle's wings up-
borne,
To heaven ascend;
I shall behold his face,
I shall his power adore,
And sing the wonders of his
grace
For evermore.

4   There dwells the Lord our
        King,
    The Lord our Righteousness,
    Triumphant o'er the world and
        sin,
        The Prince of Peace;
    On Zion's sacred height
    His Kingdom he maintains,
    And glorious with his saints in
        light
        For ever reigns.

5   *The whole triumphant host*
    Give thanks to God on high:
    'Hail, Father, Son, and Holy
        Ghost!'
        They ever cry.
    Hail, Abraham's God, and
        mine!—
    I join the heavenly lays,—
    All might and majesty are thine,
        And endless praise. Amen.
                THOMAS OLIVERS, 1725–99
                Based on the Jewish *Yigdal*

359

PRAISE the Lord, his glories
    show,
        Alleluia!
Saints within his courts below,
        Alleluia!
Angels round his throne above,
        Alleluia!
All that see and share his love.
        Alleluia!

2 Earth to heaven, and heaven to
        earth,
  Tell his wonders, sing his worth;
  Age to age and shore to shore,
  Praise him, praise him ever-
        more!

3 Praise the Lord, his mercies
        trace;
  Praise his providence and grace,
  All that he for man hath done,
  All he sends us through his Son.

4 Strings and voices, hands and
        hearts,
  In the concert bear your parts;
  All that breathe, your Lord
        adore,
  Praise him, praise him ever-
        more:
                HENRY FRANCIS LYTE, 1793–1847

360

PRAISE, my soul, the King of
    heaven;
    To his feet thy tribute bring;
Ransomed, healed, restored,
        forgiven,
    Who like me his praise should
        sing?
        Praise him! Praise him!
        Praise him! Praise him!
    Praise the everlasting King.

2 Praise him for his grace and
        favour
    To our fathers in distress;
  Praise him, still the same for
        ever,
    Slow to chide and swift to
        bless:
        Praise him! Praise him!
        Praise him! Praise him!
    Glorious in his faithfulness.

3 Father-like he tends and spares
        us;
    Well our feeble frame he
        knows;
  In his hands he gently bears
        us,
    Rescues us from all our foes:
        Praise him! Praise him!
        Praise him! Praise him!
    Widely as his mercy flows.

4 Frail as summer's flower we
        flourish;
    Blows the wind and it is
        gone;
  But, while mortals rise and
        perish,
    God endures unchanging on:
        Praise him! Praise him!
        Praise him! Praise him!
    Praise the high eternal One.

5 Angels, help us to adore him;
    Ye behold him face to face;
  Sun and moon, bow down be-
        fore him;
    Dwellers all in time and space.
        Praise him! Praise him!
        Praise him! Praise him!
    Praise with us the God of
        grace.
                HENRY FRANCIS LYTE, 1793–1847
                From Psalm 103

361

LET all the world in every
corner sing,
'My God and King!'
The heavens are not too
high,
His praise may thither fly;
The earth is not too low,
His praises there may grow.
Let all the world in every
corner sing,
'My God and King!'

Let all the world in every corner
sing,
'My God and King!'
The Church with psalms must
shout,
No door can keep them out;
But, above all, the heart
Must bear the longest part.
Let all the world in every corner
sing,
'My God and King!'

GEORGE HERBERT, 1593–1633

362

FROM all that dwell below the
skies
Let the Creator's praise arise:
Alleluia! Alleluia!
Let the Redeemer's Name be
sung
Through every land, in every
tongue.
*Alleluia, Alleluia, Alleluia,
Alleluia, Alleluia!*

Eternal are thy mercies, Lord:
Eternal truth attends thy
word:
Thy praise shall sound from
shore to shore
Till suns shall rise and set no
more:

ISAAC WATTS, 1674–1748
From Psalm 117

363

YE holy angels bright,
Who wait at God's right
hand,
Or through the realms of light
Fly at your Lord's command,
Assist our song,
Or else the theme
Too high doth seem
For mortal tongue.

2 Ye blessèd souls at rest,
Who ran this earthly race,
And now, from sin released,
Behold the Saviour's face,
His praises sound,
As in his light
With sweet delight
Ye do abound.

3 Ye saints, who toil below,
Adore your heavenly King,
And, onward as ye go,
Some joyful anthem sing;
Take what he gives,
And praise him still
Through good and ill,
Who ever lives.

4 My soul, bear thou thy part,
Triumph in God above,
And with a well-tuned heart
Sing thou the songs of love.
Let all thy days
Till life shall end,
Whate'er he send,
Be filled with praise.

RICHARD BAXTER, 1615–91
and others

364

KING of glory, King of peace,
I will love thee;
And, that love may never
cease,
I will move thee.
Thou hast granted my request,
Thou hast heard me;
Thou didst note my working
breast,
Thou hast spared me.

2 Wherefore with my utmost art
　　I will sing thee,
And the cream of all my heart
　　I will bring thee.
Though my sins against me
　　cried,
　　Thou didst clear me,
And alone, when they replied,
　　Thou didst hear me.

3 Seven whole days, not one in
　　seven,
　　I will praise thee;
In my heart, though not in
　　heaven,
　　I can raise thee.
Small it is, in this poor sort
　　To enrol thee;
E'en eternity's too short
　　To extol thee.

GEORGE HERBERT, 1593–1633

365

FOR the might of thine arm
　we bless thee, our God, our
　　fathers' God;
Thou hast kept thy pilgrim
　people by the strength of thy
　　staff and rod;
Thou hast called us to the
　journey which faithless feet
　　ne'er trod;
*For the might of thine arm we
　bless thee, our God, our
　　fathers' God.*

2 For the love of Christ con-
　　straining, that bound their
　　hearts as one;
For the faith in truth and
　freedom in which their work
　　was done;
For the peace of God's evangel
　wherewith their feet were
　　shod;

3 We are watchers of a beacon
　whose light must never die;
We are guardians of an altar
　that shows thee ever nigh;
We are children of thy freemen
　who sleep beneath the sod;

4 May the shadow of thy presen[ce]
　　around our camp be spread
Baptize us with the coura[ge]
　　thou gavest to our dead;
O keep us in the pathway the[ir]
　　saintly feet have trod:

CHARLES SILVESTER HORN[E]
1865–19[

366

SING to the Lord a joyf[ul]
　　song,
　　Lift up your hearts, yo[ur]
　　　voices raise;
To us his gracious gifts belon[g]
　To him our songs of love ar[d]
　　praise.

2 For life and love, for rest ar[d]
　　food,
　　For daily help and night[ly]
　　　care,
Sing to the Lord, for he is goo[d]
　And praise his Name, for it [is]
　　fair.

3 For strength to those who [on]
　　him wait
　　His truth to prove, his w[ill]
　　　to do,
Praise ye our God, for he [is]
　　great,
　Trust in his Name, for it [is]
　　true.

4 For joys untold, that fro[m]
　　above
　　Cheer those who love h[is]
　　　sweet employ,
Sing to our God, for he is love[,]
　Exalt his Name, for it is jo[y.]

5 *For he is Lord of heaven ar[d]
　　earth,
　　Whom angels serve and sain[ts]
　　　adore,
The Father, Son, and Ho[ly]
　　Ghost,
　To whom be praise for eve[r]
　　more.* Amen.

JOHN SAMUEL BEWLEY MONSE[LL]
1811–[

367

FOR the beauty of the earth,
  For the beauty of the skies,
For the love which from our
    birth
  Over and around us lies,
Christ, our God, to thee we raise
This our sacrifice of praise.

For the beauty of each hour
  Of the day and of the night,
Hill and vale, and tree and
    flower,
  Sun and moon and stars of
    light,

For the joy of ear and eye,
  For the heart and mind's
    delight,
For the mystic harmony
  Linking sense to sound and
    sight,

For the joy of human love,
  Brother, sister, parent, child,
Friends on earth and friends
    above,
  For all gentle thoughts and
    mild,

For each perfect gift of thine
  To our race so freely given,
Graces human and divine,
  Flowers of earth and buds of
    heaven:

FOLLIOTT SANDFORD PIERPOINT
1835–1917

368

Nun danket alle Gott

NOW thank we all our God,
  With heart and hands
    and voices,
Who wondrous things hath
    done,
  In whom his world rejoices,—
  Who, from our mothers'
    arms,
  Hath blessed us on our
    way
  With countless gifts of
    love,
  And still is ours today.

2 O may this bounteous God
    Through all our life be near
      us,
  With ever-joyful hearts
    And blessèd peace to cheer us,
    And keep us in his grace,
      And guide us when per-
        plexed,
    And free us from all ills
      In this world and the
        next.

3 *All praise and thanks to God*
    The Father now be given,
  The Son, and him who reigns
    With them in highest heaven,—
    The one, eternal God,
      Whom earth and heaven
        adore;
    For thus it was, is now,
      And shall be evermore.
        Amen.

MARTIN RINKART, 1586–1649
Tr. CATHERINE WINKWORTH
1827–78

369

GOD and Father, we adore
    thee
  For the Son, thine image
    bright,
In whom all thy holy nature
  Dawned on our once hopeless
    night.

2 Far from thee our footsteps
    wandered,
  On dark paths of sin and
    shame;
  But our midnight turned to
    morning,
  When the Lord of Glory
    came.

3 Word Incarnate, God revealing,
  Longed-for while dim ages
    ran,
  Love Divine, we bow before
    thee,
  Son of God and Son of Man.

4 Let our life be new created,
  Ever-living Lord, in thee,
  Till we wake with thy pure like-
    ness,
  When thy face in heaven we
    see;

5 Where the saints of all the ages,
　Where our fathers glorified,
Clouds and darkness far be-
　　neath them,
　In unending day abide.

6 God and Father, now we bless
　　thee
　　For the Son, thine image
　　　bright,
In whom all thy holy nature
　Dawns on our adoring sight.

Verse 1 attributed to
JOHN NELSON DARBY, 1800–82
Verses 2–5 and adaptation of verse 6
HUGH FALCONER, 1859–1931

370 *Beim frühen Morgenlicht*

WHEN morning gilds the
　skies,
My heart awaking cries,
　'May Jesus Christ be praisèd'.
When evening shadows fall,
This rings my curfew-call,
　'May Jesus Christ be praisèd'.
When mirth for music longs,
This is my song of songs,
　'May Jesus Christ be praisèd'.
God's holy house of prayer
Hath none that can compare
　With 'Jesus Christ be
　　praisèd'.

2 This greeting of great joy,
I ne'er have found it cloy,
　'May Jesus Christ be praisèd'.
When sorrow would molest,
Then sing I undistrest,
　'May Jesus Christ be praisèd'.
No lovelier antiphon
In all high heav'n is known
　Than 'Jesus Christ be
　　praisèd'.
There to the Eternal Word
The eternal psalm is heard,
　'O Jesus Christ be praisèd'.

3 Ye nations of mankind,
In this your concord find,
　'May Jesus Christ be praisèd'.
Let all the earth around
Ring joyous with the sound
　'May Jesus Christ be praisèd'.

Sing, suns and stars of space,
Sing, ye that see his face,
　Sing 'Jesus Christ be praisèd'
God's whole creation o'er,
For aye and evermore,
　Shall Jesus Christ be praisèd

Anonymous German hymn
early 19th century
Tr. ROBERT BRIDGES, 1844–193

371

O FOR a thousand tongues, t
　sing
My great Redeemer's praise,
The glories of my God and King
The triumphs of his grace!

2 Jesus! the Name that charm
　our fears,
　That bids our sorrows cease
'Tis music in the sinner's ears,
　'Tis life, and health, and
　peace.

3 He breaks the power of can
　celled sin,
　He sets the prisoner free;
His blood can make the foules
　clean,
　His blood availed for me.

4 He speaks, and, listening to hi
　voice,
　New life the dead receive,
The mournful, broken heart
　rejoice,
　The humble poor believe.

5 Hear him, ye deaf; his praise, ye
　dumb,
　Your loosened tongues em
　ploy;
Ye blind, behold your Saviour
　come;
　And leap, ye lame, for joy!

6 My gracious Master and my
　God,
　Assist me to proclaim,
To spread through all the eartl
　abroad
　The honours of thy Name.

CHARLES WESLEY, 1707–88

372

YE servants of God, your
    Master proclaim,
And publish abroad his wonder-
    ful Name;
The Name all-victorious of
    Jesus extol;
His Kingdom is glorious, and
    rules over all.

God ruleth on high, almighty to
    save;
And still he is nigh, his presence
    we have;
The great congregation his
    triumph shall sing,
Ascribing salvation to Jesus our
    King.

Salvation to God, who sits on
    the throne!
Let all cry aloud, and honour
    the Son:
The praises of Jesus the angels
    proclaim,
Fall down on their faces, and
    worship the Lamb.

Then let us adore, and give him
    his right,
All glory and power, all wisdom
    and might,
All honour and blessing, with
    angels above,
And thanks never ceasing, and
    infinite love.

          CHARLES WESLEY, 1707–88

373   *Gloriosi Salvatoris*

TO the Name of our Salvation
    Laud and honour let us pay,
Which for many a generation
    Hid in God's foreknowledge
        lay,
But with holy exultation
    We may sing aloud today.

Jesus is the Name we treasure,
    Name beyond what words
        can tell,
Name of gladness, Name of
    pleasure,
Ear and heart delighting well;
Name of sweetness passing
    measure,
    Saving us from sin and hell.

3 'Tis the Name that whoso
    preacheth
    Speaks like music to the ear;
Who in prayer this Name be-
    seecheth
    Sweetest comfort findeth
        near;
Who its perfect wisdom
    reacheth
    Heav'nly joy possesseth here.

4 Jesus is the Name exalted
    Over every other name;
In this Name, whene'er as-
    saulted,
    We can put our foes to
        shame;
Strength to them who else had
    halted,
    Eyes to blind, and feet to
    lame.

5 Therefore we, in love adoring,
    This most blessèd Name
        revere,
Holy Jesus, thee imploring
    So to write it in us here
That hereafter, heavenward
    soaring,
    We may sing with angels
    there.

                  15th century
    Tr. Compilers of *Hymns Ancient*
            and Modern, 1861
      Based on the tr. by
    JOHN MASON NEALE, 1818–66

374

TO God be the glory! great
    things he hath done!
So loved he the world that he
    gave us his Son,
Who yielded his life an atone-
    ment for sin,
And opened the life-gate that
    all may go in.

2 O perfect redemption, the
    purchase of blood!
To every believer the promise of
    God;
The vilest offender who truly
    believes,
That moment from Jesus a
    pardon receives.

3 Great things he hath taught us,
    great things he hath done,
And great our rejoicing through
    Jesus the Son:
But purer and higher and
    greater will be
Our wonder, our transport,
    when Jesus we see.

FRANCES (CROSBY) VAN ALSTYNE
1820–1915

375 *Schönster Herr Jesu*

FAIREST Lord Jesus,
    Ruler of all nature,
O thou of God and Man the
    Son;
Thee will I cherish,
Thee will I honour,
Thou my soul's glory, joy and
    crown.

2 Fair are the meadows,
    Fairer still the woodlands,
Robed in the verdure and bloom
    of spring.
Jesus is fairer,
Jesus is purer,
He makes the saddest heart to
    sing.

3 Fair are the flowers,
    Fairer still the sons of men
In all the freshness of youth
    arrayed;
Yet is their beauty
Fading and fleeting;
Lord Jesus, thine will never
    fade.

4 Fair is the sunshine,
    Fairer still the moonlight,
And fair the twinkling starry
    host;
Jesus shines brighter,
Jesus shines purer
Than all the stars that heaven
    can boast.

Münster Gesangbuch, 1677
Tr. LILIAN STEVENSON, 1870–1960
and others

376

HOW sweet the Name of
    Jesus sounds
In a believer's ear!
It soothes his sorrows, heals his
    wounds,
And drives away his fear.

2 It makes the wounded spirit
    whole,
    And calms the troubled
    breast;
'Tis manna to the hungry soul,
And to the weary rest.

3 Dear Name! the rock on which I
    build,
    My shield and hiding-place,
My never-failing treasury, filled
    With boundless stores of
    grace.

4 Jesus, my Shepherd, Husband,
    Friend,
    My Prophet, Priest, and
    King,
My Lord, my Life, my Way, my
    End,
    Accept the praise I bring.

5 Weak is the effort of my heart,
    And cold my warmest
    thought;
But, when I see thee as thou
    art,
    I'll praise thee as I ought.

6 Till then I would thy love pro-
    claim
    With every fleeting breath;
And may the music of thy
    Name
    Refresh my soul in death.

JOHN NEWTON, 1725–1807

377 *Jesu dulcis memoria*

JESUS, the very thought of
    thee
    With sweetness fills my
    breast;
But sweeter far thy face to see
    And in thy presence rest.

Nor voice can sing, nor heart
    can frame,
  Nor can the memory find
A sweeter sound than thy blest
    Name,
  O Saviour of mankind!

O Hope of every contrite heart,
  O Joy of all the meek,
To those who fall how kind thou
    art!
  How good to those who seek!

But what to those who find? Ah,
    this
  Nor tongue nor pen can show;
The love of Jesus, what it is
  None but his loved ones
    know.

Jesus, our only joy be thou,
  As thou our prize wilt be;
Jesus, be thou our glory now,
  And through eternity.

Probably 12th century
Tr. EDWARD CASWALL, 1814–78
Lyra Catholica, 1849

78   *Jesu, Rex admirabilis*

O JESUS, King most wonder-
    ful,
Thou Conqueror renowned,
Thou Sweetness most ineffa le,
  In whom all joys are found!

When once thou visitest the
    heart,
  Then truth begins to shine,
Then earthly vanities depart,
  Then kindles love divine.

O Jesus, Light of all below,
  Thou Fount of life and fire,
Surpassing all the joys we
    know,
  And all we can desire,—

May every heart confess thy
    Name,
  And ever thee adore,
And, seeking thee, itself inflame
  To seek thee more and more.

5 Thee may our tongues for ever
    bless;
  Thee may we love alone,
And ever in our lives express
  The image of thine own.

Probably 12th century
Tr. EDWARD CASWALL, 1814–78
Lyra Catholica, 1849

379   *O Deus, ego amo te*

M Y God, I love thee; not
    because
I hope for heaven thereby,
Nor yet because who love thee
    not
  Are lost eternally.

2 Thou, O my Jesus, thou didst
    me
  Upon the cross embrace;
For me didst bear the nails and
    spear,
  And manifold disgrace,

3 And griefs and torments num-
    berless,
  And sweat of agony;
Even death itself; and all for
    one
  Who was thine enemy.

4 Then why, most loving Jesus
    Christ,
  Should I not love thee well,
Not for the sake of winning
    heaven,
  Or of escaping hell;

5 Not with the hope of gaining
    aught,
  Not seeking a reward;
But as thyself hast lovèd me,
  O ever-loving Lord?

6 Even so I love thee, and will
    love,
  And in thy praise will sing,
Solely because thou art my
    God,
  And my eternal King.

17th century Latin, based on a
Spanish sonnet
Tr. EDWARD CASWALL, 1814–78

380

MAN of Sorrows! wondrous
Name
For the Son of God, who came
Ruined sinners to reclaim!
Alleluia! what a Saviour!

2 Bearing shame and scoffing rude,
In my place condemned he
stood,
Sealed my pardon with his
blood:

3 Guilty, vile, and helpless we;
Spotless Lamb of God was he:
Full atonement,—can it be?

4 Lifted up was he to die,
'It is finished' was his cry;
Now in heaven exalted high:

5 When he comes, our glorious
King,
All his ransomed home to bring,
Then anew this song we'll sing:
PHILIPP BLISS, 1838–76

381

I WILL sing the wondrous
story
Of the Christ who died for
me,—
How he left the realms of glory
For the cross on Calvary:
*Yes, I'll sing the wondrous
story*
*Of the Christ who died for
me,—*
*Sing it with his saints in
glory,*
*Gathered by the crystal
sea.*

2 I was lost: but Jesus found me,
Found the sheep that went
astray,
Raised me up and gently led me
Back into the narrow way:

3 Faint was I, and fears possessed
me,
Bruised was I from many a
fall:
Hope was gone, and shame distressed me:
But his love has pardoned all:

4 Days of darkness still may meet
me,
Sorrow's paths I oft may
tread;
But his presence still is with me
By his guiding hand I'm led:

5 He will keep me till the river
Rolls its waters at my feet:
Then he'll bear me safely over
Made by grace for glory
meet:
FRANCIS HAROLD ROWLEY
1854–195

382

ALL hail, the power of Jesus
Name!
Let angels prostrate fall;
Bring forth the royal diadem,
To *crown him Lord of all.

2 Crown him, ye martyrs of your
God,
Who from his altar call;
Extol him in whose path ye trod
And crown him Lord of all.

3 Ye seed of Israel's chosen race
Ye ransomed of the fall,
Hail him who saves you by his
grace,
And crown him Lord of all.

4 Let every tongue and every
tribe,
Responsive to the call,
To him all majesty ascribe,
And crown him Lord of all.
EDWARD PERRONET, 1726–92

* *The words 'crown him' are sung four
times in each verse.*

383   *For children*

COME, children, join to sing—
Alleluia! Amen!
Loud praise to Christ our King
Alleluia! Amen!
Let all, with heart and voice,
Before his throne rejoice;
Praise is his gracious choice:
Alleluia! Amen!

2 Come, lift your hearts on high
Alleluia! Amen!
Let praises fill the sky;
Alleluia! Amen!

He is our Guide and Friend;
To us he'll blessing send;
His love shall never end:
    Alleluia! Amen!

Praise yet the Lord again;
    Alleluia! Amen!
Life shall not end the strain;
    Alleluia! Amen!
On heaven's blissful shore
His goodness we'll adore,
    Singing for evermore,
        Alleluia! Amen!

CHRISTIAN HENRY BATEMAN
1813–89

84   *For children*

COME, let us remember the
    joys of the town:
Gay vans and bright buses that
    roar up and down,
Shop-windows and playgrounds
    and swings in the park,
And street-lamps that twinkle
    in rows after dark.

Come, let us now lift up our
    voices in praise,
And to the Creator a thanks-
    giving raise,
For towns with their buildings
    of stone, steel and wood,
For people who love them and
    work for their good.

We thank thee, O God, for the
    numberless things
And friends and adventures
    which every day brings.
O may we not rest until all that
    we see
In towns and in cities is pleasing
    to thee.

DORIS GILL
Two verses omitted

385   *For children*

IT is a thing most wonderful,
    Almost too wonderful to be,
That God's own Son should
    come from heaven,
    And die to save a child like me.
And yet I know that it is true:
    He chose a poor and humble
    lot,

And wept, and toiled, and
    mourned, and died.
For love of those who loved
    him not.

3 It is most wonderful to know
    His love for me so free and
    sure;
But 'tis more wonderful to see
    My love for him so faint and
    poor.

4 And yet I want to love thee,
    Lord;
    O light the flame within my
    heart,
And I will love thee more and
    more,
    Until I see thee as thou art.

WILLIAM WALSHAM HOW
1823–97

386   *For younger children*

PRAISE him, praise him, all
    ye little children,
    He is love, he is love;
Praise him, praise him, all ye
    little children,
    He is love, he is love.

2 Thank him, thank him, all ye
    little children,
    He is love, he is love;
Thank him, thank him, all ye
    little children,
    He is love, he is love.

3 Love him, love him, all ye little
    children,
    He is love, he is love;
Love him, love him, all ye little
    children,
    He is love, he is love.

4 Crown him, crown him, all ye
    little children,
    God is love, God is love;
Crown him, crown him, all ye
    little children,
    God is love, God is love.

Anonymous, c. 1890

The following are also suitable
Nos. 135–8, 145–6, 238, 640

AFFIRMATION

387
PSALM 23

THE Lord's my Shepherd, I'll
not want.
He makes me down to lie
In pastures green: he leadeth me
The quiet waters by.

2 My soul he doth restore again;
And me to walk doth make
Within the paths of righteous-
ness,
Even for his own Name's
sake.

3 Yea, though I walk in death's
dark vale,
Yet will I fear none ill:
For thou art with me; and thy
rod
And staff me comfort still.

4 My table thou hast furnishèd
In presence of my foes;
My head thou dost with oil
anoint,
And my cup overflows.

5 Goodness and mercy all my life
Shall surely follow me:
And in God's house for ever-
more
My dwelling-place shall be.

6 *To Father, Son, and Holy Ghost,*
The God whom we adore,
Be glory, as it was, and is,
And shall be evermore. Amen.

388

THE King of Love my Shep-
herd is,
Whose goodness faileth
never;
I nothing lack if I am his
And he is mine for ever.

2 Where streams of living water
flow
My ransomed soul he leadeth,
And where the verdant pastures
grow
With food celestial feedeth.

3 Perverse and foolish oft
strayed;
But yet in love he sought me
And on his shoulder gently laid
And home rejoicing brough
me.

4 In death's dark vale I fear no il
With thee, dear Lord, besid
me;
Thy rod and staff my comfor
still,
Thy cross before to guide me

5 Thou spread'st a table in m
sight;
Thy unction grace bestoweth
And O what transport of de
light
From thy pure chalic
floweth!

6 And so through all the length o
days
Thy goodness faileth never
Good Shepherd, may I sing th
praise
Within thy house for ever!

HENRY WILLIAMS BAKER, 1821–7
From Psalm 2

389
PSALM 23, Gelineau
version

THE Lord is my Shepherd;
There is nothing I shall want
Fresh and green are the pasture
Where he gives me repose.
Near restful waters he leads me
To revive my drooping spirit.

2 He guides me along the righ
path;
He is true to his Name.
If I should walk in the valley o
darkness
No evil would I fear.
You are there with your croo
and your staff;
With these you give me comfor

140

You have prepared a banquet
for me,
In the sight of my foes.
My head you have anointed
with oil;
My cup is overflowing.

Surely goodness and kindness
shall follow me
All the days of my life.
In the Lord's own house shall
I dwell
For ever and ever.

To the Father and Son give
glory,
Give glory to the Spirit.
To God who is, who was, and
who will be
For ever and ever.

Antiphon 1
My Shepherd is the Lord,
nothing indeed shall I want.

Antiphon 2
His goodness shall follow me
always, to the end of my
days.

Antiphon 3
The Lord is my Shepherd,
nothing shall I want; he
leads me by safe paths,
nothing shall I fear.

390   PSALM 89, verses
15, 16, 18

O GREATLY blest the people
are
The joyful sound that know;
In brightness of thy face, O
Lord,
They ever on shall go.

They in thy Name shall all the
day
Rejoice exceedingly;
And in thy righteousness shall
they
Exalted be on high.

3 For God is our defence; and he
To us doth safety bring:
The Holy One of Israel
Is our almighty King.

4 *To Father, Son, and Holy Ghost,*
The God whom we adore,
Be glory, as it was, and is,
And shall be evermore. Amen.

391   PSALM 34, verses
1, 2, 7–9, 11, 14, 15

G OD will I bless all times; his
praise
My mouth shall still express.
My soul shall boast in God: the
meek
Shall hear with joyfulness.

2 The angel of the Lord encamps,
And round encompasseth
All those about that do him fear,
And them delivereth.

3 O taste and see that God is
good:
Who trusts in him is blest.
Fear God, his saints: none that
him fear
Shall be with want oppressed.

4 O children, hither do ye come,
And unto me give ear;
I shall you teach to understand
How ye the Lord should fear.

5 Depart from ill, do good, seek
peace,
Pursue it earnestly.
God's eyes are on the just; his
ears
Are open to their cry.

6 *To Father, Son, and Holy Ghost,*
The God whom we adore,
Be glory, as it was, and is,
And shall be evermore. Amen.

392   PSALM 124 (ii)

N OW Israel may say, and that
truly,
If that the Lord had not our
cause maintained;
If that the Lord had not our
right sustained,
When cruel men against us
furiously
Rose up in wrath, to make of us
their prey;

141

2 Then certainly they had de-
voured us all,
And swallowed quick, for aught
that we could deem;
Such was their rage, as we might
well esteem.
And as fierce floods before them
all things drown,
So had they brought our soul to
death quite down.

3 The raging streams, with their
proud swelling waves,
Had then our soul o'erwhelmèd
in the deep.
But blest be God, who doth us
safely keep,
And hath not given us for a
living prey
Unto their teeth, and bloody
cruelty.

4 Even as a bird out of the
fowler's snare
Escapes away, so is our soul set
free:
Broke are their nets, and thus
escapèd we.
Therefore our help is in the
Lord's great Name,
Who heaven and earth by his
great power did frame.

5 *Glory to God the Father, God the
Son,*
*And unto God the Spirit, Three
in One.*
*From age to age let saints his
Name adore,*
*His power and love proclaim from
shore to shore,*
*And spread his fame, till time
shall be no more.* Amen.

393   PSALM 126

WHEN Zion's bondage God
turned back,
As men that dreamed were
we.
Then filled with laughter was
our mouth,
Our tongue with melody:

2 They among the heathen said,
'The Lord
Great things for them hath
wrought.'

The Lord hath done great thin
for us,
Whence joy to us is brough

3 As streams of water in th
south,
Our bondage, Lord, recall.
Who sow in tears, a reapir
time
Of joy enjoy they shall.

4 That man who, bearing preciou
seed,
In going forth doth mourn
He doubtless, bringing back h
sheaves,
Rejoicing shall return.

5 *To Father, Son, and Holy Ghos*
The God whom we adore,
Be glory, as it was, and is,
And shall be evermore. Amei

394 PARAPHRASE 22, verses 3–

ART thou afraid his powe
shall fail
When comes thy evil day?
And can an all-creating arm
Grow weary or decay?

2 Supreme in wisdom as in powe
The Rock of ages stands;
Though him thou canst not se
nor trace
The working of his hands.

3 He gives the conquest to th
weak,
Supports the fainting heart
And courage in the evil hou
His heavenly aids impart.

4 Mere human power shall fas
decay,
And youthful vigour cease;
But they who wait upon th
Lord
In strength shall still increas

5 They with unwearied feet sha
tread
The path of life divine;
With growing ardour onwar
move,
With growing brightnes
shine.

On eagles' wings they mount,
they soar,
Their wings are faith and
love,
Till, past the cloudy regions
here,
They rise to heaven above.

Scottish Paraphrases, 1781
From Isaiah 40:28–end

395 PARAPHRASE 60

FATHER of peace, and God
of love!
We own thy power to save,
That power by which our
Shepherd rose
Victorious o'er the grave.

Him from the dead thou
brought'st again,
When, by his sacred blood,
Confirmed and sealed for ever-
more
The eternal covenant stood.

O may thy Spirit seal our souls,
And mould them to thy will,
That our weak hearts no more
may stray,
But keep thy precepts still;

That to perfection's sacred
height
We nearer still may rise,
And all we think, and all we do,
Be pleasing in thine eyes.

Scottish Paraphrases, 1781
From Hebrews 13:20, 21

396 PARAPHRASE 63

BEHOLD the amazing gift of
love
The Father hath bestowed
On us, the sinful sons of men,
To call us sons of God!

2 Concealed as yet this honour
lies,
By this dark world un-
known,—
A world that knew not when he
came,
Even God's eternal Son.

3 High is the rank we now pos-
sess;
But higher we shall rise,
Though what we shall hereafter
be
Is hid from mortal eyes.

4 Our souls, we know, when he
appears,
Shall bear his image bright;
For all his glory, full disclosed,
Shall open to our sight.

5 A hope so great, and so divine,
May trials well endure;
And purge the soul from sense
and sin,
As Christ himself is pure.

Scottish Paraphrases, 1781
From 1 John 3:1–3

397 *Deus Pater credentium*

O GOD, thou art the Father
Of all that have believed:
From whom all hosts of angels
Have life and power received.
O God, thou art the Maker
Of all created things,
The righteous Judge of judges,
The Almighty King of kings.

2 High in the heavenly Zion
Thou reignest God adored;
And in the coming glory
Thou shalt be Sovereign
Lord.
Beyond our ken thou shinest,
The everlasting Light;
Ineffable in loving,
Unthinkable in might.

3 Thou to the meek and lowly
Thy secrets dost unfold;
O God, thou doest all things,
All things both new and old.
I walk secure and blessèd
In every clime or coast,
In Name of God the Father,
And Son, and Holy Ghost.

ST. COLUMBA, 521–97
Tr. DUNCAN MACGREGOR
1854–1923

143

398 ᵼm ᴀonᴀpᴀn ᴅom ᵼnᵹ ᴀn ᴩᴌiᴀᴆ

ALONE with none but thee,
my God;
I journey on my way;
What need I fear, when thou
art near,
O King of night and day?
More safe am I within thy hand,
Than if a host did round me
stand.

2 My destined time is fixed by
thee,
And Death doth know his
hour.
Did warriors strong around me
throng,
They could not stay his
power;
No walls of stone can man defend
When thou thy messenger
dost send.

3 My life I yield to thy decree,
And bow to thy control
In peaceful calm, for from thine
arm
No power can wrest my soul.
Could earthly omens e'er appal
A man that heeds the
heavenly call!

4 The child of God can fear no ill,
His chosen dread no foe;
We leave our fate with thee, and
wait
Thy bidding when to go.
'Tis not from chance our com-
fort springs,
Thou art our trust, O King of
kings.

Attributed to St. COLUMBA
521–97
Tr. anonymous

399

THOUGH in God's form he
was,
Christ Jesus would not snatch
At parity with God;

2 Himself he sacrificed,
Taking a servant's form,
Being born like ev'ry man;

3 Revealed in human shape,
Obediently he stooped
To die upon a cross.

4 Him therefore God raised high
Gave him the Name of Lord,
All other names above;

5 That at the Saviour's Name
No knee might be unbowed,
In heaven, or earth, or hell;

6 And ev'ry tongue confess,
To God the Father's praise,
That 'Jesus Christ is Lord'.
Tr. ARCHIBALD MACBRIDE HUNTE
From Phil. 2:6–1

400

FIRMLY I believe and truly
God is Three, and God i
One;
And I next acknowledge dul
Manhood taken by the Son.

2 And I trust and hope most full
In that Manhood crucified;
And each thought and deed un
ruly
Do to death, as he has died.

3 Simply to his grace and wholly
Light and life and strengt
belong,
And I love supremely, solely
Him the holy, him the strong

4 And I hold in veneration
For the love of him alone,
Holy Church as his creation,
And her teachings as his own

5 *Adoration aye be given,*
With and through the angelic
host,
To the God of earth and heaven,
Father, Son, and Holy Ghost
Amen.
JOHN HENRY NEWMAN, 1801–9(

401 ᴀᴄomᴩiuᵹ ᵼnoᵼu niuᵹᵼ ᴄᴩen

TODAY I arise,
Invoking the Blessèd
Trinity,
Confessing the Blessèd Unity
Creator of all the things
that be.

Today I arise,
    By strength of Christ and his
       mystic Birth,
    By   his   Passion,   and
       Triumph's saving worth,
    By his coming again to judge
       the earth.
    *[Today I arise, today I arise.]

Today I arise,
    By seraphs serving the Lord
       above,
    By truths his ancient heralds
       prove,
    By saints in purity, labour,
       love.

Today I arise,
    By splendour of sun and
       flaming brand,
    By rushing wind, by lightning
       grand,
    By depth of sea, by strength
       of land.

5 Today I arise,
    With God my steersman, stay
       and guide,
    To guard, to counsel, to hear,
       to bide,
    His way before, his hosts
       beside—

6 Protecting me now
    From crafty wiles of demon
       crew,
    From foemen, be they many
       or few,
    From lusts that I can scarce
       subdue.

7 Lord Jesus the Christ,
    Today surround me with
       thy might;
    Before, behind, on left and
       right,
    Be thou in breadth, in length,
       in height.

8 Direct and control
    The minds of all who think
       on me,
    The lips of all who speak to
       me,
    The eyes of all who look on
       me.

9 Today I arise,
    Invoking the Blessèd Trinity,
    Confessing the Blessèd Unity:
    Saviour, on us salvation be!

          ST. PATRICK, 372–466
    Tr. ROBERT ALEXANDER STEWART
          MACALISTER, 1870–1950

  * This refrain is to be omitted when the
Irish traditional tunes, RAMELTON and
CULRATHAIN are used.

402   Ꭿꮯomꭲιus ιnoιu nιuꭲꭲ cꭲen

I BIND unto myself today
    The strong Name of the
       Trinity,
    By invocation of the same,
       The Three in One, and One
       in Three.

2 I bind this day to me for ever,
    By power of faith, Christ's
       Incarnation;
    His baptism in the Jordan
       river;
    His death on cross for my
       salvation;
    His bursting from the spicèd
       tomb;
    His riding up the heavenly
       way;
    His coming at the day of doom:
    I bind unto myself today.

3 I bind unto myself today
    The virtues of the star-lit
       heaven,
    The glorious sun's life-giving
       ray,
    The whiteness of the moon at
       even,
    The flashing of the lightning
       free,
    The whirling wind's tem-
       pestuous shocks,
    The stable earth, the deep salt
       sea
    Around the old eternal rocks.

4 I bind unto myself today
    The power of God to hold and
       lead,
    His eye to watch, his might to
       stay,
    His ear to hearken to my
       need,

The wisdom of my God to
teach,
His hand to guide, his shield
to ward,
The word of God to give me
speech,
His heavenly host to be my
guard.

5 Christ be with me, Christ within
me,
Christ behind me, Christ before me,
Christ beside me, Christ to win
me,
Christ to comfort and restore
me,
Christ beneath me, Christ
above me,
Christ in quiet, Christ in
danger,
Christ in hearts of all that love
me,
Christ in mouth of friend and
stranger.

6 *I bind unto myself the Name,*
The strong Name of the
Trinity,
By invocation of the same,
The Three in One, and One in
Three,
Of whom all nature hath creation,
Eternal Father, Spirit, Word,
Praise to the Lord of my salva-
tion:
Salvation is of Christ the
Lord. Amen.

ST. PATRICK, 372–466
Version by CECIL FRANCES ALEXANDER
1818–95

Verses 1–4 and 6 are sung to ST. PATRICK.
Verse 5 is sung to CLONMACNOISE.

403

THEE will I love, my God and
King,
Thee will I sing, my strength
and tower:
For evermore thee will I trust,
O God most just of truth and
power,
Who all things hast in order
placed,
Yea, for thy pleasure hast
created;

And on thy throne, unseen, unknown,
Reignest alone in glory
seated.

2 Set in my heart thy love I find
My wandering mind to thee
thou leadest:
My trembling hope, my strong
desire
With heavenly fire thou
kindly feedest.
Lo, all things fair thy path prepare,
Thy beauty to my spirit
calleth,
Thine to remain in joy or
pain,
And count it gain whate'er
befalleth.

3 O more and more thy love ex-
tend,
My life befriend with
heavenly pleasure;
That I may win thy paradise,
Thy pearl of price, thy count-
less treasure;
Since but in thee I can go free
From earthly care and vain
oppression,
This prayer I make for Jesus'
sake,
That thou me take in thy
possession.

ROBERT BRIDGES, 1844–1930
Yattendon Hymnal, 1899

404

GOD is my strong salvation;
What foe have I to fear?
In darkness and temptation
My light, my help is near.

2 Though hosts encamp around
me,
Firm to the fight I stand;
What terror can confound me,
With God at my right hand?

3 Place on the Lord reliance;
My soul, with courage wait;
His truth be thine affiance,
When faint and desolate.

His might thine heart shall
    strengthen,
  His love thy joy increase;
Mercy thy days shall lengthen;
  The Lord will give thee peace.
      JAMES MONTGOMERY, 1771–1854
                From Psalm 27

5 Still from man to God eternal
    Sacrifice of praise be done,
  High above all praises praising
    For the gift of Christ his Son.
      Christ doth call
      One and all:
    Ye who follow shall not fall.
        ROBERT BRIDGES, 1844–1930
        Based on JOACHIM NEANDER
                      1650–80

* This verse may be omitted.

405 *Meine Hoffnung stehet feste*

ALL my hope on God is
    founded;
  He doth still my trust renew.
Me through change and chance
    he guideth,
  Only good and only true.
      God unknown,
      He alone
    Calls my heart to be his
      own.

2 Pride of man and earthly
    glory,
  Sword and crown betray his
    trust;
What with care and toil he
    buildeth,
  Tower and temple, fall to
    dust.
      But God's power,
      Hour by hour,
    Is my temple and my tower.

3 God's great goodness aye en-
    dureth,
  Deep his wisdom passing
    thought:
Splendour, light, and life attend
    him,
  Beauty springeth out of
    naught.
      Evermore,
      From his store
    New-born worlds rise and
      adore.

*4 Daily doth the Almighty Giver
    Bounteous gifts on us be-
    stow;
  His desire our soul delighteth,
    Pleasure leads us where we go.
      Love doth stand
      At his hand;
    Joy doth wait on his com-
      mand.

406 *Ein' feste Burg ist unser Gott*

A SAFE stronghold our God is
    still,
  A trusty shield and weapon;
He'll help us clear from all the
    ill
  That hath us now o'ertaken.
      The ancient prince of hell
      Hath risen with purpose
        fell;
      Strong mail of craft and
        power
      He weareth in this hour;
    On earth is not his fellow.

2 With force of arms we nothing
    can,
  Full soon were we down-
    ridden;
But for us fights the proper
    Man,
  Whom God himself hath
    bidden.
      Ask ye who is this same?
      Christ Jesus is his Name,
      The Lord Sabaoth's Son;
      He, and no other one,
    Shall conquer in the battle.

3 And were this world all devils
    o'er,
  And watching to devour us,
We lay it not to heart so sore;
  Not they can overpower us.
      And let the prince of ill
      Look grim as e'er he will,
      He harms us not a whit;
      For why?—his doom is
        writ;
      A word shall quickly slay
        him.

147

4 God's word, for all their craft
    and force,
  One moment will not linger,
But, spite of hell, shall have its
    course;
  'Tis written by his finger.
    And, though they take our
      life,
    Goods, honour, children,
      wife,
    Yet is their profit small;
    These things shall vanish
      all:
  The city of God remaineth.
      MARTIN LUTHER, 1483–1546
    Tr. THOMAS CARLYLE, 1795–1881

407   *Ein' feste Burg ist unser Gott*

A FORTRESS sure is God our
    King,
A shield that ne'er shall fail us;
His sword alone shall succour
    bring,
When evil doth assail us.
With craft and cruel hate
Doth Satan lie in wait,
And, armed with deadly power,
Seeks whom he may devour;
On earth where is his equal?

2 O who shall then our cham-
    pion be,
  Lest we be lost for ever?
  One sent by God—from sin 'tis
    he
  The sinner shall deliver;
  And dost thou ask his Name?
  'Tis Jesus Christ—the same
  Of Sabaoth the Lord,
  The Everlasting Word;
  'Tis he must win the battle.

3 God's word remaineth ever
    sure,
  To us his goodness showing;
  The Spirit's gifts, of sin the
    cure,
  Each day he is bestowing.
  Though naught we love be left,
  Of all, e'en life, bereft,
  Yet what shall Satan gain?
  God's kingdom doth remain,
  And shall be ours for ever.
      MARTIN LUTHER, 1483–1546
    Tr. GODFREY THRING, 1823–1903

408   *O quam iuvat fratres, Deus*

H APPY are they, they that
    love God,
    Whose hearts have Christ
      confessed,
  Who by his cross have found
    their life,
    And 'neath his yoke their
      rest.

2 Glad is the praise, sweet are the
    songs,
    When they together sing;
  And strong the prayers that
    bow the ear
    Of heaven's eternal King.

3 Christ to their homes giveth
    his peace,
    And makes their loves his
      own;
  But ah, what tares the evil one
    Hath in his garden sown!

4 Sad were our lot, evil this
    earth,
    Did not its sorrows prove
  The path whereby the sheep
    may find
    The fold of Jesus' love.

5 Then shall they know, they
    that love him,
    How all their pain was good;
  And death itself cannot unbind
    Their happy brotherhood.
      ROBERT BRIDGES, 1844–1930
      Yattendon Hymnal, 1899
    Based on CHARLES COFFIN
      1676–1749

409

A ND can it be, that I should
    gain
    An interest in the Saviour's
      blood?
Died he for me, who caused his
    pain—
    For me, who him to death
      pursued?
Amazing love! how can it be
That thou, my God, shouldst
    die for me?

AFFIRMATION

2 He left his Father's throne
    above,—
So free, so infinite his grace—
Emptied himself of all but love,
    And bled for Adam's helpless
        race:
'Tis mercy all, immense and free;
For, O my God, it found out me!

3 No condemnation now I dread;
    Jesus, and all in him, is
        mine!
Alive in him, my living Head,
    And clothed in righteousness
        divine,
Bold I approach the eternal
    throne,
And claim the crown, through
    Christ my own.
                CHARLES WESLEY, 1707–88

410

NOT what these hands have
    done
Can save this guilty soul;
Not what this toiling flesh has
    borne
Can make my spirit whole.

2   Not what I feel or do
    Can give me peace with God;
Not all my prayers, and sighs,
    and tears
    Can bear my heavy load.

3   Thy work alone, O Christ,
    Can ease this weight of sin;
Thy blood alone, O Lamb of
    God,
    Can give me peace within.

4   Thy love to me, O God,
    Not mine, O Lord, to thee,
Can rid me of this dark unrest,
    And set my spirit free.

5   Thy grace alone, O God,
    To me can pardon speak;
Thy power alone, O Son of God,
    Can this sore bondage break.

6   I bless the Christ of God,
    I rest on life divine,
And with unfaltering lip and
    heart,
    I call this Saviour mine.
        HORATIUS BONAR, 1808–89, altered

411

MY hope is built on nothing
    less
Than Jesus' blood and right-
    eousness;
I dare not trust my sweetest
    frame,
But wholly lean on Jesus'
    Name.
    On Christ, the solid rock, I
        stand;
    All other ground is sinking
        sand.

2 When darkness seems to veil
    his face,
I rest on his unchanging grace;
In every high and stormy gale,
My anchor holds within the veil:

3 His oath, his covenant, and
    blood,
Support me in the whelming
    flood;
When all around my soul gives
    way,
He then is all my hope and stay:
                EDWARD MOTE, 1797–1874

412

WILL your anchor hold in
    the storms of life,
When the clouds unfold their
    wings of strife?
When the strong tides lift, and
    the cables strain,
Will your anchor drift, or firm
    remain?
    We have an anchor that keeps
        the soul
    Steadfast and sure while the
        billows roll;
    Fastened to the Rock which
        cannot move,
    Grounded firm and deep in the
        Saviour's love!

2 Will your anchor hold in the
    straits of fear,
When the breakers roar and the
    reef is near?
While the surges rave, and the
    wild winds blow,
Shall the angry waves then your
    bark o'erflow?

149

3 Will your anchor hold in the
   floods of death,
When the waters cold chill your
   latest breath?
On the rising tide you can never
   fail,
While your anchor holds within
   the veil:

4 Will your eyes behold through
   the morning light
The city of gold and the harbour
   bright?
Will you anchor safe by the
   heavenly shore,
When life's storms are past for
   evermore?

PRISCILLA JANE OWENS, 1829–99

413

JESUS shall reign where'er the
   sun
Does his successive journeys
   run;
His Kingdom stretch from shore
   to shore,
Till moons shall wax and wane
   no more.

2 People and realms of every
   tongue
Dwell on his love with sweetest
   song;
And infant voices shall pro-
   claim
Their early blessings on his
   Name.

3 Blessings abound where'er he
   reigns:
The prisoner leaps to lose his
   chains,
The weary find eternal rest,
And all the sons of want are
   blest.

4 Let every creature rise and
   bring
Peculiar honours to our King,
Angels descend with songs
   again,
And earth repeat the long
   Amen.

ISAAC WATTS, 1674–1748

414

Wir glauben all' an einen Gott

WE believe in one true God,
   Father, Son, and Holy
Ghost,
Ever present help in need,
Praised by all the heavenly
   host;

2 We believe in Jesus Christ,
Son of God and Mary's Son,
Who descended from his
   throne,
And for us salvation won;

3 We confess the Holy Ghost,
Who from both fore'er pro-
   ceeds;
Who upholds and comforts us
In all trials, fears, and needs.

4 *Blest and Holy Trinity,*
Praise forever be to thee!
By whose mighty power alone
All is made and wrought and
   done. Amen.

TOBIAS CLAUSNITZER, 1619–84
Tr. CATHERINE WINKWORTH
1827–78, altered

415

THE great love of God is revealed in the Son,
Who came to this earth to redeem every one.
That love, like a stream flowing
   clear to the sea,
Makes clean every heart that
   from sin would be free.

2 It binds the whole world, every
   barrier it breaks,
The hills it lays low, and the
   mountains it shakes.
It's yours, it is ours, O how
   lavishly given!
The pearl of great price, and the
   treasure of heaven!

DANIEL THAMBYRAJAH NILES
1908–70

416 *For children*

GOD is love: his the care,
Tending each, everywhere.
God is love—all is there!
Jesus came to show him,
That mankind might know
  him:
Sing aloud, loud, loud!
Sing aloud, loud, loud!
  God is good!
  God is truth!
God is beauty! Praise him!

2 None can see God above;
All have here man to love;
Thus may we Godward move,
Finding him in others,
Holding all men brothers:

3 Jesus lived here for men,
Strove and died, rose again,
Rules our hearts, now as
  then;
For he came to save us
By the truth he gave us:

4 To our Lord praise we sing—
Light and life, friend and
  king,
Coming down love to bring,
Pattern for our duty,
Showing God in beauty:

PERCY DEARMER, 1867–1936

417 *For younger children*

GOD is always near me,
Hearing what I say,
Knowing all my thoughts and
  deeds,
All my work and play.

2 God is always near me;
In the darkest night
He can see me just the same
As by mid-day light.

3 God is always near me,
Though so young and small;
Not a look or word or thought,
But God knows it all.

PHILIPP BLISS, 1838–76
The Charm, 1871

418 *For younger children*

JESUS loves me! this I know
For the Bible tells me so;
Little ones to him belong;
They are weak, but he is strong.
  *Yes! Jesus loves me,
  Loves me, loves me!
  Yes! Jesus loves me;
  For the Bible tells me so!*

2 Jesus loves me! he who died
Heaven's gate to open wide;
He will wash away my sin,
Let his little child come in:

3 Jesus loves me! he will stay
Close beside me all the way;
Then his little child will take
Up to heaven, for his dear sake:

ANNA BARTLETT WARNER
1820–1915

* When Tune (ii), JESUS LOVES ME, *is
sung, the Refrain reads:*
  Yes! Jesus loves me!
  Yes! Jesus loves me!
  Yes! Jesus loves me!
  The Bible tells me so.

419 *For younger children*

LORD, I would own thy ten-
der care.
And all thy love to me;
The food I eat, the clothes I
  wear,
Are all bestowed by thee.

2 'Tis thou preservest me from
death
And dangers every hour;
I cannot draw another breath
Unless thou give me power.

3 Kind angels guard me every
night,
As round my bed they stay;
Nor am I absent from thy sight
In darkness or by day.

4 My health and friends and
parents dear
To me by God are given;
I have not any blessing here
But what is sent from heaven.

5 Such goodness, Lord, and con-
    stant care
  A child can ne'er repay;
But may it be my daily prayer
  To love thee and obey.

        JANE TAYLOR, 1783–1824

420

THE Church's one foundation
    Is Jesus Christ her Lord:
She is his new creation
  By water and the word;
From heaven he came and
    sought her
To be his holy bride;
With his own blood he bought
    her,
  And for her life he died.

2 Elect from every nation,
  Yet one o'er all the earth,
Her charter of salvation
    One Lord, one faith, one birth:
One holy Name she blesses,
  Partakes one holy food,
And to one hope she presses,
  With every grace endued.

3 'Mid toil and tribulation,
  And tumult of her war,
She waits the consummation
  Of peace for evermore,
Till with the vision glorious
  Her longing eyes are blest,
And the great Church victorious
  Shall be the Church at rest.

4 Yet she on earth hath union
  With God the Three in One,
And mystic sweet communion
  With those whose rest is won.
O happy ones and holy!
  Lord, give us grace that we,
Like them, the meek and lowly,
  On high may dwell with thee.

    SAMUEL JOHN STONE, 1839–1900

421

GLORIOUS things of thee
    are spoken,
  Zion, city of our God;
He whose word cannot be
    broken
  Formed thee for his own
    abode.

On the Rock of Ages founded,
  What can shake thy sure
    repose?
With salvation's walls sur-
    rounded,
  Thou may'st smile at all thy
    foes.

2 See! the streams of living
    waters,
  Springing from eternal love,
Well supply thy sons and
    daughters,
  And all fear of want remove.
Who can faint while such a
    river
  Ever flows their thirst to as-
    suage,—
Grace, which, like the Lord the
    Giver,
  Never fails from age to age?

3 Round each habitation hover-
    ing,
  See! the cloud and fire appear,
For a glory and a covering,
  Showing that the Lord is
    near.
Blest inhabitants of Zion,
  Washed in the Redeemer's
    blood,
Jesus, whom their souls rely on,
  Makes them kings and priests
    to God.

4 Saviour, if of Zion's city
  I, through grace, a member
    am,
Let the world deride or pity,
  I will glory in thy Name.
Fading is the worldling's
    pleasure,
  All his boasted pomp and
    show;
Solid joys and lasting treasure
  None but Zion's children
    know.

      JOHN NEWTON, 1725–1807

422

CITY of God, how broad and
    far
  Outspread thy walls sublime!
The true thy chartered freemen
    are,
  Of every age and clime.

2 One holy Church, one army
    strong,
  One steadfast, high intent;
One working band, one harvest-
    song,
  One King omnipotent.

3 How purely hath thy speech
    come down
  From man's primeval youth!
How grandly hath thine empire
    grown,
  Of freedom, love and truth!

4 How gleam thy watch-fires
    through the night
  With never-fainting ray!
How rise thy towers, serene and
    bright,
  To meet the dawning day!

5 In vain the surge's angry shock,
  In vain the drifting sands:
Unharmed upon the eternal
    Rock
  The eternal City stands.
          SAMUEL JOHNSON, 1822–82

423 *Igjennem Nat og Trængsel*

THROUGH the night of doubt
    and sorrow
  Onward goes the pilgrim
    band,
Singing songs of expectation,
  Marching to the promised
    land.

2 Clear before us, through the
    darkness,
  Gleams and burns the guid-
    ing light;
Brother clasps the hand of
    brother,
  Stepping fearless through the
    night;

3 One the light of God's own
    presence,
  O'er his ransomed people
    shed,
Chasing far the gloom and
    terror,
  Brightening all the path we
    tread;

4 One the object of our journey,
  One the faith which never
    tires,
One the earnest looking for-
    ward,
  One the hope our God in-
    spires;

5 One the strain that lips of
    thousands
  Lift as from the heart of one;
One the conflict, one the peril,
  One the march in God begun;

6 One the gladness of rejoicing
  On the far eternal shore,
Where the one Almighty Father
  Reigns in love for evermore.
      BERNHARDT SEVERIN INGEMANN
                 1789–1862
      Tr. SABINE BARING-GOULD
                 1834–1924

424

THY hand, O God, has guided
    Thy flock, from age to age;
The wondrous tale is written,
  Full clear, on every page;
Our fathers owned thy goodness,
  And we their deeds record;
And both of this bear witness,
  *One Church, one Faith, one
    Lord.*

2 Thy heralds brought glad
    tidings
  To greatest, as to least;
They bade men rise, and hasten
  To share the great King's
    feast;
And this was all their teaching,
  In every deed and word,
To all alike proclaiming,

3 Through many a day of dark-
    ness,
  Through many a scene of
    strife,
The faithful few fought bravely
  To guard the nation's life.
Their Gospel of redemption,
  Sin pardoned, man restored,
Was all in this enfolded,

4 Thy mercy will not fail us,
　Nor leave thy work undone;
With thy right hand to help us,
　The victory shall be won;
And then, by men and angels,
　Thy Name shall be adored,
And this shall be their anthem:
　　EDWARD HAYES PLUMPTRE
　　　　1821–91

425

IN Christ there is no East or
　West,
　In him no South or North,
But one great fellowship of
　love
　　Throughout the whole wide
　　earth.

2 In him shall true hearts every-
　where
　Their high communion find,
His service is the golden cord
　Close-binding all mankind.

3 Join hands, then, brothers of
　the Faith,
　Whate'er your race may be:
Who serves my Father as a son
　Is surely kin to me.

4 In Christ now meet both East
　and West,
　In him meet South and North,
All Christlike souls are one in
　him,
　　Throughout the whole wide
　　earth.
　　　　JOHN OXENHAM, 1852–1941

426 *For children*

A GLORIOUS company we
　sing,
The Master and his men,
He sent them forth to tell his
　love
　By voice and hand and pen.

2 A loving company we sing,
When Jesus sent to save
All sick and blind and hungry
　folk,
The outcast and the slave.

3 We join this glorious company
Of Jesus and his friends,
To　spread　throughout　this
　troubled world
His love that never ends.
　　　ALBERT FREDERICK BAYLY
　　The following are also suitable
　　Nos. 139, 140, 151, 169, 324, 333

427 *For younger children*

THE Church is wherever God's
　people are praising,
Singing their thanks for joy on
　this day.
The Church is wherever disciples
　of Jesus
Remember his story and walk
　in his way.

2 The Church is wherever God's
　people are helping,
Caring for neighbours in sick-
　ness and need.
The Church is wherever God's
　people are sharing
The words of the Bible in gift
　and in deed.
　　　　CAROL ROSE IKELER

DEDICATION AND DISCIPLESHIP

428

LORD of creation, to thee be
　all praise!
Most mighty thy working, most
　wondrous thy ways!
Who reignest in glory no tongue
　can e'er tell,
Yet deign'st in the heart of the
　humble to dwell.

2 Lord of all power, I give thee
　my will,
In joyful obedience thy tasks
　to fulfil.
Thy bondage is freedom; thy
　service is song;
And, held in thy keeping, my
　weakness is strong.

154

Lord of all wisdom, I give thee
my mind,
Rich truth that surpasseth
man's knowledge to find.
What eye hath not seen and
what ear hath not heard
Is taught by thy Spirit and
shines from thy Word.

Lord of all bounty, I give thee
my heart;
I praise and adore thee for all
that thou art;
Thy love to inflame me, thy
counsel to guide,
Thy presence to shield me,
whate'er may betide.

Lord of all being, I give thee
my all;
If e'er I disown thee, I stumble
and fall;
But, sworn in glad service thy
word to obey,
I walk in thy freedom to the
end of the way.

JACK COPLEY WINSLOW

429

MY God, accept my heart
this day
And make it always thine,
That I from thee no more may
stray,
No more from thee decline.

Before the cross of him who
died,
Behold, I prostrate fall;
Let every sin be crucified,
And Christ be all in all.

Anoint me with thy heavenly
grace,
And seal me for thine own;
That I may see thy glorious
face,
And worship near thy throne.

Let every thought and work
and word
To thee be ever given;
Then life shall be thy service,
Lord,
And death the gate of heaven.

5 All glory to the Father be,
All glory to the Son,
All glory, Holy Ghost, to thee,
While endless ages run. Amen.

MATTHEW BRIDGES, 1800–94

430

'TAKE up thy cross,' the
Saviour said,
'If thou wouldst my disciple
be;
Take up thy cross, with willing
heart,
And humbly follow after me.'

2 Take up thy cross; let not its
weight
Fill thy weak soul with vain
alarm;
His strength shall bear thy
spirit up,
And brace thy heart, and
nerve thine arm.

3 Take up thy cross, nor heed the
shame,
And let thy foolish pride be
still:
Thy Lord refused not e'en to die
Upon a cross, on Calvary's hill.

4 Take up thy cross, then, in his
strength,
And calmly every danger
brave;
'Twill guide thee to a better
home,
And lead to victory o'er the
grave.

5 Take up thy cross, and follow
Christ,
Nor think till death to lay
it down;
For only he who bears the cross
May hope to wear the glorious
crown.

CHARLES WILLIAM EVEREST
1814–77

431

JESUS, Master, whose I am,
Purchased, thine alone to be,
By thy blood, O spotless Lamb,
Shed so willingly for me,
Let my heart be all thine own,
Let me live to thee alone.

2 Jesus, Master, I am thine:
   Keep me faithful, keep me
      near;
Let thy presence in me shine,
   All my homeward way to
      cheer.
Jesus, at thy feet I fall,
O be thou my All in All.

3 Jesus, Master, whom I serve,
   Though so feebly and so ill,
Strengthen hand and heart and
      nerve
   All thy bidding to fulfil;
Open thou mine eyes to see
All the work thou hast for me.

4 Jesus, Master, wilt thou use
   One who owes thee more than
      all?
As thou wilt! I would not
      choose;
   Only let me hear thy call.
Jesus, let me always be
In thy service glad and free.
                FRANCES RIDLEY HAVERGAL
                            1836–79

432

MAY the mind of Christ my
   Saviour
Live in me from day to day,
By his love and power controlling
All I do or say.

2 May the word of God dwell
      richly
   In my heart from hour to
      hour,
So that all may see I triumph
Only through his power.

3 May the peace of God my Father
   Rule my life in everything,
That I may be calm to comfort
Sick and sorrowing.

4 May the love of Jesus fill me,
   As the waters fill the sea;
Him exalting, self abasing,
This is victory.

5 May I run the race before me,
   Strong and brave to face the
      foe,
Looking only unto Jesus
As I onward go.
                KATE BARCLAY WILKINSON
                            1859–1928

433

GOD be in my head, and in
   my understanding;
God be in mine eyes, and in my
   looking;
God be in my mouth, and in my
   speaking;
God be in my heart, and in my
   thinking;
God be at mine end, and at my
   departing.
            Book of Hours (London, 1514)

434

O JESUS, I have promised
   To serve thee to the end;
Be thou for ever near me,
   My Master and my Friend:
I shall not fear the battle
   If thou art by my side,
Nor wander from the pathway
   If thou wilt be my Guide.

2 O let me feel thee near me:
   The world is ever near;
I see the sights that dazzle,
   The tempting sounds I hear;
My foes are ever near me,
   Around me and within;
But, Jesus, draw thou nearer,
   And shield my soul from
      sin.

3 O let me hear thee speaking
   In accents clear and still,
Above the storms of passion,
   The murmurs of self-will;
O speak to reassure me,
   To hasten or control;
O speak, and make me listen,
   Thou Guardian of my soul.

4 O Jesus, thou hast promised,
   To all who follow thee,
That where thou art in glory
   There shall thy servant be;
And, Jesus, I have promised
   To serve thee to the end;
O give me grace to follow,
   My Master and my Friend.
                JOHN ERNEST BODE, 1816–74

35

LORD, in the fullness of my
    might,
  I would for thee be strong:
While runneth o'er each dear
    delight,
  To thee should soar my song.

I would not give the world my
    heart,
  And then profess thy love;
I would not feel my strength
    depart,
  And then thy service prove.

I would not with swift-wingèd
    zeal
  On the world's errands go,
And labour up the heavenly hill
  With weary feet and slow.

O not for thee my weak desires,
  My poorer, baser part!
O not for thee my fading fires,
  The ashes of my heart!

O choose me in my golden time:
  In my dear joys have part!
For thee the glory of my prime,
  The fullness of my heart!

THOMAS HORNBLOWER GILL
1819–1906

36

O MASTER, let me walk with
    thee
In lowly paths of service free;
Thy secret tell; help me to bear
The strain of toil, the fret of
    care.

Help me the slow of heart to
    move
By some clear winning word of
    love;
Teach me the wayward feet to
    stay,
And guide them in the home-
    ward way.

Teach me thy patience; still
    with thee
In closer, dearer company,
In work that keeps faith sweet
    and strong,
In trust that triumphs over
    wrong,

4 In hope that sends a shining ray
  Far down the future's broaden-
      ing way,
  In peace that only thou canst
      give,
  With thee, O Master, let me live.

WASHINGTON GLADDEN
1836–1918

437

LOVE Divine, all loves excell-
    ing,
  Joy of heaven, to earth come
      down,
  Fix in us thy humble dwelling,
    All   thy   faithful   mercies
      crown.
Jesus, thou art all compassion,
  Pure, unbounded love thou
      art;
Visit us with thy salvation,
  Enter every trembling heart.

2 Come, almighty to deliver;
    Let us all thy life receive;
  Suddenly return, and never,
      Never more thy temples leave.
  Thee   we   would   be   always
      blessing,
    Serve thee as thy hosts above,
  Pray, and praise thee, without
      ceasing,
      Glory in thy perfect love.

3 Finish then thy new creation:
    Pure and spotless let us be;
  Let us see thy great salvation,
      Perfectly restored in thee,
  Changed from glory into glory,
      Till in heaven we take our
      place,
  Till we cast our crowns before
      thee,
    Lost in wonder, love, and
      praise.

CHARLES WESLEY, 1707–88

438

GRACIOUS   Spirit,   Holy
    Ghost,
Taught by thee, we covet most,
Of thy gifts at Pentecost,
    Holy, heavenly love.

2 Faith that mountains could remove,
Tongues of earth or heaven
above,
Knowledge, all things, empty
prove
Without heavenly love.

3 Though I as a martyr bleed,
Give my goods the poor to feed,
All is vain if love I need;
Therefore give me love.

4 Love is kind, and suffers long;
Love is meek, and thinks no
wrong,
Love than death itself more
strong;
Therefore give us love.

5 Prophecy will fade away,
Melting in the light of day;
Love will ever with us stay;
Therefore give us love.

6 Faith and hope and love we see,
Joining hand in hand, agree;
But the greatest of the three,
And the best, is love.

CHRISTOPHER WORDSWORTH, 1807–85
From 1 Corinthians 13

439

O LORD and Master of us all,
Whate'er our name or sign,
We own thy sway, we hear thy
call,
We test our lives by thine.

2 Thou judgest us: thy purity
Doth all our lusts condemn;
The love that draws us nearer
thee
Is hot with wrath to them.

3 Our thoughts lie open to thy
sight;
And naked to thy glance
Our secret sins are, in the light
Of thy pure countenance.

4 Yet, weak and blinded though
we be,
Thou dost our service own;
We bring our varying gifts to
thee,
And thou rejectest none.

5 Apart from thee all gain is loss,
All labour vainly done;
The solemn shadow of thy cross
Is better than the sun.

6 Our Friend, our Brother, and
our Lord,
What may thy service be?
Nor name, nor form, nor ritual
word,
But simply following thee.

7 We faintly hear; we dimly see;
In differing phrase we pray;
But, dim or clear, we own in thee
The Light, the Truth, the
Way.

JOHN GREENLEAF WHITTIER
1807–9

440

'LIFT up your hearts!' We
. lift them, Lord, to thee;
Here at thy feet none other may
we see:
'Lift up your hearts!' E'en so,
with one accord,
We lift them up, we lift them
to the Lord.

2 Above the level of the former
years,
The mire of sin, the slough of
guilty fears,
The mist of doubt, the blight of
love's decay,
O Lord of light, lift all our
hearts today!

3 Lift every gift that thou thyself
hast given;
Low lies the best till lifted up
to heaven;
Low lie the bounding heart, the
teeming brain,
Till, sent from God, they mount
to God again.

4 Then, as the trumpet-call, in
after years,
'Lift up your hearts!' rings
pealing in our ears,
Still shall those hearts respond
with full accord,
'We lift them up, we lift them
to the Lord!'

HENRY MONTAGU BUTLER
1833–19

158

441

SOLDIERS of Christ! arise,
  And put your armour on,
Strong in the strength which
    God supplies
  Through his eternal Son;
Strong in the Lord of hosts,
  And in his mighty power;
Who in the strength of Jesus
    trusts
  Is more than conqueror.

Stand, then, in his great might,
  With all his strength endued;
And take, to arm you for the
    fight,
  The panoply of God.
To keep your armour bright
  Attend with constant care,
Still walking in your Captain's
    sight,
  And watching unto prayer.

From strength to strength go
    on;
  Wrestle, and fight, and pray;
Tread all the powers of darkness
    down,
  And win the well-fought
    day,—
That, having all things done,
  And all your conflicts passed,
Ye may o'ercome through Christ
    alone,
  And stand complete at last.

CHARLES WESLEY, 1707–88

442

FIGHT the good fight with
  all thy might;
Christ is thy strength, and
    Christ thy right;
  Lay hold on life, and it shall
    be
Thy joy and crown eternally.

Run the straight race through
    God's good grace,
Lift up thine eyes, and seek his
    face;
  Life with its path before us
    lies;
Christ is the way, and Christ
    the prize.

3 Cast care aside; and on thy
    Guide
Lean, and his mercy will
    provide,—
  Lean, and the trusting soul
    shall prove
Christ is its life, and Christ its
    love.

4 Faint not, nor fear; his arm is
    near;
He changeth not, and thou art
    dear;
  Only believe, and thou shalt
    see
That Christ is all in all to thee.

JOHN SAMUEL BEWLEY MONSELL
1811–75

443

WHO would true valour see,
  Let him come hither;
One here will constant be,
    Come wind, come wea-
      ther;
There's no discouragement
Shall make him once relent
His first avowed intent
    To be a pilgrim.

2 Whoso beset him round
    With dismal stories,
Do but themselves confound;
      His strength the more is.
No lion can him fright,
He'll with a giant fight,
But he will have a right
    To be a pilgrim.

3 Hobgoblin nor foul fiend
    Can daunt his spirit;
He knows he at the end
      Shall life inherit.
Then fancies fly away;
He'll fear not what men say;
He'll labour night and day
    To be a pilgrim.

JOHN BUNYAN, 1628–88

444

I FEEL the winds of God to-
    day;
  Today my sail I lift,
Though heavy oft with drench-
    ing spray,
  And torn with many a rift;

159

If hope but light the water's
    crest,
  And Christ my bark will use,
I'll seek the seas at his behest,
  And brave another cruise.

2 It is the wind of God that dries
  My vain regretful tears,
Until with braver thoughts shall
    rise
  The purer, brighter years;
If cast on shores of selfish ease
  Or pleasure I should be,
Lord, let me feel thy freshening
    breeze,
  And I'll put back to sea.

3 If ever I forget thy love
    And how that love was
      shown,
Lift high the blood-red flag
    above:
  It bears thy Name alone.
Great Pilot of my onward way,
  Thou wilt not let me drift;
I feel the winds of God today,
  Today my sail I lift.

        JESSIE ADAMS, 1863–1954

445

M AKE me a captive, Lord,
    And then I shall be
  free;
Force me to render up my
    sword,
  And I shall conqueror be.
I sink in life's alarms
  When by myself I stand;
Imprison me within thine
    arms,
  And strong shall be my
    hand.

2 My heart is weak and poor
  Until it master find;
It has no spring of action sure—
  It varies with the wind.
It cannot freely move
  Till thou hast wrought its
    chain;
Enslave it with thy matchless
    love,
  And deathless it shall reign.

3 My power is faint and low
   Till I have learned to serve;
It wants the needed fire to glow
  It wants the breeze to nerve;
It cannot drive the world,
  Until itself be driven;
Its flag can only be unfurled
  When thou shalt breathe from
    heaven.

4 My will is not my own
   Till thou hast made it thine;
If it would reach a monarch's
    throne
  It must its crown resign;
It only stands unbent,
  Amid the clashing strife,
When on thy bosom it has lean
  And found in thee its life.

        GEORGE MATHESON, 1842–190

446

*L AND of our Birth, w
    pledge to thee
Our love and toil in the year
  to be;
When we are grown and tak
  our place,
As men and women with ou
  race.

2 Father in heaven, who loves
  all,
O help thy children when the
  call;
That they may build from ag
  to age
An undefilèd heritage.

3 Teach us to bear the yoke i
  youth,
With steadfastness and caref
  truth;
That, in our time, thy grac
  may give
The truth whereby the nation
  live.

4 Teach us to rule ourselves a
  way,
Controlled and cleanly nigh
  and day;
That we may bring, if need aris
No maimed or worthless sacr
  fice.

Teach us to look, in all our ends,
On thee for Judge, and not our
friends;
That we, with thee, may walk
uncowed
By fear or favour of the crowd.

Teach us the strength that cannot seek,
By deed or thought, to hurt the
weak;
That, under thee, we may
possess
Man's strength to succour man's
distress.

Teach us delight in simple
things,
And mirth that has no bitter
springs;
Forgiveness free of evil done,
And love to all men 'neath the
sun!

8 Land of our Birth, our faith,
our pride,
For whose dear sake our fathers
died;
O Motherland, we pledge to
thee,
Head, heart, and hand through
the years to be!

RUDYARD KIPLING, 1865–1936

*The complete poem is given here, but
verses 1 and 8 should be omitted unless the
occasion warrants their use.*

447

LORD and Master, who hast
called us
All our days to follow thee,
We have heard thy clear com-
mandment,
'Bring the children unto Me.'

2 So we come to thee, the teacher,
At thy feet we kneel to pray:
We can only lead the children
When thyself shalt show the
way.

3 Teach us thy most wondrous
method,
As of old in Galilee
Thou didst show thy chosen
servants
How to bring men unto thee.

4 Give us store of wit and wisdom,
Give us love which never tires,
Give us thine abiding patience,
Give us hope which aye inspires.

5 Mighty Wisdom of the God-
head,
Thou the One eternal Word,
Thou the counsellor, the teacher,
Fill us with thy fullness, Lord.

FLORENCE MARGARET SMITH
1886–1958

448 *For young people*

JUST as I am, thine own to be,
Friend of the young, who
lovest me;
To consecrate myself to thee,
O Jesus Christ, I come.

2 In the glad morning of my
day,
My life to give, my vows to
pay,
With no reserve and no delay,
With all my heart I come.

3 I would live ever in the light,
I would work ever for the right,
I would serve thee with all my
might,
Therefore to thee I come.

4 Just as I am, young, strong and
free,
To be the best that I can be
For truth, and righteousness,
and thee,
Lord of my life, I come.

MARIANNE FARNINGHAM
1834–1909

The following are also suitable
Nos. 211, 88

449 *For children*

LOOKING upward every day,
Sunshine on our faces;
Pressing onward every day
Toward the heavenly places;
Growing every day in awe,
For thy Name is holy;
Learning every day to love
With a love more lowly;

2 Walking every day more close
   To our Elder Brother;
Growing every day more true
   Unto one another;
Leaving every day behind
   Something which might hin-
      der;
Running swifter every day;
   Growing purer, kinder,—

3 Lord, so pray we every day:
   Hear us in thy pity,
That we enter in at last
   To the holy city.
Looking upward every day,
   Sunshine on our faces;
Press we onward every day
   Toward the heavenly places.
                    MARY BUTLER, 1841–1916

450 *For children*

SAVIOUR, teach me, day by
   day,
Love's sweet lesson to obey;

Sweeter lesson cannot be,
Loving him who first loved me.

2 With a child's glad heart of love
At thy bidding may I move,
Prompt to serve and follow
   thee,
Loving him who first loved me.

3 Teach me thus thy steps to
   trace,
Strong to follow in thy grace,
Learning how to love from thee,
Loving him who first loved me.

4 Love in loving finds employ,
In obedience all her joy;
Ever new that joy will be,
Loving him who first loved me.

5 Thus may I rejoice to show
That I feel the love I owe;
Singing, till thy face I see,
Of his love who first loved me.
                    JANE ELIZA LEESON, 1807–8.

STEWARDSHIP AND SERVICE

451

ALMIGHTY Father of all
   things that be,
Our life, our work, we consecrate to thee,
Whose heavens declare thy
   glory from above,
Whose earth below is witness to
   thy love.

2 For well we know this weary,
   soilèd earth
Is yet thine own by right of its
   new birth,
Since that great cross upreared
   on Calvary
Redeemed it from its fault and
   shame to thee.

3 Thine still the changeful beauty
   of the hills,
The purple valleys flecked with
   silver rills,
The ocean glistening 'neath the
   golden rays;
They all are thine, and voiceless
   speak thy praise.

4 Thou dost the strength to work
   man's arm impart;
From thee the skilled musician's
   mystic art,
The grace of poet's pen or
   painter's hand
To teach the loveliness of sea
   and land.

5 Then grant us, Lord, in all
   things thee to own,
To dwell within the shadow of
   thy throne,
To speak and work, to think
   and live, and move,
Reflecting thine own nature
   which is love;

6 That so, by Christ redeemed
   from sin and shame,
And hallowed by thy Spirit's
   cleansing flame,
Ourselves, our work, and all our
   powers may be
A sacrifice acceptable to thee.
                    ERNEST EDWARD DUGMORE
                    1843–1925

452

GOD, who hast given us
power to sound
Depths hitherto unknown;
To probe earth's hidden mys-
teries,
And make their might our
own;
Great are thy gifts: yet greater
far
This gift, O God, bestow,
That as to knowledge we attain
We may in wisdom grow.

Let wisdom's godly fear dispel
All fears that hate impart;
Give understanding to the mind,
And with new mind new
heart.

So for thy glory and man's good
May we thy gifts employ,
Lest, maddened by the lust of
power,
Man shall himself destroy.

GEORGE WALLACE BRIGGS
1875–1959

453

BEHOLD us, Lord, a little
space
From daily tasks set free,
And met within thy holy place
To rest awhile with thee.
Yet these are not the only walls
Wherein thou mayst be
sought;
On homeliest work thy blessing
falls,
In truth and patience
wrought.

Thine is the loom, the forge, the
mart,
The wealth of land and sea,
The worlds of science and of art,
Revealed and ruled by thee.
Work shall be prayer, if all be
wrought
As thou wouldst have it done,
And prayer, by thee inspired
and taught,
Itself with work be one.

JOHN ELLERTON, 1826–93

454

SON of God, eternal Saviour,
Source of life and truth and
grace,
Son of Man, whose birth in-
carnate
Hallows all our human race;
Thou, our Head, who, throned
in glory,
For thine own dost ever plead,
Fill us with thy love and pity,
Heal our wrongs, and help
our need.

2 As thou, Lord, hast lived for
others,
So may we for others live;
Freely have thy gifts been
granted,
Freely may thy servants give.
Thine the gold and thine the
silver,
Thine the wealth of land and
sea,
We but stewards of thy bounty,
Held in solemn trust for thee.

3 Come, O Christ, and reign
among us,
King of Love, and Prince of
Peace;
Hush the storm of strife and
passion,
Bid its cruel discords cease.
Ah, the past is dark behind us,
Strewn with wrecks and
stained with blood;
But before us gleams the vision
Of the coming brotherhood.

4 See the Christlike host advancing,
High and lowly, great and
small,
Linked in bonds of common
service
For the common Lord of all.
Thou who prayedst, thou who
willest
That thy people should be
one,
Grant, O grant our hope's
fruition:
Here on earth thy will be
done.

SOMERSET CORRY LOWRY
1855–1932

163

455

ANGEL voices, ever singing
　　Round thy throne of light,
Angel harps, for ever ringing,
　　Rest not day nor night;
Thousands only live to bless
　　　thee,
　　And confess thee
　　　　Lord of might.

2 Yea, we know that thou re-
　　　joicest
　　O'er each work of thine;
Thou didst ears and hands and
　　　voices
　　For thy praise design;
Craftsman's art and music's
　　　measure
　　For thy pleasure
　　　　All combine.

3 In thy house, great God, we
　　　offer
　　Of thine own to thee,
And for thine acceptance
　　　proffer,
　　All unworthily,
Hearts and minds and hands
　　　and voices,
　　In our choicest
　　　　Psalmody.

4 *Honour, glory, might, and merit*
　　Thine shall ever be,
Father, Son, and Holy Spirit,
　　Blessèd Trinity.
Of the best that thou hast given,
　　Earth and heaven
　　　　Render thee. Amen.
　　　　　FRANCIS POTT, 1832–1909

456

WE give thee but thine
　　　own,
　　Whate'er the gift may be;
All that we have is thine alone,
　　A trust, O Lord, from thee.

2 May we thy bounties thus
　　As stewards true receive,
And gladly, as thou blessest
　　　us,
　　To thee our first-fruits give.

3 O hearts are bruised and dead,
　　And homes are bare and cold,
And lambs for whom the
　　　Shepherd bled
　　Are straying from the fold.

4 To comfort and to bless,
　　To find a balm for woe,
To tend the lone and fatherless
　　Is angels' work below.

5 The captive to release,
　　To God the lost to bring,
To teach the way of life and
　　　peace,
　　It is a Christ-like thing.

6 And we believe thy word,
　　Though dim our faith may
　　　be,—
Whate'er for thine we do, O
　　　Lord,
　　We do it unto thee.
　　　WILLIAM WALSHAM HOW, 1823–9

457

FILL thou our life, O Lord
　　　our God,
　　In every part with praise,
That our whole being may
　　　proclaim
　　Thy being and thy ways.

2 Not for the lip of praise alone,
　　Nor ev'n the praising heart
We ask, but for a life made up
　　Of praise in every part.

3 Praise in the common things of
　　　life,
　　Its goings out and in;
Praise in each duty and each
　　　deed,
　　However small and mean.

4 So shalt thou, gracious Lord,
　　　receive
　　From us the glory due;
And so shall we begin on earth
　　The song for ever new.

5 So shall no part of day or night
　　From sacredness be free;
But all our life, in every step,
　　Be fellowship with thee.
　　　HORATIUS BONAR, 1808–8
　　　　　altered

164

458

LORD of all good, our gifts
we bring to thee,
Use them thy holy purpose to
fulfil;
Tokens of love and pledges they
shall be
That our whole life is offered
to thy will.

Father, whose bounty all creation shows,
Christ, by whose willing sacrifice we live,
Spirit, from whom all life in
fullness flows,
To thee with grateful hearts
ourselves we give.

ALBERT FREDERICK BAYLY

459

FOUNTAIN of good, to own
thy love
Our thankful hearts incline;
What can we render, Lord, to
thee,
When all the worlds are
thine?

But thou hast needy brethren
here,
Partakers of thy grace,
Whose names thou wilt thyself
confess
Before the Father's face.

And in their accents of distress
Thy pleading voice is heard;
In them thou mayst be clothed
and fed,
And visited and cheered.

Thy face, with reverence and
with love,
We in thy poor would see;
O may we minister to them,
And in them, Lord, to thee.

PHILIP DODDRIDGE, 1702–51

460

O BROTHER man, fold to
thy heart thy brother!
Where pity dwells, the peace
of God is there;

To worship rightly is to love
each other,
Each smile a hymn, each
kindly deed a prayer.

2 For he whom Jesus loved hath
truly spoken:
The holier worship which he
deigns to bless
Restores the lost, and binds the
spirit broken,
And feeds the widow and the
fatherless.

3 Follow with reverent steps the
great example
Of him whose holy work was
doing good;
So shall the wide earth seem our
Father's temple,
Each loving life a psalm of
gratitude.

4 Then shall all shackles fall; the
stormy clangour
Of wild war-music o'er the
earth shall cease;
Love shall tread out the baleful
fire of anger,
And in its ashes plant the
tree of peace.

JOHN GREENLEAF WHITTIER
1807–92

461

O GOD of mercy, God of
might,
In love and pity infinite,
Teach us, as ever in thy sight,
To live our life to thee.

2 And thou, who cam'st on earth
to die
That fallen man might live
thereby,
O hear us, for to thee we cry,—
In hope, O Lord, to thee.

3 Teach us the lesson thou hast
taught,
To feel for those thy blood hath
bought,
That every word and deed and
thought
May work a work for thee.

4 For all are brethren, far and wide,
　Since, thou, O Lord, for all hast
　　died;
　Then teach us, whatsoe'er be-
　　tide,
　To love them all in thee.

5 In sickness, sorrow, want, or
　　care;
　Whate'er it be, 'tis ours to
　　share;
　May we, where help is needed,
　　there
　Give help as unto thee.

6 And may thy Holy Spirit move
　All those who live, to live in
　　love,
　Till thou shalt greet in heaven
　　above
　All those who give to thee.

GODFREY THRING, 1823–1903

462

TAKE my life, and let it be
　　Consecrated, Lord, to thee.
Take my moments and my
　days;
Let them flow in ceaseless
　praise.

2 Take my hands, and let them
　move
At the impulse of thy love.
Take my feet, and let them be
Swift and beautiful for thee.

3 Take my voice, and let me sing
Always, only, for my King.
Take my intellect, and use
Every power as thou shalt
　choose.

4 Take my will, and make it thine;
It shall be no longer mine.
Take my heart—it is thine own;
It shall be thy royal throne.

5 Take my love; my Lord, I pour
At thy feet its treasure-store.
Take myself, and I will be
Ever, only, all for thee.

FRANCES RIDLEY HAVERGAL
1836–79, altered

463

FORTH in thy Name, O
　　Lord, I go,
My daily labour to pursue,
Thee, only thee, resolved to
　know
In all I think, or speak, or do.

2 The task thy wisdom hath
　assigned
O let me cheerfully fulfil,
In all my works thy presence
　find,
And prove thy good and
　perfect will.

3 Thee may I set at my right
　hand,
Whose eyes mine inmost sub-
　stance see,
And labour on at thy command
And offer all my works to
　thee.

4 Give me to bear thy easy yoke,
And every moment watch
　and pray,
And still to things eternal look,
And hasten to thy glorious
　day;

5 For thee delightfully employ
Whate'er thy bounteous grace
　hath given,
And run my course with even
　joy,
And closely walk with thee
　to heaven.

CHARLES WESLEY, 1707–88
altered

464   *For children*

THE wise may bring their
　learning,
The rich may bring their
　wealth,
And some may bring their
　greatness,
And some their strength and
　health:
We too would bring our trea-
　sures
To offer to the King;
We have no wealth or learning,
What gifts then shall we
　bring?

166

We'll bring the many duties
 We have to do each day;
We'll try our best to please him,
 At home, at school, at play:
And better are these treasures
 To offer to our King
Than richest gifts without
 them;
 Yet these we all may bring.

We'll bring him hearts that love
 him,
 We'll bring him thankful
 praise,
And souls for ever striving
 To follow in his ways:
And these shall be the treasures
 We offer to the King,
And these are gifts that ever
 Our grateful hearts may
 bring.

Book of Praise for Children (1881)
 and Compilers of
 The BBC Hymn Book, 1951

465 *For younger children*

HANDS to work and feet to
 run—
 God's good gifts to me and
 you;
Hands and feet he gave to us
 To help each other the whole
 day through.

2 Eyes to see and ears to hear—
 God's good gifts to me and
 you;

Eyes and ears he gave to us
 To help each other the whole
 day through.

3 Minds to think and hearts to
 love—
 God's good gifts to me and
 you;
Minds and hearts he gave to us
 To help each other the whole
 day through.

HILDA MARGARET DODD

466 *For younger children*

OUR thoughts go round the
 world
To children everywhere;
So much of joy is ours, O God,
Help us to love and share.

JESSIE ELEANOR MOORE, 1887–1969

467 *For younger children*

TAKE our gifts, O loving
 Jesus,
 Use them in some lovely way,
For the happiness and comfort
 Of the whole wide world
 today.

2 Let us be allowed to help you,
 In some plan of loving care,
In some venture for the king-
 dom,
 By our pence and by our
 prayer.

MARGARET CROPPER

WITNESS AND ENCOURAGEMENT

468

SPEAK forth thy word, O
 Father,
Men's hungry minds to feed:
The people starve and perish,
Unconscious of their need;
For so, Lord, thou hast made us
That not alone by bread,
But by thy word of comfort
Our hunger must be fed.

2 The secrets of the atom,
 The universe of light,
 All wonders of creation
 Proclaim thy boundless
 might:
 But only through the witness
 From man to man passed on
 Dost thou reveal in fullness
 The Gospel of thy Son.

3 To each man in his language,
  To each man in his home,
  By many paths and channels
  The faith of Christ may come:
  How shall men hear its message
  If there be none to preach?
  How shall they learn its lesson
  If there be none to teach?

4 Take us, then, Lord, and use us
  Thy messengers to be:
  Our prayers, our gifts, our ser-
      vice
  We offer here to thee,
  That every man and nation
  May learn what we have heard,
  And all the minds of millions
  Shall feed upon thy word.

            CHARLES JEFFRIES

469   *Dieu, nous avons vu
           ta gloire*

* G OD, your glory we have seen
      in your Son,
  Full of truth, full of heavenly grace:
  In Christ make us live, his love
  shine on our face,
  And the nations shall see in us the
  triumph you have won.

2 In the fields of this world his
    good news he has sown,
  And sends us out to reap till the
    harvest is done.

3 In his love like a fire that con-
    sumes he passed by.
  The flame has touched our lips;
    let us shout, 'Here am I'.

4 He was broken for us, God-for-
    saken his cry,
  And still the bread he breaks;
    to ourselves we must die.

5 He has trampled the grapes of
    new life on his cross.
  Now drink the cup and live; he
    has filled it for us.

6 He has founded a kingdom that
    none shall destroy;
  The corner-stone is laid. Go to
    work: build with joy!

            DIDIER RIMBAUD
      Refrain tr. ROLAND JOHNSON
      Verses tr. BRIAN WREN

  * Verse 1 is repeated as a refrain after
each verse.

470

G O ye, said Jesus, and preach
      the word,
  All through the world let it
      voice be heard,
  Publish the tidings o'er land
      and sea,
  Tell men the truth that shall
      make them free
  And carry the Gospel on!

2 Lo, I am with you the whole
      way through,
  Blessing and guiding in all that
      you do,
  Go ye wherever man's feet have
      trod,
  Bearing the gift of the word of
      God
  And carry the Gospel on!

3 Swiftly and surely the truth
      shall spread,
  Winning its way as the word is
      read,
  Lifting the nations till old and
      young,
  Hearing God's voice in their
      native tongue,
  Shall carry the Gospel on!

4 Saviour, obeying thy great
      command,
  Safe in the grasp of thy guiding
      hand,
  Strong in the faith of thy holy
      word,
  Gladly we answer our risen
      Lord,
  And carry the Gospel on!

            GEORGE OSBORNE GREGORY

471

L IFT up your heads, ye gates
      of brass,
    Ye bars of iron, yield,
  And let the King of Glory pass
    The cross is in the field.

2 Ye armies of the living God,
    His sacramental host,
  Where hallowed footstep never
      trod,
    Take your appointed post.

Follow the cross; the ark of
  peace
Accompany your path,
To slaves and rebels bring re-
  lease
  From bondage and from
    wrath.

Though few and small and weak
  your bands,
  Strong in your Captain's
    strength,
Go to the conquest of all
  lands;
  All must be his at length.

O fear not, faint not, halt not
  now;
  Quit you like men, be strong;
To Christ shall every nation
  bow,
  And sing with you this song:

'Uplifted are the gates of brass;
  The bars of iron yield;
Behold the King of Glory pass!
  The cross hath won the field.'

JAMES MONTGOMERY, 1771–1854

472(i) *Verzäge nicht, du Häuflein klein*

FEAR not, thou faithful
  Christian flock;
God is thy shelter and thy
  rock;
Fear not for thy salvation.
Though fierce the foe and dark
  the night,
The Lord of hosts shall be thy
  might,
Christ thine illumination.
Arise! Arise! thy foe defy!
Call on the Name of God most
  high,
With heavenly succour arm
  you!
'Gainst world and flesh and
  powers of hell,
Now for his honour quit you
  well.
Lo! there is naught can harm
  you.

ROBERT BRIDGES, 1844–1930
Based on JOHANN MICHAEL
ALTENBURG, 1584–1640
Verse 2 omitted

472(ii)

FAITH of our fathers, taught
  of old
By faithful shepherds of the fold,
  The hallowing of our nation;
Thou wast through many a
  wealthy year,
Through many a darkened day
  of fear,
  The rock of our salvation.
Arise, arise, good Christian men,
Your glorious standard raise
  again,
  The cross of Christ who calls
    you;
Who bids you live and bids you
  die
For his great cause, and stands
  on high
  To witness what befalls you.

2 Our fathers held the faith re-
  ceived,
By saints declared, by saints
  believed,
  By saints in death defended;
Through pain of doubt and
  bitterness,
Through pain of treason and
  distress,
  They for the right contended.
Arise, arise, good Christian men,
Your glorious standard raise
  again,
  The cross of Christ who
    bought you;
Who leads you forth in this new
  age,
With long-enduring hearts to
  wage
  The warfare he has taught
    you.

THOMAS ALEXANDER LACEY
1853–1931
Verses 2, 4 omitted

473

LORD, who in thy perfect
  wisdom
Times and seasons dost arrange,
Working out thy changeless
  purpose
In a world of ceaseless change;

Thou didst form our ancient
    nation,
Guiding it through all the days,
To unfold in it thy purpose
To thy glory and thy praise.

2 To our shores remote, benighted,
Barrier of the western waves,
Tidings in thy love thou sentest,
Tidings of the cross that saves.
Saints and heroes strove and
    suffered
Here thy gospel to proclaim;
We, the heirs of their en-
    deavour,
Tell the honour of their name.

3 Still thine ancient purpose
    standeth
Every change and chance
    above;
Still thine ancient Church re-
    maineth,
Witness to thy changeless love.
Grant us vision, Lord, and
    courage
To fulfil thy work begun;
In the Church and in the nation,
Kings of kings, thy will be
    done.
    TIMOTHY REES, 1874–1939, altered

474

CHRIST is the King! O
    friends rejoice;
Brothers and sisters, with one
    voice
Make all men know he is your
    choice.

2 O magnify the Lord, and raise
Anthems of joy and holy praise
For Christ's brave saints of
ancient days,

3 Who with a faith for ever new
Followed the King, and round
    him drew
Thousands of faithful men and
true.

4 Let Love's unconquerable might
Your scattered companies unite
In service to the Lord of light:

5 So shall God's will on earth ║
    done,
New lamps be lit, new tasl║
    begun,
And the whole Church at la║
    be one.
    GEORGE KENNEDY ALLEN BE║
    1883–19║

475

WE have heard a joyf║
    sound,—
    'Jesus saves!'
Spread the gladness all aroun║
    'Jesus saves!'
Bear the news to every land,
    Climb the steeps and cro║
    the waves;
Onward!—'tis our Lord's cor║
    mand.
    Jesus saves!

2 Waft it on the rolling tide:
    'Jesus saves!'
Tell to sinners far and wide,
    'Jesus saves!'
Sing, ye islands of the sea;
    Echo back, ye ocean caves
Earth shall keep her jubilee:
    Jesus saves!

3 Sing above the battle's strife
    'Jesus saves!'
By his death and endless li║
    'Jesus saves!'
Sing it softly through th║
    gloom,
    When the heart for mer║
    craves;
Sing in triumph o'er the tomb
    'Jesus saves!'

4 Give the winds a mighty voi║
    'Jesus saves!'
Let the nations now rejoice:
    Jesus saves!
Shout salvation full and free
    To every strand that ocea║
    laves,—
This our song of victory,
    'Jesus saves!'
    PRISCILLA JANE OWE║
    1829–19║

476

'FOR my sake and the
Gospel's, go
And tell redemption's story';
His heralds answer, 'Be it so,
And thine, Lord, all the glory!'
They preach his birth, his life,
his cross,
The love of his atonement
For whom they count the world
but loss,
His Easter, his enthronement.

Hark! hark! the trump of
jubilee
Proclaims to every nation,
From pole to pole, by land and
sea,
Glad tidings of salvation.
Still on and on the anthems
spread,
Of alleluia voices;
In concert with the holy dead,
The warrior Church rejoices.

He comes whose advent-
trumpet drowns
The last of time's evangels,
Immanuel, crowned with many
crowns,
The Lord of saints, and
angels.
O Life, Light, Love, the great
I AM
Triune, who changest never,
The throne of God and of the
Lamb
Is thine, and thine for ever.

EDWARD HENRY BICKERSTETH
1825–1906, altered

477

RISE up, O men of God!
Have done with lesser
things;
Give heart and soul and mind
and strength
To serve the King of kings.

Rise up, O men of God!
His Kingdom tarries long;
Bring in the day of brother-
hood,
And end the night of wrong.

3 Rise up, O men of God!
The Church for you doth
wait:
His strength shall make your
spirit strong,
Her service make you great.

4 Lift high the cross of Christ!
Tread where his feet have
trod;
As brothers of the Son of Man
Rise up, O men of God!

WILLIAM PIERSON MERRILL
1867–1954, altered

478

SOLDIERS of the cross, arise!
Gird you with your armour
bright;
Mighty are your enemies,
Hard the battle ye must fight.

2 O'er a faithless fallen world
Raise your banner in the
sky;
Let it float there wide unfurled;
Bear it onward; lift it high.

3 'Mid the homes of want and woe,
Strangers to the living word,
Let the Saviour's herald go,
Let the voice of hope be heard.

4 Where the shadows deepest lie,
Carry truth's unsullied ray;
Where are crimes of blackest
dye,
There the saving sign display.

5 To the weary and the worn
Tell of realms where sorrows
cease;
To the outcast and forlorn
Speak of mercy and of peace.

6 Guard the helpless; seek the
strayed;
Comfort troubles; banish
grief;
In the might of God arrayed,
Scatter sin and unbelief.

7 Be the banner still unfurled,
Still unsheathed the Spirit's
sword,
Till the kingdoms of the world
Are the Kingdom of the Lord.

WILLIAM WALSHAM HOW, 1823–97

479

WHO is on the Lord's side?
　　Who will serve the King?
Who will be his helpers
　Other lives to bring?
Who will leave the world's side?
　Who will face the foe?
Who is on the Lord's side?
　Who for him will go?
　　By thy call of mercy,
　　　By thy grace divine,
　We are on the Lord's side;
　　Saviour, we are thine.

2 Jesus, thou hast bought us,
　　Not with gold or gem,
But with thine own life-blood,
　For thy diadem.
With thy blessing filling
　Each who comes to thee,
Thou hast made us willing,
　Thou hast made us free.
　　By thy grand redemption,
　　　By thy grace divine,
　We are on the Lord's side;
　　Saviour, we are thine.

3 Fierce may be the conflict,
　　Strong may be the foe,
But the King's own army
　None can overthrow.
Round his standard ranging,
　Victory is secure,
For his truth unchanging
　Makes the triumph sure.
　　Joyfully enlisting,
　　　By thy grace divine,
　We are on the Lord's side;
　　Saviour, we are thine.

4 Chosen to be soldiers
　　In an alien land,
Chosen, called, and faithful,
　For our Captain's band,
In the service royal
　Let us not grow cold;
Let us be right loyal,
　Noble, true, and bold.
　　Master, thou wilt keep us,
　　　By thy grace divine,
　Always on the Lord's side,
　　Saviour, always thine.

FRANCES RIDLEY HAVERGAL
1836–79

480

ONWARD! Christian soldiers,
　　Marching as to war,
With the cross of Jesus
　Going on before.
Christ, the Royal Master,
　Leads against the foe;
Forward into battle,
　See! his banners go:
　　Onward! Christian soldiers,
　　　Marching as to war,
　　With the cross of Jesus
　　　Going on before.

2 At the sign of triumph
　　Satan's legions flee;
On then, Christian soldiers,
　On to victory!
Hell's foundations quiver
　At the shout of praise;
Brothers, lift your voices,
　Loud your anthems raise:

3 Like a mighty army
　　Moves the Church of God;
Brothers, we are treading
　Where the saints have trod.
We are not divided,
　All one body we,
One in hope, in doctrine,
　One in charity:

4 Crowns and thrones may
　　perish,
　Kingdoms rise and wane,
But the Church of Jesus
　Constant will remain;
Gates of hell can never
　'Gainst that Church prevail;
We have Christ's own
　promise,
　And that cannot fail:

5 Onward, then, ye people!
　　Join our happy throng;
Blend with ours your voices
　In the triumph song:
'Glory, laud, and honour
　Unto Christ the King!'
This, through countless ages,
　Men and angels sing:

SABINE BARING-GOULD
1834–1924

81

STAND up! stand up for Jesus,
   Ye soldiers of the cross!
Lift high his royal banner!
   It must not suffer loss.
From victory to victory
   His army he shall lead,
Till every foe is vanquished,
   And Christ is Lord indeed.

Stand up! stand up for Jesus!
   The trumpet-call obey;
Forth to the mighty conflict
   In this his glorious day!
Ye that are men, now serve him
   Against unnumbered foes;
Your courage rise with danger,
   And strength to strength
      oppose.

Stand up! stand up for Jesus!
   Stand in his strength alone;
The arm of flesh will fail you;
   Ye dare not trust your own.
Put on the gospel armour,
   Each piece put on with prayer;
Where duty calls, or danger,
   Be never wanting there.

Stand up! stand up for Jesus!
   The strife will not be long;
This day the noise of battle,
   The next the victor's song.
To him that overcometh
   A crown of life shall be;
He with the King of Glory
   Shall reign eternally.

GEORGE DUFFIELD, 1818–88

82

YIELD not to temptation, for
   yielding is sin;
Each victory will help you some
   other to win;
Fight manfully onward; dark
   passions subdue;
Look ever to Jesus, he will carry
   you through.
   Ask the Saviour to help you,
   Comfort, strengthen, and
      keep you;
   He is willing to aid you;
   He will carry you through.

2 Shun evil companions; bad
      language disdain;
God's Name hold in reverence,
   nor take it in vain;
Be thoughtful and earnest,
   kind-hearted and true;
Look ever to Jesus, he will carry
   you through.

3 To him that o'ercometh God
      giveth a crown;
Through faith we shall conquer,
   though often cast down;
He who is our Saviour our
   strength will renew;
Look ever to Jesus, he will carry
   you through.

HORATIO RICHMOND PALMER
1834–1907

483

GO, labour on: spend and be
      spent,
   Thy joy to do the Father's
      will;
It is the way the Master went;
   Should not the servant tread
      it still?

2 Go, labour on while it is day:
   The world's dark night is
      hastening on;
Speed, speed thy work; cast
      sloth away;
   It is not thus that souls are
      won.

3 Men die in darkness at thy
      side,
   Without a hope to cheer the
      tomb;
Take up the torch and wave it
      wide,
   The torch that lights time's
      thickest gloom.

4 Toil on, faint not, keep watch,
      and pray;
   Be wise the erring soul to
      win;
Go forth into the world's high-
      way,
   Compel the wanderer to come
      in.

5 Toil on, and in thy toil rejoice;
   For toil comes rest, for exile
     home;
   Soon shalt thou hear the Bride-
     groom's voice,
   The midnight peal, 'Behold,
     I come!'

HORATIUS BONAR, 1808–89

484

COURAGE, brother! do not
   stumble,
   Though thy path be dark as
     night;
   There's a star to guide the
     humble;
   'Trust in God, and do the
     right'.
   Let the road be rough and
     dreary,
   And its end far out of sight,
   Foot it bravely; strong or
     weary,
   *Trust in God, and do the right.

2 Perish policy and cunning,
   Perish all that fears the light!
   Whether losing, whether win-
     ning,
   Trust in God, and do the right.
   Some will hate thee, some will
     love thee,
   Some will flatter, some will
     slight;
   Cease from man, and look above
     thee:
   Trust in God, and do the right.

3 Simple rule, and safest guiding,
   Inward peace, and inward
     might,
   Star upon our path abiding,—
   Trust in God, and do the right.
   Courage, brother! do not
     stumble,
   Though thy path be dark as
     night;
   There's a star to guide the
     humble:
   'Trust in God, and do the
     right.'

NORMAN MACLEOD, 1812–72

* When this hymn is sung to Tune (ii)
COURAGE, BROTHER, the words 'Trust in
God' must be sung three times in the last
line of each verse.

485

LORD, speak to me, that
   may speak
   In living echoes of thy ton
   As thou hast sought, so let m
     seek
   Thy erring children lost an
     lone.

2 O lead me, Lord, that I ma
     lead
   The wandering and th
     wavering feet;
   O feed me, Lord, that I ma
     feed
   Thy hungering ones wit
     manna sweet.

3 O strengthen me, that, while
     stand
   Firm on the rock, and stron
     in thee,
   I may stretch out a loving han
   To wrestlers with the trouble
     sea.

4 O teach me, Lord, that I ma
     teach
   The precious things thou do
     impart;
   And wing my words, that the
     may reach
   The hidden depths of many
     heart.

5 O give thine own sweet rest t
     me,
   That I may speak with sooth
     ing power
   A word in season, as from the
   To weary ones in needf
     hour.

6 O fill me with thy fullness, Lor
   Until my very heart o'erflo
   In kindling thought and glowin
     word,
   Thy love to tell, thy prais
     to show.

7 O use me, Lord, use even me,
   Just as thou wilt, and whe
     and where,
   Until thy blessèd face I see,
   Thy rest, thy joy, thy glor
     share.

FRANCES RIDLEY HAVERGA
1836–7

486

1 LOVER of souls and Lord of
all the living,
Whose service maketh free,
Hear us who once again our-
selves are giving
Thy servants sure to be.

2 Thou who dost bear the whole
world's tribulation
Upon thy heart alone,
Thou who hast bought us by
thy cross and passion,
And chosen us for thine own,

3 Show us thyself, that we may
know their sorrow
Who have not seen thy face;
Show us their darkness, and
the radiant morrow
Of thine eternal grace.

4 Show us the love wherewith
thy heart is burning,
The travail of thy soul:
Grant us to share thy heart's
desire and yearning
That thou mightest make them
whole.

*5 Make strong our hands, by
thine own great hand grasp-
ing,
Avail and guide our youth;
Grant to us now life that is
everlasting,
And then to know thy truth.

HELEN WADDELL, 1889–1965

* *This verse may be omitted.*

487

1 AND did those feet in ancient
time
Walk upon England's moun-
tains green?
And was the Holy Lamb of God
On England's pleasant pastures seen?

And did the countenance divine
Shine forth upon our clouded
hills?
And was Jerusalem builded here
Among these dark satanic
mills?

2 Bring me my bow of burning
gold!
Bring me my arrows of desire!
Bring me my spear! O clouds,
unfold!
Bring me my chariot of fire!
I will not cease from mental
fight,
Nor shall my sword sleep in
my hand,
Till we have built Jerusalem
In England's green and
pleasant land.

WILLIAM BLAKE, 1757–1827

488 *For younger children*

1 JESUS bids us shine, with a
pure, clear light,
Like a little candle burning in
the night.
In this world is darkness; so let
us shine,
You in your small corner, and I
in mine.

2 Jesus bids us shine, first of all
for him;
Well he sees and knows it, if our
light grows dim:
He looks down from heaven to
see us shine,
You in your small corner, and I
in mine.

3 Jesus bids us shine, then, for all
around;
Many kinds of darkness in the
world are found—
Sin, and want, and sorrow; so
we must shine,
You in your small corner, and I
in mine.

SUSAN WARNER, 1819–85

175

RESPONSE TO THE WORD OF GOD

INTERCESSION: FOR THE CHURCH

489 PSALM 122, verses 1, 2, 6–9

I JOY'D when to the house
of God,
Go up, they said to me.
Jerusalem, within thy gates
Our feet shall standing be.

2 Pray that Jerusalem may have
Peace and felicity:
Let them that love thee and thy
peace
Have still prosperity.

3 Therefore I wish that peace may
still
Within thy walls remain,
And ever may thy palaces
Prosperity retain.

4 Now, for my friends' and
brethren's sakes,
Peace be in thee, I'll say.
And for the house of God our
Lord,
I'll seek thy good alway.

5 *To Father, Son, and Holy Ghost,*
The God whom we adore,
Be glory, as it was, and is,
And shall be evermore. Amen.

490

J ESUS, with thy Church abide;
Be her Saviour, Lord, and
Guide,
While on earth her faith is tried:
We beseech thee, hear us.

2 Keep her life and doctrine pure;
Grant her patience to endure,
Trusting in thy promise sure:

3 May she one in doctrine be,
One in truth and charity,
Winning all to faith in thee:

4 May her scattered children be
From reproach of evil free,
Blameless witnesses for thee:

5 May she thus all glorious be,
Spotless and from wrinkle fre[e]
Pure and bright, and worth[y]
thee:

THOMAS BENSON POLLOC[K]
1836–9[ ]

491 *Christe, du Beistand deiner*
Kreuzgemeine

L ORD of our life, and God o[f]
our salvation,
Star of our night, and Hope o[f]
every nation,
Hear and receive thy Church[']s
supplication,
Lord God Almighty.

2 See round thine ark the hungr[y]
billows curling;
See how thy foes their banne[rs]
are unfurling;
Lord, while their darts en[-]
venomed they are hur[l-]
ing,
Thou canst preserve us.

3 Lord, thou canst help whe[n]
earthly armour faileth;
Lord, thou canst save whe[n]
deadly sin assaileth;
Lord, o'er thy rock nor deat[h]
nor hell prevaileth;
Grant us thy peace, Lord[.]

4 Grant us thy help till foes ar[e]
backward driven;
Grant them thy truth that the[y]
may be forgiven;
Grant peace on earth, and, afte[r]
we have striven,
Peace in thy heaven.

PHILIP PUSEY, 1799–185[ ]
Based on MATTHÄUS APELLES VO[N]
LÖWENSTERN, 1594–164[ ]

492

O THOU, who at th[y]
Eucharist didst pray
That all thy Church migh[t]
be for ever one,

FOR THE CHURCH

Grant us at every Eucharist to say,
With longing heart and soul,
'Thy will be done'.
O may we all one bread, one body be,
One through this sacrament of unity.

2 For all thy Church, O Lord, we intercede;
Make thou our sad divisions soon to cease;
Draw us the nearer each to each, we plead,
By drawing all to thee, O Prince of Peace;
Thus may we all one bread, one body be,
One through this sacrament of unity.

3 We pray thee too for wanderers from thy fold;
O bring them back, good Shepherd of the sheep,

Back to the faith which saints believed of old,
Back to the Church which still that faith doth keep;
Soon may we all one bread, one body be,
One through this sacrament of unity.

4 So, Lord, at length when sacraments shall cease,
May we be one with all thy Church above,
One with thy saints in one unbroken peace,
One with thy saints in one unbounded love:
More blessèd still, in peace and love to be
One with the Trinity in Unity.

WILLIAM HARRY TURTON
1856–1938
Based on St. John 17:11

INTERCESSION:
FOR THE CHURCH'S MISSION

493 PSALM 67

LORD, bless and pity us,
Shine on us with thy face:
That the earth thy way, and nations all
May know thy saving grace.

2 Let people praise thee, Lord;
Let people all thee praise.
O let the nations all be glad,
In songs their voices raise:

3 Thou wilt justly people judge,
On earth rule nations all.
Let people praise thee, Lord;
let them
Praise thee, both great and small.

4 The earth her fruit shall yield,
Our God shall blessing send.
God shall us bless; men shall him fear
Unto earth's utmost end.

5 *To thee be glory, Lord,*
Whom heaven and earth adore,
To Father, Son, and Holy Ghost,
One God for evermore. Amen.

494

THOU whose almighty word
Chaos and darkness heard
And took their flight,
Hear us, we humbly pray,
And, where the gospel day
Sheds not its glorious ray,
Let there be light.

2 Thou who didst come to bring,
On thy redeeming wing,
Healing and sight,
Health to the sick in mind,
Sight to the inly blind,
O now to all mankind
Let there be light.

177

3 Spirit of truth and love,
Life-giving, holy Dove,
Speed forth thy flight;
Move o'er the waters' face,
Bearing the lamp of grace,
And in earth's darkest place
Let there be light.

4 Blessèd and holy Three,
Glorious Trinity,
Wisdom, Love, Might,
Boundless as ocean's tide
Rolling in fullest pride,
Through the world far and wide
Let there be light.

JOHN MARRIOTT, 1780–1825

495

O LORD our God, arise!
The cause of truth
maintain,
And wide o'er all the peopled
world
Extend her blessèd reign.

2 Thou Prince of Life, arise!
Nor let thy glory cease;
Far spread the conquests of thy
grace,
And bless the earth with
peace.

3 Thou Holy Ghost, arise!
Expand thy quickening wing,
And o'er a dark and ruined
world
Let light and order spring.

4 All on the earth, arise!
To God the Saviour sing;
From shore to shore, from earth
to heaven,
Let echoing anthems ring.

RALPH WARDLAW, 1779–1853

496

O SPIRIT of the living God,
In all thy plenitude of
grace,
Where'er the foot of man hath
trod,
Descend on our apostate race.

2 Give tongues of fire and hearts
of love,
To preach the reconciling
word;
Give power and unction from
above,
Whene'er the joyful sound is
heard.

3 Be darkness, at thy coming,
light;
Confusion order, in thy path;
Souls without strength inspire
with might;
Bid mercy triumph over
wrath.

4 O Spirit of the Lord, prepare
All the round earth her God
to meet;
Breathe thou abroad like morning air,
Till hearts of stone begin to
beat.

5 Baptize the nations; far and
nigh
The triumphs of the cross
record;
The Name of Jesus glorify,
Till every kindred call him
Lord.

JAMES MONTGOMERY, 1771–1854

497

GOD of mercy, God of grace,
Show the brightness of
thy face;
Shine upon us, Saviour, shine,
Fill thy Church with light divine,
And thy saving health extend
Unto earth's remotest end.

2 Let the people praise thee, Lord;
Be by all that live adored;
Let the nations shout and sing
Glory to their Saviour King,
At thy feet their tribute pay,
And thy holy will obey.

3 Let the people praise thee, Lord;
Earth shall then her fruits afford,
God to man his blessing give,
Man to God devoted live—
All below and all above,
One in joy and light and love.

HENRY FRANCIS LYTE, 1793–1847

498

ARM of the Lord, awake, awake!
Put on thy strength, the nations shake,
And let the world, adoring, see
Triumphs of mercy wrought by thee.

Say to the heathen from thy throne,
'I am Jehovah, God alone';
Thy voice their idols shall confound,
And cast their altars to the ground.

Let Zion's time of favour come;
O bring the tribes of Israel home;
And let our wondering eyes behold
Gentiles and Jews in Jesus' fold.

Almighty God, thy grace proclaim
In every clime of every name;
Let adverse powers before thee fall,
And crown the Saviour Lord of all.

WILLIAM SHRUBSOLE, 1759–1829

499

ETERNAL God, whose power upholds
Both flower and flaming star,
To whom there is no here nor there,
No time, no near nor far,
No alien race, no foreign shore,
No child unsought, unknown,
O send us forth, thy prophets true,
To make all lands thine own!

O God of love, whose spirit wakes
In every human breast,
Whom love, and love alone, can know,
In whom all hearts find rest,
Help us to spread thy gracious reign,
Till greed and hate shall cease,
And kindness dwell in human hearts,
And all the earth find peace!

3 O God of truth, whom science seeks
And reverent souls adore,
Who lightest every earnest mind
Of every clime and shore,
Dispel the gloom of error's night,
Of ignorance and fear,
Until true wisdom from above
Shall make life's pathway clear!

4 O God of beauty, oft revealed
In dreams of human art,
In speech that flows to melody,
In holiness of heart;
Teach us to ban all ugliness
That blinds our eyes to thee,
Till all shall know the loveliness
Of lives made fair and free.

5 O God of righteousness and grace,
Seen in the Christ, thy Son,
Whose life and death reveal thy face,
By whom thy will was done,
Inspire thy heralds of good news
To live thy life divine,
Till Christ is formed in all mankind,
And every land is thine!

HENRY HALLAM TWEEDY
1868–1953

500

CHRIST for the world we sing!
The world to Christ we bring
With fervent prayer;
The wayward and the lost,
By restless passions tossed,
Redeemed at countless cost
From dark despair.

2 Christ for the world we sing!
  The world to Christ we bring
      With one accord;
  With us the work to share,
  With us reproach to dare,
  With us the cross to bear,
      For Christ our Lord.

3 Christ for the world we sing!
  The world to Christ we bring
      With joyful song;
  The new-born souls, whose days,
  Reclaimed from error's ways,
  Inspired with hope and praise,
      To Christ belong.

SAMUEL WOLCOTT, 1813–86

501 *For children*

FAR round the world thy
    children sing their song:
From East and West their
    voices sweetly blend,
Praising the Lord in whom
    young lives are strong,
Jesus our Guide, our Hero, and
    our Friend.

2 Where thy wide ocean, wave on
      rolling wave,
  Beats through the ages, on each
      island shore,
  They praise their Lord, whose
      hand alone can save,
  Whose sea of love surrounds
      them evermore.

3 Still there are lands where none
      have seen thy face,
  Children whose hearts have
      never shared thy joy;

Yet thou wouldst pour on thes
    thy radiant grace,
Give thy glad strength to ever
    girl and boy.

4 All round the world let childre
      sing thy song:
  From East and West thei
      voices sweetly blend,
  Praising the Lord in whom
      young lives are strong,
  Jesus our Guide, our Hero, an
      our Friend.

BASIL JOSEPH MATHEW
1879–195

502 *For children*

GOD of heaven, hear ou
    singing;
Only little ones are we,
Yet, a great petition bringing
Father, now we come to thee

2 Let thy Kingdom come, w
      pray thee;
  Let the world in thee find rest
  Let all know thee, and obey thee
      Loving, praising, blessing
      blest.

3 Let the sweet and joyful stor
      Of the Saviour's wondrou
      love,
  Wake on earth a song of glory
  Like the angels' song above

4 Father, send the glorious hour
  Every heart be thine alone,
  For the Kingdom, and th
      power,
      And the glory are thine ow
FRANCES RIDLEY HAVERGA
1836–7

INTERCESSION: FOR THE WORLD

503

THY love, O God, has all man-
    kind created,
  And led thy people to this
      present hour:
  In Christ we see love's glory
      consummated;
  Thy Spirit manifests his
      living power.

2 We bring thee, Lord, in ferver
      intercession
  The children of thy world
      wide family:
  With contrite hearts we offe
      our confession,
  For we have sinned agains
      thy charity.

3 From out the darkness of our
    hope's frustration;
From all the broken idols of
    our pride;
We turn to seek thy truth's
    illumination;
And find thy mercy waiting
    at our side.

4 In pity look upon thy children's
    striving
For life and freedom, peace
    and brotherhood;
Till, at the fullness of thy truth
    arriving,
We find in Christ the crown
    of every good.

5 Inspire thy Church, mid earth's
    discordant voices,
To preach the gospel of her
    Lord above;
Until the day this warring world
    rejoices
To hear the mighty harmonies
    of love,

6 Until the tidings men have long
    awaited,
From north to south, from
    east to west shall ring;
And all mankind, by Jesus
    liberated,
Proclaims in jubilation, Christ
    is King!

ALBERT FREDERICK BAYLY

504

O GOD of love, O King of
    peace,
Make wars throughout the
    world to cease;
The wrath of sinful man re-
    strain:
Give peace, O God, give peace
    again.

2 Remember, Lord, thy works of
    old,
The wonders that our fathers
    told;
Remember not our sin's dark
    stain:
Give peace, O God, give peace
    again.

3 Whom shall we trust but thee,
    O Lord?
Where rest but on thy faithful
    word?
None ever called on thee in vain:
Give peace, O God, give peace
    again.

4 Where saints and angels dwell
    above,
All hearts are knit in holy love;
O bind us in that heavenly
    chain:
Give peace, O God, give peace
    again.

HENRY WILLIAMS BAKER, 1821–77

505

CHRIST is the world's true
    light,
Its captain of salvation,
The daystar clear and bright
Of every man and nation;
New life, new hope awakes,
Where'er men own his sway:
Freedom her bondage breaks,
And night is turned to day.

2 In Christ all races meet,
    Their ancient feuds forgetting,
The whole round world com-
    plete,
From sunrise to its setting:
When Christ is throned as Lord,
Men shall forsake their fear,
To ploughshare beat the sword,
To pruning-hook the spear.

3 One Lord, in one great name
Unite us all who own thee;
    Cast out our pride and shame
    That hinder to enthrone thee;
The world has waited long,
Has travailed long in pain;
To heal its ancient wrong,
    Come, Prince of Peace, and
    reign.

GEORGE WALLACE BRIGGS
1875–1959

506

O GOD of our divided world,
    Light up thy way where
    our ways part.
Restore the kinship of our birth,
Revive in us a single heart—

2 A heart that sees in Christ its
goal
And cares with Christ for every
man,
That seeks beyond all outward
forms
The brotherhood of God's own
plan.

3 Where we have failed to understand
Our brother's heart, O Lord
forgive.
Grant us the confidence to share
The lights whereby our brothers
live.

4 Then shall we know a richer
world
Where all divisions are dis-
owned,
Where heart joins heart and
hand joins hand,
Where man is loved and Christ
enthroned.

ALAN NORMAN PHILLIPS

507

FATHER Eternal, Ruler of
Creation,
Spirit of Life, which moved
ere form was made,
Through the thick darkness
covering every nation,
Light to man's blindness, O
be thou our aid!
*Thy Kingdom come, O Lord,
thy will be done.*

2 Races and peoples, lo! we stand
divided,
And, sharing not our griefs,
no joy can share;
By wars and tumults Love is
mocked, derided,
His conquering cross no kingdom wills to bear;

3 Envious of heart, blind-eyed,
with tongues confounded,
Nation by nation still goes
unforgiven;
In wrath and fear, by jealousies
surrounded,
Building proud towers which
shall not reach to heaven.

4 Lust of possession worketh
desolations;
There is no meekness in the
sons of earth.
Led by no star, the rulers of
the nations
Still fail to bring us to the
blissful birth.

5 How shall we love thee, holy,
hidden Being,
If we love not the world
which thou hast made?
O, give us brother-love, for
better seeing
Thy Word made flesh and in
a manger laid.

LAURENCE HOUSMAN, 1865–1959

508

ALMIGHTY Father, who dost
give
The gift of life to all who live,
Look down on all earth's sin and
strife,
And lift us to a nobler life.

2 Lift up our hearts, O King of
kings,
To brighter hopes and kindlier
things,
To visions of a larger good,
And holier dreams of brotherhood.

3 Thy world is weary of its
pain,
Of selfish greed and fruitless
gain,
Of tarnished honour, falsely
strong,
And all its ancient deeds of
wrong.

4 Hear thou the prayer thy ser-
vants pray,
Uprising from all lands today,
And o'er the vanquished powers
of sin
O bring thy great salvation in.

JOHN HOWARD BERTRAM
MASTERMAN, 1867–1933

509

O HOLY City, seen of John,
Where Christ, the Lamb,
doth reign,
Within whose four-square walls
shall come
No night, nor need, nor pain,
And where the tears are wiped
from eyes
That shall not weep again!

2 O shame to us who rest content
While lust and greed for gain
In street and shop and tenement
Wring gold from human pain,
And bitter lips in blind despair
Cry, 'Christ hath died in
vain!'

3 Give us, O God, the strength to
build
The City that hath stood
Too long a dream, whose laws
are love,
Whose ways are brotherhood,
And where the sun that shineth
is
God's grace for human good.

4 Already in the mind of God
That City riseth fair:
Lo, how its splendour challenges
The souls that greatly dare—
Yea, bids us seize the whole of
life
And build its glory there.
WALTER RUSSELL BOWIE
1882–1969
(suggested by St. John's vision
in Revelation 21)

510

L ORD of light, whose Name
out-shineth
All the stars and suns of
space,
Deign to make us thy co-
workers
In the Kingdom of thy grace;
Use us to fulfil thy purpose
In the gift of Christ thy Son:
Father, as in highest heaven,
So on earth thy will be done.

2 By the toil of lowly workers
In some far outlying field;
By the courage where the
radiance
Of the cross is still revealed;
By the victories of meekness,
Through reproach and suffer-
ing won,—

3 Grant that knowledge, still in-
creasing,
At thy feet may lowly kneel;
With thy grace our triumphs
hallow,
With thy charity our zeal;
Lift the nations from the sha-
dows
To the gladness of the sun:

4 By the prayers of faithful watch-
men,
Never silent day or night;
By the cross of Jesus bringing
Peace to men, and healing
light;
By the love that passeth know-
ledge,
Making all thy children one:
HOWELL ELVET LEWIS, 1860–1953

511

O DAY of God, draw nigh
In beauty and in power,
Come with thy timeless judg-
ment now
To match our present hour.

2 Bring to our troubled minds,
Uncertain and afraid,
The quiet of a steadfast faith,
Calm of a call obeyed.

3 Bring justice to our land,
That all may dwell secure,
And finely build for days to
come
Foundations that endure.

4 Bring to our world of strife
Thy sovereign word of peace,
That war may haunt the earth
no more
And desolation cease.

5   O Day of God, draw nigh
        As at creation's birth;
    Let there be light again, and set
        Thy judgments in the earth.
       ROBERT BALGARNIE YOUNG SCOTT

512

W HERE cross the crowded
      ways of life,
  Where sound the cries of race
      and clan,
Above the noise of selfish strife,
  We hear thy voice, O Son of
    Man.

2 In haunts of wretchedness and
     need,
      On shadowed thresholds dark
       with fears,
  From paths where hide the lures
     of greed,
      We catch the vision of thy
       tears.

3 From tender childhood's help-
     lessness,
      From woman's grief, man's
       burdened toil,
  From famished souls, from
     sorrow's stress,
      Thy heart has never known
       recoil.

4 The cup of water given for thee
     Still holds the freshness of thy
       grace;
  Yet long these multitudes to see
     The sweet compassion of thy
      face.

5 O Master, from the mountain
     side
      Make haste, to heal these
       hearts of pain;
  Among these restless throngs
     abide,
      O tread the city's streets
       again:

6 Till sons of men shall learn thy
     love,
      And follow where thy feet
       have trod;
  Till glorious from thy heaven
     above,
      Shall come the City of our
       God.

       FRANK MASON NORTH, 1850–1935

513

G OD of the pastures, hear our
      prayer,
Lord of the growing seed,
Bless thou the fields, for to thy
    care
We look in all our need.

2 God of the rivers in their course,
  Lord of the swelling sea,
  Where man must strive with
    nature's force,
  Do thou his guardian be.

3 God of the dark and sombre
    mine,
  Lord of its hard-won store,
  In toil and peril all be thine;
  Thy help and strength are sure.

4 God of the city's throbbing
    heart,
  Lord of its industry,
  Bid greed and base deceit de-
    part,
  Give true prosperity.

5 God of authority and right,
  Lord of all earthly power,
  To those who rule us grant thy
    light,
  Thy wisdom be their dower.

6 God of the nations, King of men,
  Lord of each humble soul,
  We seek thy gracious aid again,
  Come down and make us whole.

       THOMAS CHARLES HUNTER CLARE

514

E TERNAL Ruler of the
      ceaseless round
    Of circling planets singing on
      their way,
Guide of the nations from the
    night profound
    Into the glory of the perfect
      day:
Rule in our hearts, that we may
    ever be
Guided and strengthened and
    upheld by thee.

2 We are of thee, the children of
    thy love,
    The brothers of thy well-
      belovèd Son;
Descend, O Holy Spirit, like a
    dove,
    Into our hearts, that we may
      be as one;
As one with thee, to whom we
    ever tend;
As one with him, our Brother
    and our Friend.

3 We would be one in hatred of
    all wrong,
    One in our love of all things
      sweet and fair,
One with the joy that breaketh
    into song,
    One with the grief that
      trembleth into prayer,
One in the power that makes the
    children free
To follow truth, and thus to
    follow thee.

4 O clothe us with thy heavenly
    armour, Lord,
    Thy trusty shield, thy sword
      of love divine;
Our inspiration be thy constant
    word;
    We ask no victories that are
      not thine:
Give or withhold, let pain or
    pleasure be;
Enough to know that we are
    serving thee.

JOHN WHITE CHADWICK
1840–1904

515

FATHER, who on man dost
    shower
Gifts of plenty from thy dower,
To thy people give the power
    All thy gifts to use aright.

2 Give pure happiness in leisure,
Temperance in every pleasure,
    Holy use of earthly treasure,
      Bodies clear and spirits
        bright.

3 Lift from this and every nation
All that brings us degradation;
Quell the forces of temptation;
    Put thine enemies to flight.

4 Be with us, thy strength supply-
    ing,
That with energy undying,
Every foe of man defying,
    We may rally to the fight.

5 Thou who art our Captain ever,
Lead us on to great endeavour;
May thy Church the world
    deliver:
    Give us wisdom, courage,
      might.

6 Father, who hast sought and
    found us,
Son of God, whose love has
    bound us,
Holy Ghost, within us, round
    us—
    Hear us, Godhead infinite.

PERCY DEARMER, 1867–1936

The following are also suitable
Nos. 340, 214, 322

INTERCESSION: FOR THE NATION

516

GOD the Omnipotent! King,
    who ordainest
Great winds thy clarions,
    lightnings thy sword:
Show forth thy pity on high
    where thou reignest;
    Give to us peace in our time,
      O Lord.

2 God the All-merciful! earth
    hath forsaken
Meekness and mercy, and
    slighted thy word;
Bid not thy wrath in its terrors
    awaken;
    Give to us peace in our time,
      O Lord.

3 God the All-righteous One! man
    hath defied thee;
    Yet to eternity standeth thy
      word;
Falsehood and wrong shall not
    tarry beside thee;
Give to us peace in our time,
    O Lord.

4 God the All-wise! by the fire of
    thy chastening,
    Earth shall to freedom and
      truth be restored;
Through the thick darkness thy
    Kingdom is hastening;
Thou wilt give peace in our
    time, O Lord.

5 So shall thy children, with
    thankful devotion,
    Praise him who saved them
      from peril and sword,
Singing in chorus, from ocean
    to ocean,
Peace to the nations, and
    praise to the Lord.

        HENRY FOTHERGILL CHORLEY
                  1808–72
      and JOHN ELLERTON, 1826–93

517

GOD of Eternity, Lord of
    the Ages,
Father and Spirit and Saviour
    of men!
Thine is the glory of time's
    numbered pages;
Thine is the power to revive
    us again.

2 Thankful, we come to thee,
    Lord of the nations,
    Praising thy faithfulness,
      mercy, and grace
Shown to our fathers in past
    generations,
Pledge of thy love to our
    people and race.

*3 Far from our ancient home,
    sundered by oceans,
    Zion is builded, and God is
      adored:
Lift we our hearts in united
    devotions!
Ends of the earth, join in
    praise to the Lord!

*4 Beauteous this land of ours
    bountiful Giver!
    Brightly the heavens thy glory
      declare;
Streameth the sunlight on hill,
    plain, and river,
Shineth thy cross over fields
    rich and fair.

5 Pardon our sinfulness, God of
    all pity,
    Call to remembrance thy
      mercies of old;
Strengthen thy Church to
    abide as a city
Set on a hill for a light to thy
    fold.

6 Head of the Church on earth,
    risen, ascended!
    Thine is the honour that dwells
      in this place:
As thou hast blessed us
    through years that have
      ended,
Still lift upon us the light of
    thy face.

      ERNEST NORTHCROFT MERRINGTON
                  1876–1953

* Verse 3 for use overseas. Verse 4 for
use in the Southern Hemisphere, the refer-
ence being to the Southern Cross.

518

LORD, while for all mankind
    we pray,
Of every clime and coast,
O hear us for our native land,
The land we love the most.

2 Our fathers' sepulchres are
    here,
    And here our kindred dwell,
Our children too; how should
    we love
Another land so well?

3 O guard our shores from every
    foe;
    With peace our borders bless;
With prosperous times our cities
    crown,
Our fields with plenteousness.

4 Unite us in the sacred love
    Of knowledge, truth, and
      thee;
  And let our hills and valleys
      shout
    The songs of liberty.

5 Lord of the nations, thus to
      thee
  Our country we commend;
  Be thou her refuge and her
      trust,
    Her everlasting Friend.

JOHN REYNELL WREFORD
1800–81

519

JUDGE Eternal, throned in
    splendour,
    Lord of lords and King of
      kings,
  With thy living fire of judgment
    Purge this land of bitter
      things;
  Solace all its wide dominion
    With the healing of thy
      wings.

2 Still the weary folk are pining
    For the hour that brings
      release;
  And the city's crowded clangour
    Cries aloud for sin to cease;
  And the homesteads and the
      woodlands
    Plead in silence for their
      peace.

3 Crown, O God, thine own
      endeavour;
    Cleave our darkness with thy
      sword;
  Feed the faithless and the
      hungry
    With the richness of thy
      word;
  Cleanse the body of this Nation
    Through the glory of the
      Lord.

HENRY SCOTT HOLLAND
1847–1918, altered

520

O GOD of earth and altar,
    Bow down and hear our
      cry;
  Our earthly rulers falter,
    Our people drift and die;
  The walls of gold entomb us,
    The swords of scorn divide,
  Take not thy thunder from
      us,
    But take away our pride.

2 From all that terror teaches,
    From lies of tongue and pen,
  From all the easy speeches
    That comfort cruel men,
  From sale and profanation
    Of honour and the sword,
  From sleep and from damnation,
    Deliver us, good Lord!

3 Tie in a living tether
    The prince and priest and
      thrall;
  Bind all our lives together,
    Smite us and save us all;
  In ire and exultation,
    Aflame with faith, and free,
  Lift up a living nation,
    A single sword to thee.

GILBERT KEITH CHESTERTON
1874–1936

521

GOD save our gracious Queen,
    Long live our noble Queen;
  God save the Queen!
  Send her victorious,
  Happy and glorious,
  Long to reign over us:
    God save the Queen!

2 Thy choicest gifts in store
  On her be pleased to pour;
    Long may she reign;
  May she defend our laws,
  And ever give us cause
  To sing with heart and voice,
    'God save the Queen!'

From the version of 1745

INTERCESSION: FOR THE FAMILY

522

OUR Father, by whose Name
   All fatherhood is known,
Who dost in love proclaim
   Each family thine own,
Bless thou all parents, guarding well,
With constant love as sentinel,
   The homes in which thy people dwell.

2 O Christ, thyself a child
   Within an earthly home,
With heart still undefiled,
   Thou didst to manhood come;
Our children bless, in ev'ry place,
That they may all behold thy face,
   And knowing thee may grow in grace.

3 O Spirit, who dost bind
   Our hearts in unity,
Who teachest us to find
   The love from self set free,
In all our hearts such love increase,
That ev'ry home by this release,
   May be the dwelling place of peace.

FRANCIS BLAND TUCKER

523   *O selig Haus, wo man dich aufgenommen*

O HAPPY home, where thou art loved the dearest,
   Thou loving Friend, and Saviour of our race,
And where among the guests there never cometh
   One who can hold such high and honoured place!

2 O happy home, where two in heart united
   In holy faith and blessèd hope are one,
Whom death a little while alone divideth,
   And cannot end the union here begun!

3 O happy home, whose little ones are given
   Early to thee, in humble faith and prayer,—
To thee, their Friend, who from the heights of heaven
   Dost guide and guard with more than mother's care!

4 O happy home, where each one serves thee, lowly,
   Whatever his appointed work may be,
Till every common task seems great and holy,
   When it is done, O Lord, as unto thee!

5 O happy home, where thou art not forgotten
   When joy is overflowing, full and free;
O happy home, where every wounded spirit
   Is brought, Physician, Comforter, to thee:

6 Until at last, when earth's day's work is ended,
   All meet thee in the blessèd home above,
From whence thou camest, where thou hast ascended,
   Thy everlasting home of peace and love!

KARL JOHANN PHILIPP SPITTA
1801–59
Tr. SARAH LAURIE FINDLATER
1823–1907

524

THY Kingdom come; yea, bid it come,
But, when thy Kingdom first began
On earth, thy Kingdom was a home,
A child, a woman, and a man.

2 The child was in the midst thereof,
O blessèd Jesus, holiest one!
The centre and the fount of love,
Mary and Joseph's little Son.

Wherever on this earth shall be
A child, a woman, and a man,
The image of that trinity
Wherewith thy Kingdom first began,

4 Establish there thy Kingdom!
Yea,
And o'er that trinity of love
Send down, as in thy appointed day,
The brooding spirit of thy Dove.

KATHARINE TYNAN-HINKSON
1861–1931

INTERCESSION:
FOR THE MINISTRY OF HEALING

525

FROM thee all skill and science flow,
All pity, care, and love,
All calm and courage, faith and hope;
O pour them from above.

And part them, Lord, to each and all,
As each and all shall need,
To rise like incense, each to thee,
In noble thought and deed.

And hasten, Lord, that perfect day
When pain and death shall cease,
And thy just rule shall fill the earth
With health, and light, and peace;

When ever blue the sky shall gleam,
And ever green the sod;
And man's rude work deface no more
The Paradise of God.

CHARLES KINGSLEY, 1819–75

526

FATHER, whose will is life and good
For all of mortal breath,
Bind strong the bond of brotherhood
Of those who fight with death.

2 Empower the hands and hearts and wills
Of friends in lands afar,
Who battle with the body's ills,
And wage thy holy war.

3 Where'er they heal the maimed and blind,
Let love of Christ attend:
Proclaim the good Physician's mind,
And prove the Saviour friend.

4 For still his love works wondrous charms,
And, as in days of old,
He takes the wounded to his arms,
And bears them to the fold.

5 O Father, look from heaven and bless,
Where'er thy servants be,
Their works of pure unselfishness,
Made consecrate to thee!

HARDWICKE DRUMMOND RAWNSLEY
1851–1920

RESPONSE TO THE WORD OF GOD

INTERCESSION:
FOR TRAVELLERS AND THE ABSENT

527

ETERNAL Father, strong to
save,
Whose arm hath bound the
restless wave,
Who bidd'st the mighty ocean
deep
Its own appointed limits keep:
  O hear us when we cry to
thee
  For those in peril on the
sea.

2 O Christ, whose voice the waters
heard,
And hushed their raging at thy
word,
Who walkedst on the foaming
deep,
And calm amid the storm didst
sleep:
  O hear us when we cry to
thee
  For those in peril on the
sea.

3 O Holy Spirit, who didst
brood
Upon the waters dark and
rude,
And bid their angry tumult
cease,
And give, for wild confusion,
peace:
  O hear us when we cry to
thee
  For those in peril on the
sea.

4 O Trinity of love and power,
Our brethren shield in danger's
hour;
From rock and tempest, fire and
foe,
Protect them wheresoe'er they
go:
  Thus evermore shall rise to
thee
  Glad hymns of praise from
land and sea.

    WILLIAM WHITING, 1825–78

528

THOU who dost rule on
high,
  Our Father and our Friend,
All those who ride the sky
  We now to thee commend,
For though among the stars
they move,
They cannot rise beyond thy
love.

2   Alone in boundless space,
    May they be still with thee
  The glory of thy face
    Among the heavens see;
For thou, by land and sea and
air,
Art with thy children every-
where.

3   When tempests loose their
power
    And dangers gather round
  In thee, in that dread hour,
    May their defence be found;
O may that peace possess their
mind
Which all thy trusting children
find.

4   And soon from pole to pole,
    Thy Kingdom, Lord, arise;
  And peace alone control
    The commerce of the skies;
Till all the gifts thou givest
men,
We to thy glory give again.

    ROBERT WESLEY LITTLEWOOD

529

HOLY Father, in thy mercy,
  Hear our anxious prayer;
Keep our loved ones, now far
distant,
  'Neath thy care.

Jesus, Saviour, let thy presence
    Be their light and guide;
Keep, O keep them, in their
    weakness,
    At thy side.

When in sorrow, when in
    danger,
    When in loneliness,
In thy love look down and
    comfort
    Their distress.

May the joy of thy salvation
    Be their strength and
    stay;

May they love and may they
    praise thee
    Day by day.

5 Holy Spirit, let thy teaching
    Sanctify their life;
Send thy grace that they may
    conquer
    In the strife.

6 Father, Son, and Holy Spirit,
    God the One in Three,
Bless them, guide them, save
    them, keep them
    Near to thee.
        ISABEL STEPHANA STEVENSON
        1843–90

THE CHURCH TRIUMPHANT

530 PARAPHRASE 61

BLEST be the everlasting God,
    The Father of our Lord!
Be his abounding mercy praised,
    His majesty adored!

2 When from the dead he raised
    his Son,
    And called him to the sky,
He gave our souls a lively hope
    That they should never die.

3 To an inheritance divine
    He taught our hearts to rise;
'Tis uncorrupted, undefiled,
    Unfading in the skies.

4 Saints by the power of God are
    kept,
    Till the salvation come:
We walk by faith as strangers
    here
But Christ shall call us home.
        Scottish Paraphrases, 1781
        From 1 Peter 1: 3–5

531 PARAPHRASE 59, verses
        1–4, 13

BEHOLD what witnesses un-
    seen
    Encompass us around;
Men, once like us, with suffer-
    ing tried,
But now with glory crowned.

2 Let us, with zeal like theirs
    inspired,
    Begin the Christian race,
And, freed from each encumber-
    ing weight,
    Their holy footsteps trace.

3 Behold a witness nobler still,
    Who trod affliction's path,
Jesus, at once the finisher
    And author of our faith.

4 He for the joy before him set,
    So generous was his love,
Endured the cross, despised the
    shame,
    And now he reigns above.

5 Then let our hearts no more
    despond,
    Our hands be weak no more;
Still let us trust our Father's love,
    His wisdom still adore.
        Scottish Paraphrases, 1781
        From Hebrews Ch. 12

532 PARAPHRASE 65,
      verses 5, 6, 8, 9, 11

HARK how the adoring hosts
    above
    With songs surround the
    throne!
Ten thousand thousand are
    their tongues;
But all their hearts are one.

2 Worthy the Lamb that died,
    they cry,
To be exalted thus;
Worthy the Lamb, let us reply;
For he was slain for us.

3 Thou hast redeemed us with thy
    blood,
And set the prisoners free;
Thou mad'st us kings and
    priests to God,
And we shall reign with thee.

4 From every kindred, every
    tongue,
Thou brought'st thy chosen
    race;
And distant lands and isles
    have shared
The riches of thy grace.

5 *To him who sits upon the throne,*
    The God whom we adore,
And to the Lamb that once was
    slain,
Be glory evermore. Amen.

        Scottish Paraphrases, 1781
        From Revelation 5:11–14

533   PARAPHRASE 66

HOW bright these glorious
    spirits shine!
Whence all their white array?
How came they to the blissful
    seats
Of everlasting day?
Lo! these are they, from suffer-
    ings great
Who came to realms of light,
And in the blood of Christ have
    washed
Those robes which shine so
    bright.

2 Now, with triumphal palms
    they stand
Before the throne on high,
And serve the God they love,
    amidst
The glories of the sky.
His presence fills each heart
    with joy,
Tunes every mouth to sing:
By day, by night, the sacred
    courts
With glad hosannas ring.

3 Hunger and thirst are felt no
    more,
Nor suns with scorching ray;
God is their sun, whose cheering
    beams
Diffuse eternal day.
The Lamb who dwells amidst
    the throne
Shall o'er them still preside,
Feed them with nourishment
    divine,
And all their footsteps guide.

*4 'Mong pastures green he'll lead
    his flock,
Where living streams appear;
And God the Lord from every
    eye
Shall wipe off every tear.

        Scottish Paraphrases, 1781
        From Revelation 7:13–en

* *Verse 4 is sung to the second half*
of the tune.

534

FOR all the saints who from
    their labours rest,
Who thee by faith before the
    world confessed,
Thy Name, O Jesus, be for ever
    blest.

        Alleluia! Alleluia!

2 Thou wast their Rock, their
    Fortress, and their Might;
Thou, Lord, their Captain in the
    well-fought fight;
Thou, in the darkness drear,
    their one true Light:

3 O may thy soldiers, faithful,
    true, and bold,
Fight as the saints who nobly
    fought of old,
And win, with them, the victor's
    crown of gold:

4 O blest communion, fellowship
    divine!
We feebly struggle, they in
    glory shine;
Yet all are one in thee, for all
    are thine:

5 And when the strife is fierce,
    the warfare long,
Steals on the ear the distant
    triumph song,
And hearts are brave again, and
    arms are strong:

6 The golden evening brightens
    in the west;
Soon, soon to faithful warriors
    cometh rest;
Sweet is the calm of Paradise
    the blest:

7 But, lo! there breaks a yet more
    glorious day;
The saints triumphant rise in
    bright array;
The King of Glory passes on his
    way:

8 From earth's wide bounds, from
    ocean's farthest coast,
Through gates of pearl streams
    in the countless host,
Singing to Father, Son, and
    Holy Ghost:
        WILLIAM WALSHAM HOW, 1823–97

535

*O quanta, qualia sunt
illa sabbata*

O WHAT their joy and their
    glory must be,
Those endless Sabbaths the
    blessèd ones see!
Crown for the valiant; to weary
    ones rest;
God shall be all, and in all ever
    blest.

2 What are the Monarch, his
    court, and his throne?
What are the peace and the joy
    that they own?
Tell us, ye blest ones, that in it
    have share,
If what ye feel ye can fully de-
    clare.

3 Truly Jerusalem name we that
    shore,
'Vision of peace,' that brings
    joy evermore!
Wish and fulfilment can severed
    be ne'er,
Nor the thing prayed for come
    short of the prayer.

4 We, where no trouble distrac-
    tion can bring,
Safely the anthems of Zion shall
    sing;
While for thy grace, Lord, their
    voices of praise
Thy blessèd people shall ever-
    more raise.

5 *Low before him with our praises*
    we fall,
Of whom, and in whom, and
    through whom are all;
Of whom, the Father; and
    through whom, the Son;
In whom, the Spirit, with these
    ever One.   Amen.
        PETER ABELARD, 1079–1142
    Tr. JOHN MASON NEALE, 1818–66

536

THERE is a land of pure
    delight,
Where saints immortal reign;
Infinite day excludes the night,
And pleasures banish pain;

2 There everlasting spring abides,
And never-withering flowers:
Death, like a narrow sea, divides
This heavenly land from ours.

3 Sweet fields beyond the swell-
    ing flood
Stand dressed in living green;
So to the Jews old Canaan stood,
While Jordan rolled between.

4 But timorous mortals start and
    shrink
To cross this narrow sea,
And linger, shivering on the
    brink,
And fear to launch away.

5 O could we make our doubts
    remove—
Those gloomy doubts that
    rise—
And see the Canaan that we
    love,
With unbeclouded eyes;

6 Could we but climb where
 Moses stood,
And view the landscape o'er,
Not Jordan's stream, nor
 death's cold flood,
Should fright us from the
 shore.

ISAAC WATTS, 1674–1748

---

537 *Urbs Sion aurea, patria*
 lactea

JERUSALEM the golden,
 With milk and honey blest,
Beneath thy contemplation
Sink heart and voice
 oppressed:
I know not, O I know not
 What social joys are there,
What radiancy of glory,
 What light beyond compare.

2 They stand, those halls of Zion,
 Conjubilant with song,
And bright with many an angel,
 And all the martyr throng:
The Prince is ever in them;
 The daylight is serene;
The pastures of the blessèd
 Are decked in glorious sheen.

3 There is the throne of David,
 And there, from care re-
 leased,
The shout of them that
 triumph,
The song of them that feast;
And they who, with their
 Leader,
Have conquered in the fight,
For ever and for ever
 Are clad in robes of white.

4 O sweet and blessèd country,
 The home of God's elect!
O sweet and blessèd country,
 That eager hearts expect!
Jesus, in mercy bring us
 To that dear land of rest,
Who art, with God the Father
 And Spirit, ever blest. Amen.

Verses 1–3 BERNARD OF CLUNY
 12th century
Tr. JOHN MASON NEALE, 1818–66
Verse 4 Compilers of
Hymns Ancient and Modern, 1861

538

FOR those we love within the
 veil,
Who once were comrades of
 our way,
We thank thee, Lord; for they
 have won
To cloudless day;

2 And life for them is life indeed,
 The splendid goal of earth's
 strait race;
And where no shadows inter-
 vene
They see thy face.

3 Not as we knew them any more,
 Toilworn, and sad with
 burdened care,—
Erect, clear-eyed, upon their
 brows
Thy Name they bear.

4 Free from the fret of mortal
 years,
 And knowing now thy perfect
 will,
With quickened sense and
 heightened joy
They serve thee still.

5 O fuller, sweeter is that life,
 And larger, ampler is the air:
Eye cannot see nor heart con-
 ceive
The glory there;

6 Nor know to what high purpose
 thou
 Dost yet employ their ripened
 powers,
Nor how at thy behest they
 touch
This life of ours.

7 There are no tears within their
 eyes;
 With love they keep per-
 petual tryst;
And praise and work and rest
 are one,
With thee, O Christ.

WILLIAM CHARTER PIGGOTT
1872–1943

539 *Caelestis aulae principes*

CAPTAINS of the saintly band,
Lights who lighten ev'ry land,
Princes who with Jesus dwell,
Judges of his Israel,

On the nations sunk in night
Ye have shed the Gospel light;
Sin and error flee away,
Truth reveals the promised day.

Not by warrior's spear and sword,
Not by art of human word,
Preaching but the cross of shame,
Rebel hearts for Christ ye tame.

Earth, that long in sin and pain
Groaned in Satan's deadly chain,
Now to serve its God is free
In the law of liberty.

Distant lands with one acclaim
Tell the honour of your name,
Who, wherever man has trod,
Teach the mysteries of God.

Glory to the Three in One
While eternal ages run,
Who from deepest shades of night
Called us to his glorious light.
Amen.

JEAN-BAPTISTE DE SANTEÜIL
1630–97
Tr. HENRY WILLIAMS BAKER
1821–77

540 *Aeterna Christi munera*

THE eternal gifts of Christ the King,
The apostles' glorious deeds, we sing;
And while due hymns of praise we pay,
Our thankful hearts cast grief away.

2 The Church in these her princes boasts,
These victor chiefs of warrior hosts;
The soldiers of the heavenly hall,
The lights that rose on earth for all.

3 'Twas thus the yearning faith of saints,
The unconquered hope that never faints,
The love of Christ that knows not shame,
The prince of this world overcame.

4 In these the Father's glory shone;
In these the will of God the Son;
In these exults the Holy Ghost;
Through these rejoice the heavenly host.

5 Redeemer, hear us of thy love,
That, with this glorious band above,
Hereafter, of thine endless grace,
Thy servants also may have place.

Attributed to ST. AMBROSE
c. 340–97
Tr. JOHN MASON NEALE, 1818–66
and others

541

THE Son of God goes forth to war,
A kingly crown to gain;
His blood-red banner streams afar:
Who follows in his train?
Who best can drink his cup of woe,
Triumphant over pain,
Who patient bears his cross below,
He follows in his train.

2 The martyr first, whose eagle
      eye
   Could pierce beyond the
      grave,
   Who saw his Master in the
      sky,
   And called on him to save;
   Like him, with pardon on his
      tongue
   In midst of mortal pain,
   He prayed for them that did the
      wrong:
   Who follows in his train?

3 A glorious band, the chosen
      few
   On whom the Spirit came,
   Twelve valiant saints, their
      hope they knew,
   And mocked the cross and
      flame;
   They climbed the steep ascent
      of heaven,
   Through peril, toil, and pain:
   O God, to us may grace be given
   To follow in their train.
                REGINALD HEBER, 1783–1826

542 *Alleluia piis edite laudibus*

SING Alleluia forth in duteous
   praise,
Ye citizens of heaven; O
      sweetly raise
   An *endless Alleluia*.

2 Ye powers, who stand before
      the eternal Light,
   In hymning choirs re-echo to
      the height:

3 Ye who have gained at length
      your palms in bliss,
   Victorious ones, your chant
      shall still be this:

4 There, in one grand acclaim,
      for ever ring
   The strains which tell the
      honour of your King:

   While thee, by whom were all
      things made, we praise
   For ever, and tell out in sweetest
      lays:

6 Almighty Christ, to thee ou
      voices sing
   Glory for evermore; to thee w
      bring:
   Mozarabic Breviary, 5th–8th centur
          Tr. JOHN ELLERTON, 1826–9

543

LET saints on earth in concer
   sing
   With those whose work i
      done;
For all the servants of our Kin
   In earth and heaven are on

2 One family, we dwell in him,
   One Church, above, beneath
Though now divided by th
      stream,
   The narrow stream of death.

3 One army of the living God,
   To his command we bow;
Part of his host hath crosse
   the flood,
   And part is crossing now.

4 Even now to their eternal hom
   There pass some spirits blest
While others to the margi
   come,
   Waiting their call to rest.

5 Jesus, be thou our constan
      Guide;
   Then, when the word is given
Bid Jordan's narrow stream
   divide,
   And bring us safe to heaven
          CHARLES WESLEY, 1707–8

544 *O fryniau Caersalem ceir gweled*

FROM heavenly Jerusalem's
   towers,
   The path through the deser
      they trace;
And every affliction they suf
      fered
   Redounds to the glory o
      grace;

Their look they cast back on
    the tempests,
  On fears, on grim death and
    the grave,
Rejoicing that now they're in
    safety,
  Through him that is mighty
    to save.

2 And we, from the wilds of the
    desert,
  Shall flee to the land of the
    blest;
Life's tears shall be changed to
    rejoicing,
  Its labours and toil into rest:
There we shall find refuge
    eternal,
  From sin, from affliction,
    from pain,
And in the sweet love of the
    Saviour,
  A joy without end shall
    attain.

DAVID CHARLES, 1762–1834
Tr. LEWIS EDWARDS, 1809–87

545

FAR off I see the goal—
  O Saviour, guide me;
I feel my strength is small—
  Be thou beside me;
With vision ever clear,
With love that conquers fear,
And grace to persevere,
  O Lord, provide me.

2 Whene'er thy way seem
    strange,
  Go thou before me;
And, lest my heart should
    change,
  O Lord, watch o'er me;
But, should my faith prove
    frail,
And I through blindness fail,
O let thy grace prevail,
  And still restore me.

3 Should earthly pleasures wane,
    And joy forsake me,
And lonely hours of pain
    At length o'ertake me,—
My hand in thine hold fast
Till sorrow be o'er-past,
And gentle death at last
  For heaven awake me.

4 There, with the ransomed
    throng
    Who praise for ever
The love that made them
    strong
    To serve for ever,
I, too, would see thy face,
Thy finished work re-trace,
And magnify thy grace,
  Redeemed for ever.

ROBERT ROWLAND ROBERTS
1865–1945

*The following are also suitable
No.*
14 We come unto our father's God
473 Lord, who in thy perfect wisdom

IV

THE SACRAMENTS

HOLY BAPTISM

546

THE APOSTLES'
CREED

I believe in
GOD THE FATHER ALMIGHTY,
MAKER OF HEAVEN AND
EARTH
and in
JESUS CHRIST HIS ONLY SON OUR
LORD
who was conceived by the
Holy Ghost,
born of the Virgin Mary,
suffered under Pontius Pilate,
was crucified, dead, and
buried;
he descended into hell.
The third day he rose again
from the dead,
he ascended into heaven, and
sitteth on the right hand
of God the Father Al-
mighty;
from thence he shall come to
judge the quick and the
dead.
I believe in
the HOLY GHOST;
the HOLY CATHOLIC CHURCH;
the COMMUNION OF SAINTS;
the FORGIVENESS OF SINS;
the RESURRECTION OF THE
BODY;
and the LIFE EVERLASTING.
Amen.

547 PSALM 78, verses 4(b)–7

THE praises of the Lord our
God,
And his almighty strength,
The wondrous works that he
hath done,
We will show forth at length.

2 His testimony and his law
In Israel he did place,
And charged our fathers it to
show
To their succeeding race;

3 That so the race which was to
come
Might well them learn and
know;
And sons unborn, who should
arise,
Might to their sons them
show:

4 That they might set their hope
in God,
And suffer not to fall
His mighty works out of their
mind,
But keep his precepts all.

5 *To Father, Son, and Holy Ghost,*
The God whom we adore,
Be glory, as it was, and is,
And shall be evermore. Amen.

548 PARAPHRASE 47
verses 2–4

WHEN to the sacred font we
came,
Did not the rite proclaim,
That, washed from sin, and all
its stains,
New creatures we became?

2 With Christ the Lord we died
to sin;
With him to life we rise,
To life which, now begun on
earth,
Is perfect in the skies.

Too long enthralled to Satan's
    sway,
  We now are slaves no more;
For Christ hath vanquished
    death and sin,
  Our freedom to restore.

To Father, Son, and Holy Ghost,
  The God whom we adore,
Be glory, as it was, and is,
  And shall be evermore. Amen.
                        Scottish Paraphrases, 1781
                        From Romans 6:3–7

549

OUR children, Lord, in faith
    and prayer,
  We now devote to thee;
Let them thy covenant mercies
    share,
  And thy salvation see.

2 Such helpless babes thou didst
    embrace,
  While dwelling here below;
To us and ours, O God of grace,
  The same compassion show.

3 O thou whose infant feet were
    found
  Within thy Father's shrine,
Whose years, with changeless
    virtue crowned,
  Were all alike divine,

4 Dependent on thy bounteous
    breath,
  We seek thy grace alone,
In childhood, manhood, age,
    and death,
  To keep us still thine own.
            vv. 1, 2 THOMAS HAWEIS, 1734–1820
            vv. 3, 4 REGINALD HEBER, 1783–1826

550

* *LIFT high the cross, the love of*
    Christ proclaim
  Till all the world adore his sacred
    name.

2 Come, brethren, follow where
    our Captain trod,
  Our King victorious, Christ the
    Son of God:

3 Led on their way by this
    triumphant sign,
  The hosts of God in conquering
    ranks combine:

4 Each new-born soldier of the
    Crucified
  Bears on his brow the seal of
    him who died:

5 This is the sign which Satan's
    legions fear
  And angels veil their faces to
    revere:

6 O Lord, once lifted on the
    glorious tree,
  As thou hast promised, draw
    men unto thee:

7 From farthest regions let them
    homage bring,
  And on his cross adore their
    Saviour King:
                    MICHAEL ROBERT NEWBOLT
                                1874–1956
                    Based on GEORGE WILLIAM
                        KITCHIN, 1827–1912

  * *Verse 1 is repeated as a refrain after*
each verse.

551

A LITTLE child the Saviour
    came,
  The Mighty God was still his
    Name,
And angels worshipped as he
    lay
  The seeming infant of a day.

2 He who, a little child, began
  The life divine to show to man,
Proclaims from heaven the
    message free,
  'Let little children come to me.'

3 We bring them, Lord, and with
    the sign
  Of sprinkled water name them
    thine:
Their souls with saving grace
    endow;
  Baptize them with thy Spirit
    now.

4 O give thine angels charge, good
    Lord,
  Them safely in thy way to
    guard;
Thy blessing on their lives com-
    mand,
And write their names upon thy
    hand.

5 O thou who by an infant's
    tongue
  Dost hear thy perfect glory
    sung,
May these, with all the heavenly
    host,
Praise Father, Son, and Holy
    Ghost.

        WILLIAM ROBERTSON, 1820–64

552 *Liebster Jesu, wir sind hier*

BLESSÈD Jesus, here we
    stand,
  Met to do as thou hast
    spoken;
And this child, at thy com-
    mand,
  Now we bring to thee in token
That to Christ it here is given,
For of such shall be his
    heaven.

2 Therefore hasten we to thee;
  Take the pledge we bring, O
    take it;
Let us here thy glory see,
  And in tender pity make it
Now thy child, and leave it
    never—
Thine on earth, and thine for
    ever.

3 Make it, Head, thy member
    now;
  Shepherd, take thy lamb and
    feed it;
Prince of Peace, its peace be
    thou;
  Way of life, to heaven O lead
    it;
Vine, this branch may noth-
    ing sever,
Grafted firm in thee for ever.

4 Now upon thy heart it lies,
  What our hearts so dearly
    treasure;
Heavenward lead our burdened
    sighs;
  Pour thy blessing without
    measure;
Write the name we now have
    given,
Write it in the book of
    heaven.

      BENJAMIN SCHMOLK, 1672–1737
      Tr. CATHERINE WINKWORTH
          1827–78

553

O FATHER, in thy father-
    heart
We know our children have
    their part;
We sign them in thy threefold
    Name,
And by the sprinkled water
    claim
Thy covenant in Christ revealed,
To us and to our children
    sealed:

2 Name of the Father, pledge that
    we
  Our inmost being draw from
    thee;
Name of the Son, whereby we
    know
The Father's love to men below;
Name of the Spirit, blessèd sign
That now we share the life
    divine.

        ELLA SOPHIA ARMITAGE
          1841–1931

554

O GOD, thy life-creating love
  This sacred trust to
    parents gave.
In Christ thou camest from
    above
Thy children's souls to claim
    and save.

Help us who now our pledges
give
The young to train and guard
and guide,
To learn of Christ, and so to live
That they may in thy love abide.

Grant, Lord, as strength and
wisdom grow,
That every child thy truth may
learn.
Impart thy light, that each may
know
Thy will and life's true way
discern.

Then home and child, kept in
thy peace,
And guarded, Father, by thy
care,
Will in the grace of Christ increase,
And all thy Kingdom's blessings
share.

ALBERT FREDERICK BAYLY

55 *After baptism*

O LOVING Father, to thy
care
We give again this child of
thine,
Baptized and blessed with faithful prayer
And sealed with Love's
victorious sign.

As Christ, thy Son, did not refuse
The homage of the children's
cry,
So teach *him* childhood's gifts
to use
Thy Name to praise and
magnify.

3 Through youth and age, through
shine and shade,
Grant *him* to run *his* earthly
race,
Forgetting not that man was
made
To show thy glory and thy
grace:

4 Till, at the last, before thy
throne
He lays *his* earthly armour
down,
His task of loving service done,
And, in thy mercy, takes *his*
crown.

CYRIL ARGENTINE ALINGTON
1872–1955
The following are also suitable Nos. 402
(vv. 1, 2, 4, 6); 420 (vv. 1, 2); 421
(vv. 1–3); 429.

556

T HE Lord bless you, and keep
you: the Lord make his face
to shine upon you, and be
gracious unto you: the Lord
lift up his countenance upon
you, and give you peace.

557 *For younger children Cradle Roll*

F ATHER, hear us as we pray
For these little ones today:
Good and gentle may they be;
Early may they come to thee.

2 Bless, we pray thee, Saviour
dear,
All whose names are written
here;
Guard and keep them safe from
harm;
Hold them with thy loving arm.

EDITH FLORENCE BOYLE
MACALISTER, 1873–1950

HOLY COMMUNION

558

THE NICENE CREED

WE believe in
ONE GOD THE FATHER
ALMIGHTY, Maker of heaven

and earth, and of all things
visible and invisible:
and in
ONE LORD JESUS CHRIST, the
only begotten Son of God, begotten of his Father before all
worlds, GOD OF GOD, LIGHT OF

LIGHT, VERY GOD OF VERY GOD, begotten, not made, being of one substance with the Father, by whom all things were made:

WHO, for us men, and for our salvation, came down from heaven, and was incarnate by the Holy Ghost of the Virgin Mary, AND WAS MADE MAN, and was crucified also for us under Pontius Pilate.

HE suffered and was buried; and the third day he rose again according to the Scriptures, and ascended into heaven, and sitteth on the right hand of the Father. And he shall come again with glory to judge both the quick and the dead, whose Kingdom shall have no end.

And we believe in

THE HOLY GHOST, the Lord and Giver of Life, who proceedeth from the Father and the Son; who with the Father and the Son together is worshipped and glorified; who spake by the prophets.

And we believe

ONE HOLY CATHOLIC AND APOSTOLIC CHURCH.

We acknowledge

ONE BAPTISM for the remission of sins.

And we look for

THE RESURRECTION OF THE DEAD, and the LIFE OF THE WORLD TO COME. Amen.

559

SALUTATION

Minister The Lord be with you;
People   And with thy spirit.

SURSUM CORDA

Minister Lift up your hearts;
People   We lift them up unto the Lord.
Minister Let us give thanks unto our Lord God;
People   It is meet and right so to do.

560

SANCTUS

Holy, Holy, Holy, Lord God of Hosts,
Heaven and earth are full of thy glory.
Glory be to thee, O Lord Most High. Amen.

561

BENEDICTUS QUI VENIT

Blessèd is he that cometh in the Name of the Lord:
*Hosanna in the highest.

* The word Hosanna is sung three times

562

THE LORD'S PRAYER

First form

OUR Father which art in heaven,
Hallowed be thy Name.
Thy Kingdom come.
Thy will be done in earth, as it is in heaven.
Give us this day our daily bread.
And forgive us our debts, as we forgive our debtors.
And lead us not into temptation, but deliver us from evil:
For thine is the Kingdom, and the power, and the glory, for ever. Amen.

Second form

OUR Father, who art in heaven,
Hallowed be thy Name.
Thy Kingdom come.
Thy will be done, on earth as it is in heaven.
Give us this day our daily bread.
And forgive us our trespasses, as we forgive those who trespass against us.

And lead us not into tempta-
on, but deliver us from evil:
For thine is the Kingdom, the
ower, and the glory, for ever and
ver. Amen.

St Matthew 6:9–13

563   AGNUS DEI

O LAMB of God, that takest
away the sins of the world,
have mercy upon us.
O Lamb of God, that takest away
the sins of the world, have
mercy upon us.
O Lamb of God, that takest away
the sins of the world, grant us
thy peace.

564   PSALM 26, verses 6–8

MINE hands in innocence, O
Lord,
I'll wash and purify;
So to thine holy altar go,
And compass it will I:

That I, with voice of thanks-
giving,
May publish and declare,
And tell of all thy mighty
works,
That great and wondrous are.

The habitation of thy house,
Lord, I have lovèd well;
Yea, in that place I do delight
Where doth thine honour
dwell.

To Father, Son, and Holy Ghost,
The God whom we adore,
Be glory, as it was, and is,
And shall be evermore. Amen.

565   PSALM 116, verses 13, 14,
17–19

I'LL of salvation take the cup,
On God's name will I call:
I'll pay my vows now to the
Lord
Before his people all.

2 Thank-offerings I to thee will
give,
And on God's name will call.
I'll pay my vows now to the
Lord
Before his people all;

3 Within the courts of God's own
house,
Within the midst of thee,
O city of Jerusalem.
Praise to the Lord give ye.

4 *To Father, Son, and Holy Ghost,*
The God whom we adore,
Be glory, as it was, and is,
And shall be evermore. Amen.

566   PSALM 24

THE earth belongs unto the
Lord,
And all that it contains;
The world that is inhabited,
And all that there remains.
For the foundations of the same
He on the seas did lay,
And he hath it establishèd
Upon the floods to stay.

2 Who is the man that shall
ascend
Into the hill of God?
Or who within his holy place
Shall have a firm abode?
Whose hands are clean, whose
heart is pure.
And unto vanity
Who hath not lifted up his soul,
Nor sworn deceitfully.

3 This is the man who shall re-
ceive
The blessing from the Lord;
The God of his salvation shall
Him righteousness accord.
This is the generation who
Do after him inquire;
They Jacob are, who seek thy
face
With their whole hearts' de-
sire.
———

4 Ye gates, lift up your heads on
high;
Ye doors that last for aye,
Be lifted up, that so the King
Of glory enter may.

But who of glory is the King?
The mighty Lord is this;
*Even that same Lord that great
in might
And strong in battle is.

5 Ye gates, lift up your heads; ye
doors,
Be lifted up, that so the King
Of glory enter may.
But who is he that is the King,
The King of glory? who is
this?
*The Lord of hosts, and none but
he,
The King of glory is.
†(Alleluia! Amen).

Metrical Psalter, 1650 (Irish)
* *These two lines are repeated.*
† *The Alleluia is sung five times and
the Amen three times.*

567 *Schmücke dich, o liebe Seele*

DECK thyself, my soul, with
gladness,
Leave the gloomy haunts of
sadness,
Come into the daylight's splendour,
There with joy thy praises
render
Unto him whose grace un-
bounded
Hath this wondrous banquet
founded;
High o'er all the heavens he
reigneth,
Yet to dwell with thee he
deigneth.

2 Hasten as a bride to meet him,
And with loving reverence greet
him,
For with words of life im-
mortal
Now he knocketh at thy portal;
Haste to ope the gates before
him,
Saying, while thou dost adore
him,
'Suffer, Lord, that I receive
thee,
And I never more will leave
thee.'

3 Sun, who all my life dost
brighten;
Light, who dost my soul en-
lighten;
Joy, the sweetest man e'er
knoweth;
Fount, whence all my being
floweth:
At thy feet I cry, my Maker,
Let me be a fit partaker
Of this blessèd food from
heaven,
For our good, thy glory, given.

4 Jesus, Bread of Life, I pray
thee,
Let me gladly here obey thee;
Never to my hurt invited,
Be thy love with love requited
From this banquet let me
measure,
Lord, how vast and deep its
treasure;
Through the gifts thou here
dost give me,
As thy guest in heaven receive
me.

JOHANN FRANCK, 1618–7?
Tr. CATHERINE WINKWORTH
1827–7?

568

FATHER most loving, listen
to thy children
Who as thy family joyfully
foregather,
Singing the praises of thy Son
our Brother,
Jesus beloved!

2 We stand attentive, listening to
God's Gospel,
Welcoming Jesus as he speaks
among us,
Mind and heart open, ready to
receive him,
Lips to proclaim him!

3 Father in heaven, bless the gifts
we offer,
Signs of our true love, hearts in
homage given!
Make them the one gift that is
wholly worthy,
Christ, spotless victim!

Father, we thank thee for thy
    Son's dear presence,
Coming to feed us as the Bread
    of heaven,
Making us one with him in
    sweet communion,
One with each other!

Praised be our Father, lovingly
    inviting
Guests to this banquet, praised
    the Son who feeds us,
Praised too the Spirit, sent by
    Son and Father,
Making us Christ-like! Amen.
                JAMES QUINN

69 救世之身爲
衆生擘

THE bread of life, for all men
    broken!
He drank the cup on Golgotha.
His grace we trust, and spread
    with reverence
    This holy feast, and thus re-
    member.

With godly fear we seek thy
    presence;
    Our hearts are sad, people
    distressed.
Thy holy face is stained with
    bitter tears,
    Our human pain still bearest
    thou with us.

O Lord, we pray, come thou
    among us,
Lighten our eyes, brightly
    appear!
Immanuel, heav'n's joy un-
    ending,
    Our life with thine for ever
    blending.
        TIMOTHY TINGFANG LEW
                1891–1947
    Tr. WALTER REGINALD OXENHAM
                TAYLOR

70

I AM not worthy, holy Lord,
    That thou shouldst come to
    me;
Speak but the word; one
    gracious word
    Can set the sinner free.

2 I am not worthy; cold and bare
    The lodging of my soul;
How canst thou deign to enter
    there?
    Lord, speak, and make me
    whole.

3 I am not worthy; yet, my God,
    How can I say thee nay,—
Thee, who didst give thy flesh
    and blood
    My ransom price to pay?

4 O come, in this sweet morning*
    hour,
    Feed me with food divine;
And fill me with all thy love and
    power
    This worthless heart of mine.
      HENRY WILLIAMS BAKER, 1821–77

    * Or evening.

571   *Jesu, dulcedo cordium*

JESUS, thou Joy of loving
    hearts,
    Thou Fount of life, thou
    Light of men,
From the best bliss that earth
    imparts
    We turn unfilled to thee
    again.

2 Thy truth unchanged hath ever
    stood;
    Thou savest those that on
    thee call:
To them that seek thee thou
    art good,
    To them that find thee, all in
    all.

3 We taste thee, O thou living
    Bread,
    And long to feast upon thee
    still;
We drink of thee, the Fountain-
    head,
    And thirst our souls from
    thee to fill.

4 Our restless spirits yearn for
    thee,
    Where'er our changeful lot is
    cast,—
Glad when thy gracious smile
    we see,
    Blest when our faith can
    hold thee fast.

5 O Jesus, ever with us stay;
   Make all our moments calm
      and bright;
   Chase the dark night of sin away;
   Shed o'er the world thy holy
      light.

12th century
Tr. RAY PALMER, 1808-87

572

COME, risen Lord, and deign
   to be our guest;
Nay, let us be thy guests;
   the feast is thine;
Thyself at thine own board
   make manifest,
   In thine own sacrament of
      bread and wine.

2 We meet, as in that upper room
      they met;
   Thou at the table, blessing,
      yet dost stand;
   'This is my body': so thou
      givest yet;
   Faith still receives the cup as
      from thy hand.

3 One body we, one body who
      partake,
   One Church united in com-
      munion blest;
   One name we bear, one bread of
      life we break,
   With all thy saints on earth
      and saints at rest.

4 One with each other, Lord, for
      one in thee,
   Who art one Saviour and one
      living Head;
   Then open thou our eyes, that
      we may see;
   Be known to us in breaking
      of the bread.

GEORGE WALLACE BRIGGS
1875-1959
altered

573   *Before Communion*

HERE, O my Lord, I see
   thee face to face;
Here would I touch and
   handle things unseen,
Here grasp with firmer hand
   the eternal grace,
And all my weariness upon
   thee lean.

2 Mine is the sin, but thine th[e]
      righteousness;
   Mine is the guilt, but thin[e]
      the cleansing blood;
   Here is my robe, my refuge, an[d]
      my peace—
   Thy blood, thy righteousnes[s]
      O Lord my God.

3 Here would I feed upon th[e]
      bread of God,
   Here drink with thee th[e]
      royal wine of heaven;
   Here would I lay aside eac[h]
      earthly load,
   Here taste afresh the calm [of]
      sin forgiven.

4 This is the hour of banquet an[d]
      of song;
   This is the heavenly tab[le]
      spread for me;
   Here let me feast, and, feastin[g]
      still prolong
   The hallowed hour of fellow[-]
      ship with thee.

After Communion

5 Too soon we rise; the symbo[l]
      disappear;
   The feast, though not th[e]
      love, is past and gone;
   The bread and wine remov[ed]
      but thou art here,
   Nearer than ever, still m[y]
      Shield and Sun.

6 I have no help but thine; n[or]
      do I need
   Another arm save thine t[o]
      lean upon;
   It is enough, my Lord, enoug[h]
      indeed;
   My strength is in thy migh[t,]
      thy might alone.

7 Feast after feast thus com[es]
      and passes by,
   Yet, passing, points to th[e]
      glad feast above,
   Giving sweet foretaste of th[e]
      festal joy,
   The Lamb's great brid[al]
      feast of bliss and love.

HORATIUS BONAR, 1808-[?]
Order of verses altere[d]

574

BREAD of the world, in
mercy broken,
Wine of the soul, in mercy shed,
By whom the words of life were
spoken,
And in whose death our sins
are dead:
Look on the heart by sorrow
broken,
Look on the tears by sinners
shed;
And be thy feast to us the token
That by thy grace our souls
are fed.

REGINALD HEBER, 1783–1826

575

THOU standest at the altar,
Thou offerest every
prayer;
In faith's unclouded vision
We see thee ever there.

Out of thy hand the incense
Ascends before the throne,
Where thou art interceding,
Lord Jesus, for thine own.

And, through thy blood ac-
cepted,
With thee we keep the feast:
Thou art the one Oblation;
Thou only art the Priest.

We come, O only Saviour;
On thee, the Lamb, we feed:
Thy flesh is bread from heaven;
Thy blood is drink indeed.

To thee, Almighty Father;
Incarnate Son, to thee;
To thee, Anointing Spirit,—
All praise and glory be. Amen.

EDWARD WILTON EDDIS
1825–1905, altered

576

O CHRIST, who sinless art
alone,
Our frailty and our sin who
knowest,
We stand in thee before the
throne
And plead the death thou
showest.

2 O Christ, our sacrifice and
Priest,
Who in the glory intercedest,
We in the shadow keep the feast
And show the death thou
pleadest.

3 *To thee in endless life enthroned,*
O Christ, eternal praise be
given,
With Holy Ghost and Father
owned
One God in earth and heaven.
Amen.

ARTHUR WELLESLEY WOTHERSPOON
1853–1936

577   Σιγησάτω πᾶσα σάρξ
βροτεία

LET all mortal flesh keep
silence,
And with fear and trembling
stand;
Ponder nothing earthly-minded,
For with blessing in his hand
Christ our God to earth de-
scendeth,
Our full homage to demand.

2 King of kings, yet born of
Mary,
As of old on earth he stood,
Lord of lords, in human ves-
ture—
In the body and the blood—
He will give to all the faithful
His own self for heavenly food.

3 Rank on rank the host of
heaven
Spreads its vanguard on the
way,
As the Light of light descendeth
From the realms of endless
day,
That the powers of hell may
vanish
As the darkness clears away.

4 At his feet the six-winged
Seraph;
Cherubim with sleepless eye,
Veil their faces to the Presence,
As with ceaseless voice they
cry,
'Alleluia, Alleluia,
Alleluia, Lord most high'.

Liturgy of St. James
Tr. GERARD MOULTRIE, 1829–85

578 *Pange, lingua, gloriosi*
Corporis mysterium

†NOW, my tongue, the mystery tĕlling
Öf the glorious Body sing,
And the Blood, all price excelling,
Which the Gentiles' Lord and Kïng,
In a Virgin's womb once dwelling,
Shed for this wörld's ransoming.

2 That last night, at supper lÿing,
'Mïd the Twelve, his chosen bänd,
Jesus, with the law complying
Keeps the feast its rites demänd;
Then, more precious food supplying,
Gives himself with his own hand.

3 Word-made-flesh, true bread he mäketh
Bÿ his word his Flesh to bĕ,
Wine his Blood; which whoso taketh
Must from carnal thoughts be frëe;
Faith alone, though sight forsaketh,
Shows true hearts thĕ mystery.

———

*4 Therefore we, before him bënding,
Thïs great sacrament reverë;
Types and shadows have their ending,
For the newer rite is hëre;
Faith, our outward sense befriending,
Makes our inwärd vision clear.

5 *Unto God be praise and hönour*
Tö the Father, to the Sön,
To the mighty Spirit, glory—
Ever Three and ever Onë:
Power and glory in the highest
While eternäl ages run. Ämën.

ST. THOMAS AQUINAS
1227–7[
Tr. EDWARD CASWALL, 1814–7[
and Compilers o[
Hymns Ancient and Modern, 186[

† *The pointing is for use with tune (*[
PANGE LINGUA only.
* *Verses* 4, 5 *may be sung to* TANTU[
ERGO SACRAMENTUM, *no.* 373.

579

ALMIGHTY Father, Lor[
most high,
Who madest all, who fillest al[
Thy Name we praise an[
magnify,
For all our needs on thee we cal[

2 We offer to thee of thine own,
Ourselves and all that we ca[
bring,
In bread and cup before thee[
shown,
Our universal offering.

3 All that we have we bring t[
thee,
Yet all is naught when all i[
done,
Save that in it thy love can se[
The sacrifice of thy dear Son.

4 By his command in bread and
cup
His body and his blood we
plead;
What on the cross he offered u[
Is here our sacrifice indeed.

5 For all thy gifts of life and
grace,
Here we thy servants humbly
pray
That thou wouldst look upon
the face
Of thine anointed Son today.

VINCENT STUCKEY STRATTON
COLES, 1845–1929

HOLY COMMUNION

580

AND now, O Father, mindful of
    the love
  That bought us, once for all,
    on Calvary's Tree,
And having with us him that
    pleads above,
  We here present, we here
    spread forth to thee
That only offering perfect in
    thine eyes,
  The one true, pure, immortal
    sacrifice.

2 Look, Father, look on his
    anointed face,
  And only look on us as found
    in him;
Look not on our misusings of
    thy grace,
  Our prayer so languid, and
    our faith so dim:
For lo! between our sins and
    their reward
  We set the Passion of thy Son
    our Lord.

3 And then for those, our dearest
    and our best,
  By this prevailing presence
    we appeal;
O fold them closer to thy
    mercy's breast,
  O do thine utmost for their
    souls' true weal;
From tainting mischief keep
    them white and clear,
  And crown thy gifts with
    strength to persevere.

4 And so we come: O draw us to
    thy feet,
  Most patient Saviour, who
    canst love us still;
And by this food, so awesome
    and so sweet,
  Deliver us from every touch
    of ill:
In thine own service make us
    glad and free,
  And grant us never more to
    part with thee.

WILLIAM BRIGHT, 1824–1901
Based on *Unde et memores, Domine,
nos servi tui*

581

*Verbum supernum
prodiens, nec Patris*

FORTH from on high the
    Father sends
His Son, who yet stays by his
    side.
The Word made man for man
    then spends
His life till life's last eventide.

2 While Judas plans the traitor's
    sign,
The mocking kiss that Love
    betrays,
Jesus in form of bread and wine
His loving sacrifice displays.

3 He gives himself that faith may
    see
The heavenly Food on which
    men feed,
That flesh and blood of man
    may be
Fed by his flesh and blood in-
    deed.

4 By birth he makes himself
    man's kin;
As Food before his guests he
    lies;
To death he bears man's cross
    of sin;
In heaven he reigns as man's
    blest prize.

5 O Priest and Victim, Lord of
    Life,
Throw wide the gates of Para-
    dise!
We face our foes in mortal
    strife;
Thou art our strength! O heed
    our cries!

6 *To Father, Son, and Spirit blest,
One only God, be ceaseless praise!
May he in goodness grant us rest
In heaven, our home, for endless
    days! Amen.*

JAMES QUINN
From the Latin of
ST. THOMAS AQUINAS, 1227–74

582

IN love, from love, thou camest
    forth, O Lord,
Sent from the Father, his in-
    carnate Word;

That in that perfect Name, by
  thee confessed,
Our hearts with thine might
  find their perfect rest.

2 Within the veil, thy mortal
  travail o'er,
Thou livest unto God to die no
  more;
And now, made sons of God,
  with thee we stand,
Girt with the grace of thy con-
  firming hand.

3 Thou art our Royal Priest before the throne;
Our priesthood is in thee, from
  thee alone;
In thee we offer at our Father's
  feet
The offering pure, with holy
  incense sweet.

4 The sacred rite its ordered
  course hath run,
All that thy Love ordained our
  love hath done,
Still showing forth before our
  Father's eyes
The one, pure, perfect, filial
  sacrifice.

5 And now, O Lord, from out thy
  chosen place
Thy voice proclaims anew the
  feast of grace.
Cleanse thou us, Lord, in this
  most holy hour
By thine own breath of resurrection power.

6 Lord of the living and the tran-
  quil dead,
Reveal thyself, our one all-
  glorious Head;
And through these hallowed
  gifts of bread and wine
Feed thy one Body with the
  Life divine.

7 O perfect Brother, and true
  Son of God,
Impart to us thy Body and thy
  Blood,
That through communion of
  one mind, one heart,
We may advance to see thee
  as thou art.

8 *Jesus, Immanuel, evermore*
  adored,
At thy great Name we bow, we
  own thee Lord:
Glory be thine, O Father, thine,
  O Son,
And thine, O Holy Spirit, ever
  One. Amen.
        JOHN MACLEOD, 1840–9

583

LORD, enthroned in heavenly
  splendour,
  First-begotten from the dead
Thou alone, our strong defender
  Liftest up thy people's head
      Alleluia! Alleluia!
  Jesus, true and living Bread.

2 Here our humblest homage pay
    we;
  Here in loving reverence
    bow;
Here for faith's discernment
    pray we,
  Lest we fail to know thee
    now.
      Alleluia! Alleluia!
  Thou art here, we ask not
    how.

3 Though the lowliest form doth
    veil thee,
  As of old in Bethlehem,
Here as there thine angels hail
    thee,
  Branch and Flower of Jesse's
    stem.
      Alleluia! Alleluia!
  We in worship join with
    them.

4 Paschal Lamb, thine offering,
    finished
  Once for all when thou wast
    slain,
In its fullness undiminished
  Shall for evermore remain,
      Alleluia! Alleluia!
  Cleansing souls from every
    stain.

5 Life-imparting, heavenly
    Manna,
  Stricken Rock with stream-
    ing side,

Heaven and earth with loud
    hosanna
Worship thee, the Lamb who
    died,
    Alleluia! Alleluia!
Risen, ascended, glorified.
      GEORGE HUGH BOURNE, 1840–1925

---

584   *Adoro te devote, latens*
               Deitas

THEE we adore, O hidden
    Saviour, thee,
Who in thy sacrament dost
    deign to be:
Both flesh and spirit at thy
    presence fail,
Yet here thy presence we de-
    voutly hail.

O blest memorial of our dying
    Lord!
Thou living Bread, who life dost
    here afford,
O may our souls for ever live
    by thee,
And thou to us for ever precious
    be.

Fountain of goodness, Jesus,
    Lord, and God,
Cleanse us, unclean, with thy
    most cleansing blood;
Make us in thee devoutly to
    believe,
In thee to hope, to thee in love
    to cleave.

O Christ, whom now beneath a
    veil we see,
May what we thirst for soon our
    portion be,
There in the glory of thy dwell-
    ing-place
To gaze on thee unveiled, and
    see thy face.
      ST. THOMAS AQUINAS, 1227–74
      Tr. JAMES RUSSELL WOODFORD
      1820–85, altered

585

ACCORDING to thy gracious
    word,
In meek humility,
This will I do, my dying Lord,
    I will remember thee.

2 Thy body, broken for my sake,
    My bread from heaven shall
      be;
Thy testamental cup I take,
    And thus remember thee.

3 Gethsemane can I forget?
    Or there thy conflict see,
Thine agony and bloody sweat,
    And not remember thee?

4 When to the cross I turn mine
    eyes,
    And rest on Calvary,
O Lamb of God, my sacrifice,
    I must remember thee,—

5 Remember thee, and all thy
    pains,
    And all thy love to me;
Yea, while a breath, a pulse re-
    mains,
Will I remember thee.

6 And when these failing lips
    grow dumb,
    And mind and memory flee,
When thou shalt in thy King-
    dom come,
Jesus, remember me.
      JAMES MONTGOMERY, 1771–1854

586

FATHER, we thank thee who
    hast planted
    Thy holy name within our
      hearts,
Knowledge and faith and life
    immortal
Jesus thy Son to us imparts.

2 Thou, Lord, didst make all for
    thy pleasure,
Didst give man food for all
    his days,
Giving in Christ the bread
    eternal;
Thine is the power, be thine
    the praise.

3 Watch o'er thy Church, O Lord,
    in mercy,
    Save it from evil, guard it
      still,
Perfect it in thy love, unite it,
    Cleansed and conformed unto
      thy will.

4 As grain, once scattered on the
    hillsides,
    Was in the bread we break
      made one,
So may thy world-wide Church
    be gathered
    Into thy Kingdom by thy
      Son.

From prayers in the *Didache*, probably
second century. Tr. and versified by
FRANCIS BLAND TUCKER
altered

587

AUTHOR of life divine,
    Who hast a table spread,
Furnished with mystic wine
    And everlasting bread,
Preserve the life thyself hast
    given,
And feed and train us up for
    heaven.

2   Our needy souls sustain
    With fresh supplies of love,
Till all thy life we gain,
    And all thy fullness prove,
And, strengthened by thy per-
    fect grace,
Behold without a veil thy face.

CHARLES WESLEY, 1707–88

588

بنيلا ضني (تيا وفجهت

STRENGTHEN for service,
    Lord, the hands
    That holy things have taken;
Let ears that now have heard
    thy songs
    To clamour never waken.

2 Lord, may the tongues which
    'Holy' sang
    Keep free from all deceiving;
The eyes which saw thy love be
    bright,
    Thy blessèd hope perceiving.

3 The feet that tread thy holy
    courts
    From light do thou not
    banish;
The bodies by thy body fed
    With thy new life replenish.

Liturgy of Malabar
Tr. CHARLES WILLIAM HUMPHREY
1840–192
PERCY DEARMER, 1867–1936
and others

589

FORTH in the peace of Christ
    we go;
Christ to the world with joy we
    bring;
Christ in our minds, Christ on
    our lips,
Christ in our hearts, the world's
    true King.

2 King of our hearts, Christ
    makes us kings;
Kingship with him his servants
    gain;
With Christ, the Servant-Lord
    of all,
Christ's world we serve to
    share Christ's reign.

3 Priests of the world, Christ
    sends us forth
The world of time to consecrate,
The world of sin by grace to
    heal,
Christ's world in Christ to re-
    create.

4 Christ's are our lips, his word
    we speak;
Prophets are we whose deeds
    proclaim
Christ's truth in love that we
    may be
Christ in the world, to spread
    Christ's name.

5 We are the Church; Christ bids
    us show
That in his Church all nations
    find
Their hearth and home where
    Christ restores
True peace, true love, to all
    mankind.

JAMES QUINN

590 PARAPHRASE 38, verses
8, 10, 11

NOW, Lord! according to thy
word,
Let me in peace depart;
Mine eyes have thy salvation
seen,
And gladness fills my heart.

2 This great salvation, long pre-
pared,
And now disclosed to view,
Hath proved thy love was con-
stant still,
And promises were true.

3 That Sun I now behold, whose
light
Shall heathen darkness chase,

And rays of brightest glory pour
Around thy chosen race.

4 *To Father, Son, and Holy Ghost,*
The God whom we adore,
Be glory, as it was, and is,
And shall be evermore. Amen.

Scottish Paraphrases, 1781
From St. Luke 2:29–32

The following are also suitable

7 O send thy light forth and thy truth

307 'Lift up your hearts': I hear the
summons calling

351 O thou my soul, bless God the Lord

492 O thou, who at thy Eucharist didst
pray

V

OTHER ORDINANCES

CONFIRMATION

591 PARAPHRASE 54

I'M not ashamed to own my
    Lord,
  Or to defend his cause,
Maintain the glory of his cross,
  And honour all his laws.

2 Jesus, my Lord! I know his
    Name,
  His Name is all my boast;
Nor will he put my soul to
    shame,
  Nor let my hope be lost.

3 I know that safe with him re-
    mains,
  Protected by his power,
What I've committed to his
    trust,
  Till the decisive hour.

4 Then will he own his servant's
    name
  Before his Father's face,
And in the New Jerusalem
  Appoint my soul a place.
            Scottish Paraphrases, 1781
            From 2 Timothy 1:12

592

WE come, O Christ, to thee,
  True Son of God and man,
By whom all things consist,
  In whom all life began:
In thee alone we live and move,
And have our being in thy love.

2 Thou art the way to God,
  Thy blood our ransom paid;
In thee we face our Judge
  And Maker unafraid.
Before the throne absolved we
    stand:
Thy love has met thy law's
    demand.

3 Thou art the living truth!
  All wisdom dwells in thee,
Thou source of every skill,
  Eternal verity!
Thou great I AM! In thee we
    rest,
True answer to our every quest.

4 Thou only art true life,
  To know thee is to live
The more abundant life
  That earth can never give:
O risen Lord! We live in thee
And thou in us eternally!

5 We worship thee, Lord Christ,
  Our Saviour and our King,
To thee our youth and strength
  Adoringly we bring:
So fill our hearts that men may
    see
Thy life in us and turn to thee!
            EDITH MARGARET CLARKSON

593

YE that know the Lord is
    gracious,
  Ye for whom a Corner-stone
Stands, of God elect and pre-
    cious,
  Laid that ye may build
    thereon,
See that on that sure founda-
    tion
  Ye a living temple raise,
Towers that may tell forth
    salvation,
  Walls that may re-echo
    praise.

2 Living stones, by God ap-
    pointed
  Each to his allotted place,
Kings and priests, by God
    anointed,
  Shall ye not declare his grace?

214

Ye, a royal generation,
  Tell the tidings of your birth,
Tidings of a new creation
  To an old and weary earth.

3 Tell the praise of him who
    called you
  Out of darkness into light,
Broke the fetters that en-
    thralled you,
  Gave you freedom, peace
    and sight:
Tell the tale of sins forgiven,
  Strength renewed and hope
    restored,
Till the earth, in tune with
    heaven,
  Praise and magnify the Lord!
                CYRIL ARGENTINE ALINGTON
                          1872–1955
                From 1 Peter 2:3–10

594

WITNESS, ye men and
    angels, now,
  Before the Lord we speak;
To him we make our solemn
    vow,
  A vow we dare not break;

2 That, long as life itself shall last,
    Ourselves to Christ we yield;
  Nor from his cause will we de-
    part,
  Or ever quit the field.

3 We trust not in our native
    strength,
  But on his grace rely,
That, with returning wants,
    the Lord
  Will all our need supply.

4 O guide our doubtful feet aright,
  And keep us in thy ways;
And while we turn our vows to
    prayers,
  Turn thou our prayers to
    praise.
                BENJAMIN BEDDOME, 1717–95

595

WE magnify thy Name, O
    God,
  That to thy people thou hast
    given
A covenant sign eternal.
Baptized into the Triune Name
Of Father, Son, and Holy
    Ghost
Thou didst them seal for ever.

2 Nurtured within thy family,
  Thy servants now proclaim to
    all
  Their faith in Christ their
    Saviour.
Confirm and strengthen them,
    O God,
Increase in them the Spirit's
    grace;
Grant them thy benediction.

3 May they, at Christ's own Table,
    be
  Partakers of his flesh and blood
With grateful adoration.
May they in all things live like
    Christ,
And thereby witness to all men
That he is Lord eternal.
                JOHN MONTEITH BARKLEY
        The following are also suitable
        Nos. 629, 342, 550 and hymns from sec-
        tion III. nos. 387–488.

ORDINATION

596   PSALM 103, verses 19–22

THE Lord preparèd hath his
    throne
  In heavens firm to stand;
And every thing that being
    hath
  His kingdom doth command.

2 O ye his angels, that excel
    In strength, bless ye the
      Lord;
  Ye who obey what he com-
    mands,
    And hearken to his word.

215

3 O bless and magnify the Lord,
Ye glorious hosts of his:
Ye ministers, that do fulfil
Whate'er his pleasure is.

4 O bless the Lord, all ye his
works,
Wherewith the world is
stored
In his dominions everywhere.
My soul, bless thou the Lord.

5 To Father, Son, and Holy Ghost,
The God whom we adore,
Be glory, as it was, and is,
And shall be evermore. Amen.

597

POUR out thy Spirit from
on high;
Lord, thine ordainèd servants
bless;
Graces and gifts to each supply,
And clothe thy priests with
righteousness.

2 Within thy temple when they
stand,
To teach the truth, as taught
by thee,

Saviour, like stars in thy right
hand
The angels of the churches
be!

3 Wisdom and zeal and faith impart,
Firmness with meekness,
from above,
To bear thy people on their
heart,
And love the souls whom
thou dost love.

4 To watch and pray, and never
faint;
By day and night strict
guard to keep;
To warn the sinner, cheer
the saint,
Nourish thy lambs, and feed
thy sheep;

5 Then, when their work is
finished here,
In humble hope their charge
resign.
When the Chief Shepherd shall
appear,
O God, may they and we be
thine.

JAMES MONTGOMERY, 1771–1854
The following is also suitable
No. 342 Come, Holy Ghost, our souls
inspire

MARRIAGE

598

PSALM 67

GOD be merciful unto ' us
and ' bless us : and cause
his ' face to ' shine up- ' on
us :
That thy way may be ' known
upon ' earth : thy saving '
health a- ' mong all ' nations.

2 Let the people ' praise thee
O ' God : let ' all the ' people '
praise thee :
O let the nations be glad
and ' sing for ' joy : for thou
shalt judge the people
righteously and ' govern
the ' nations up · on ' earth.

3 Let the people ' praise thee
O ' God : let ' all the '
people ' praise thee :
Then shall the earth ' yield
her ' increase : and God
even ' our own ' God shall '
bless us.

†4 God ' shall ' bless us : and all
the ' ends of the ' earth
shall ' fear him.

*Glory ' be to the ' Father : and
to the Son ' and to the '
Holy ' Ghost
As it ' was in the be- ' ginning:
is now and ever shall be '
world without ' end.*

A- ' men.

† *Second half of Chant*

599

O FATHER, by whose
  sovereign sway
The sun and stars in order
  move,
Yet who hast made us bold to
  say
Thy nature and thy Name is
  love:

2 O royal Son, whose every deed
  Showed love and love's
    divinity,
Yet didst not scorn the hum-
    blest need
At Cana's feast in Galilee:

3 O Holy Spirit, who dost speak
  In saint and sage since time
    began,
Yet givest courage to the weak
  And teachest love to selfish
    man:

4 Be present in our hearts today,
  All powerful to bless, and give
To these thy children grace
  that they
May love, and through their
  loving live.
                CYRIL ARGENTINE ALINGTON
                1872–1955

600

O FATHER, all creating,
  Whose wisdom, love, and
    power
First bound two lives together
  In Eden's primal hour,
The lives of these thy children
  With thy best gifts endue,
A home by thee made happy,
  A love by thee kept true.

2 O Saviour, Guest most boun-
    teous
  Of old in Galilee,
Vouchsafe today thy presence
  With these who call on thee;
Their store of earthly gladness
  Transform to heavenly wine,
And teach them, in the tasting,
  To know the gift is thine.

3 O Spirit of the Father,
  Breathe on them from above,
So mighty in thy pureness,
  So tender in thy love;
That, guarded by thy presence,
  From sin and strife kept free,
Their lives may own thy
    guidance,
  Their hearts be ruled by
    thee.

4 Except thou build it, Father,
  The house is built in vain;
Except thou, Saviour, bless it,
  The joy will turn to pain;
But naught can break the union
  Of hearts in thee made one;
And love thy Spirit hallows
  Is endless love begun.
                JOHN ELLERTON, 1826–93, altered

601

O GOD, whose loving hand
  has led
Thy children to this joyful day,
We pray that thou wilt bless
  them now
As, one in thee, they face life's
  way.

2 Grant them the will to follow
    Christ
  Who graced the Feast in Galilee,
And through his perfect life of
    love
  Fulfilment of their love to see.

3 Give them the power to make
    a home
  Where peace and honour shall
    abide,
Where Christ shall be the
    gracious Head,
  The trusted Friend, the con-
    stant Guide.

4 *To Father, Son, and Holy Ghost,*
  The God whom heaven and earth
    adore,
Be glory, as it was of old,
  Is now, and shall be evermore.
    Amen.
                JOHN BOYD MOORE

602

O GOD of Love, to thee we bow,
And pray for these before thee now,
That, closely knit in holy vow,
They may in thee be one.

2 When days are filled with pure delight,
When paths are plain and skies are bright,
Walking by faith and not by sight,
May they in thee be one.

3 When stormy winds fulfil thy will,
And all their good seems turned to ill,

Then, trusting thee completely, still
May they in thee be one.

4 Whate'er in life shall be their share
Of quickening joy or burdening care,
In power to do and grace to bear,
May they in thee be one.

5 Eternal Love, with them abide;
In thee for ever may they hide,
For even death cannot divide
Those whom thou makest one.

WILLIAM VAUGHAN JENKINS
1868–1920

The following are also suitable
Nos. 9, 115, 368, 388, 457, 360

FUNERAL SERVICES

603   PSALM 103, verses 13–17

SUCH pity as a father hath
Unto his children dear;
Like pity shows the Lord to such
As worship him in fear.

2 For he remembers we are dust,
And he our frame well knows.
Frail man, his days are like the grass,
As flower in field he grows:

3 For over it the wind doth pass,
And it away is gone;
And of the place where once it was
It shall no more be known.

4 But unto them that do him fear
God's mercy never ends;
And to their children's children still
His righteousness extends.

5 *To Father, Son, and Holy Ghost,*
The God whom we adore,
Be glory, as it was, and is,
And shall be evermore. Amen.

604

GO, happy soul, thy days are ended,
Thy pilgrimage on earth below:
Go, by angelic guard attended,
To God's own Paradise now go.

2 Go; Christ, the Shepherd good, befriend thee,
Who gave his life thy soul to win;
'Tis even he that shall defend thee,
Thy going out and coming in.

3 Go forth in peace: farewell to sadness:
May rest in Paradise be thine;
In Jesus' presence there is gladness:
Light everlasting on thee shine.

GEORGE RATCLIFFE WOODWARD
1849–1934
and Compilers of
The BBC Hymn Book

218

605 *Jesus lebt, mit ihm auch ich*

JESUS lives! thy terrors now
  Can, O Death, no more
    appal us;
Jesus lives! by this we know
  Thou, O grave, canst not
    enthral us.
                    Alleluia!

2 Jesus lives! henceforth is death
    But the gate of life immortal;
This shall calm our trembling
      breath
  When we pass its gloomy
      portal.

3 Jesus lives! for us he died;
    Then, alone to Jesus living,
Pure in heart may we abide,
    Glory to our Saviour giving.

4 Jesus lives! our hearts know
      well
    Naught from us his love shall
      sever;
Life, nor death, nor powers of
      hell
    Tear us from his keeping ever.

5 Jesus lives! to him the throne
    Over heaven and earth is
      given;
May we go where he is gone,
    Live and reign with him in
      heaven.
        CHRISTIAN FÜRCHTEGOTT GELLERT
                      1715–69
        Tr. FRANCES ELIZABETH COX
                      1812–97

606

O LORD of life, where'er they
      be,
Safe in thine own eternity,
Our dead are living unto thee.
  Alleluia! Alleluia! Alleluia!

2 All souls are thine, and, here or
      there,
They rest within thy sheltering
      care;
One providence alike they
      share.

3 Thy word is true, thy ways are
      just;
Above the requiem, 'Dust to
      dust,'
Shall rise our psalm of grateful
      trust,

4 O happy they in God who rest,
No more by fear and doubt
      oppressed;
Living or dying, they are blest:
        FREDERICK LUCIAN HOSMER
                      1840–1929

607

GOD of the living, in whose
      eyes
Unveiled thy whole creation
      lies,
All souls are thine; we must not
      say
That those are dead who pass
      away;
From this our world of flesh
      set free,
We know them living unto thee.

2 Released from earthly toil and
      strife,
With thee is hidden still their
      life;
Thine are their thoughts, their
      works, their powers,
All thine, and yet most truly
      ours;
For well we know, where'er
      they be,
Our dead are living unto thee.
        JOHN ELLERTON, 1826–93

608

THERE is a blessèd home
    beyond this land of woe,
Where trials never come.
    nor tears of sorrow flow;
Where faith is lost in sight,
    and patient hope is crowned,
And everlasting light
    its glory throws around.

2 O joy all joys beyond!
  to see the Lamb who died,
For ever there enthroned,
  for ever glorified;
To give to him the praise
  of every triumph won,
And sing, through endless days,
  the great things he hath
  done.

3 *There is a land of peace;*
  the angels know it well;
Glad songs that never cease
  within its portals swell;
Around its glorious throne
  ten thousand saints adore
Christ, with the Father one
  and Spirit, evermore. Amen.

HENRY WILLIAMS BAKER
1821–77

DEDICATION OF CHURCH BUILDINGS

609

THIS stone to thee in faith
  we lay;
We build the temple, Lord,
  to thee:
Thine eye be open, night and
  day,
To guard this house and
  sanctuary.

2 Here, when thy people seek thy
  face,
  And dying sinners pray to
  live,
Hear thou, in heaven thy
  dwelling-place,
  And when thou hearest, O
  forgive!

3 Here, when thy messengers pro-
  claim
  The blessèd Gospel of thy
  Son,
Still, by the power of his great
  Name,
  Be mighty signs and wonders
  done.

4 'Hosanna!' to their heavenly
  King
  When children's voices raise
  that song,
'Hosanna!' let their angels sing,
  And heaven, with earth, the
  strain prolong.

5 But will the eternal Father
  deign
  Here to abide, no transient
  guest?
Will here the world's Re-
  deemer reign,
  And here the Holy Spirit
  rest?

6 That glory never hence depart
  Yet choose not, Lord, this
  house alone;
Thy Kingdom come to every
  heart:
  In all the world be thine the
  throne.

JAMES MONTGOMERY, 1771–1854
altered

610

ALL things are thine; no gift
  have we,
Lord of all gifts, to offer thee;
And hence with grateful hearts
  today,
Thine own before thy feet we lay.

2 Thy will was in the builders'
  thought;
  Thy hand unseen amidst us
  wrought;
Through mortal motive, scheme
  and plan,
Thy wise eternal purpose ran.

3 In weakness and in want we call
  On thee for whom the heavens
  are small;
Thy glory is thy children's good,
Thy joy thy tender Father-hood.

4 O Father, deign these walls to
  bless;
  Fill with thy love their emptiness;
And let their door a gateway be
  To lead us from ourselves to
  thee.

JOHN GREENLEAF WHITTIER
1807–92

The following is also suitable
No. 10 Christ is made the sure foundation

VI

TIMES AND SEASONS

NEW YEAR

11

O GOD, our help in ages past,
　Our hope for years to come,
Our shelter from the stormy blast,
　And our eternal home!

Under the shadow of thy throne
　Thy saints have dwelt secure;
Sufficient is thine arm alone,
　And our defence is sure.

Before the hills in order stood,
　Or earth received her frame,
From everlasting thou art God,
　To endless years the same.

A thousand ages in thy sight
　Are like an evening gone;
Short as the watch that ends the night
　Before the rising sun.

Time, like an ever-rolling stream,
　Bears all its sons away;
They fly forgotten, as a dream
　Dies at the opening day.

O God, our help in ages past,
　Our hope for years to come,
Be thou our guard while troubles last,
　And our eternal home.

ISAAC WATTS, 1674–1748

12

FOR thy mercy and thy grace,
　Faithful through another year,
Hear our song of thankfulness;
　Jesus, our Redeemer, hear.

2 Lo! our sins on thee we cast,
　Thee, our perfect sacrifice,
And, forgetting all the past,
　Press towards our glorious prize.

3 Dark the future; let thy light
　Guide us, Bright and Morning Star;
Fierce our foes, and hard the fight;
　Arm us, Saviour, for the war.

4 In our weakness and distress,
　Rock of strength, be thou our stay;
In the pathless wilderness
　Be our true and living way.

5 Keep us faithful, keep us pure,
　Keep us evermore thine own;
Help, O help us to endure;
　Fit us for the promised crown.

HENRY DOWNTON, 1818–85

613

GREAT God, we sing that mighty hand
　By which supported still we stand;
The opening year thy mercy shows,
　And mercy crowns its lingering close.

2 By day, by night, at home, abroad,
　Still are we guarded by our God,
By his incessant bounty fed,
　By his unerring counsel led.

3 With grateful hearts the past we own;
The future, all to us unknown,
We to thy guardian care commit,
And peaceful leave before thy feet.

4 In scenes exalted or depressed
Thou art our joy, and thou our rest;
Thy goodness all our hopes shall raise,
Adored through all our changing days.

5 When death shall interrupt these songs,
And seal in silence mortal tongues,
Our helper God, in whom we trust,
Shall keep our souls and guard our dust.

PHILIP DODDRIDGE, 1702–51

614

MARCH on, my soul, with strength,
March forward, void of fear;
He who hath led will lead,
While year succeedeth year;
* And as thou goest on thy way,
His hand shall hold thee day by day.

2 March on, my soul, with strength,
In ease thou dar'st not dwell;
High duty calls thee forth;
Then up, and quit thee well!
Take up thy cross, take up thy sword,
And fight the battles of thy Lord!

3 March on, my soul, with strength,
With strength, but not thine own;
The conquest thou shalt gain,
Through Christ thy Lord alone;
His grace shall nerve thy feeble arm,
His love preserve thee safe from harm.

4 March on, my soul, with strength,
From strength to strength march on;
Warfare shall end at length,
All foes be overthrown.
Then, O my soul, if faithful now,
The crown of life awaits thy brow.

WILLIAM WRIGHT, 1859–192

* The last line of each verse is repeated

615

HEAVENLY Father, thou hast brought us
Safely to the present day,
Gently leading on our footsteps,
Watching o'er us all the way;
Friend and Guide through life's long journey,
Grateful hearts to thee we bring;
But for love so true and changeless
How shall we fit praises sing?

2 Mercies new and never-failing
Brightly shine through all the past,
Watchful care and loving kindness,
Always near from first to last,
Tender love, divine protection,
Ever with us day and night,
Blessings more than we can number
Strew the path with golden light.

3 Shadows deep have crossed our pathway;
We have trembled in the storm;
Clouds have gathered round so darkly
That we could not see thy form;
Yet thy love hath never left us
In our griefs alone to be,
And the help each gave the other
Was the strength that came from thee.

Many that we loved have left
  us,
  Reaching first their journey's
  end;
Now they wait to give us welcome—
  Brother, sister, child, and
  friend.
When at last our journey's
  over,
  And we pass away from
  sight,
Father, take us through the
  darkness
  Into everlasting light.

HESTER PERIAM HAWKINS
1846 -1928

616

AT thy feet, our God and
  Father,
  Who hast blessed us all our
  days,
We with grateful hearts would
  gather,
  To begin the year with
  praise,—

Praise for light so brightly
  shining
  On our steps from heaven
  above,
Praise for mercies daily twining
  Round us golden cords of love.

2 Jesus, for thy love most tender,
  On the cross for sinners
  shown,
  We would praise thee, and sur-
  render
  All our hearts to be thine own.
With so blest a Friend provided,
  We upon our way would go,
Sure of being safely guided,
  Guarded well from every foe.

3 Every day will be the brighter
  When thy gracious face we see;
Every burden will be lighter
  When we know it comes from
  thee.
Spread thy love's broad banner
  o'er us;
  Give us strength to serve and
  wait,
Till the glory breaks before us,
  Through the city's open gate.

JAMES DRUMMOND BURNS
1823–64

617

PSALM 145 (ii), verses 9,
10, 15, 16

GOOD unto all men is the
  Lord:
O'er all his works his mercy is.
Thy works all praise to thee
  afford:
Thy saints, O Lord, thy Name
  shall bless.

The eyes of all things, Lord,
  attend,
And on thee wait that here do
  live,
And thou, in season due, dost
  send
Sufficient food them to relieve.

Yea, thou thine hand dost open
  wide,
And every thing dost satisfy
That lives, and doth on earth
  abide,
Of thy great liberality.

4 To Father, Son, and Holy Ghost,
  The God whom earth and heaven
  adore,
  Be glory, as it was of old,
  Is now, and shall be evermore.
  Amen.

618

THE glory of the spring how
  sweet!
  The new-born life how glad!
What joy the happy earth to
  greet,
  In new, bright raiment clad!

2 Divine Renewer, thee I bless;
  I greet thy going forth;
I love thee in the loveliness
  Of thy renewèd earth.

3 But O these wonders of thy grace,
   These nobler works of thine,
These marvels sweeter far to
   trace,
   These new births more divine,

4 This new-born glow of faith so
   strong,
   This bloom of love so fair,
This new-born ecstasy of song,
   And fragrancy of prayer!

5 Creator Spirit, work in me
   These wonders sweet of
   thine;
Divine Renewer, graciously
   Renew this heart of mine.
                THOMAS HORNBLOWER GILL
                        1819–1906

619

B Y the rutted roads we
   follow,
Fallow fields are rested now;
All along the waking country
   Soil is waiting for the plough.

2 In the yard the plough is ready,
   Ready to the ploughman's
   hand,
Ready for the crow-straight
   furrow,
   Farmer's sign across God's
   land.

3 God, in this good land you lend
   us,
   Bless the service of the share;
Light our thinking with your
   wisdom,
   Plant your patience in our
   care.

4 This is first of all man's labours,
   Man must always plough the
   earth;
God, be with us at the ploughing,
   Touch our harvest at its
   birth.
                        JOHN ARLOTT

620

Wir pflügen und wir streuen

W E plough the fields, and
   scatter
The good seed on the land,
But it is fed and watered
By God's almighty hand;

He sends the snow in winter,
   The warmth to swell the
   grain,
The breezes and the sunshine
   And soft refreshing rain.
      *All good gifts around us
      Are sent from heaven above,
   Then thank the Lord, O thank
      the Lord,
      For all his love.*

2 He only is the Maker
   Of all things near and far;
He paints the wayside flower,
   He lights the evening star;
The winds and waves obey
   him,
   By him the birds are fed;
Much more to us, his children,
   He gives our daily bread.

3 We thank thee then, O Father,
   For all things bright and
   good,
The seed-time and the harvest,
   Our life, our health, our
   food.
Accept the gifts we offer
   For all thy love imparts,
And, what thou most desirest,
   Our humble, thankful hearts.
          MATTHIAS CLAUDIUS, 1740–1815
          Tr. JANE MONTGOMERY CAMPBELL
                             1817–7

621

For younger children

S EE the farmer sow the seed
   While the field is brown;
See the furrows deep and
   straight
   Up the field and down:
      *Farmer, farmer, sow your
      seed
      Up the field and down;
   God will make the golden
      corn
      Grow where all is brown.*

2 Wait awhile and look again
   Where the field was bare;
See how God has sent the corn
   Growing golden there:
          FREDERICK ARTHUR JACKSON
                         1867–194

SPRING

522   *For younger children*

IN the lanes and in the parks
    Little flowers are showing;
God, who made and loves the
    flowers,
Watches o'er their growing.

2 In the bushes and the trees,
    Birdsong is beginning;
God, who made and loves the
    birds,
    Listens to their singing.

M. TEMPLE FRERE

SUMMER

523

THE summer days are come
    again;
    Once more the glad earth
        yields
Her golden wealth of ripening
    grain,
    And breath of clover fields,
And deepening shade of summer
    woods,
    And glow of summer air,
And winging thoughts, and
        happy moods
    Of love and joy and prayer.

2 The summer days are come
    again;
    The birds are on the wing;
God's praises, in their loving
    strain,
    Unconsciously they sing.
We know who giveth all the
    good
    That doth our cup o'erbrim;
For summer joy in field and
    wood,
    We lift our song to him.

SAMUEL LONGFELLOW, 1819–92

624

SUMMER suns are glowing
    Over land and sea;
Happy light is flowing,
    Bountiful and free.
Everything rejoices
    In the mellow rays;
All earth's thousand voices
    Swell the psalm of praise.

2 God's free mercy streameth
    Over all the world,
And his banner gleameth,
    Everywhere unfurled.
Broad and deep and glorious
    As the heaven above,
Shines in might victorious
    His eternal love.

3 Lord, upon our blindness
    Thy pure radiance pour;
For thy loving-kindness
    Make us love thee more.
And, when clouds are drifting
    Dark across our sky,
Then, the veil uplifting,
    Father, be thou nigh.

4 We will never doubt thee,
    Though thou veil thy light;
Life is dark without thee;
    Death with thee is bright.
Light of light, shine o'er us
    On our pilgrim way;
Go thou still before us,
    To the endless day.

WILLIAM WALSHAM HOW, 1823–97

625   *For younger children*

LET us sing our song of praise;
    Thank you, God! Thank
        you, God!
For the happy summer days,
    Thank you, God! Thank you,
        God!

2 For the sunshine and the
        showers,
    Thank you, God! Thank you,
        God!
Bringing us the lovely flowers,
    Thank you, God! Thank you,
        God!

For the green and shady trees,
Thank you, God! Thank you,
God!

For the gentle cooling breeze,
Thank you, God! Thank you,
God!

WINIFRED EVA BARNARD

SEEDTIME AND HARVEST

626 PSALM 65, verses 9, 11–13

EARTH thou dost visit,
watering it,
Making it rich to grow
With thy full flood, providing
corn;
Thou hast prepared it so.

2 So thou the year most liberally
Dost with thy goodness
crown;
And all thy paths abundantly
On us drop fatness down.

3 They drop upon the pastures
wide,
That do in deserts lie;
The little hills on every side
Rejoice right pleasantly.

4 With flocks the pastures clothèd
be,
The vales with corn are clad;
And now they shout and sing to
thee,
For thou hast made them
glad.

5 *To Father, Son, and Holy Ghost,*
The God whom we adore,
Be glory, as it was, and is,
And shall be evermore. Amen.

2 All this world is God's own
field,
Fruit unto his praise to yield;
Wheat and tares together sown
Unto joy or sorrow grown;
First the blade, and then the ear
Then the full corn shall appear
Lord of harvest, grant that we
Wholesome grain and pure
may be.

3 For the Lord our God shall
come,
And shall take his harvest
home;
From his field shall in that day
All offences purge away;
Give his angels charge at last
In the fire the tares to cast;
But the fruitful ears to store
In his garner evermore.

4 Even so, Lord, quickly come,
Bring thy final harvest home:
Gather thou thy people in,
Free from sorrow, free from sin,
There, for ever purified,
In thy garner to abide:
Come, with all thine angels,
come,
Raise the glorious harvest-
home!

HENRY ALFORD, 1810–71

627

COME, ye thankful people,
come,
Raise the song of harvest-home:
All is safely gathered in,
Ere the winter storms begin;
God, our Maker, doth provide
For our wants to be supplied:
Come to God's own temple,
come,
Raise the song of harvest-
home.

628

FOUNTAIN of mercy, God of
love,
How rich thy bounties are!
The rolling seasons, as they
move,
Proclaim thy constant care.

2 When in the bosom of the earth
The sower hid the grain,
Thy goodness marked its secret
birth,
And sent the early rain.

The spring's sweet influence
    was thine;
  The plants in beauty grew;
Thou gavest summer suns to
    shine,
  And mild refreshing dew.

These various mercies from
    above
Matured the swelling grain;
A yellow harvest crowns thy
    love,
  And plenty fills the plain.

Seed-time and harvest, Lord,
    alone
Thou dost on man bestow;
Let him not then forget to own
  From whom his blessings flow.

Fountain of love, our praise is
    thine;
  To thee our songs we'll raise,
And all created nature join
  In glad exultant praise.

       ALICE FLOWERDEW, 1759–1830
               altered
Also suitable are hymns in Section 11

29

FAIR waved the golden
    corn
In Canaan's pleasant land,
When full of joy, some shining
    morn,
Went forth the reaper band.

To God, so good and great,
  Their cheerful thanks they
    pour,
Then carry to his temple gate
  The choicest of their store.

For thus the holy word,
  Spoken by Moses, ran:
'The first ripe ears are for the
    Lord,
  The rest he gives to man.'

Like Israel, Lord, we give
  Our earliest fruits to thee,
And pray that, long as we shall
    live,
  We may thy children be.

Thine is our youthful prime,
  And life and all its powers;
Be with us in our morning time,
  And bless our evening hours.

6 In wisdom let us grow,
    As years and strength are
      given,
  That we may serve thy Church
      below,
    And join thy saints in heaven.

       JOHN HAMPDEN GURNEY, 1802–62

630   *For children*

THE fields and vales are thick
    with corn,
The reapers now are there,
They gather in the sheaves
    where once
The earth was brown and bare.

2 The empty barns will soon be
    filled
  With ripe and golden grain,
For God has given the harvest
    fruit,
  Who gave the sun and rain.

       FREDERICK ARTHUR JACKSON
               1867–1942

631   *For younger children*

WE thank thee, Lord, for all
    thy gifts
Of sunshine warm, and showers
    of rain
That ripened all the lovely
    fruits
And fields of golden grain.

2 We thank thee for the joy that
    comes
  To us, when harvest gifts we
      bring—
That others, too, may know thy
    love,
  Which speaks through every-
      thing.

3 O give us loving, thankful
    hearts,
  For all thy goodness, love, and
      care;
And help us always to be glad
To give away and share.

       JESSIE MARGARET MACDOUGALL
            FERGUSON, 1895–1964
               altered

WINTER

632

'TIS winter now; the fallen
   snow
  Has left the heavens all
   coldly clear;
Through leafless boughs the
   sharp winds blow,
  And all the earth lies dead
   and drear.

2 And yet God's love is not with-
   drawn;
  His life within the keen air
   breathes;
His beauty paints the crimson
   dawn,
  And clothes the boughs with
   glittering wreaths.

3 And though abroad the sharp
   winds blow,
  And skies are chill, and frosts
   are keen,
Home closer draws her circle
   now,
  And warmer glows her light
   within.

4 O God! who giv'st the winter
   cold,
  As well as summer's joyous
   rays,
Us warmly in thy love enfold,
  And keep us through life's
   wintry days.
     SAMUEL LONGFELLOW, 1819–

633   *For younger children*

LITTLE birds in winter time
  Hungry are and poor;
Feed them, for the Father's
   sake,
Till the winter's o'er.

2 Throw them crumbs that you
   can spare
Round about your door;
Feed them, for the Father's
   sake,
Till the winter's o'er.
    FREDERICK ARTHUR JACKSON,
     1867–194

CLOSE OF SERVICE

CLOSE OF SERVICE

534

MAY the grace of Christ our Saviour,
And the Father's boundless love,
With the Holy Spirit's favour,
Rest upon us from above.

Thus may we abide in union
With each other and the Lord,
And possess in sweet communion
Joys which earth cannot afford.

JOHN NEWTON, 1725–1807
Based on 2 Corinthians 13:14

535

ALMIGHTY God, thy word is cast
Like seed into the ground;
Now let the dew of heaven descend,
And righteous fruits abound.

Let not the foe of Christ and man
This holy seed remove,
But give it root in every heart
To bring forth fruits of love.

Let not the world's deceitful cares
The rising plant destroy,
But let it yield a hundredfold
The fruits of peace and joy.

Oft as the precious seed is sown,
Thy quickening grace bestow,
That all whose souls the truth receive
Its saving power may know.

JOHN CAWOOD, 1775–1852

636

AND now the wants are told that brought
Thy children to thy knee;
Here lingering still, we ask for naught,
But simply worship thee.

2 For thou art God, the One, the Same,
O'er all things high and bright;
And round us, when we speak thy Name,
There spreads a heaven of light.

3 O thou, above all blessing blest,
O'er thanks exalted far,
Thy very greatness is a rest
To weaklings as we are;

4 For when we feel the praise of thee
A task beyond our powers,
We say, 'A perfect God is he,
And he is fully ours'.

5 *All glory to the Father be,*
All glory to the Son,
All glory, Holy Ghost, to thee,
While endless ages run. Amen.
WILLIAM BRIGHT, 1824–1901

637

COME, dearest Lord, descend and dwell
By faith and love in every breast;
Then shall we know, and taste, and feel
The joys that cannot be expressed.

2 Come, fill our hearts with inward strength,
Make our enlargèd souls
possess
And learn the height and
breadth and length
Of thine unmeasurable grace.

3 *Now to the God whose power can
do*
*More than our thoughts or
wishes know,*
Be everlasting honours done
*By all the Church, through
Christ his Son. Amen.*
ISAAC WATTS, 1674–1748

638

LORD, dismiss us with thy
blessing;
Fill our hearts with joy and
peace;
Let us each, thy love possessing,
Triumph in redeeming grace;
O refresh us, O refresh us,
Travelling through this
wilderness.

2 Thanks we give and adoration
For thy Gospel's joyful
sound;
May the fruits of thy salvation
In our hearts and lives
abound,
May thy presence, may thy
presence
With us evermore be found.
JOHN FAWCETT, 1740–1817

639

NOW may he who from the
dead
Brought the Shepherd of the
sheep,

Jesus Christ, our King and
Head,
All our souls in safety keep.

2 May he teach us to fulfil
What is pleasing in his sight,
Perfect us in all his will,
And preserve us day and
night.

3 To that dear Redeemer's praise,
Who the covenant sealed with
blood,
Let our hearts and voices raise
Loud thanksgivings to our
God.
JOHN NEWTON, 1725–1807

640

Αἰνεῖτε, παῖδες, Κύριον

PRAISE ye the Lord, ye
servants of the Lord:
Praise ye his name; his lordly
honour sing:
Thee we adore; to thee glad
homage bring;
Thee we acknowledge; God to
be adored
For thy great glory,
Sovereign, Lord, and King.

2 Father of Christ—of him whose
work was done,
When by his death he took our
sins away—
To thee belongeth worship, day
by day,
Yea, Holy Father, everlasting
Son,
And Holy Ghost, all praise be
thine for aye! Amen.
Apostolic Constitutions, 3rd century
Tr. GEORGE RATCLIFFE
WOODWARD, 1849–1934
and Compilers of
The BBC Hymn Book

The following are also suitable
Nos. 204, 46

EVENING

641

ALL praise to thee, my God,
this night,
For all the blessings of the
light!

Keep me, O keep me, King of
kings,
Beneath thy own almighty
wings.

Forgive me, Lord, for thy dear
    Son,
The ill that I this day have done,
That with the world, myself,
    and thee,
I, ere I sleep, at peace may be.

Teach me to live, that I may
    dread
The grave as little as my bed;
Teach me to die, that so I may
Rise glorious at the awesome
    day.

O may my soul on thee repose,
And may sweet sleep mine eye-
    lids close,—
Sleep that may me more
    vigorous make
To serve my God when I awake.

When in the night I sleepless lie,
My soul with heavenly thoughts
    supply;
Let no ill dreams disturb my
    rest,
No powers of darkness me
    molest.

Praise God, from whom all
    blessings flow;
Praise him, all creatures here
    below;
Praise him above, ye heavenly
    host;
Praise Father, Son, and Holy
    Ghost. Amen.

                THOMAS KEN, 1637–1711

642
Ach bleib bei uns, Herr
Jesu Christ

NOW cheer our hearts this
    eventide,
Lord Jesus Christ, and with us
    bide;
Thou that canst never set in
    night,
Our heavenly Sun, our glorious
    Light.

2 May we and all who bear thy
    Name
By gentle love thy cross pro-
    claim,

Thy gift of peace on earth
    secure,
And for thy truth the world
    endure.

         ROBERT BRIDGES, 1844–1930
          Yattendon Hymnal, 1899
     Based on NICOLAUS SELNECKER
                 1532–92

643
Die Nacht ist kommen, drin
wir ruhen sollen

NOW God be with us, for the
    night is closing;
The light and darkness are of
    his disposing,
And 'neath his shadow here to
    rest we yield us,
    For he will shield us.

2 Let evil thoughts and spirits
    flee before us;
Till morning cometh, watch,
    Protector, o'er us;
In soul and body thou from
    harm defend us;
    Thine angels send us.

3 Let holy thoughts be ours when
    sleep o'ertakes us;
Our earliest thoughts be thine
    when morning wakes
    us;
All day serve thee, in all that
    we are doing
    Thy praise pursuing.

4 We have no refuge, none on
    earth to aid us,
Save thee, O Father, who thine
    own hast made us;
But thy dear Presence will not
    leave them lonely
    Who seek thee only.

5 Father, thy Name be praised,
    thy Kingdom given,
Thy will be done on earth as 'tis
    in heaven;
Keep us in life, forgive our sins,
    deliver
    Us now and ever.

            PETRUS HERBERT, ?–1571
      Tr. CATHERINE WINKWORTH
                 1827–78

644

Holy Father, cheer our way
With thy love's perpetual ray;
Grant us, every closing day,
Light at evening time.

2 Holy Saviour, calm our fears
When earth's brightness disappears;
Grant us in our latter years
Light at evening time.

3 Holy Spirit, be thou nigh
When in mortal pains we lie;
Grant us, as we come to die,
Light at evening time.

4 Holy, blessèd Trinity,
Darkness is not dark to thee;
Those thou keepest always see
Light at evening time.

RICHARD HAYES ROBINSON
1842–92

645

Τὴν ἡμέραν διελθών

The day is past and over:
All thanks, O Lord, to thee;
I pray thee now that sinless
The hours of dark may be.
O Jesus, keep me in thy sight,
And guard me through the coming night.

2 The joys of day are over:
I lift my heart to thee,
And pray thee that offenceless
The hours of dark may be.
O Jesus, keep me in thy sight,
And guard me through the coming night.

3 The toils of day are over:
I raise the hymn to thee,
And pray that free from peril
The hours of dark may be.
O Jesus, keep me in thy sight,
And guard me through the coming night.

4 Be thou my soul's Preserver,
O God, for thou dost know
How many are the perils
Through which I have to go.
Lover of men, O hear my call,
And guard and save me from them all.

6th century
Tr. JOHN MASON NEALE, 1818–66

646

The day thou gavest, Lord, is ended;
The darkness falls at thy behest;
To thee our morning hymns ascended,
Thy praise shall sanctify our rest.

2 We thank thee that thy Church unsleeping,
While earth rolls onward into light,
Through all the world her watch is keeping,
And rests not now by day or night.

3 As o'er each continent and island
The dawn leads on another day,
The voice of prayer is never silent,
Nor dies the strain of praise away.

4 The sun that bids us rest is waking
Our brethren 'neath the western sky,
And hour by hour fresh lips are making
Thy wondrous doings heard on high.

5 So be it, Lord! thy throne shall never,
Like earth's proud empires, pass away;
Thy Kingdom stands and grows for ever,
Till all thy creatures own thy sway.

JOHN ELLERTON, 1826–93

47

SUN of my soul, thou Saviour
dear,
It is not night if thou be near:
O may no earth-born cloud arise
To hide thee from thy servant's
eyes.

Abide with me from morn till
eve,
For without thee I cannot live;
Abide with me when night is
nigh,
For without thee I dare not die.

Watch by the sick; enrich the
poor
With blessings from thy boundless store;
Be every mourner's sleep tonight,
Like infant's slumbers, pure
and light.

Come near and bless us when
we wake,
Ere through the world our way
we take,
Till in the ocean of thy love
We lose ourselves in heaven
above.

JOHN KEBLE, 1792–1866

48

ERE I sleep, for every favour
This day showed
By my God,
I will bless my Saviour.

O my Lord, what shall I render
To thy Name,
Still the same,
Gracious, good, and tender?

Visit me with thy salvation;
Let thy care
Now be near,
Round my habitation.

Thou my Rock, my Guard, my
Tower,
Safely keep,
While I sleep,
Me, with all thy power.

5 So, whene'er in death I slumber,
Let me rise
With the wise,
Counted in their number.

JOHN CENNICK, 1718–55

649

SAVIOUR, again to thy dear
Name we raise
With one accord our parting
hymn of praise.
Guard thou the lips from sin,
the hearts from shame,
That in this house have called
upon thy Name.

2 Grant us thy peace, Lord,
through the coming night;
Turn thou for us its darkness
into light;
From harm and danger keep
thy servants free;
For dark and light are both
alike to thee.

3 Grant us thy peace throughout
our earthly life;
Peace to thy Church from error
and from strife;
Peace to our land, the fruit of
truth and love;
Peace in each heart, thy Spirit
from above:

4 Thy peace in sorrow, balm of
every pain;
Thy peace in death, the hope
to rise again;
Then, when thy voice shall bid
our conflict cease,
Call us, O Lord, to thine eternal
peace.

JOHN ELLERTON, 1826–93

650

ROUND me falls the night;
Saviour, be my light:
Through the hours in darkness
shrouded
Let me see thy face unclouded;
Let thy glory shine
In this heart of mine.

2 Earthly work is done,
  Earthly sounds are none;
Rest in sleep and silence seeking,
Let me hear thee softly speaking;
  In my spirit's ear
  Whisper, 'I am near'.

3 Blessèd, heavenly Light,
  Shining   through   earth's
    night;
Voice that oft of love hast told
    me;
Arms so strong to clasp and
    hold me;
  Thou thy watch wilt keep,
  Saviour, o'er my sleep.

WILLIAM ROMANIS, 1824–99

651

A SOVEREIGN Protector I
  have,
  Unseen, yet for ever at hand,
Unchangeably faithful to save,
  Almighty to rule and com-
    mand.
He smiles, and my comforts
    abound;
  His grace as the dew shall
    descend,
And walls of salvation surround
  The soul he delights to defend.

2 Inspirer and Hearer of prayer,
  Thou Shepherd and Guardian
    of thine,
My all to thy covenant care
  I sleeping and waking resign.
If thou art my Shield and my
    Sun,
  The night is no darkness to
    me;
And, fast as my moments roll on,
  They bring me but nearer to
    thee.

AUGUSTUS MONTAGUE TOPLADY
1740–78

652   Christe, qui lux es et dies

O CHRIST who art the Light
  and Day,
Thou drivest darksome night
  away,
We know thee as the Light of
  light,
Illuminating mortal sight.

2 All holy Lord, we pray to the
  Keep us tonight from dang
    free,
Grant us, dear Lord, in thee
    rest,
So be our sleep in quiet blest

3 And while the eyes soft slumb
    take,
Still be the heart to thee awak
Be thy right hand upheld abov
Thy servants resting in th
    love.

4 Yes, our Defender, be the
    nigh
To bid the powers of darkne
    fly,
Keep us from sin, and guide f
    good
Thy servants purchased by th
    blood.

5 *All praise to God the Father be*
  All praise, eternal Son, to thee
  Whom with the Spirit we adore
  For ever and for evermore. Ame

6th centu
Verses 1–4 tr. RICHARD RUNCIMA
TERRY, 1865–19
Verse 5 tr. WILLIAM JOHN COPELAN
1804–

653   *For younger children*

N OW the day is over,
  Night is drawing nigh,
Shadows of the evening
  Steal across the sky.

2 Now the darkness gathers,
  Stars begin to peep,
Birds, and beasts, and flowers
  Soon will be asleep.

3 Jesus, give the weary
  Calm and sweet repose;
With thy tender blessing
  May mine eyelids close.

4 Grant to little children
  Visions bright of thee;
Guard the sailors tossing
  On the deep blue sea.

5 Comfort every sufferer
  Watching late in pain;
Those who plan some evil
  From their sin restrain.

Through the long night-watches,
  May thine angels spread
Their white wings above me,
  Watching round my bed.

When the morning wakens,
  Then may I arise
Pure, and fresh, and sinless
  In thy holy eyes.

Glory to the Father,
  Glory to the Son,
And to thee, blest Spirit,
  Whilst all ages run. Amen.
        SABINE BARING-GOULD
          1834–1924

54 *For younger children*

GENTLE Jesus, hear our
  prayer,
Keep us in thy loving care;
And when evening shadows
  fall,
Casting darkness over all,
Loving Jesus, be thou near,
For with thee we have no
  fear.
      JESSIE MARGARET MACDOUGALL
         FERGUSON, 1895–1964

655 *For younger children*

INTO thy loving care,
  Into thy keeping,
Lord, who art everywhere,
Take us, we pray.
             Author unknown

656 *For younger children*

JESUS, tender Shepherd, hear
  me;
  Bless thy little lamb tonight;
Through the darkness be thou
  near me;
  Watch my sleep till morning
    light.

2 All this day thy hand has led me,
  And I thank thee for thy care;
Thou hast clothed me, warmed
  and fed me;
  Listen to my evening prayer.

3 Let my sins be all forgiven;
  Bless the friends I love so
    well;
Take me, when I die, to heaven,
  Happy there with thee to
    dwell.
      MARY LUNDIE DUNCAN, 1814–40

DOXOLOGIES

57

NOW to him who loved us,
  gave us
Every pledge that love could
  give,
Freely shed his blood to save us,
  Gave his life that we might
    live,
    Be the Kingdom
    And dominion
And the glory evermore.
            Amen.
      SAMUEL MILLER WARING
          1792–1827

58

PRAISE God, from whom all
  blessings flow;
Praise him, all creatures here
  below;

Praise him above, ye heavenly
  host;
Praise Father, Son, and Holy
  Ghost. Amen.
      THOMAS KEN, 1637–1711

659 *Lob, Ehr' und Preis sei Gott*

ALL praise and thanks to God
  The Father now be given,
The Son, and him who reigns
  With   them   in   highest
    heaven,—
  The one, eternal God,
    Whom earth and heaven
    adore;
For thus it was, is now,
  And shall be evermore.
             Amen.
    MARTIN RINKART, 1586–1649
    Tr. CATHERINE WINKWORTH
            1827–78

I

660

Gloria et honor Deo

UNTO God be praise and
 honour:
To the Father, to the Son,
To the mighty Spirit, glory—
 Ever Three and ever One:
Power and glory in the highest
While eternal ages run. Amen.

Tr. WILLIAM MAIR, 1830–1920
and ARTHUR WELLESLEY
WOTHERSPOON, 1853–1936

661

Gloria et honor Deo

LAUD and honour to the
 Father,
 Laud and honour to the Son,
Laud and honour to the Spirit,
 Ever Three and ever One,
One in might, and One in glory,
 While unending ages run.
 Amen.

7th or 8th century
Tr. JOHN MASON NEALE, 1818–66

*The following Doxologies are included
elsewhere in the book*

No.
1, v. 5 (*and elsewhere*) To Father, Son, a...
 Holy Ghost (L.M.)
5, v. 6 (*and elsewhere*) To Father, Son, a...
 Holy Ghost (C.M.)
30, v. 7 Let all things their Creator ble...
70, v. 3 (*ll.* 5–8) Now glory be to G...
74, v. 6 To thee be glory, Lord 135, v...
To God the Father, Son
198. v. 5 Christ to thee, with God t...
 Father
301, v. 4 Glory to God the Father, t...
 unbegotten One
392, v. 5 Glory to God the Father, G...
 the Son

*The following hymns also end in Dox...
 logies*
31, 37, 41, 43, 56, 73, 75, 118, 182, 18...
199, 208, 209, 223, 257, 264, 305, 32...
330, 348, 352, 358, 366, 400, 402, 4...
429, 455, 493, 532, 535, 539, 568, 57...
576, 581, 582, 636, 640, 652, 653.
Gloria Patri appears at No. 344

662

AMENS.

VIII

PERSONAL FAITH AND DEVOTION

563

O FOR a closer walk with God,
    A calm and heavenly frame,
A light to shine upon the road
    That leads me to the Lamb!

Where is the blessedness I knew
    When first I saw the Lord?
Where is the soul-refreshing view
    Of Jesus and his word?

What peaceful hours I once enjoyed!
    How sweet their memory still!
But they have left an aching void
    The world can never fill.

Return, O Holy Dove! return,
    Sweet messenger of rest!
I hate the sins that made thee mourn,
    And drove thee from my breast.

The dearest idol I have known,
    Whate'er that idol be,
Help me to tear it from thy throne,
    And worship only thee.

So shall my walk be close with God,
    Calm and serene my frame;
So purer light shall mark the road
    That leads me to the Lamb.

WILLIAM COWPER, 1731–1800

564

O FOR a faith that will not shrink,
    Though pressed by many a foe,
That will not tremble on the brink
    Of poverty or woe,

2 That will not murmur nor complain
    Beneath the chastening rod,
But, in the hour of grief or pain,
    Can lean upon its God;

3 A faith that shines more bright and clear
    When tempests rage without,
That when in danger knows no fear,
    In darkness feels no doubt;

4 A faith that keeps the narrow way
    Till life's last spark is fled,
And with a pure and heavenly ray
    Lights up a dying bed!

5 Lord, give me such a faith as this,
    And then, whate'er may come,
I taste even now the hallowed bliss
    Of an eternal home.

WILLIAM HILEY BATHURST
1796–1877

665

O GOD, thou art my God alone,
    Early to thee my soul shall cry,
A pilgrim in a land unknown,
    A thirsty land whose springs are dry.

237

2 O that it were as it hath been
  When, praying in the holy
    place,
Thy power and glory I have
    seen,
  And marked the footsteps of
    thy grace!

3 Yet through this rough and
    thorny maze
  I follow hard on thee, my
    God;
Thine hand unseen upholds my
    ways;
  I safely tread where thou hast
    trod.

4 Thee, in the watches of the
    night,
  When I remember on my bed,
Thy presence makes the dark-
    ness light;
  Thy guardian wings are
    round my head.

5 Better than life itself thy love,
  Dearer than all beside to me;
For whom have I in heaven
    above,
  Or what on earth, compared
    with thee?

6 Praise, with my heart, my
    mind, my voice,
  For all thy mercy I will give;
My soul shall still in God rejoice;
  My tongue shall bless thee
    while I live.

JAMES MONTGOMERY, 1771–1854

666

O THOU, my Judge and
    King—
  My broken heart, my voice-
    less prayer,
My poverty, and blind des-
    pair,
To thee, O Christ, I bring.

2 O thou, my Judge and King—
  My treason to thy love most
    sweet,
My pride that pierced thy
    weary feet,
To thee, O Christ, I bring.

3 O thou, my Judge and King—
  My tearful hope, my faith'
    distress,
For thee to pardon and to
    bless,
To thee, O Christ, I bring.

4 O thou, my Judge and King—
  With no excuse, for thou art
    just,
My sins, that set me in the
    dust,
To thee, O Christ, I bring.

5 O thou, my Judge and King—
  My soul, from depths of my
    disgrace,
To seek for mercy at thy face
To thee, O Christ, I bring.

LAUCHLAN MACLEAN WATT
1867–1957

667

A PPROACH, my soul, the
    mercy-seat,
  Where Jesus answers prayer;
There humbly fall before his
    feet,
  For none can perish there.

2 Thy promise is my only plea;
  With this I venture nigh:
Thou callest burdened souls to
    thee,
  And such, O Lord, am I.

3 Bowed down beneath a load of
    sin,
  By Satan sorely pressed,
By war without and fears with-
    in,
  I come to thee for rest.

4 Be thou my Shield and Hiding-
    place,
  That, sheltered near thy side,
I may my fierce accuser face,
  And tell him thou hast died.

5 O wondrous love! to bleed and
    die,
  To bear the cross and shame,
That guilty sinners, such as I,
  Might plead thy gracious
    Name!

JOHN NEWTON, 1725–1807

668

*Wer nur den lieben Gott
lässt walten*

IF thou but suffer God to guide
  thee,
  And hope in him through all
    thy ways,
He'll give thee strength,
  whate'er betide thee,
  And bear thee through the
    evil days;
Who trusts in God's unchanging
  love
Builds on the rock that naught
  can move.

2 What can these anxious cares
    avail thee,
  These never-ceasing moans
    and sighs?
What can it help if thou bewail
  thee
  O'er each dark moment as it
    flies?
Our cross and trials do but press
The heavier for our bitterness.

3 Only be still, and wait his leisure
  In cheerful hope, with heart
    content
  To take whate'er thy Father's
    pleasure
  And all-discerning love have
    sent;
Nor doubt our inmost wants are
  known
To him who chose us for his own.

4 Sing, pray, and keep his ways
    unswerving;
  So do thine own part faith-
    fully,
  And trust his word,—though
    undeserving,
  Thou yet shalt find it true for
    thee;
God never yet forsook at need
The soul that trusted him in-
  deed.

GEORG NEUMARK, 1621–81
Tr. CATHERINE WINKWORTH
1827–78

669

Befiehl du deine Wege

PUT thou thy trust in God,
  In duty's path go on;
Walk in his strength with faith
  and hope,
  So shall thy work be done.

Give to the winds thy fears;
  Hope, and be undismayed;
God hears thy sighs and counts
    thy tears,
  God shall lift up thy head.

2 Through waves, and clouds,
    and storms
  He gently clears thy way;
Wait thou his time; so shall this
    night
  Soon end in joyous day.
Leave to his sovereign sway
  To choose and to command;
So shalt thou, wondering, own
    his way
  How wise, how strong his
    hand.

3 Thou seest our weakness,
    Lord;
  Our hearts are known to thee:
O lift thou up the sinking hand,
  Confirm the feeble knee.
Let us, in life, in death,
  Thy steadfast truth declare,
And publish, with our latest
    breath,
  Thy love and guardian care.

PAUL GERHARDT, 1607–76
Par. JOHN WESLEY, 1703–91
and others

670

WORKMAN of God! O lose
  not heart,
  But learn what God is like,
And, in the darkest battle-field,
  Thou shalt know where to
    strike.

2 Thrice blest is he to whom is
    given
  The instinct that can tell
That God is on the field when he
  Is most invisible.

3 He hides himself so won-
    drously,
  As though there were no God;
He is least seen when all the
    powers
  Of ill are most abroad.

4 Ah! God is other than we think;
  His ways are far above,
Far beyond reason's height, and
    reached
  Only by childlike love.

5 Then learn to scorn the praise
     of men,
   And learn to lose with God;
For Jesus won the world
     through shame,
   And beckons thee his road.

6 For right is right, since God is
     God,
   And right the day must win;
To doubt would be disloyalty,
   To falter would be sin.

FREDERICK WILLIAM FABER
1814–63

671   *Wem in Leidenstagen*

O LET him whose sorrow
    No relief can find,
Trust in God, and borrow
   Ease for heart and mind.

2 Where the mourner, weeping,
   Sheds the secret tear,
God his watch is keeping,
   Though none else be near.

3 God will never leave thee;
   All thy wants he knows,
Feels the pains that grieve thee,
   Sees thy cares and woes.

4 If in grief thou languish,
   He will dry the tear,
Who his children's anguish
   Soothes with succour near.

5 All thy woe and sadness,
   In this world below,
Balance not the gladness
   Thou in heaven shalt know,

6 When thy gracious Saviour,
   In the realms above,
Crowns thee with his favour,
   Fills thee with his love.

HEINRICH SIEGMUND OSWALD
1751–1834
Tr. FRANCES ELIZABETH COX
1812–97

672

CHRIST who knows all his
    sheep
Will all in safety keep,
   He will not lose one soul,
     Nor ever fail us;
Nor we the promised goal,
   Though hell assail us.

2 I know my God is just;
   To him I wholly trust
     All that I have and am,
       All that I hope for:
All's sure and seen to him,
   Which here I grope for.

3 Lord Jesus, take this spirit:
   We trust thy love and merit.
     Take home the wandering
       sheep,
   For thou hast sought it;
This soul in safety keep,
   For thou hast bought it.

RICHARD BAXTER, 1615–91
altered

673   *Stille, mein Wille; dein*
       Jesus hilft siegen

BE still, my soul: the Lord is
    on thy side;
   Bear patiently the cross of
     grief or pain;
Leave to thy God to order and
   provide;
   In every change he faithful
     will remain.
Be still, my soul: thy best, thy
   heavenly Friend
Through thorny ways leads to
   a joyful end.

2 Be still, my soul: thy God doth
   undertake
     To guide the future as he has
       the past.
Thy hope, thy confidence let
   nothing shake;
     All now mysterious shall be
       bright at last.
Be still, my soul: the waves
   and winds still know
His voice who ruled them while
   he dwelt below.

3 Be still, my soul: when dearest
     friends depart,
     And all is darkened in the
       vale of tears,
Then shalt thou better know
   his love, his heart,
     Who comes to soothe thy
       sorrow and thy fears.
Be still, my soul: thy Jesus can
   repay,
From his own fullness, all he
   takes away.

240

Be still, my soul: the hour is
    hastening on
When we shall be forever
    with the Lord,
When disappointment, grief,
    and fear are gone,
    Sorrow forgot, love's purest
    joys restored.
Be still, my soul: when change
    and tears are past,
All safe and blessèd we shall
    meet at last.

> KATHARINA VON SCHLEGEL
> 1697–?
> Tr. JANE LAURIE BORTHWICK
> 1813–97

674

JESUS, these eyes have never
    seen
That radiant form of thine;
The veil of sense hangs dark
    between
    Thy blessèd face and mine.

I see thee not, I hear thee not,
    Yet art thou oft with me;
And earth hath ne'er so dear a
    spot
    As where I meet with thee.

Like some bright dream that
    comes unsought,
When slumbers o'er me roll,
Thine image ever fills my
    thought,
    And charms my ravished
    soul.

Yet, though I have not seen,
    and still
Must rest in faith alone,
I love thee, dearest Lord, and
    will,
    Unseen but not unknown.

When death these mortal eyes
    shall seal,
    And still this throbbing heart,
The rending veil shall thee re-
    veal
    All glorious as thou art.

> RAY PALMER, 1808–87

675

'TWIXT gleams of joy and
    clouds of doubt
Our feelings come and go;
Our best estate is tossed about
    In ceaseless ebb and flow.
No mood of feeling, form of
    thought,
    Is constant for a day;
But thou, O Lord, thou changest
    not:
    The same thou art alway.

2 I grasp thy strength, make it
    mine own,
    My heart with peace is blest;
I lose my hold, and then comes
    down
    Darkness, and cold unrest.
Let me no more my comfort
    draw
    From my frail hold of thee,
In this alone rejoice with awe—
    Thy mighty grasp of me.

3 Out of that weak, unquiet drift
    That comes but to depart,
To that pure heaven my spirit lift
    Where thou unchanging art.
Lay hold of me with thy strong
    grasp,
    Let thy almighty arm
In its embrace my weakness
    clasp,
    And I shall fear no harm.

4 Thy purpose of eternal good
    Let me but surely know;
On this I'll lean—let changing
    mood
    And feeling come or go—
Glad when thy sunshine fills my
    soul,
    Not lorn when clouds o'ercast,
Since thou within thy sure con-
    trol
    Of love dost hold me fast.

> JOHN CAMPBELL SHAIRP, 1819–85

676

HARK, my soul! it is the
    Lord;
'Tis thy Saviour, hear his word;
Jesus speaks, and speaks to thee:
'Say, poor sinner, lov'st thou me?

2 'I delivered thee when bound,
    And, when bleeding, healed thy
        wound;
  Sought thee wandering, set thee
        right;
  Turned thy darkness into light.

3 'Can a woman's tender care
    Cease towards the child she bare?
  Yes, she may forgetful be,
  Yet will I remember thee.

4 'Mine is an unchanging love,
    Higher than the heights above,
  Deeper than the depths be-
        neath,
  Free and faithful, strong as
        death.

5 'Thou shalt see my glory soon,
    When the work of grace is done;
  Partner of my throne shalt be;
  Say, poor sinner, lov'st thou
        me?'

6 Lord, it is my chief complaint
    That my love is weak and faint;
  Yet I love thee, and adore;
  O for grace to love thee more!
        WILLIAM COWPER, 1731–1800

677

O LOVE that wilt not let me
    go,
I rest my weary soul in thee:
I give thee back the life I owe,
That in thine ocean depths its
        flow
    May richer, fuller be.

2 O Light that followest all my
        way,
    I yield my flickering torch
        to thee:
  My heart restores its borrowed
        ray,
  That in thy sunshine's blaze its
        day
    May brighter, fairer be.

3 O Joy that seekest me through
        pain,
    I cannot close my heart to
        thee:
  I trace the rainbow through the
        rain,
  And feel the promise is not vain,
    That morn shall tearless be.

4 O Cross that liftest up my head,
    I dare not ask to fly from thee;
  I lay in dust life's glory dead,
  And from the ground there
        blossoms red
    Life that shall endless be.
        GEORGE MATHESON, 1842–190

678
Ich will Dich lieben,
meine Stärke

THEE will I love, my
    Strength, my Tower;
Thee will I love, my Joy, my
        Crown;
Thee will I love with all my
        power,
    In all thy works, and thee
        alone;
Thee will I love, till sacred fire
Fill my whole soul with pure
        desire.

2 I thank thee, uncreated Sun,
    That thy bright beams on me
        have shined;
  I thank thee, who hast over-
        thrown
    My foes, and healed my
        wounded mind;
  I thank thee, whose enlivening
        voice
  Bids my freed heart in thee
        rejoice.

3 Thee will I love, my Joy, my
        Crown;
    Thee will I love, my Lord,
        my God;
  Thee will I love, beneath thy
        frown
    Or smile, thy sceptre or thy
        rod;
  What though my flesh and
        heart decay,
  Thee shall I love in endless day.
        JOHANN SCHEFFLER, 1624–7
        Tr. JOHN WESLEY, 1703–9
            altered

679

LORD, it belongs not to my
    care
  Whether I die or live;
To love and serve thee is my
        share,
    And this thy grace must give

242

2 If life be long, I will be glad,
　　That I may long obey;
If short, yet why should I be sad
　　To welcome endless day?

3 Christ leads me through no darker rooms
　　Than he went through before;
He that into God's Kingdom comes
　　Must enter by this door.

4 Come, Lord, when grace hath made me meet
　　Thy blessèd face to see;
For, if thy work on earth be sweet,
　　What will thy glory be?

5 My knowledge of that life is small,
　　The eye of faith is dim;
But 'tis enough that Christ knows all,
　　And I shall be with him.

RICHARD BAXTER, 1615–91

680

MY times are in thy hand:
　　My God, I wish them there;
My life, my friends, my soul I leave
　　Entirely to thy care.

2 My times are in thy hand,
　　Whatever they may be,
Pleasing or painful, dark or bright,
　　As best may seem to thee.

3 My times are in thy hand:
　　Why should I doubt or fear?
My Father's hand will never cause
　　His child a needless tear.

4 My times are in thy hand,
　　Jesus, the Crucified;
Those hands my cruel sins had pierced
　　Are now my guard and guide.

5 My times are in thy hand:
　　I'll always trust in thee;
And, after death, at thy right hand
　　I shall for ever be.

WILLIAM FREEMAN LLOYD
1791–1853

681

IN heavenly love abiding,
　　No change my heart shall fear;
And safe is such confiding,
　　For nothing changes here:
The storm may roar without me,
　　My heart may low be laid;
But God is round about me,
　　And can I be dismayed?

2 Wherever he may guide me,
　　No want shall turn me back;
My Shepherd is beside me,
　　And nothing can I lack.
His wisdom ever waketh,
　　His sight is never dim:
He knows the way he taketh,
　　And I will walk with him.

3 Green pastures are before me,
　　Which yet I have not seen;
Bright skies will soon be o'er me,
　　Where the dark clouds have been.
My hope I cannot measure:
　　My path to life is free:
My Saviour has my treasure,
　　And he will walk with me.

ANNA LAETITIA WARING
1820–1910

682

LEAD, kindly Light, amid the encircling gloom,
　　Lead thou me on;
The night is dark, and I am far from home;
　　Lead thou me on.
Keep thou my feet; I do not ask to see
The distant scene,—one step enough for me.

2 I was not ever thus, nor prayed that thou
　　Shouldst lead me on;
I loved to choose and see my path, but now
　　Lead thou me on.
I loved the garish day, and, spite of fears,
Pride ruled my will: remember not past years.

3 So long thy power hath blest
me, sure it still
Will lead me on,
O'er moor and fen, o'er crag
and torrent, till
The night is gone,
And with the morn those angel
faces smile,
Which I have loved long since,
and lost awhile.

JOHN HENRY NEWMAN, 1801–90

683

I HEAR thy welcome voice
That calls me, Lord, to thee,
For cleansing in thy precious
blood
That flowed on Calvary.
   I am coming, Lord,
     Coming now to thee;
   Wash me, cleanse me in the
   blood
     That flowed on Calvary.

2 'Tis Jesus calls me on
To perfect faith and love,
To perfect hope and peace and
trust,
For earth and heaven above.

3 'Tis Jesus who confirms
The blessèd work within,
By adding grace to welcomed
grace,
Where reigned the power of sin.

4 All hail, atoning blood!
All hail, redeeming grace!
All hail, the gift of Christ our
Lord,
Our Strength and Righteous-
ness!

LEWIS HARTSOUGH, 1828–72

684

BENEATH the cross of Jesus
I fain would take my
stand—
The shadow of a mighty rock
Within a weary land;
A home within a wilderness,
A rest upon the way,
From the burning of the noon-
tide heat
And the burden of the day.

2 O safe and happy shelter,
O refuge tried and sweet,
O trysting-place where heaven's
love
And heaven's justice meet!
As to the exiled patriarch
That wondrous dream was
given,
So seems my Saviour's cross
to me—
A ladder up to heaven.

3 Upon that cross of Jesus,
Mine eye at times can see
The very dying form of One
Who suffered there for me;
And from my smitten heart
with tears,
Two wonders I confess—
The wonder of his glorious love,
And my own worthlessness.

4 I take, O cross, thy shadow
For my abiding-place;
I ask no other sunshine than
The sunshine of his face:
Content to let the world go by,
To know no gain nor loss—
My sinful self my only shame,
My glory all, the cross.

ELIZABETH CECILIA CLEPHANE
1830–69

685

I AM trusting thee, Lord Jesus,
Trusting only thee,
Trusting thee for full salvation,
Great and free.

2 I am trusting thee for pardon;
At thy feet I bow,
For thy grace and tender mercy
Trusting now.

3 I am trusting thee to guide me;
Thou alone shalt lead,
Every day and hour supplying
All my need.

4 I am trusting thee for power:
Thine can never fail;
Words which thou thyself shalt
give me
Must prevail.

I am trusting thee, Lord Jesus;
  Never let me fall;
I am trusting thee for ever,
  And for all.

    FRANCES RIDLEY HAVERGAL
        1836–79

686

JESUS, I will trust thee,—
  Trust thee with my soul;
Guilty, lost, and helpless,
  Thou canst make me whole.
There is none in heaven
  Or on earth like thee;
Thou hast died for sinners—
  Therefore, Lord, for me.

Jesus, I will trust thee;
  Name of matchless worth,
Spoken by the angel
  At thy wondrous birth,
Written, and for ever,
  On thy cross of shame:
Sinners read and worship,
  Trusting in that Name.

Jesus, I will trust thee,
  Pondering thy ways
Full of love and mercy
  All thine earthly days.
Sinners gathered round thee,
  Lepers sought thy face,
None too vile or loathsome
  For a Saviour's grace.

Jesus, I will trust thee,
  Trust without a doubt;
Whosoever cometh
  Thou wilt not cast out.
Faithful is thy promise;
  Precious is thy blood;
These my soul's salvation,
  Thou my Saviour God!

    MARY JANE WALKER, 1816–78

687

I AM not skilled to understand
  What God hath willed,
    what God hath planned;
I only know at his right hand
  Stands One who is my
    Saviour.

2 I take God at his word and
    deed:
  'Christ died to save me', this
    I read;
And in my heart I find a need
  Of him to be my Saviour.

3 And was there then no other
    way
  For God to take?—I cannot say;
I only bless him, day by day,
  Who saved me through my
    Saviour.

4 That he should leave his place
    on high
And come for sinful man to die,
You count it strange?—so do
    not I,
  Since I have known my
    Saviour.

5 And O that he fulfilled may see
The travail of his soul in me,
And with his work contented
    be,
  As I with my dear Saviour!

6 Yea, living, dying, let me bring
My strength, my solace, from
    this spring,
That he who lives to be my King
  Once died to be my Saviour.

    DORA GREENWELL, 1821–82

688

I NEED thee every hour,
  Most gracious Lord;
No tender voice but thine
  Can peace afford.

2 I need thee every hour;
  Stay thou near by;
Temptations lose their power
  When thou art nigh.

3 I need thee every hour,
  In joy or pain;
Come quickly and abide,
  Or life is vain.

4 I need thee every hour;
  Teach me thy will;
And thy rich promises
  In me fulfil.

    ANNIE SHERWOOD HAWKS
        1835–1918

689

NEARER, my God, to thee,
  Nearer to thee!
Ev'n though it be a cross
  That raiseth me,
Still all my song would be,
'Nearer, my God, to thee,
  *Nearer to thee!'

2 Though, like the wanderer,
    The sun gone down,
  Darkness be over me,
    My rest a stone,
  Yet in my dreams I'd be
  Nearer, my God, to thee,
    Nearer to thee!

3 There let the way appear
    Steps unto heaven,
  All that thou send'st to me
    In mercy given,
  Angels to beckon me
  Nearer, my God, to thee,
    Nearer to thee!

4 Then, with my waking thoughts
    Bright with thy praise,
  Out of my stony griefs
    Bethel I'll raise,
  So by my woes to be
  Nearer, my God, to thee,
    Nearer to thee!

5 Or if on joyful wing
    Cleaving the sky,
  Sun, moon, and stars forgot,
    Upwards I fly,
  Still all my song shall be,
  'Nearer, my God, to thee,
    Nearer to thee!'
        SARAH FLOWER ADAMS, 1805–48

* When Tune (ii) PROPRIOR DEO is used,
the last line of each verse is repeated.

690

TEACH me to serve thee,
  Lord,
I humbly pray.
Help me the path to tread
In thine own way.
As thou hast promised, Lord,
O let thy living Word
New strength to me afford
For every day.

2 Teach me, O Lord, to give,
    Nor count the cost,
  For what is given for thee
    Is never lost.
  Whate'er I lend to thee
  Thou first didst give to me,
  Thy debtor I must be
  Till Jordan's crossed.

3 Teach me, O Lord, to fight,
    Nor heed the pain:
  Since he who fights for thee
    Ne'er fights in vain.
  Help me to stand for right,
  Be thou my guiding light,
  And daily by thy might
  I shall attain.

4 Teach me to labour on,
    Nor ask reward,
  To toil, nor seek for rest
    While sin's abroad.
  And should I faithful be,
  Grant I may dwell with thee
  Through all eternity,
  My King, my Lord.
        EDNA MARTHA PHILLIPS

691

DEAR MASTER, in whose
  life I see
All that I would but fail to be,
Let thy clear light for ever shine
To shame and guide this life
  of mine.

2 Though what I dream and what
    I do
  In my weak days are always
    two,
  Help me, oppressed by things
    undone,
  O thou, whose deeds and dreams
    were one!
        JOHN HUNTER, 1848–1917

692

TEACH me, my God and
  King,
In all things thee to see;
And what I do in anything,
  To do it as for thee!

A man that looks on glass,
On it may stay his eye;
Or if he pleaseth, through it
    pass,
And then the heaven espy.

All may of thee partake;
Nothing can be so mean,
Which with this tincture, 'for
    thy sake',
Will not grow bright and
    clean.

A servant with this clause
Makes drudgery divine:
Who sweeps a room, as for thy
    laws,
Makes that and the action
    fine.

This is the famous stone
That turneth all to gold;
For that which God doth touch
    and own
Cannot for less be told.

GEORGE HERBERT, 1593–1633

693

MY soul, there is a country
    Afar beyond the stars,
Where stands a wingèd sentry
All skilful in the wars.

2 There, above noise, and danger,
    Sweet peace sits, crowned
        with smiles,
And One born in a manger
    Commands the beauteous
        files.

3 He is thy gracious friend,
    And—O my soul, awake!—
Did in pure love descend,
    To die here for thy sake.

4 If thou canst get but thither,
    There grows the flower of
        peace,
The rose that cannot wither,
    Thy fortress, and thy ease.

5 Leave then thy foolish ranges;
    For none can thee secure,
But One, who never changes,
    Thy God, thy Life, thy Cure.

HENRY VAUGHAN, 1621–95

694

THE sands of time are
    sinking;
The dawn of heaven breaks;
The summer morn I've sighed
    for,
The fair, sweet morn, awakes.
Dark, dark hath been the mid-
    night,
    But dayspring is at hand,
And glory, glory dwelleth
    In Immanuel's land.

2 O Christ! He is the fountain,
    The deep, sweet well of love;
The streams on earth I've tasted
    More deep I'll drink above:
There to an ocean fullness
    His mercy doth expand,
And glory, glory dwelleth
    In Immanuel's land.

3 With mercy and with judgment
    My web of time he wove,
And aye the dews of sorrow
    Were lustred by his love;
I'll bless the hand that guided,
    I'll bless the heart that
        planned,
When throned where glory
        dwelleth
    In Immanuel's land.

4 I've wrestled on towards
        heaven,
    'Gainst storm and wind and
        tide;
Now, like a weary traveller
    That leaneth on his guide,
Amid the shades of evening,
    While sinks life's lingering
        sand,
I hail the glory dawning
    In Immanuel's land.

ANNE ROSS COUSIN, 1824–1906

695

ABIDE with me: fast falls the
    eventide;
The darkness deepens; Lord,
    with me abide:
When other helpers fail, and
    comforts flee,
Help of the helpless, O abide
    with me.

2 Swift to its close ebbs out life's
    little day;
Earth's joys grow dim, its
    glories pass away;
Change and decay in all around
    I see:
O thou who changest not,
    abide with me.

3 I need thy presence every
    passing hour;
What but thy grace can foil the
    tempter's power?
Who like thyself my guide and
    stay can be?
Through cloud and sunshine,
    O abide with me.

4 I fear no foe with thee at hand
    to bless;
Ills have no weight, and tears
    no bitterness:
Where is death's sting? where
    grave, thy victory?
I triumph still if thou abide
    with me.

5 Hold thou thy cross before my
    closing eyes,
Shine through the gloom, and
    point me to the skies;
Heaven's morning breaks, and
    earth's vain shadows flee:
In life and death, O Lord, abide
    with me.

HENRY FRANCIS LYTE, 1793–1847

INDEX OF PSALMS

The metrical psalms have been taken from the *Scottish Metrical Psalter* of 1650 and the *Irish Metrical Psalter* of 1880.

Psalms taken from other sources are printed in *italic* and the sources are given. AV = Authorized Version; NEB = New English Bible.

Psalm 2 vv. 1, 2, 6–8, 11, 12b (AV)	*Why do the heathen rage*	*166*
Psalm 8 vv. 1, 3–5	How excellent in all the earth	138
Psalm 9 vv. 7–11	God shall endure for aye; he doth	23
Psalm 15	Within thy tabernacle, Lord	5
Psalm 19 vv. 7–10, 14	God's law is perfect, and converts	125
Psalm 19 vv. 7–14 (NEB adapted)	*God's perfect law revives the soul*	*126*
Psalm 22 vv. 1–9, 11, 15–19, 22–24, 27, 30, 31 (AV)	*My God, my God, why hast thou forsaken me*	*239*
Psalm 23	The Lord's my Shepherd, I'll not want	387
Psalm 23 (Gelineau 22)	*The Lord is my Shepherd*	*389*
Psalm 24 vv. 1–6	The earth belongs unto the Lord	566
Psalm 24 vv. 7–10	Ye gates lift up your heads on high	566
Psalm 25 vv. 4, 5a, 6–10	Show me thy ways, O Lord	74
Psalm 26 vv. 6–8	Mine hands in innocence, O Lord	564
Psalm 27 vv. 1, 3–5, 14	The Lord's my light and saving health	26
Psalm 33 vv. 1–5	Ye righteous, in the Lord rejoice	27
Psalm 34 vv. 1, 2, 7–9, 11, 14, 15	God will I bless all times; his praise	391
Psalm 36 vv. 5–9	Thy mercy, Lord, is in the heavens	6
Psalm 40 vv. 1–4	I waited for the Lord my God	73
Psalm 42 vv. 1–5, 8–11 (AV)	*As the hart panteth after the water brooks*	*231*
Psalm 43 vv. 3–5	O send thy light forth and thy truth	7
Psalm 46 vv. 1–5	God is our refuge and our strength	24
Psalm 47	*O clap your hands all ye people*	*284*
Psalm 50 vv. 1–6, 14, 23	*The mighty God even the Lord hath spoken*	*310*
Psalm 51 vv. 1–4, 6–12 (AV)	*Have mercy upon me O God*	*63*
Psalm 51 (NEB adapted)	*O God be gracious to me in Thy love*	*64*
Psalm 61 vv. 1–4	O God, give ear unto my cry	71
Psalm 62 vv. 5–8	Only on God do thou, my soul	25
Psalm 63 vv. 1–4	Lord, thee my God, I'll early seek	41
Psalm 65 vv. 1–4	Praise waits for thee in Sion, Lord	28
Psalm 65 vv. 9, 11–13	Earth thou dost visit, watering it	626
Psalm 67	Lord, bless and pity us	493
Psalm 67	*God be merciful unto us and bless us*	*598*
Psalm 68 vv. 18a, 19, 20	Thou hast, O Lord, most glorious	285
Psalm 72 vv. 1, 2, 5, 11, 17–19	*Give the king thy judgments O God*	*158*
Psalm 72 vv. 8, 10, 11, 17–19	His large and great dominion shall	167
Psalm 78 vv. 4b–7	The praises of the Lord our God	547
Psalm 84 vv. 1–5	How lovely is thy dwelling-place	4
Psalm 85 (ii) vv. 1, 2, 5–7	Lord, thine heart in love hath yearned	75

INDEX OF PSALMS

Psalm 89 vv. 15, 16, 18	O greatly blest the people are	390
Psalm 90 vv. 1, 2, 14, 16, 17	Lord, thou hast been our dwelling-place	102
Psalm 92 vv. 1–4	To render thanks unto the Lord	29
Psalm 93	The Lord doth reign, and clothed is he	140
Psalm 95 vv. 1–6	O come and let us to the Lord	19
Psalm 95 from vv. 1–7 (Coverdale)	*O come let us sing unto the Lord*	*20*
Psalm 95 vv. 1–7 (AV)	*O come let us sing unto the Lord*	*21*
Psalm 96 vv. 1, 2, 6–8	O sing a new song to the Lord	22
Psalm 96 vv. 9, 11–13	In beauty of his holiness	311
Psalm 98 from vv. 1–3, 5–9	*Sing a new song to Jehovah*	*348*
Psalm 98	*O sing unto the Lord a new song*	*349*
Psalm 100	All people that on earth do dwell	1
Psalm 100 (Coverdale)	*O be joyful in the Lord all ye lands*	*3*
Psalm 102 (ii) vv. 13–18	Thou shalt arise, and mercy yet	333
Psalm 103 vv. 1–5	O thou my soul, bless God the Lord	351
Psalm 103 vv. 13–17	Such pity as a father hath	603
Psalm 103 vv. 19–22	The Lord prepared hath his throne	596
Psalm 104 vv. 1–5, 30–34	*Bless the Lord, O my soul*	*326*
Psalm 106 vv. 1–5, 48	Give praise and thanks unto the Lord	101
Psalm 116 vv. 1–7	I love the Lord, because my voice	8
Psalm 116 vv. 13, 14, 17–19	I'll of salvation take the cup	565
Psalm 118 vv. 15–24	*The voice of rejoicing and salvation*	*262*
Psalm 118 vv. 19–25, 28, 29	O set ye open unto me	263
Psalm 118 vv. 19–29	*Open to me the gates of righteousness*	*232*
Psalm 119 vv. 33–40	Teach me, O Lord, the perfect way	127
Psalm 121	I to the hills will lift mine eyes	139
Psalm 122 vv. 1, 2, 6–9	I joy'd when to the house of God	489
Psalm 124 (ii)	Now Israel may say	392
Psalm 126	When Sion's bondage God turned back	393
Psalm 130 from vv. 1–8	Lord, from the depths to thee I cried	65
Psalm 130 (Gelineau 129)	*Out of the depths I cry to you, O Lord*	*67*
Psalm 130 (AV)	*Out of the depths have I cried unto thee O Lord*	*66*
Psalm 136 (ii) vv. 1–5, 23–26	Praise God, for he is kind	137
Psalm 136 (Gelineau 135)	*O give thanks to the Lord for he is good*	*350*
Psalm 139 (NEB adapted)	*Thou art before me, Lord, thou art behind*	*68*
Psalm 143 (ii) vv. 1, 6, 8	Oh, hear my prayer, Lord	70
Psalm 145 (ii) vv. 1–6	O Lord, thou art my God and King	346
Psalm 145 (ii) vv. 9, 10, 15, 16	Good unto all men is the Lord	617
Psalm 147 vv. 1–5	Praise ye the Lord; for it is good	136
Psalm 148(ii)	The Lord of heaven confess	135
Psalm 150	Praise ye the Lord. God's praise within	347

TABLE OF LITURGICAL ITEMS

Agnus Dei | O Lamb of God, that takest away the sins of the world | 563

Apostles' Creed, The, | I believe in God the Father Almighty | 546

Benediction | The Lord bless you, and keep you | 556

Benedictus qui venit | Blessèd is he that cometh in the Name of the Lord | 561

Gloria in excelsis | Glory be to God on high | 62

Gloria Patri | Glory be to the Father, and to the Son | 344

Kyrie eleison
  First form | Lord have mercy | 60
  Second form | Lord, have mercy upon us | 60

Lord's Prayer, The,
  First form | Our Father, which art in heaven | 562
  Second form | Our Father, who art in heaven | 562

Nicene Creed, The, | We believe in one God, the Father Almighty | 558

Salutation | The Lord be with you | 559

Sanctus | Holy, Holy, Holy, Lord God of Hosts | 560

Sursum Corda | Lift up your hearts | 559

INDEX OF FIRST LINES

Hymns for Children are marked with an asterisk

A fortress sure is God our King	40
A gladsome hymn of praise we sing	14
*A glorious company we sing	42
A great and mighty wonder	19
*A little child may know	18
A little child the Saviour came	55
A safe stronghold our God is still	40
A Sovereign Protector I have	6?
Abide with me: fast falls the eventide	69
According to thy gracious word	58
Again the morn of gladness	29
Ah, holy Jesus, how hast thou offended	2?
All creatures of our God and King	?
All glory, laud, and honour	2?
All hail, the power of Jesus' Name	38
All my heart this night rejoices	1?
All my hope on God is founded	40
All people that on earth do dwell	?
All poor men and humble	18
All praise and thanks to God (*Doxology*)	65
All praise to thee, for thou, O King divine	29
All praise to thee, my God, this night	64
All things are thine; no gift have we	61
*All things bright and beautiful.	15
Alleluia (*Settings*)	34
Almighty Father, Lord most high	57
Almighty Father of all things that be	4?
Almighty Father, who dost give	50
Almighty God, thy word is cast	6.
Alone thou goest forth, O Lord	24
Alone with none but thee, my God	39
Amen (*Settings*)	66
And can it be, that I should gain	40
And did those feet in ancient time	48
And now, belovèd Lord, thy soul resigning	2?
And now, O Father, mindful of the love	58
And now the wants are told that brought	63
Angel voices, ever singing	45
Angel voices, richly blending	17
Angels from the realms of glory	18
Approach, my soul, the mercy-seat	66
Arm of the Lord, awake, awake	49
Art thou afraid his power shall fail (*Paraphrase 22*)	39
As now the day draws near its ending	?
As the hart panteth after the water brooks	23
As with gladness men of old	20
*At Eastertime the lilies fair	28
At eve, when now he breathed no more	2?
At even, when the sun was set	2?
At the cross, her station keeping	24

252

INDEX OF FIRST LINES

At the Name of Jesus . . .		.	. 300
At thy feet, our God and Father		.	. 616
Author of life divine . .		.	. 587
Awake, my soul, and with the sun		.	. 42
Away in a manger, no crib for a bed		.	. 195
Away with gloom, away with doubt		.	. 292
Be still, my soul: the Lord is on thy side		.	. 674
Be thou my Vision, O Lord of my heart		.	. 87
Before all time the Word existed		.	. 162
Before Jehovah's awesome throne		.	. 2
Before the day draws near its ending		.	. 53
Behold a little Child . .		.	. 207
Behold he comes! your leader comes (*Paraphrase 26*)		.	. 159
Behold the amazing gift of love (*Paraphrase 63*)		.	. 396
Behold the great Creator makes .		.	. 197
Behold! the mountain of the Lord (*Paraphrase 18*)		.	. 312
Behold us, Lord, a little space .		.	. 453
Behold what witnesses unseen (*Paraphrase 59*) .		.	. 531
Beneath the cross of Jesus . .		.	. 684
Bethlehem, of noblest cities .		.	. 199
Bless the Lord O my soul .		.	. 326
Blessèd be the Lord God of Israel (*Benedictus*) .		.	. 161
Blessèd is he that cometh in the Name of the Lord (*Benedictus Qui Venit*)		.	. 561
Blessèd Jesus, here we stand .		.	. 552
Blessing and honour and glory and power		.	. 299
Blest are the pure in heart . .		.	. 113
Blest be the everlasting God (*Paraphrase 61*) .		.	. 530
Blest is the man, O God .		.	. 324
Blest morning, whose first dawning rays		.	. 273
Book of books, our people's strength .		.	. 128
Bread of the world, in mercy broken .		.	. 574
Break forth, O living light of God		.	. 133
Breathe on me, Breath of God . .		.	. 103
Brightest and best of the sons of the morning		.	. 201
By Jesus' grave on either hand .		.	. 261
By the rutted roads we follow . .		.	. 619
Captains of the saintly band .		.	. 539
Child in the manger . .		.	. 180
Children of Jerusalem . .		.	. 236
Christ for the world we sing .		.	. 500
Christ is coming! let creation .		.	. 313
Christ is made the sure foundation .		.	. 10
Christ is the King! O friends rejoice		.	. 474
Christ is the world's Redeemer .		.	. 301
Christ is the world's true light .		.	. 505
Christ Jesus lay in death's strong bands		.	. 268
Christ the Lord is risen to-day .		.	. 275
Christ who knows all his sheep .		.	. 672
Christ, whose glory fills the skies		.	. 114
Christians, awake, salute the happy morn		.	. 190
City of God, how broad and far .		.	. 422
Come, children, join to sing .		.	. 383
Come, dearest Lord, descend and dwell		.	. 637
Come down, O Love Divine . .		.	. 115

INDEX OF FIRST LINES

Come, gracious Spirit, heavenly Dove 116
Come, Holy Ghost, our hearts inspire 122
Come, Holy Ghost, our souls inspire 342
Come, Holy Spirit, come 104
*Come, let us remember the joys of the town . . . 38
Come, let us to the Lord our God (*Paraphrase 30*) . . 6
Come, risen Lord, and deign to be our guest . . . 572
Come, thou Holy Paraclete 10
Come, thou long-expected Jesus 320
*Come, ye children, sing to Jesus 28
Come, ye faithful, raise the strain 26
Come, ye thankful people, come 62
Command thy blessing from above 11
Courage, brother! do not stumble 48
Creator Spirit! by whose aid 118
Crown him with many crowns 29

Dear Lord and Father of mankind 7
Dear Master, in whose life I see 69
Deck thyself, my soul, with gladness 56
Defend me, Lord, from hour to hour 9

Earth thou dost visit, watering it 62
Easter glory fills the sky 27
Enter thy courts, thou Word of life 11
Ere I sleep, for every favour 64
Eternal Father, strong to save 52
Eternal God, whose power upholds 49
Eternal Light! eternal light 35
Eternal Ruler of the ceaseless round 51

Fair waved the golden corn 62
Fairest Lord Jesus 37
Faith of our fathers, taught of old . . . . 472(ii)
Far off I see the goal 54
*Far round the world thy children sing their song . . 50
Father Eternal, Ruler of Creation 50
*Father, hear us as we pray 55
*Father, lead me, day by day 9
Father most holy, merciful and loving 3
Father most loving, listen to thy children . . . 56
Father of heaven, whose love profound 7
Father of peace, and God of love (*Paraphrase 60*) . . 39
Father, we praise thee, now the night is over . . . 4
*Father, we thank thee for the night 9
Father, we thank thee who hast planted 58
Father, who on man dost shower 51
Father, whose will is life and good 52
Fear not, thou faithful Christian flock . . . . 472(i)
Fight the good fight with all thy might 44
Fill thou our life, O Lord our God 45
Firmly I believe and truly 40
For all the saints who from their labours rest . . . 53
For my sake and the Gospel's, go 47
For the beauty of the earth 36
For the might of thine arm we bless thee, our God . . 36
For those we love within the veil 53
For thy gift of God the Spirit 33

254

INDEX OF FIRST LINES

For thy mercy and thy grace 612
Forth from on high the Father sends . . . 581
Forth in the peace of Christ we go . . . 589
Forth in thy Name, O Lord, I go . . . 463
Forty days and forty nights 210
Fountain of good, to own thy love . . . 459
Fountain of mercy, God of love . . . 628
From all that dwell below the skies . . . 362
From east to west, from shore to shore . . 189
From glory to glory advancing, we praise thee, O Lord 325
From heavenly Jerusalem's towers . . . 544
From thee all skill and science flow . . . 525

*Gentle Jesus, hear our prayer 654
Give heed, my heart, lift up thine eyes . . 188
Give praise and thanks unto the Lord . . . 101
Give the King thy judgments O God . . . 158
Gloomy night embraced the place . . . 177
Glorious things of thee are spoken . . . 421
Glory be to God on high (Gloria in excelsis) . . 62
Glory be to God the Father 354
Glory be to the Father, and to the Son (Gloria Patri) 344
Go, happy soul, thy days are ended . . . 604
Go, labour on: spend and be spent . . . 483
Go ye, said Jesus, and preach the word . . 470
God and Father, we adore thee . . . 369
God be in my head, and in my understanding . 433
God be merciful unto us and bless us . . . 598
*God is always near me 417
God is ascended up on high 290
God is Love: his mercy brightens . . . 144
*God is love: his the care 416
God is my strong salvation 24
God is our refuge and our strength . . . 303
God is working his purpose out, as year succeeds to year 147
God moves in a mysterious way . . . 517
God of Eternity, Lord of the Ages . . . 88
God of grace and God of glory . . . 502
*God of heaven, hear our singing . . . 497
God of mercy, God of grace 607
God of the living, in whose eyes . . . 513
God of the pastures, hear our prayer . . . 184
God rest you merry, gentlemen . . . 355
God reveals his presence 521
God save our gracious Queen 23
God shall endure for aye; he doth . . . 516
God the Omnipotent! King, who ordainest . . 452
God, who hast given us power to sound . . 151
*God, who made the earth 155
*God who put the stars in space . . . 391
God will I bless all times; his praise . . . 469
God, your glory we have seen in your Son . . 125
God's law is perfect, and converts . . . 126
God's perfect law revives the soul . . . 183
Good Christian men, rejoice 270
Good Christian men, rejoice and sing . . . 280
*Good Joseph had a garden 617
Good unto all men is the Lord . . . .

255

INDEX OF FIRST LINES

Gracious Spirit, Holy Ghost 438
Great God, we sing that mighty hand 613
Guide me, O thou great Jehovah . . . 89

Hail, gladdening Light, of his pure glory poured . . 54
Hail thee, Festival Day 328
Hail to the Lord's Anointed 317
*Hands to work and feet to run 465
Happy are they, they that love God . . . 408
Hark how the adoring hosts above (*Paraphrase 65*) . 532
Hark, my soul! it is the Lord 676
Hark, the glad sound! the Saviour comes (*Paraphrase 39*) 160
Hark! the herald angels sing 169
Hark what a sound, and too divine for hearing . 314
Have mercy upon me, O God, according to thy loving-kindness 63
Heavenly Father, may thy blessing . . . 134
Heavenly Father, thou hast brought us . . 615
Here, O my Lord, I see thee face to face . . 573
His large and great dominion shall . . . 167
Holy Father, cheer our way 644
Holy Father, in thy mercy 529
Holy God, holy and mighty (*Trisagion*) . . 61, 240
Holy, Holy, Holy, Lord God Almighty . . . 352
Holy, Holy, Holy, Lord God of Hosts (*Sanctus*) . 560
Holy Spirit, ever living 334
*Holy Spirit, hear us 124
Holy Spirit, Truth Divine 106
*Hosanna, loud hosanna 235
How bright these glorious spirits shine (*Paraphrase 66*) 533
How brightly beams the morning star . . 202
How excellent in all the earth 138
How glorious Sion's courts appear (*Paraphrase 20*) . 294
How great the harvest is 341
How lovely is thy dwelling-place . . . 4
How sweet the Name of Jesus sounds . . 376
How vain the cruel Herod's fear . . . 209
*How wonderful this world of thine . . 152
*Hushed was the evening hymn . . . 123

I am not skilled to understand 687
I am not worthy, holy Lord 570
I am trusting thee, Lord Jesus 685
I believe in God the Father Almighty (*The Apostles' Creed*) 546
I bind unto myself today 402
*I can picture Jesus toiling 226
I feel the winds of God today 444
I greet thee, who my sure Redeemer art . . 86
I hear thy welcome voice 683
I heard the voice of Jesus say 212
I joy'd when to the house of God . . . 489
*I like to think of Jesus 229
I love the Lord, because my voice . . . 8
*I love to hear the story 227
*I love to think that Jesus saw 156
I need thee every hour 688
I to the hills will lift mine eyes 139
I waited for the Lord my God 73
I will sing the wondrous story 381

256

INDEX OF FIRST LINES

If I come to Jesus	.	58
If thou but suffer God to guide thee	.	668
I'll of salvation take the cup	.	565
I'm not ashamed to own my Lord (*Paraphrase 54*)	.	591
Immortal, invisible, God only wise	.	32
Immortal Love, for ever full	.	306
In beauty of his holiness	.	311
In Christ there is no East or West	.	425
In heavenly love abiding	.	681
In love, from love, thou camest forth, O Lord	.	582
In the bleak mid-winter	.	178
In the cross of Christ I glory	.	259
In the lanes and in the parks	.	622
Infant holy	.	186
Into thy loving care	.	655
It came upon the midnight clear	.	170
It fell upon a summer day	.	213
It is a thing most wonderful	.	385
Jerusalem the golden	.	537
Jesus bids us shine, with a pure, clear light	.	488
Jesus calls us! O'er the tumult	.	211
Jesus Christ, I look to thee	.	112
Jesus Christ is risen today	.	264
Jesus Christ, our Lord and King	.	59
Jesus, Friend of little children	.	100
Jesus, good above all other	.	111
Jesus' hands were kind hands, doing good to all	.	228
Jesus, I will trust thee	.	686
Jesus lives! thy terrors now	.	605
Jesus, Lord, Redeemer	.	283
Jesus, Lover of my soul	.	78
Jesus loves me! this I know	.	418
Jesus, Master, whose I am	.	431
'Jesus!' Name of wondrous love	.	205
Jesus, our hope, our heart's desire	.	302
Jesus, Saviour ever mild	.	98
Jesus shall reign where'er the sun	.	413
Jesus, stand among us	.	11
Jesus, tender Shepherd, hear me	.	656
Jesus, these eyes have never seen	.	674
Jesus, the very thought of thee	.	377
Jesus, thou Joy of loving hearts	.	571
Jesus, whose all-redeeming love	.	215
Jesus, with thy Church abide	.	490
Join all the glorious names	.	304
Judge Eternal, throned in splendour	.	519
Just as I am, thine own to be	.	448
Just as I am, without one plea	.	79
King of glory, King of peace	.	364
King of kings and Lord of lords	.	203
Land of our Birth, we pledge to thee	.	446
Laud and honour to the Father (*Doxology*)	.	661
Lead, kindly Light, amid the encircling gloom	.	682
Lead us, heavenly Father, lead us	.	90
Let all mortal flesh keep silence	.	577

INDEX OF FIRST LINES

Let all the world in every corner sing . . . 36
Let saints on earth in concert sing . . . 54
*Let us sing our song of praise . . . 62
Let us with a gladsome mind . . . 3
Lift high the cross, the love of Christ proclaim . . 55
Lift up your heads, ye gates of brass . . . 47
Lift up your heads, ye mighty gates . . .
Lift up your hearts (*Sursum Corda*) . . . 55
'Lift up your hearts': I hear the summons calling . . 36
'Lift up your hearts!' We lift them, Lord, to thee . . 44
Light of the anxious heart . . . 1
Light of the world! for ever, ever shining . . . 13
*Little birds in winter time . . . 63
Lo! he comes, with clouds descending . . . 31
Look upon us, blessèd Lord . . . 12
Look, ye saints! the sight is glorious . . . 28
*Looking upward every day . . . 44
Lord and Master, who hast called us . . . 44
Lord, bless and pity us . . . 49
Lord Christ, when first thou cam'st to men . . 25
Lord, dismiss us with thy blessing . . . 63
Lord, enthroned in heavenly splendour . . 58
Lord, from the depths to thee I cried . . . 6
Lord God, the Holy Ghost . . . 33
Lord have mercy (*Kyrie eleison. First form*) . . 6
Lord have mercy upon us (*Kyrie eleison. Second form*) . 6
*Lord, I would own thy tender care . . . 41
Lord, in the fullness of my might . . . 43
Lord, it belongs not to my care . . . 67
*Lord Jesus, be thou with us now . . . 1
Lord Jesus, think on me . . . 8
Lord, now lettest thou thy servant depart in peace (*Nunc dimittis*) . . . 20
Lord of all being, throned afar . . . 1
Lord of all good, our gifts we bring to thee . . 45
Lord of all hopefulness, Lord of all joy . . . 9
Lord of beauty, thine the splendour . . . 12
Lord of creation, to thee be all praise . . . 42
Lord of light, whose Name outshineth . . . 51
Lord of our life, and God of our salvation . . 49
Lord, speak to me, that I may speak . . . 48
Lord, thee my God, I'll early seek . . . 4
Lord, thine heart in love hath yearned . . .
Lord, thou hast been our dwelling-place . . 10
Lord, thy word abideth . . . 13
Lord, when thy Kingdom comes, remember me . . 24
Lord, while for all mankind we pray . . . 51
Lord, who in thy perfect wisdom . . . 47
Love came down at Christmas . . . 19
Love Divine, all loves excelling . . . 43
Love of the Father, Love of God the Son . . 33
Lover of souls and Lord of all the living . . 48
Loving Shepherd of thy sheep . . . 9

Make me a captive, Lord . . . 44
Man of Sorrows! wondrous Name . . . 38
March on, my soul, with strength . . . 61
May the grace of Christ our Saviour . . . 63

258

INDEX OF FIRST LINES

May the mind of Christ my Saviour . . . 432
Mine eyes have seen the glory of the coming of the Lord . 318
Mine hands in innocence, O Lord . . . 564
Most glorious Lord of Life, that on this day . . 44
My faith looks up to thee . . . 81
My God, accept my heart this day . . . 429
My God, how wonderful thou art . . . 356
My God, I love thee; not because . . . 379
My God, I thank thee, who hast made . . 146
My God my God why hast thou forsaken me . 239
My hope is built on nothing less . . . 411
My song is love unknown . . . 224
My soul doth magnify the Lord (*Magnificat*) . 163
My soul, there is a country . . . 693
My times are in thy hand . . . 680

Nearer, my God, to thee . . . 689
New every morning is the love . . . 47
Not what these hands have done . . . 410
Now at last he takes his throne . . . 308
Now cheer our hearts this eventide . . 642
Now God be with us, for the night is closing . 643
Now Israel may say, and that truly . . 392
Now, Lord! according to thy word (*Paraphrase 38*) . 590
Now may he who from the dead . . . 639
Now, my tongue, the mystery telling . . 578
Now thank we all our God . . . 368
Now that the daylight fills the sky . . 45
Now the day is over . . . 653
Now the green blade riseth from the buried grain . 278
Now to him who loved us, gave us (*Doxology*) . 657

O be joyful in the Lord all ye lands (*Jubilate Deo*) . 3
O breath of life, come sweeping through us . 339
O brother man, fold to thy heart thy brother . 460
O Christ who art the Light and Day . . 652
O Christ, who sinless art alone . . . 576
O clap your hands all ye people . . . 284
O come, all ye faithful . . . 191
O come, and let us to the Lord . . . 19
O come and mourn with me awhile . . 243
O come let us sing unto the Lord (*Venite exultemus*) . 20
O come let us sing unto the Lord (*Psalm 95* AV) . 21
O come, O come, Emmanuel . . . 165
O day of God, draw nigh . . . 511
O day of joy and wonder . . . 327
O dearest Lord, thy sacred head . . . 252
O Father, all creating . . . 600
O Father, by whose sovereign sway . . 599
O Father, in thy father-heart . . . 553
O for a closer walk with God . . . 663
O for a faith that will not shrink . . 664
O for a heart to praise my God . . . 85
O for a thousand tongues, to sing . . 371
O give thanks to the Lord for he is good . 350
O gladsome Light, O grace . . . 55
O God be gracious to me in thy love . . 64
O God, give ear unto my cry . . . 71

O God of Bethel! by whose hand (*Paraphrase 2*) . . . 7
O God of earth and altar 52
O God of love, O King of peace 50
O God of Love, to thee we bow 60
O God of mercy, God of might. 46
O God of our divided world 50
O God, our help in ages past 61
O God, the joy of heaven above 14
O God, thou art my God alone 66
O God, thou art the Father 39
O God, thy life-creating love 55
O God, whose loving hand has led . . . 60
O greatly blest the people are 39
O happy home, where thou art loved the dearest . 52
O, hear my prayer, Lord 7
O Holy City, seen of John 50
O Jesus, I have promised 43
O Jesus, King most wonderful 37
O Jesus, strong and pure and true 9
O joy! because the circling year 32
O Lamb of God that takest away the sins of the world (*Agnus Dei*) 56
O let him whose sorrow 67
O Light that knew no dawn 9
O little town of Bethlehem 17
O Lord and Master of us all 43
O Lord of every shining constellation . . . 14
O Lord of heaven and earth and sea . . . 14
O Lord of life, thy quickening voice . . . 4
O Lord of life, where'er they be 60
O Lord, thou art my God and King . . . 34
O Lord our God, arise 49
O Love, how deep, how broad, how high . . 22
O Love that wilt not let me go. 67
O loving Father, to thy care 55
O Master, let me walk with thee 43
O my people, what have I done to thee (*The Reproaches*) 24
O perfect God, thy love 24
O perfect life of love 24
O Sacred Head, sore wounded 25
O send thy light forth and thy truth . . . 26
O set ye open unto me. 7
O sing a new song to the Lord 2
O sing a song of Bethlehem 22
O sing unto the Lord a new song for he hath done marvellous
   things 34
*O Son of Man, our Hero strong and tender . . 30
O sons and daughters, let us sing 27
O Spirit of the living God 49
O thou, my Judge and King 66
O thou my soul, bless God the Lord . . . 35
O thou, who at thy Eucharist didst pray . . 49
O thou who camest from above 11
O Trinity, O blessèd Light 5
O what their joy and their glory must be . . 53
O wondrous type, O vision fair 21
O word of pity, for our pardon pleading . . 24
O worship the King all-glorious above . . . 3

INDEX OF FIRST LINES

f the Father's love begotten 198
n Christmas night all Christians sing . . . 181
n Jordan's bank the Baptist's cry . . . 208
nce in royal David's city 193
ne who is all unfit to count 82
nly on God do thou, my soul 25
nward! Christian soldiers 480
pen to me the gates of righteousness . . . 232
ur blest Redeemer, ere he breathed . . . 336
ur children, Lord, in faith and prayer . . . 549
ur Father, by whose Name 522
ur Father which art in heaven (*The Lord's Prayer. First form*) . 562
ur Father who art in heaven (*The Lord's Prayer. Second form*) . 562
ur thoughts go round the world 466
ut of the depths have I cried unto thee O Lord . . 66
ut of the depths I cry to you, O Lord . . . 67

our out thy Spirit from on high 597
raise God, for he is kind 137
raise God, from whom all blessings flow (*Doxology*) . 658
raise him, praise him, all ye little children . . 386
raise, my soul, the King of heaven . . . 360
raise the Lord, his glories show . . . 359
raise the Lord! ye heavens, adore him . . . 37
raise to the Holiest in the height . . . 238
raise to the Lord, the Almighty, the King of creation . 9
raise waits for thee in Sion, Lord . . . 28
raise ye the Lord; for it is good . . . 136
raise ye the Lord. God's praise within . . 347
raise ye the Lord, ye servants of the Lord . . 640
ut thou thy trust in God 669

Rejoice, the Lord is King 296
ejoice! the year upon its way . . . 330
ide on! ride on in majesty 234
ise up, O men of God 477
ock of Ages, cleft for me 83
ound me falls the night 650
ound the Lord in glory seated . . . 353

aviour, again to thy dear Name we raise . . 649
aviour, teach me, day by day . . . 450
ee! in yonder manger low 179
ee the farmer sow the seed 621
erve the Lord with joy and gladness . . . 17
how me thy ways, O Lord 74
ing a new song to Jehovah 348
ing Alleluia forth in duteous praise . . . 542
ing, my tongue, how glorious battle . . . 256
ing praise to God who reigns above . . . 142
ing to the Lord a joyful song . . . 366
ing we triumphant hymns of praise . . . 305
oldiers of Christ! arise 441
oldiers of the cross, arise 478
on of God, eternal Saviour 454
on of the Lord Most High 219
ongs of praise the angels sang . . . 38

INDEX OF FIRST LINES

Speak forth thy word, O Father . . . .
Spirit Divine, attend our prayers . . . .
Spirit of God, descend upon my heart . . .
Spirit of God, that moved of old . . . .
Spirit of Light—Holy . . . .
Spirit of mercy, truth and love . . . .
Stand up, and bless the Lord . . . .
Stand up! stand up for Jesus . . . .
Still the night, holy the night . . . .
Strengthen for service, Lord, the hands . .
Such pity as a father hath . . . .
Summer suns are glowing . . . .
Sun of my soul, thou Saviour dear . . .

Take my life, and let it be . . . .
*Take our gifts, O loving Jesus . . . .
'Take up thy cross,' the Saviour said . .
Teach me, my God and King . . . .
Teach me, O Lord, the perfect way . . .
Teach me to serve thee, Lord . . . .
Tell me the old, old story . . . .
Tell out, my soul, the greatness of the Lord .
The bread of life, for all men broken . .
*The Church is wherever God's people are praising
The Church's one foundation . . . .
The day is past and over . . . .
The day of resurrection . . . .
The day thou gavest, Lord, is ended . .
The duteous day now closeth . . . .
The earth belongs unto the Lord . . .
The eternal gates are lifted up . . .
The eternal gifts of Christ the King . .
*The fields and vales are thick with corn . .
The first Nowell the angel did say . . .
The glory of the spring how sweet . . .
The God of Abraham praise . . . .
The great love of God is revealed in the Son .
The Head that once was crowned with thorns .
The King of Love my Shepherd is . . .
The Lord ascendeth up on high . . .
The Lord be with you (*Salutation*) . . .
The Lord bless you, and keep you (*Benediction*) .
The Lord doth reign, and clothed is he . .
The Lord is King! lift up thy voice . . .
The Lord is my shepherd . . . .
The Lord is risen indeed . . . .
The Lord of heaven confess . . . .
The Lord prepared hath his throne . . .
The Lord will come and not be slow . .
The Lord's my light and saving health . .
The Lord's my Shepherd, I'll not want . .
The mighty God even the Lord hath spoken .
*The morning bright, with rosy light . . .
The praises of the Lord our God . . .
The race that long in darkness pined (*Paraphrase 19*)
The royal banners forward go . . . .
The sands of time are sinking . . .
The Saviour died but rose again (*Paraphrase 48*) .

INDEX OF FIRST LINES

The Son of God goes forth to war	541
The spacious firmament on high	143
The strife is o'er, the battle done	266
The summer days are come again	623
The sun is sinking fast	50
The voice of rejoicing and salvation is in the tabernacles of the righteous	262
The wise may bring their learning	464
The world itself keeps Easter Day	274
Thee we adore, O hidden Saviour, thee	584
Thee will I love, my God and King	403
Thee will I love, my Strength, my Tower	678
There is a blessèd home beyond this land of woe	608
There is a green hill far away	241
There is a land of pure delight	536
There's a wideness in God's mercy	218
Therefore we, before him bending	578
Thine arm, O Lord, in days of old	214
Thine be the glory, risen, conquering Son	279
This is God's holy house	18
This is the day of light	46
This joyful Eastertide	271
This stone to thee in faith we lay	609
Thou art before me, Lord, thou art behind	68
Thou art the Way: to thee alone	121
Thou hast, O Lord, most glorious	285
Thou hidden Love of God, whose height	96
Thou shalt arise, and mercy yet	333
Thou standest at the altar	575
Thou who dost rule on high	528
Thou whose almighty word	494
Though in God's form he was	399
Throned upon the awesome Tree	247
Through the night of doubt and sorrow	423
Thy hand, O God, has guided	424
Thy Kingdom come, O God	322
'Thy Kingdom come!'—on bended knee	323
Thy Kingdom come; yea bid it come	524
Thy love, O God, has all mankind created	503
Thy mercy, Lord, is in the heavens	6
'Tis winter now; the fallen snow	632
Today I arise	401
To God be the glory! great things he hath done	374
To render thanks unto the Lord	29
To the Name of our Salvation	373
Too soon we rise; the symbols disappear	573
Turn back, O man, forswear thy foolish ways	84
'Twas on that night when doomed to know (*Paraphrase 35*)	237
'Twixt gleams of joy and clouds of doubt	675
Unto God be praise and honour (*Doxology*)	660
Unto us is born a Son	187
Wake, awake! for night is flying	315
We believe in one God the Father Almighty (*The Nicene Creed*)	558
We believe in one true God	414
We come, O Christ, to thee	592
We come unto our fathers' God	14

INDEX OF FIRST LINES

We give thee but thine own 4
We have heard a joyful sound 4
We love the place, O God . . . . .
We magnify thy Name, O God 5
We plough the fields, and scatter 6
We praise thee, O God (*Te Deum laudamus*) . . . 3
We sing the praise of him who died 2
*We thank thee, God, for eyes to see 1
*We thank thee Lord, for all thy gifts 6
'Welcome, happy morning!'—age to age shall say . . 2
What grace, O Lord, and beauty shone . . . 2
When all thy mercies, O my God 1
When Christ was born in Bethlehem 1
When God of old came down from heaven . . . 3
When I survey the wondrous cross 2
*When Jesus saw the fishermen 2
When Mary brought her treasure 2
When morning gilds the skies 3
When to the sacred font we came (*Paraphrase 47*) . . 3
When Sion's bondage God turned back . . . 3
Where cross the crowded ways of life 5
Where high the heavenly temple stands (*Paraphrase 58*) . 2
While humble shepherds watched their flocks (*Paraphrase 37*) . 1
Who is he, in yonder stall 2
Who is on the Lord's side 4
Who would true valour see 4
Why do the heathen rage 1
Will your anchor hold in the storms of life . . . 4
Wise men seeking Jesus 2
Within thy tabernacle, Lord . . . . .
Witness, ye men and angels, now 5
Workman of God! O lose not heart 6
Worship the Lord in the beauty of holiness . . .

Ye holy angels bright 3
Ye righteous, in the Lord rejoice . . . .
Ye servants of God, your Master proclaim . . . 3
Ye servants of the Lord 3
Ye that know the Lord is gracious 5
Ye who the Name of Jesus bear (*Paraphrase 52*) . . 2
Yield not to temptation, for yielding is sin . . . 4